Errata for *Russian Conservatism* by Paul Robinson

Page references in the index entries are off by two pages in this printing of the book; add two to each page reference to arrive at the correct location in the text to which the entry refers.

RUSSIAN CONSERVATISM

A volume in the NIU Series in
SLAVIC, EAST EUROPEAN, AND EURASIAN STUDIES
Edited by Christine D. Worobec

For a list of books in the series,
visit our website at cornellpress.cornell.edu.

✳ RUSSIAN ✳
CONSERVATISM

P A U L   R O B I N S O N

Northern Illinois University Press
an imprint of
Cornell University Press
Ithaca and London

Copyright © 2019 by Cornell University

All rights reserved. Except for brief quotations in a review, this book, or parts
thereof, must not be reproduced in any form without permission in writing
from the publisher. For information, address Cornell University Press, Sage
House, 512 East State Street, Ithaca, New York 14850. Visit our website at
cornellpress.cornell.edu.

First published 2019 by Cornell University Press

Printed in the United States of America

ISBN 978-1-5017-4734-2 (cloth : alk. paper)
ISBN 978-1-5017-4736-6 (pdf)
ISBN 978-1-5017-4735-9 (epub/mobi)

Book and cover design by Yuni Dorr

Librarians: A CIP record is available with the Library of Congress.

Contents

PREFACE

I would like to thank Amy Farranto of Northern Illinois University Press for suggesting that I write this book and for supporting the project thereafter. Thanks also to my wife Chione, Aleksandr Churkin, Oksana Drozdova, Aleksandr Dugin, Paul Grenier, Gary Hamburg, Egor Kholmogorov, Iury Lisitsa, Alexander Martin, Mikhail Remizov, and Alison Rowley.

All dates in this book are new style. In the notes and bibliography, I have strictly followed the Library of Congress system for transliterating Russian words and names. In cases where I have used translations from Russian, the transliteration of names may vary according to the translator, so that one author's name may appear in several versions. In the main text, I have altered the Library of Congress system in a number of ways to reflect normal English usage and to bring it closer to how words sound in English. For this reason, I have transliterated the Russian *ё* as *yo* not *e*. Because Russian authors whose names end in *ий* are popularly rendered as ending in *y* not *ii*, I have used the former—Dostoevsky, not Dostoevskii. I have also generally used a *y* for the Russian soft sign—thus Ilyin, not Il'in—although on some occasions I have omitted the soft sign entirely—Tretiakov, not Tret'iakov. Where there is a generally accepted transliteration for a Russian name, I have used that—Yeltsin not El'tsin, Wrangel not Vrangel', and so on. The names of tsars are given in English—for instance, Nicholas I and Alexander I, not Nikolai I and Aleksandr I. Again, this is to reflect common practice.

Russian Conservatism

INTRODUCTION

This is a book about the complex ideological phenomenon known as Russian conservatism. Given the enormous upheavals that Russia has experienced in the past 250 years—Napoleon Bonaparte's invasion, the emancipation of the serfs, large-scale industrialization and urbanization, revolution, communism, the Second World War, the disintegration of the Soviet Union and the subsequent collapse of the Russian economy—Russians have been continually concerned with managing change and looking for ways to soften its impact. One response has been conservatism: an ideology that seeks to ensure that change is in accord with Russia's nature, its history, and its traditions.

In writing this book, I work from the assumption that there is continuity in the ideology of Russian conservatism and thus it can be said to have a "history." I therefore examine the evolution of conservatism in Russia from about 1800 to today and analyze how successive Russian conservatives have tried to manage change in the areas of culture, politics, and economics.

"Today" is an ever-changing concept, and in their efforts to explain how they ended up where they are different generations of historians have found different things significant. From 1917 to 1991, the "today" that those studying Russia wished to explain was communism and the Soviet Union. Historians were drawn to subjects that contributed to explaining these things, while other matters were consigned to what Leon Trotsky called "the dustbin of history," dismissed as historically irrelevant dead ends. As Lesley Chamberlain points out, "the Cold War approach to Russian philosophy . . . selected those themes in the history of ideas that apparently led to the Bolshevik Revolution of 1917."[1] This meant that books on prerevolutionary Russian intellectual history tended to focus on Westernizers, Populists, Anarchists, Nihilists, Socialist Revolutionaries, and Marxists.[2] Western historians largely (although not entirely) ignored conservatism of all types.

Meanwhile, within the Soviet Union the study of conservatism did not fit the regime's communist ideology and could even be considered dangerous. Consequently, as Gary Hamburg says, "among Soviet historians Russian conservatism commanded scant attention ... before the late 1980s the history of conservative and right-wing political parties remained virtually unknown, although not an explicitly forbidden topic."[3]

Despite a general dislike of communism, there was little sympathy in the West for Russian conservatives. Alternatives to Bolshevism were sought instead in the writings of Mensheviks, Trotskyists, or others of a more moderate socialist or liberal disposition. Few historians wished to spend their time studying conservatives, whom they regarded as historical failures and whose anti-Western and anti-liberal opinions were considered distasteful. Marc Raeff, for instance, commented in his cultural history of the interwar Russian emigration, *Russia Abroad*, that "only the liberal and socialist publicists had anything of interest to say in their analyses of events in the Soviet Union. The conservative and reactionary monarchists thought only in terms of a restoration."[4] Raeff's dismissive (and quite inaccurate) attitude led him to entirely ignore important conservative figures such as the philosopher Ivan Ilyin. The interwar Russian emigration was for the most part conservative in disposition. To write about a society while ignoring its prevailing intellectual current is, to say the least, inadequate.

The same could be said of studies of other periods of Russian history, be they nineteenth-century Imperial Russia, the twentieth-century Soviet Union, or twenty-first-century post-Soviet Russia. For instance, the attention historians have paid to the prerevolutionary intelligentsia can easily lead one to believe that educated Russians as a whole were alienated from the tsarist system. This was not so, as is obvious from the tens of thousands of educated Russians who served loyally within the state administration, in the military, and in business, as well as from the writings of prominent conservatives such as Nikolai Danilevsky, Fyodor Dostoevsky, Mikhail Katkov, Konstantin Leontyev, and Konstantin Pobedonostsev. Indeed, one could make a case that from 1800 to 1917 conservatism was much more common than radicalism and was "the dominant political outlook of Russia's 19th-century ruling elite."[5] A history of Russia that fails to acknowledge conservative thought is necessarily an incomplete and inaccurate one. Restoring conservatism to its rightful place is an important task for contemporary historians.

Furthermore, conservatism does have intellectual value. As Alexander Martin comments with regard to the early nineteenth century, "conservative thinkers made significant contributions to Russian culture ... they promoted the development of a civil society involved with public affairs. ... They also encouraged a more humane attitude towards the peasantry. ... Finally, they strengthened Russia's sense of cultural identity."[6] Speaking of the same period, Arkady Minakov similarly notes that "Russian conservatives of the 'first wave' were talented people in many ways, as a rule splendidly educated, and conceding nothing in terms of their intellectual capacity to their liberal and radical opponents."[7] The same is true of conservatives in other eras.

The "today" of today is not the same as that of twenty-five years ago. Communism and the Soviet Union have vanished, and in their place a new Russian state has arisen. Since 2012 there has been considerable talk of a "conservative turn" in Russian politics.[8] At the time of writing (in early 2018), it is often said that Russia's president Vladimir Putin has moved from an essentially pragmatic outlook to a more ideological one.[9] According to Melik Kaylan, "Putin has changed . . . and now espouses a discernible, exportable, full-fledged '-ism.' . . . That '-ism' is conservatism."[10]

There is some truth to this. In recent years Russia has seen a revival in the influence of the Orthodox Church, growing anti-Westernism, and the passage of socially conservative legislation. Putin does not cite liberal or socialist thinkers of the nineteenth century in his speeches, such as Vissarion Belinsky, Nikolai Chernyshevsky, Aleksandr Herzen, or Ivan Turgenev. Instead, he makes reference to Alexander III, Fyodor Dostoevsky, Ivan Ilyin, Nikolai Karamzin, Aleksandr Solzhenitsyn, Pyotr Stolypin, and other luminaries of Russia's conservative past.[11] Similar references appear in the speeches and writings of other leading politicians,[12] as well as in government documents.[13] Meanwhile, government-sponsored and independent conservative think tanks have come into being, and some intellectuals are making a concerted effort to revive Russia's conservative tradition. In a recent survey of international relations (IR) experts at Russian universities, "the most important Russian thinkers of the nineteenth to twentieth centuries relevant to the development of Russian IR" were identified as Nikolai Danilevsky, Konstantin Leontyev, and Aleksandr Panarin, all of whom are generally labeled as "conservative."[14] Conservative thought is undoubtedly influential in contemporary Russia.

All this gives the study of Russian conservatism a particular salience at this moment, at the start of Putin's fourth term as president. Russian scholar Aleksandr Repnikov concludes that "in the current situation, when some of the postulates of conservative ideology are being echoed not only by the Russian political elite, but also by society, formulating an adequate representation of conservatism in autocratic Russia acquires great significance."[15] To this one may add "formulating an adequate representation of conservatism" during the Soviet period, both within the Soviet Union and among the Russian emigration. Conservatism from all these periods has shaped Russian politics and society today.

In recent years, Russian scholars have published books and articles on various aspects of the subject of Russian conservatism.[16] This output is, however, dominated by studies of specific people[17] and specific time periods.[18] There has been little effort to bring the studies of individual people and particular periods together to produce an overall analysis of the subject. The one notable exception is V. A. Gusev's 2001 book *Russkii konservatizm: Osnovnye napravleniia i etapy razvitiia* (Russian conservatism: Basic directions and stages of development).[19] It covers Imperial Russia, the interwar emigration, and the post-Soviet period, and includes an analysis of what Gusev calls "state conservatism" and "cultural-Orthodox conservatism." This makes it the most comprehensive single-authored volume published to date. There is, however, no equivalent in English.

During the Cold War, scholars did publish several English-language studies of Russian nationalism.[20] Similarly, post–Cold War scholarship on the topic of Russian conservatism has focused on various facets of contemporary nationalism, most notably neo-Eurasianism.[21] But while nationalism is closely connected to Russian conservatism, the two isms are far from being synonymous, and a focus strictly on nationalism paints an incomplete picture of conservative thought. Another element of Russian conservatism is Orthodoxy. This too has attracted some attention,[22] but in general studies of Orthodoxy, nationalism, statism, and other aspects of Russian conservatism have remained fragmented.

Similarly, English-language authors have yet to produce a historical narrative of Russian conservative thought from its earliest manifestations through to today. In recent years, there have been several studies of conservatism in various periods of Russian history,[23] as well as biographies of conservative politicians and thinkers,[24] but nothing that brings them all together. Richard Pipes's 2005 book *Russian Conservatism and Its Critics: A Study in Political Culture* covers the largest period, including the eighteenth and nineteenth centuries, but it stops at the Russian Revolution of 1917.[25] Pipes also defines Russian conservatism in a very narrow way, solely in terms of a belief in a strong, centralized state, unrestrained by law. Not only does Pipes's definition leave out all facets of conservatism not connected to strong state power (such as religious, economic, and social conservatism), but it also ignores the thinking of the many Russian conservatives who have argued in favor of limits on state authority. In short, until now there has been no English-language study of the entire history of Russian conservatism from its origins to the present day and encompassing all its many parts.

This book aims to provide the comprehensive overview of the topic that has previously been lacking. To this end, it examines the history of Russian conservatism in Imperial Russia, the Soviet Union, the emigration, and post-Soviet Russia, and looks at all the aspects mentioned above. I hope that this will provide readers with a better understanding both of Russia's past and of its present.

CHAPTER 1

DEFINING RUSSIAN CONSERVATISM

Anybody wishing to study conservatism confronts an immediate problem: scholars do not agree on what it is. Nor do they agree about its origins, while some argue that there is not a single type of conservatism, but several.[1] The problem is further complicated by the fact that many of conservatism's most commonly cited features appear at best to fit uneasily together and at worst to contradict each other entirely. Conservatism is universalistic, but also anti-universalistic; seems to oppose change, but also to promote it; can be vehemently anti-liberal, but also can be liberal; and so on. Different groups labeled "conservative" often hold views diametrically opposed to one another—modern day American "paleoconservatives," for instance, are bitter enemies of American "neoconservatives." Readers of this book will come across seemingly paradoxical phrases such as "liberal conservative," "conservative modernization," and even "revolutionary conservatism." But different conservatives do all have something in common. Tying them together is the thread of a preference for organic change. Following this thread, this book will demonstrate that Russian conservatism is not a philosophy of the status quo. Rather, it is one that endorses change, but change of a certain, gradual sort that is in keeping, as much as possible, with national traditions.

Defining Conservatism

Untangling the various complications of conservatism requires recognizing what one Russian scholar calls its "binary nature."[2] On the one hand, there are those who view conservatism as an ideology, containing immutable values that transcend time and space. On the other hand, there are those who view conservatism as a "natural attitude"[3] in favor of existing institutions, which manifests itself in entirely different ways in different times and places, according to what the existing institutions happen to be.[4] In reality, these two types of conservatism tend to exist side by side, creating tensions within conservatism that are not easily reconciled.

Regardless of whether conservatism is viewed as an ideology, an attitude, or some synthesis of the two, the question arises of what constitutes its core. Scholars often see this core as consisting of a preference for the status quo and a consequent inclination to resist change. Samuel Huntington, for instance, calls conservatism "the articulate, systematic, theoretical resistance to change."[5] Michael Oakeshott writes:

> To be conservative is to be disposed to think and behave in certain manners . . . a propensity to use and to enjoy what is available rather than to wish for or to look for something else; to delight in what is present rather than what was or what may be. . . . To be conservative, then, is to prefer the familiar to the unknown, to prefer the tried to the untried, fact to mystery, the actual to the possible, the limited to the unbounded, the near to the distant. . . . The man of conservative temperament believes that a known good is not lightly to be surrendered for an unknown better.[6]

The "known good" will, however, vary considerably from time to time, from place to place, and from person to person. A conservative's preferences will therefore vary too. As the Russian philosopher Konstantin Leontyev put it, "Everyone's conservatism is his own—the Turk's is Turkish, the Englishman's is English, and the Russian's is Russian."[7] If one accepts the idea that conservatism is a preference for the status quo, then a conservative in a communist society will be a communist, whereas a conservative in a free-market liberal democracy will be a free-market liberal democrat. A conservative, in effect, can be almost anything. Michael Freeden calls this "the chameleon theory of conservatism."[8] It posits that, "conservatism is relative to a society . . . conservatism is a *positional* ideology. The content of a political programme will vary dramatically from nation to nation, from state to state."[9]

Indeed, people labeled as conservatives have proposed vastly different programs at different times and in different places. Russian conservatives of today do not hold precisely the same views as Russian conservatives of 150 years ago. Nevertheless, numerous scholars of conservatism have concluded that conservatism "is not an ideal of the *status quo*. It is predominantly about *change*."[10] Conservatism is about "managing change," "an ideology concerned with change," writes Kieron O'Hara.[11] "Conservatism . . . is *not* an ideology of the *status quo*," says Freeden. "Rather, it is an ideology predominantly *concerned* with the problem of change: not necessarily proposing to eliminate it."[12]

This is very true of Russian conservatism. More often than not, far from taking "delight in what is present," Russian conservatives have been deeply dissatisfied with the status quo and have longed to change it, sometimes proposing quite radical reforms. As will become obvious throughout this book, Russian conservatism is, and for the most part always has been, deeply interested in change.

What differentiates conservatism from other ideologies such as liberalism or socialism is not, therefore, opposition to change, but its preferences concerning the form that change should take. Conservatives are willing to countenance reform, but it has to be of a certain sort,[13] that is to say of a sort that avoids revolutionary breaks and retains ties with the past. As Eduard Popov writes, "conservatism is directed to the *future*, but unlike progressivism, not by means of a rupture with the past."[14]

This is the principle of organicism. To the conservative, a society is a "living organism."[15] Plants and animals grow and develop, gradually, and in accordance with their own nature. An attempt to change an organism's nature, or to transplant an alien organism into it, will bring it no benefit, and may even kill it. The same applies to human societies. Writing in the late nineteenth century, Konstantin Pobedonostsev, a prominent conservative member of the Russian government under tsars Alexander III and Nicholas II, remarked:

> A flower develops from a bud, and the makeup of the bud fully defines its development. If we want to give the latter a different character, which contradicts the constitution of the bud—then we will achieve nothing but death. The development of a people is also inextricably linked with the spiritual center crystalized by its history, which defines the uniqueness of the state, and makes the popular organism accept one direction of development and reject others.[16]

Russian conservatives have regularly compared Russia and Russian society to plants of one kind or another, and used words such as "organism" and "organic." Perhaps one of the best definitions of conservatism is that produced by the émigré Russian philosopher Nikolai Berdiaev in 1923:

> The conservative principle ... is a free, organic principle. It consists of a healthy reaction to violation of organic nature. ... The conservative principle is not by itself opposed to development, it merely demands that development be organic, that the future not destroy the past but continue to develop it.[17]

The organic principle provides the thread that ties conservatism together and solidifies it from merely an attitude or worldview into a fully developed ideology. According to many historians, European conservatism first coalesced into a formal ideology in the late eighteenth and early nineteenth centuries in reaction to the excesses of the French Revolution and Napoleonic Wars.[18] In the eyes of some Europeans of the time, those excesses were a natural product of the rationalism, atheism, and universalism introduced in the eighteenth century by the intellectual movement known as the Enlightenment. The Enlightenment encouraged people to believe that they could determine the rules governing human society and apply universally applicable solutions to human problems. Conservatism was a reaction to this. It argued that it is necessary to recognize that human reason is limited; that there is truth in religion, custom, and tradition; that societies differ; and that there are no universally applicable policies for the betterment of all human beings everywhere.

In the place of rationalism, universalism, and, arguably, also liberalism, conservatives in general propose organicism and religious truth. As Michael Freeden says, conservatism consists of two "core concepts"—the "understanding of organic change" and "a belief in the extra-human origins of the social order."[19] These two concepts do not fit easily together. Organicism is by nature particularistic: it suggests that each society is different and should develop differently, and that there are no universally suitable social values or institutions. "A belief in the extra-human origins of the social order," by contrast, suggests that there are universal, usually God-given values. Conservatism therefore contains an inherent contradiction between universalism and particularism. This can be seen very clearly in Russian conservatism. On the one hand, Russian conservatives of all types consistently claim that Russia is different from the West and that Western claims regarding universal human values are false. But the characteristic most often used to justify Russia's claim to difference is its Orthodox religion, which is said to be a bearer of universal truth. Russian conservatism thus strives to be both universalistic and anti-universalistic at the same time. How conservatives have tried to resolve this paradox will be one of the major themes of this book.

Conservative ideology tends to be defined by what it is *against*. This differentiates it from ideologies such as liberalism and socialism, which more clearly articulate what they are *for*: liberty, equality, and so forth. Saying what conservatism is *for* is difficult. In efforts to do so, conservative intellectuals have often resorted to creating lists of what are believed to be the key conservative principles and values.[20] The lists, however, vary from person to person. Freeden points out that one of the reasons for this is that "fixed conservative lists . . . are almost entirely composed of adjacent and peripheral concepts which are in principle eliminable."[21] Consequently, as Noel O'Sullivan remarks, "not every conservative thinker will be found to subscribe to all the ideas found on the list of 'canons of conservative thought'; and there is the further difficulty that not all who do subscribe to them would invariably be described as conservative."[22]

Nevertheless, certain features of organisms, and therefore of the organic worldview, tend to produce distinct preferences, each of which is more or less discernible in a conservative according to the person, time, and place. The first relevant feature is that organisms are not unchanging; they grow, flourish, and die. Organicism, therefore, is not inherently hostile to change. Rather, it considers change quite normal. But the organic principle will tend to produce a preference for slow and gradual, rather than revolutionary, change. Associated with this is a preference for order and stability, and a belief in the value of customs and tradition. From these will often flow a belief in the importance of "traditional" institutions, such as the nuclear family consisting of a married man and woman and their children.

Second, the fact that organisms eventually die can incline conservatives toward a cyclical view of progress. Like a living being, every civilization will eventually come to an end. No one can claim, therefore, to embody a set of values and institutions which constitute the perfection of human progress. This conclusion can lead conservatives to adopt a particularist or morally relativist position.

Third, just as different organisms have different natures, and so must be structured and develop in different ways, so too must societies. This leads to a rejection of ideas such as universal human rights and toward the adoption of nationalism. It is important to note, however, that this type of nationalism is founded on a recognition of difference rather than on the idea of the superiority of any one nation compared to another. This may result in a belief in the value of national diversity, and a rejection of processes (capitalism, globalization, and so on) that are seen as leading to homogenization.

Fourth, because a living organism is a single whole, made up of specialized but different parts, and is not merely a collection of identical and autonomous cells, organicism lends itself to a belief in the supremacy of collective interests and rights over individual interests and rights. It also lends itself to a belief in hierarchy: just as each cell has its own role to play in the organism, so does each individual in society, and it makes little sense for individuals to think that they should be the same as others, or substitute themselves for others. In this view, just as the gut cannot suddenly decide that it would rather be the brain, a cook cannot suddenly decide that he or she would rather be president. According to this line of thought, every individual should be content with his or her own place in the system. This assumption can render conservatives suspicious of democratic and liberal ideas.

Fifth, as religion is an important part of the cultural traditions of almost all societies, the priority given to tradition can produce a belief in whatever absolute and universal values are associated with the religion in question.

As will become clear in the chapters that follow, all of these preferences appear at one point or another in the history of Russian conservatism.

THE ELEMENTS OF RUSSIAN CONSERVATISM

Russian conservatism is as hard to define as conservatism in general. One recent analysis lists three types of Russian conservatism,[23] another identifies seven,[24] and a third argues that there are nine.[25] Russian conservatism is extremely heterogeneous. One should be very wary of saying that Russian conservatives believe this or that. Over the past two hundred years, Russian conservatives have believed many things, and have often disagreed as much with each other as with their common political opponents.

The matter is complicated by the fact that Russian conservatives have been influenced by certain strains of thought that in some ways overlap with conservatism but in other ways are not conservative at all. An example would be the late nineteenth-century philosopher Vladimir Solovyov who, it is said, produced a "synthesis of Christian-theocratic and liberal-universalist values."[26] Solovyov was highly critical of many of the conservatives of his own day,[27] and cannot easily be designated a conservative himself. He therefore falls outside the scope of this book. But his example reveals the difficulty of applying labels such as "conservative" or "liberal" to Russian thinkers, or of defining conservatism by means of a simple conservative-liberal dichotomy.

Despite these problems, it is possible to identify certain core concerns that can structure a study of the subject. In the 1830s, the then-minister of popular enlightenment, Count Sergei Uvarov, formulated an official ideology for the Russian state, coining the slogan "Orthodoxy, Autocracy, Nationality." This provides a good starting point for a definition of Russian conservatism. As modern Russian scholar Aleksandr Repnikov writes, "At all stages of conservatism's development *elements* of the formula 'Orthodoxy, Autocracy, Nationality' were present."[28] The three elements are not entirely distinct. In particular, conservatives' views of Russian national identity have often been tightly bound up with Orthodoxy, and it is hard to disentangle the two. Autocracy is also closely connected to ideas of Orthodoxy and nationality, although the term "autocracy" is perhaps not appropriate after 1917.

Russian conservatism is as much a cultural as a political phenomenon. In line with this, Gusev identifies two types of Russian conservatism: "state-protective conservatism," which stresses the special nature of Russian statehood and the need for a strong state, and "Orthodox-Russian (Slavophile) conservatism," which stresses the distinct nature of Russia's culture.[29] This classification, however, omits any discussion of economic and social issues. The latter have generally occupied the minds of Russian conservatives far less than matters of culture and politics. Nevertheless, in certain periods, notably the final years of the Russian Empire and the post-Soviet era, Russian conservatives have actually paid close attention to economic and social matters. For this reason, it is necessary to add another element to the list, namely "social-economic conservatism."

This book, therefore, divides the history of Russian conservatism into three strands: cultural (which includes the Orthodoxy and nationality parts of Uvarov's triad); political (which includes but is not restricted to the question of autocracy); and social-economic. There is considerable overlap between these strands, but dividing the subject up in this manner enables a focus on issues rather than personalities.

For several hundred years, Russia has been perceived by many as lagging culturally, politically, and economically behind that part of Europe and North America known as the "West." Russian conservatism has responded to the challenge of modernizing in order to catch up with the West. Specifically, the questions Russian conservatives have tried to answer are: how to create a modern society while preserving the "traditional values" of Russian Orthodoxy; how to develop an advanced and influential culture while preserving a distinct Russian national identity; how to develop a powerful state, able to defend Russia and its people and provide the stability required for cultural and economic progress, without unleashing destructive revolutionary processes; and how to forge a modern economy, without similarly unleashing the forces of social unrest. As Repnikov explains, Russian conservatism is not the opposite of reform and modernization but about finding *"another path"* that does not involve blind copying of Western examples, while "taking into account the necessity of social-political reform and the value of traditional points of view."[30] This effort to find another path manifests itself differently in each of the three strands of Russian conservatism mentioned above—cultural conservatism, political conservatism, and social-economic conservatism.

Cultural Conservatism

Russian historians disagree about the origins of conservatism in their country. Some adhere to the traditional formula that regards the rise of conservatism as a reaction to the Enlightenment and the French Revolution. This would indicate that Russian conservatism is part of a much broader European phenomenon. Others, however, view the roots of Russian conservatism as lying a hundred years further back in Russian history—in the campaign of Westernization begun by Tsar Peter the Great at the start of the eighteenth century. Seen that way, Russian conservatism is a phenomenon distinct from European conservatism,[31] and is primarily concerned with defending Russian culture against the forces of Westernization.

There is an element of truth to both propositions. On the one hand, Russian conservatism came into being as a formal ideology only in the early nineteenth century, at much the same time as conservatism in the rest of Europe. Furthermore, many of the most fervent proponents of early Russian conservatism were extremely well versed in European philosophy, were educated in European universities or traveled regularly to Western Europe, and were great admirers of European cultural and technological achievements. Referring to them as "anti-Western" is in some ways true, but in other ways not true at all. Russian conservatism owes a lot to European conservatism more generally.

On the other hand, preserving Russia's distinct national identity (or perhaps even constructing a distinct national identity) has been a central aspect of Russian conservatism since at least 1800.[32] Russian conservatism is strongly connected to a desire for organic development that avoids "Western assimilation."[33] The term "the West" is, of course, ill-defined. For nineteenth-century Russians, it primarily meant Western Europe. Nowadays, it includes also North America. The West is far from monolithic, and it is debatable whether the differences between Russia and the West are really greater than the differences within the West itself. But whatever the objective reality of the West, the idea of it exists in people's minds, and it has been the crucial "other" against which Russian national identity has been defined for over two hundred years. This concern with avoiding Western assimilation marks Russian conservatism out as somewhat different from Western conservatism. It also places cultural concerns at the center of Russian conservatism.

Defining the national identity that needs protecting has proven difficult. Russian conservatives have had to struggle with the fact that their country has historically been far from homogeneous in ethnic, cultural, or religious terms. They have made various attempts to overcome this difficulty and to determine what constitutes Russian-ness. This will be seen in the variations of Russian nationalism examined below, such as Slavophilism, Pan-Slavism, and Eurasianism. The importance of issues of nationality in Russian conservatism is such that one scholar has concluded that "the ideological complex usually known as 'Russian conservatism' would more correctly be called nationalism."[34]

Other scholars reject this conclusion. Arkady Minakov, for instance, holds that "Russian conservatism can't be equated with nationalism."[35] In part, the differences in opinion reflect the subjects of study. It is important to draw a clear distinction between, on the one hand, the Russian state, its rulers, and its leading officials, and, on the other hand, conservative intellectuals. Despite occasional forays into policies of Russification, the former have more often regarded Russian ethnic and cultural nationalism with suspicion, as likely to destabilize a multinational empire. They have preferred to emphasize a civic nationalism, or rather patriotism, based on loyalty to the imperial dynasty, the state, and its ideology (whether Orthodoxy or communism). The Russian state has consistently given nationalists the cold shoulder.

More significantly, nationalism has often been more of a religious/spiritual than a political phenomenon. The desire to avoid assimilation into the West has led Russian conservatives to seek to identify what makes Russia different, and by and large they have picked Orthodox Christianity as Russia's distinctive characteristic. Orthodoxy and conservatism have thus become tightly intertwined.

Orthodoxy has historically been a central part of Russian national identity; it has had a deep influence on Russian political thought, shaping Russians' view of the nature of the state;[36] and there are certain characteristics of Orthodoxy that cause many observers to consider it an inherently conservative religion. The key role that Orthodoxy plays in Russian conservatism means that any discussion of the latter must begin with a digression into Orthodox theology.

Orthodoxy means "right opinion," "true faith," or "true worship." A modern textbook on Orthodoxy describes the religion in the following way:

> The Roman Catholics and the Protestants adulterated the ancient faith and either added or subtracted from that which our Lord and the Apostles taught. We who, by God's grace, are Orthodox are most thankful to Him for preserving in us the True Faith. . . . Orthodoxy . . . possesses Christianity in its original form; her worship is unadulterated and genuine, and her teaching unchanged.[37]

Similarly, Paul Evdokimov writes that "the unprejudiced observer will see one consistent principle running right through every detail of Orthodox life: faithfulness to the primitive edition."[38]

These definitions bring to light a number of key points. First, as the "true faith," Orthodoxy is open to all and bears a universal message. Second, Orthodoxy defines itself to a large extent in opposition to Western Catholicism and Protestantism. This can lend it a national and particularist slant, which fits uneasily with its universalism. Third, Orthodoxy places great stress on keeping its "teaching unchanged."

The importance of tradition in Orthodoxy was well described by émigré Russian theologian Sergei Bulgakov, who linked tradition also to the organic principle. According to Bulgakov:

> The fullness of the true faith, the true doctrine, is much too vast to be held in the consciousness of an isolated member of the Church; it is guarded by the whole Church and transmitted from generation to generation, as the tradition of the Church. Tradition is the living memory of the Church, containing the true doctrine that manifests itself in history. It is not an archeological museum, not a scientific catalogue; it is not, furthermore, a dead depository. No, tradition is a living power inherent in a living organism.[39]

John Anthony McGuckin writes that "Orthodoxy does not just hold to tradition. . . . It *is* the tradition."[40] Authority is derived from "the ancient traditions manifested in the sacred liturgy and the church's ritual practices . . . the creeds and professions of the ecumenical councils . . . the great patristic writings."[41] Following this logic, Orthodoxy places firm limits upon human reason.[42] The individual must subordinate his or her own reasoning to the collective wisdom of current and past generations, and recognize the importance of faith. As St. John of Kronstadt put it, "Remember that the intellect is the servant of the heart. . . . We must, above all, attend to the heart, for the heart is life."[43]

Associated with the "heart" is the concept of "inner freedom," a form of freedom that differs from that envisaged by secular liberals, and that consists of being freed from temptation and the passions. It has been a regular concern of Russian conservatives. Nikolai Berdiaev, for instance, wrote as follows:

> Orthodoxy . . . is not an external form of behavior but spiritual life, spiritual experience, and the spiritual path. It sees inner, spiritual activity as the essence of Christianity. . . . In Protestantism, as in all Western thought, freedom is understood individualistically, as the right of the individual who protects himself from encroachment by other individuals and determines himself and his actions autonomously. Individualism is foreign to Orthodoxy, which is characterized by a distinctive form of collectivism.[44]

External political freedom is not, in this way of thinking, the most important thing. An autocratic state that restricts external freedoms but does not intrude upon people's inner freedom is acceptable. That said, in the absence of external freedom, the exercise of inner freedom obviously becomes harder. Many Russian conservatives have, therefore, been fervent supporters of free speech, and have resolutely opposed totalitarianism.

Freedom in Russian thought is often seen as inextricably linked to ideas of the good. Freedom of this sort is different from that of classical liberalism. Whereas liberalism grants people autonomy to define their own subjective version of the good and pursue it in their lives, the concept of inner freedom recognizes a single objective version of the good (normally defined in Christian terms). Inner freedom means freeing people from the internal barriers (passions, desires, and so on) that prevent them from seeking this good. Seen this way, freedom does not favor the isolated individual desiring autonomy from society or from moral laws.

In line with this, Orthodox thought draws a distinction between the "individual" and the "person." According to Metropolitan Hierotheos of Nafpaktos, "In the Orthodox Church we speak about the person using the phrase 'I love, therefore I am.' And when we talk about love, we do not mean sentimental love, but the human being's real relationship and communion with God and other people."[45] An individual is an isolated being. A person is not.

A connected idea is that of kenoticism (derived from the Greek word *kenosis*, meaning "emptying"). Orthodox Christians are encouraged to empty themselves of all their own desires, to learn true humility, and in this way to achieve holiness. Orthodox theologian Pavel Florensky remarked in a 1914 book, *The Pillar and Ground of the Truth*, that "in another person, through its kenosis, the image of my being finds its 'redemption' from under the power of sinful self-assertion, is liberated from the sin of isolated existence."[46] It is through kenosis and through relationships with others that one becomes a person and so achieves the freedom that is not available to the isolated individual.

Kenoticism has come to imply "voluntary suffering in the imitation of Christ."[47] Kenotic phrases appear regularly in the writings of Russian conservatives. They imply that people should accept their suffering, and so accept also the existing order in the world. It has been claimed that rather than promoting freedom, as suggested above, this leads to "a widespread attitude of submissiveness toward authority."[48]

According to critics, such as Richard Pipes, Russian Orthodoxy has consistently undermined its moral independence by subordinating itself to the state.[49] The church's willingness to do so is supposedly accentuated by the "otherworldly" focus of Orthodox teaching,[50] which holds that the church should leave the material world and its affairs to temporal authority, and instead concentrate on the saving of souls.

One should be careful, though, about exaggerating the degree of the church's otherworldliness and subordination to the state.[51] Moreover, at the level of individual parishes the "lived religion" of Orthodox communities has included a genuine concern for the conditions of life of these communities' members.[52] Gregory Freeze has convincingly demonstrated that in Imperial Russia, the Orthodox Church was far from being the "handmaiden of the state."[53] Argyrio Pisiotis records that "between the reigns of Peter the Great and Catherine II no fewer than fifteen major prelates were deprived of their rank and clerical dignity, forcibly retired in monasteries, imprisoned, knouted, tortured, decapitated, or burnt. Their crime was that they had resisted state policy."[54]

In fact, the Orthodox ideal of church-state relations is far from being one of unquestioning obedience. In the Byzantine tradition, which Orthodoxy follows, autocracy is "a radically limited notion."[55] The ideal is that of "symphony." According to Sergei Bulgakov, symphony is the

> mutual harmony and independence of the two parts. The state recognized the ecclesiastical law as an interior guide for its activity; the Church considered itself as

under the state. This was not Caesaro-papism in which the ecclesiastical supremacy belonged to the Emperor. Caesaro-papism was always an abuse; never was it recognized, dogmatically or canonically.[56]

The idea of symphony is that the church and the state each have their own autonomous sphere of responsibility.[57] In the words of Stanley Harakas, "the Church and the state cooperate as parts of an organic whole in the fulfilment of their purposes, each supporting and strengthening the other without this causing the subordination of the one to the other."[58] Church and state thus cooperate and "complement each other."[59]

Many of the features of Orthodoxy mentioned above tend to oppose it to the individualism and rationalism of Western liberalism. This accentuates Orthodoxy's anti-Westernism. In this regard, it is interesting to note that the Russian Orthodox Church has often regarded the West as more dangerous than the East. The West is seen as a source of heresy,[60] and also as a force pressing Russians to abandon their faith. The same is not true of the East. Thus, the Orthodox Church canonized Aleksandr Nevsky, who fought the Teutonic Knights, but made peace with the Mongols.[61] Russia's current foreign minister, Sergei Lavrov, praised this choice in an article, writing:

> Let us recall in this connection the policy pursued by Grand Prince Alexander Nevsky, who opted to temporarily submit to Golden Horde rulers, who were tolerant of Christianity, in order to uphold the Russians' right to have a faith of their own and to decide their fate, despite the European West's attempts to put Russian lands under full control and to deprive Russians of their identity. I am confident that this wise and forward-looking policy is in our genes.[62]

While promoting a patriotic identity separate from, and to some degree opposed to, that of Western Europe, in the tsarist era Orthodoxy retained its claim to be the bearer of universal truth. In this way Russia acquired a mission—namely, to preserve the truth that had been adulterated in the West, and eventually to persuade the West to see the error of its ways and to adopt the one true faith. Russia became the "Third Rome"—a term first coined by the monk Filofei of Pskov in the 1530s, which implied that Russia had inherited the mantle of Rome and Byzantium as the world's spiritual center. Russia's tsars generally did not put much stock in the concept of Russia as the Third Rome,[63] but the idea that Russia had a special spiritual mission did acquire some popular support, and in due course an important place in conservative thinking. In the process, it gave Russian Orthodoxy, and through it Russian conservatism, a sometimes messianic tinge. This to some extent offsets its anti-Westernism. While Russian conservatism often sees the West as a threat and identifies itself in opposition to it, at the same time, its holy mission is deeply connected to the West; indeed, it is to save the West. In this way, particularism and universalism come together and are reconciled. For it is precisely by protecting Russia's particular identity that Russia defends the universal truth, which it will one day restore to the rest of the world. Seen in this light, the relationship between Russian conservatism and the West is more complex than mere anti-Westernism.

Political Conservatism

Russian political conservatism has consistently desired institutions that are in accordance with Russia's own heritage and that are capable of providing Russians with peace, stability, and inner freedom. For the most part, this has meant powerful and centralized, but at the same time very limited, state authority, in other words what was known as "autocracy" before the 1917 revolution.

Richard Pipes writes that "the quintessence of Russian conservatism is autocracy. . . . The dominant strain in Russian political thought throughout history has been a conservatism that insisted on a strong, centralized authority, unrestrained by law or parliament."[64] The association of Russian conservatism with a "strong, centralized authority" is common, and not inaccurate, but it needs some qualification. First, Pipes's definition ignores the cultural aspects of Russian conservatism. Second, while Russian conservatives in the nineteenth century generally did oppose legal or parliamentary restraints on autocratic authority, they were far from being believers in unlimited state power. Some even favored the creation of representative assemblies. The idea of legal restraints also did gradually gain traction. And third, the Russian state has often been a radical, modernizing force in Russian life. Support for strong, centralized authority has come not only from conservatives but also from liberals and socialists hoping to use state power to advance their own goals. Conservatives have regularly found themselves in opposition to the state, and arguing in favor of restricting intrusions by the government bureaucracy into the lives of local communities. Autocracy, in the ideology of Russian conservatism, means *limited* government.

Historians often look to Russia's geography and climate to explain the supposed preference for a strong, centralized state. Due to its size and lack of clearly defined and easily defensible borders, Russia has been subject to repeated invasions from its earliest days right up to the Second World War. Insecurity supposedly led to militarization and the creation of a centralized authority to mobilize the population for war.[65] As a result, claims Pipes, Russia developed in a different manner from Western Europe. There was a "virtual absence of private property," even in the towns. Medieval Muscovy lacked "an independent nobility and middle class, and private property in land." It never experienced the institution of feudalism, with its reciprocal obligations between rulers and ruled. Russia's rulers regarded everything and everybody in Russia as their own personal property, to dispose of as they wished.[66] The result was that "the tsar and his officials neither then nor later conceived of society as independent of the state, as having its own rights, interests, and wishes to which they were accountable."[67]

An alternative way of looking at the issue is to view Russia as having had not a strong state but a weak one.[68] Russia's size and the poor communications between its far-flung regions have made it extremely difficult for the country's rulers to exercise control over areas far removed from the capital. The country has tradi- tionally been "undergoverned," with the state having a "weak" presence in the prov- inces.[69] To compensate, in medieval times the grand princes of Muscovy resorted to a system known as *kormlenie* ("feeding"), in which regional governors were permitted to "feed" (in other words, extract resources) off the territories under their control in order to support the local administration. This system was inevita- bly subject to abuse, allowing corrupt governors to extort an excessive amount of resources from the local population. Later, the tsars relied on the landed nobility to control the population on their behalf, in large part through the system of serf- dom, a system that contained few safeguards to prevent owners from abusing their serfs. Consequently, Russians, it could be argued, came to see local authority as inherently abusive. Their only recourse to protect themselves was to appeal to the person of the tsar, who therefore came to represent the locus of just authority. This is a pattern still evident today, when Russians' faith in the person of the president far outstrips their confidence in other state institutions.

In this light, autocracy is not, at least in theory, an oppressive form of govern- ment. On the contrary, it is a system designed to protect the people's freedoms against the oppressive actions of state officials. This also explains nineteenth-cen- tury Russian conservatives' suspicions of the state bureaucracy and also of par- liamentary institutions. Universal suffrage is a relatively new phenomenon. In the nineteenth century, European parliaments were elected using a very limited franchise, generally based upon property. Parliaments did not mean democracy as understood today. Instead, they guaranteed the power of the wealthier segment of a given society's population. Many Russians felt that such institutions would merely serve the interests of a narrow group of elites at the expense of the broader population. And in fact, attempts to introduce representative institutions with leg- islative power in Russia often hid a desire to halt social and economic reform and protect aristocratic interests.

This could be seen, for instance, in proposals put forward by Prince Mikhail Shcherbatov to Catherine II's Legislative Commission of 1767–68. Shcherbatov was a determined defender of the nobility's preeminent position in Russian society and "opposed all concessions to the peasantry ... opposed anything, in fact, that might help to undermine the traditional privileges of the aristocracy."[70] He also supported giving Russia a formal constitution and a system of checks and balances on monarchical power, and converting the noble-dominated Senate into the supreme legislative body.[71] This combination of reactionary social and economic policies with proposals for apparently liberal political reform was repeated later. An example was the support of the "aristocratic opposition" for some form of representative institutions in the 1860s and 1870s, as discussed in chapter 5.[72] As a result, those seeking to promote what might be called "the common good" were likely to be skeptical of representative institutions and likely to consider that this common good required power to be concentrated in the hands of a neutral person standing above all groups within society.[73] Only an autocrat could fulfill that role.

Autocracy is not the same as absolutism.[74] Conservative support for autocracy is not so much a belief in a strong state as a belief that the state's power should be controlled by a single individual. This is the literal meaning of "autocracy" (in Russia *samoderzhavie*, and sometimes also *samovlastie* or *edinovlastie*, all of which imply individual power). "Autocracy" says nothing about how much power the state should have, nor what spheres of life it should have competency over. It merely stipulates where power should rest,[75] namely in the hands of one person. In Russian conservative thought that person is meant to be bound by custom, tradition, religion, and even in some later thinking by law. As Ivan Ilyin put it, "The first thing which must be understood with regard to the Sovereign is the limited nature of his power, and the unlimited nature of his concomitant obligations."[76] The autocrat should care for the defense of the realm, for the maintenance of law and order, and for the economic well-being of society. Individuals' inner, spiritual life is outside of his or her competence. Excessive intrusion by the bureaucracy in local affairs is also discouraged. In conservative thought, a preference for centralized power often goes hand in hand with a belief in local autonomy.

According to Liubov Ulyanova, "historically, the state has been the main organizer and executor of reforms in Russia. During the past 200 years it is hard to find an example of any reform or smaller-scale reorganization which has been developed by social forces without the initiative and participation of the state in one form or another, or of representatives of the bureaucratic elite."[77] This has put Russian conservatives in an awkward position when such reforms have been of a radical, non-organic nature of which they do not approve. They support the state as a matter of principle, but oppose the specific policies it pursues. Leonid Poliakov notes that "Russian conservatives have at all times had to support a power, which was persistently anti-conservative, in carrying out radical changes."[78] As another Russian conservative writer puts it, "Not being in a position to resist revolution from above, conservatives at every historical moment have found themselves politically offside."[79] Consequently, says Poliakov, "conservatism in Russia has never turned into a real force, and all Russian conservatives have felt the tragedy of their alienation from power."[80]

Social-Economic Conservatism

In the first half of the nineteenth century, conservatives' primary socioeconomic concern was the issue of serfdom. Following the abolition of serfdom in 1861, conservatives turned their attention toward developing and industrializing the Russian economy without creating social tension and revolution. In the Soviet era, environmental concerns became important for some conservatives. And in the post-Soviet era, Russian conservatism has become closely associated with anti-globalism.

Like all major states, Russia has sought to build strong armed forces. This has required an advanced economy capable of producing the weaponry needed to compete with real and potential enemies. It has also meant having an educated population. Russia, though, has for several hundred years been seen by many as lagging behind the West in terms of technology and industrial output. This has created a dilemma for Russian conservatives. On the one hand, economic development and social reform are essential for the strong state and secure sovereignty they desire. On the other hand, economic and social progress tend to undermine the traditional values and institutions that conservatives support, and in extreme circumstances they unleash destructive revolutionary forces that can destroy the existing political, economic, and social system. With the exception of the Soviet era, economic progress has also tended to involve integration into the global economy. This threatens both national sovereignty and national culture. The problem has been how to enjoy the benefits of progress while avoiding the worst consequences.

One view of Russian economic history regards it as a series of cycles of alternating stagnation and rapid state-led development.[81] In the late nineteenth century and after the fall of the Soviet Union, Russian leaders sought foreign capital to facilitate economic growth. Top-down, state-driven attempts to force rapid economic progress are, however, incompatible with the organic worldview. In both the late imperial period and post-Soviet Russia, conservatives have found themselves opposing the official model of development and have sought an alternative more in keeping with the organic principle and less likely, in their view, to create social unrest or sacrifice Russia's sovereignty to foreign powers and foreign culture.

Some Russian conservatives have responded to the dilemma by denying the need for economic development and social reform. In the early nineteenth century these included landowners who wished to preserve the institution of serfdom. From the late Soviet period onward, the association of industrialization with pollution and environmental degradation also led some to call for an end to the pursuit of economic growth. But most conservatives have thought that growth is necessary. For some conservatives, this has been a very reluctant recognition, but others have been quite enthusiastic promoters of modernization. There has, therefore, never been one universally accepted school of economic thought among Russian conservatives.

Generally, though, conservatives have tended to seek gradual but steady growth rather than rapid bursts of state-led development, and have combined this inclination with a tendency toward protectionism, and in the modern era a deep suspicion of globalism. This has led to a preference for small businesses rather than large-scale industrial development, and also for encouraging economic growth by boosting consumer demand rather than by promoting large investment projects. The aim is to produce organic, bottom-up growth rather than the top-down growth so often favored by state planners, and thereby to put money in the pockets of ordinary people rather than in the pockets of wealthy oligarchs, industrialists, or financiers (often equated with foreigners). There is a definite anti-capitalist strand within Russian conservatism.

At the same time, to prevent social unrest, conservatives have shown an interest in preserving systems of social welfare, be they the peasant commune of the nineteenth century or the welfare state created in the Soviet era. This is sometimes combined with an appeal to Orthodox values of social justice and a belief in an equitable distribution of wealth. As a recent conservative manifesto, entitled the *Russian Doctrine*, puts it:

> The principle of justice is extremely important. . . . If we genuinely don't want to subject the country to another social revolution, we need to find a way of satisfying this need, which is basic for the Russian people. An unsatisfied demand for justice, and radical methods of achieving it, have systematically led Russia to catastrophe.[82]

On occasion, therefore, Russian conservatism can have much in common with what is generally considered the political and economic "left."[83] But the same desire to avoid upheaval that pushes Russian conservatism to the left on economic matters pushes it to the right on social ones, in particular toward a defense of what are seen as traditional social institutions, such as the two-parent family. The support of "traditional" or "family" values is also part of the conservative mix.

There are, of course, exceptions to the above, all of which represent tendencies rather than absolutes. Nevertheless, on the whole it is fair to say that the association of conservatism with free market economics so common in the West does not fit Russia well.

CONCLUSION

Since at least the early nineteenth century, Russian conservatism may be seen as having arisen as a reaction to processes of modernization and Westernization. Russian conservatives have been deeply concerned about the preservation and development of national identity, in which Orthodoxy has played an important, though not exclusive, role. They have favored a centralized but limited government, designed to provide order and stability and avoid revolutionary shocks, and have prioritized inner rather than outer freedom. Conservatives have searched for methods of steady economic development other than rapid, state-led modernization. Far from being satisfied with the status quo, Russian conservatives have generally disliked it and sought to alter it. Conservatism has had to move beyond merely criticizing change to proposing changes of its own. Russian conservatism is thus an ideology of organic change; it does not oppose change per se, but insists that as much as possible it should occur in accordance with existing traditions. As the chapters that follow will show, this attitude has manifested itself in different ways at different times, but the basic approach has remained consistent throughout.

CHAPTER 2

THE REIGN OF ALEXANDER I

In March 1801, a palace coup overthrew and killed the unpopular tsar of Russia, Paul I. His son and successor, Alexander I (1801–25), was only twenty-three years old when he took the reins of power and found himself immediately under intense pressure due to a volatile international situation. France, energized by the revolution of 1789, which had deposed King Louis XVI, had become the dominant military power on the European continent. Attempts by other European powers, including Russia, to curb French expansion had led to a succession of wars, known as the Napoleonic Wars, following the coronation of Napoleon Bonaparte as emperor of France in 1804.

Russia fought several wars with France during Alexander's reign. The first—the War of the Third Coalition—ended soon after the defeat of a combined Russian-Austrian army at the Battle of Austerlitz in December 1805. The second—the War of the Fourth Coalition—culminated in another Russian defeat, at Friedland in June 1807, and resulted in a peace treaty signed by Alexander and Napoleon at Tilsit in July 1807. The third and most dramatic began when the French army invaded Russia in June 1812. After defeating the invading French, the Russian army pursued Napoleon back through Germany and into France, and in March of 1814 the Russians entered Paris and brought Napoleon's rule to an end.

Alexander also faced serious challenges in domestic politics. The Russian state system remained essentially unaltered from the time of Peter the Great one hundred years previously. In theory, Alexander possessed absolute power, bound by neither constitution nor law. Various attempts had been made to change this situation during the eighteenth century, an example being an effort in 1730 to persuade Empress Anna to agree to share power with a group of advisors known as the Supreme Privy Council. Anna initially agreed to this proposal, but then changed her mind. Likewise her successors balked whenever faced with the prospect of surrendering any of their authority.

Nevertheless, Russia was "an autocracy only in theory."[1] The Russian state practiced "government light, with a mere few thousand servants"[2] to govern millions of square kilometers and nearly 40 million inhabitants. Lacking a sufficient bureaucracy or a properly codified and enforced system of law, Russia's emperors and empresses had to rely on patronage to rule. In the countryside, where the vast majority of the Russian population lived, it was largely the nobility that provided government. This system worked reasonably well for most of the eighteenth century, but by the reign of Catherine II (1762–96) it was becoming inadequate. In 1767, therefore, Catherine summoned a Legislative Commission whose purpose was to codify Russian laws. This is often described as an attempt to fundamentally reform Russian government by introduction of the rule of law, but rather than rule *of* law it would perhaps be better to describe Catherine's objective as rule *through* law. She sought not legal restrictions on her own power but rather the replacement of government by patronage with a more modern state system in which she could exercise power through law.[3] The attempt failed due to divisions among delegates to the Legislative Commission and the distraction of a war against the Ottoman Empire that began in 1768. The Commission never completed its work.

Catherine's son, Paul I, took a different approach, trying to bypass the existing patronage networks and restrict noble privileges.[4] Unsurprisingly, this proved very unpopular among the nobility and resulted in his murder in 1801. It was therefore left to Alexander I to pick up the pieces and attempt to modernize the Russian state, a task that acquired special urgency in the face of the external threat from revolutionary France. To this end, Alexander made a number of attempts to institute political change, both before and after the French invasion. These began with the establishment of the so-called "Unofficial Committee," which met from 1801 to 1803 and whose work led to various minor reforms in areas such as the rights of non-nobles to own land. More substantial were: the proposition of a major reform program by Alexander's state secretary, Mikhail Speransky, in 1809; the granting of a constitution to the Kingdom of Poland (as an autonomous part of the Russian Empire) in 1815; and the drawing up of a draft constitution (which was never enacted) for Russia itself in 1819.[5] Over time, however, the tsar's reforming zeal rather subsided, and the final years of his reign became marked instead by his increasing religiosity. This manifested itself in external affairs by the creation of a Holy Alliance between Russia, Austria, and Prussia, and in domestic affairs by efforts to propagate religious values, most notably in the educational system.

This was the setting for the first manifestations of what could be called a conservative ideology in Russia. This took some of its inspiration from Western European ideas but in other respects it continued older, Russian, modes of thought. In his history of Russian political philosophy from 1500 to 1801, Gary

Hamburg notes that "to a degree almost unfathomable for twenty-first century secular people, Russian thinking about politics before the eighteenth century rested on religious assumptions."[6] In the eighteenth century, the influx of ideas from the West changed this to some degree, but not entirely. By the nineteenth century Russian thinkers had come to accept the importance of reason but they did not for the most part believe that this required them to abandon faith. Instead they regarded themselves "as both Orthodox and rational" and viewed enlightenment as "mixing science, reason, and ethical duty."[7] In this way, nineteenth-century Russian conservatives shared a general approach that combined reason and religious faith. As Hamburg notes, Western influences on Russian thought were great but "neither displaced nor discredited the Orthodox Christian value system that had come into being in Russia in preceding centuries."[8] In the prevailing mode of thought, politics and morality were seen "more as conjoined than as discrete spheres."[9]

Developing a conservative ideology required the existence of an educated elite willing and able to engage in political philosophy. Creating this elite was a slow process, which took the length of the eighteenth century. By about 1800, several trends had come together: growing Russian nationalism; the influence of German Romanticism; the French Revolution and the Napoleonic Wars; and Alexander's efforts to carry out political reform. These factors combined to produce several different types of conservatism. The first type was cultural in form, and has been called "Romantic Nationalism." It sought to develop Russian culture and to protect it against what was seen as excessive foreign influence, especially from France, while fostering a sense of national pride. Key personalities in this movement were Admiral Aleksandr Shishkov (1754–1841), the writer Sergei Glinka (1774–1847), and prominent Moscow nobleman Count Fyodor Rostopchin (1763–1826). The second strand of conservatism was religious in form and was strongly influenced by religious ideas picked up by Alexander I while leading his army through Germany in 1814. Notable figures in this second strand were Prince Aleksandr Golitsyn (1773–1844), who from 1817 headed what was known as the "Dual Ministry," responsible for religious and educational matters; Aleksandr Sturdza (1791–1854), an official in the Russian foreign ministry and later in the Dual Ministry; and another Dual Ministry official, Mikhail Magnitsky (1778–1844). A third strand of conservatism, associated with the Russian Orthodox Church, objected to the rising influence of Western European religious ideas. Particularly prominent in this was the head of the Iuryev Monastery, Archimandrite Fotii (1792–1838). Finally, Alexander's reform plans prompted a form of political conservatism that sought to defend Russia's traditional autocratic order against the encroachment of models borrowed from Western Europe. The most famous of the political conservatives was historian Nikolai Karamzin (1766–1826). Karamzin also defended the institution of serfdom, as did some other conservatives of the era, such as Admiral Shishkov and Count Rostopchin. Others, such as Aleksandr Sturdza, favored the abolition of serfdom.

Russian conservativism in the reign of Alexander I was multifaceted, often in opposition to state policy, and far from united. But there was a common core among its various strands. Men such as Shishkov, Rostopchin, Glinka, Sturdza, and Karamzin fused reason and faith to support a form of enlightened autocracy unlimited by law but firmly bound by morality. They also shared a concern with creating a modern Russian culture and a strong state that would be able to unite the country and provide stability in the face of internal and external pressures. In these ways they set the tone for Russian conservatives of future generations.

CULTURAL CONSERVATISM

As noted above, Russian conservatism did not appear suddenly out of nowhere in 1800. Its elements slowly came together throughout the length of the eighteenth century, in effect making Russia ripe for conservatism by the start of the nineteenth century. The triad formulated by Uvarov in the 1830s (Orthodoxy, Autocracy, Nationality) could be observed as far back as the reign of Peter the Great (1672–1725) in the writings of Ivan Pososhkov (1652–1726), who praised many of Peter's reforms, but strongly condemned his introduction of Western cultural innovations, as well as the foreigners who accompanied them.[10] A. V. Cherniaev describes Pososhkov as a representative of a form of "pre-conservatism, proto-conservatism."[11] Other examples of eighteenth-century proto-conservatives included historian Ivan Boltin (1735–92); Prince Mikhail Shcherbatov (1733–90), who served as a prominent member of Catherine the Great's Legislative Commission; and playwright Denis Fonvizin (1744–92). Together they laid the groundwork for the type of organic nationalism that would become a feature of Russian conservatism from the early nineteenth century onward.

Boltin, for instance, argued that although Russia shared some characteristics with Western Europe, in other ways it was quite different, and that Russia should not be judged according to Western standards.[12] Shcherbatov, meanwhile, blamed the fact that Peter had cut Russia's connections with its traditional values for what he considered to be a catastrophic decline in Russian morals. In a classic example of organic thinking, Shcherbatov complained that Peter was like "an unskilled gardener who, from a weak tree, cuts off the water shoots which absorb its sap."[13] And Fonvizin reacted strongly against the passion for all things French (known as "Gallomania") that was so common among the Russian aristocracy of the era. After visiting France in 1777 and 1778, Fonvizin commented:

> I have acquired many benefits from my journey. Apart from better health, I have learnt to be more tolerant of the deficiencies which offended me in my fatherland. I saw that there are far more bad people than good people in the world, that people everywhere are people, that intelligent people are always rare, that there is always an abundance of idiots, and, in a word, that our nation is no worse than others and that one can enjoy a true happiness, for which there is no need to roam around in foreign lands.[14]

The examples of men like Boltin, Shcherbatov, and Fonvizin lead Russian historian Aleksandr Repnikov to conclude that Russian conservatism began as "a reaction to radical Westernization."[15] There is some truth to this, but there were also several other influences at play at the start of the nineteenth century.

The first of these was the French Revolution. This strengthened the dislike of Gallomania expressed by Fonvizin. It also seemed to confirm the dangers that resulted from demolishing traditional institutions in the name of abstract reason. Later, much of Russia's intellectual elite regarded the treaty signed by Alexander I and Napoleon at Tilsit in 1807 as a humiliation. The accord raised anti-French feeling and thereby boosted patriotism and Russian conservatism. The French invasion of Russia in 1812 strengthened the patriotic mood further.[16]

Another important influence on Russian thinking was the philosophy of German Romanticism, which gave Russians a way of intellectualizing their patriotic feelings. In particular, Romanticism provided Russian thinkers with a sense of the importance of the spiritual and the aesthetic aspects of nature; of the value of national custom; and of the limits of human reason. It thereby produced an "intellectual atmosphere" that made conservatism possible.[17]

Also important was Freemasonry, which was very popular among members of the Russian nobility in the late eighteenth century. Through it Western ideas of spirituality infiltrated Russia's ruling class. This made the Russian Orthodox Church regard it with considerable hostility. Following the French Revolution Catherine II suppressed Freemasonry, regarding it as potentially subversive. Most notably, Catherine ordered the arrest and imprisonment of Russia's most prominent Freemason, the journalist Nikolai Novikov.[18] Paul I freed Novikov and Freemasonry continued to enjoy considerable popularity in the reign of Alexander I, including among some conservatives.

A final influence was Western European conservatism. In the first decade of the nineteenth century, the writings of various European conservatives were translated into Russian. Émigrés from revolutionary France also helped spread conservative ideas.[19]

At first, the new Russian conservatism was largely cultural in form. If the title of "founder of Russian conservatism" had to be awarded to a single person, a strong candidate would be Admiral Aleksandr Shishkov. A naval officer who fought in the Russo-Swedish War of 1788–90, Shishkov played a key role in introducing German ideas of Romantic nationalism into Russia. As Alexander Martin writes, under the influence of Romantic thought, Shishkov "regarded Russia as a part of Europe politically but demanded that they part ways culturally. He believed in the inherent value of 'tradition,' which each nation should derive from its own sources."[20]

Being a highly educated member of one of the most powerful nations in Europe, Shishkov felt that Russia should have a great literature comparable to that of other European countries. Russia still had no equivalent of William Shakespeare or Molière. Intellectuals disagreed about how to create a great literature and what it should be like. Some authors, such as Nikolai Karamzin, sought to develop a new, light style, writing in what has been called "a literary language modeled on the French-influenced Russian" spoken by the Russian nobility.[21] Shishkov opposed this "new style," arguing that Russia could not create a great literature by aping the French. In place of the "new style," he campaigned for a more authentically Russian "old style."

Shishkov laid out his views in a book published in 1803, entitled *Discussion of the Old and New Styles of the Russian Language*. In it he wrote:

> Our slavish imitation of the French is like somebody who sees a neighbour who has lived in a sandy spot and has through hard labor turned the sand into fertile soil, and instead of working on his own rich black earth with the same industry, decides to fertilize it by transferring onto it some of his neighbour's barren sand. That is precisely what we are doing with our language.[22]

In Shishkov's opinion, the Russian language was rich in vocabulary, and did not need to borrow from others. He asked: "Where has the ridiculous idea come from that we have to throw out our indigenous, ancient, rich language, and found a new one based on the rules of the alien and poor language of the French?"[23] Shishkov argued that Russian literature ought to rest on the foundations of Church Slavonic. "I'm not saying," he wrote, "that we must write exactly in the Slavonic style, but I do say that the Slavonic language is the root and foundation of the Russian language; it gives it its richness, intellect, strength, and beauty."[24]

To Shishkov, all this was of more than literary importance. Literature shaped culture.[25] Building a Russian literature with close connections to Russia's linguistic traditions would reinforce the country's Orthodox identity and morals, and bring literature closer to the ordinary people. By contrast, the refined, Gallicized new style would weaken that identity and further accentuate the gap between the ruling elite and the masses. It would also undermine Russian Orthodoxy, and so promote atheism and lead to a decline in moral values.[26]

The argument about the old and new styles was an argument about Russia's future. This is an important point. It is easy to see Shishkov as backward-looking, but he was not trying to turn his back on high culture. Rather he was trying to *create* it, where it did not exist, but do so in an organic fashion. The "old style" was not actually old, just a different type of new.

Shishkov's anti-French position grouped him with those who after the 1807 Treaty of Tilsit formed the so-called "Russian Party," a loose collection of conservative-minded Russians who opposed the treaty as well as Alexander I's reform plans. Another member of the Russian Party was Count Fyodor Rostopchin, a Moscow nobleman of Tatar descent who from 1798 to 1801 had served as foreign minister under Emperor Paul. Moscow was the home of a considerable proportion of Russia's conservative intellectuals in the nineteenth century, reflecting its status as Russia's traditional capital in opposition to the Western-oriented St. Petersburg. Rostopchin had initially favored staying out of the wars that engulfed Europe in the aftermath of the French revolution,[27] but Napoleon's victory over Prussia and Russia in 1807 convinced him that France posed a serious danger to Russian security. He therefore dedicated himself to promoting Russian patriotism and purging Russia of what he considered subversive French elements. In an 1807 pamphlet, he wrote that there was no reason to copy France, for "What don't we have? We have or can have everything. A merciful Tsar, a generous nobility, rich merchants, and a hard-working people."[28]

Another important activist was Sergei Glinka, editor of the journal *Russkii vestnik*, which published the work of many prominent conservatives, including Shishkov and Rostopchin.[29] *Russkii vestnik* promoted a patriotic view of Russian history, celebrating heroes from Russia's past, attacking alleged French decadence, and supporting Shishkov's opposition to the new literary style.[30] Glinka expounded a utopian view of Russia as having been a harmonious society prior to Peter the Great,[31] and supported the idea that the Russian people embodied an exceptional way of life.[32] He and Shishkov helped to lay the groundwork for the development of Slavophilism thirty years later.

Conservatism in Russia began as an opposition movement. The French invasion of 1812 changed the situation. Suddenly, the tsar had need of eloquent anti-French patriots. Alexander appointed Rostopchin governor of Moscow, and named Shishkov as his state secretary, in which capacity the admiral was responsible for drafting the tsar's official proclamations. Shishkov used these to portray the war as being one between two civilizations: decadent, irreligious France, and peaceful, pious Russia. The war, wrote Shishkov on behalf of the tsar, was "for belief against unbelief, for freedom against love of power, for humanity against brutality."[33]

Conservatives were united in resisting the French invasion, but once the French had been driven out of Russia they disagreed on what to do next. Some, such as Glinka, felt that Russia should pursue the war and depose Napoleon. This was the policy that Alexander followed, leading Glinka to comment later that "it was Russia in 1813–1814 that saved Europe from itself and gave its civilization new light."[34] Shishkov, however, opposed carrying the war beyond Russia's borders, fearing the effects of exposing the troops to foreign influences.[35] "[War] be damned!" he wrote. "If you killed all scholars . . . all people would be turned into wicked boors; whereas if you killed all soldiers . . . all people would live in peace."[36] Shishkov thus fits into what one might call the "isolationist" tradition within Russian conservatism. Due to the attention given to Russian imperialism and messianism, this isolationist tendency tends to be ignored, but it is important nonetheless. Not every Russian conservative has believed in Russia's mission to save the West.

Shishkov was not entirely wrong to fear that the Russian advance into Europe would expose Russia to foreign influences. In 1814, as the Russian army marched through Germany, Roksandra Sturdza, a maid of honor to Alexander I's wife, Empress Elizaveta Alekseevna, introduced Alexander to two leading figures of the German "Awakening," Juliane von Krüdener and Johann Heinrich Jung-Stilling.[37] The Awakening was a form of religious revival that rejected dogmatism and emphasized the possibility of a direct relationship between man and God without the requirement of the intercession of priests.[38] These characteristics reflected the Awakening's Protestant origin, and as such challenged traditional Orthodoxy. Tsar Alexander nevertheless found the movement attractive and gave it his blessing.

Russia's triumph over France helped to create in Alexander's mind a sense of his own historical mission. His thinking became more and more mystically inclined. Perhaps the most obvious manifestation of this was the Holy Alliance, agreed by the rulers of Russia, Prussia, and Austria in September 1815. One of the prime architects of the Holy Alliance was Roksandra Sturdza's brother Aleksandr, who was an official in the Russian diplomatic service. Sturdza regarded the Alliance as a means of uniting all of Christianity against, as he put it, "the non-belief of rationalism." In an 1815 book entitled *Thoughts on the Study and Spirit of the Orthodox Church*, Aleksandr Sturdza argued that only Orthodoxy had remained true to Christian principles. The French Revolution had been God's punishment for the rationalism of Western Europe, but through the Holy Alliance, Russia could morally resurrect Europe as a whole.[39] Sturdza was of Romanian origin, wrote in

French, and married a German.[40] He was not a xenophobe. But he also accepted the Romantic view of the world, and "believed nations should assert their cultural identity rather than permit it to be dictated by foreigners . . . he also held that the 'people,' in particular the peasants, were closer to nature, God, and Truth than were the more decadent people of the cities."[41]

Alexander's new religious zeal had domestic as well as international consequences. In 1816 the tsar appointed one of Russia's most prominent "awakened," Prince Aleksandr Golitsyn, to be the minister of enlightenment, with responsibility for matters such as education and censorship. In 1817 this post was retitled minister of spiritual affairs and popular enlightenment. As it combined both religious and educational matters, Golitsyn's department became known as the "Dual Ministry." The new organization reflected the fact that religion was now seen as forming the foundation of Russia's educational system. The ministry has been described as "intended to be nothing less than a major step towards the salvation of Russian society by means of a wholesale application of Christian principles . . . to the entire range of intellectual life."[42]

Golitsyn was strongly influenced by Western European mystical literature. He regarded all Christian confessions as equal and wished to unite them in a universal Christianity.[43] As head of the Dual Ministry, Golitsyn encouraged the work of the newly formed Russian Bible Society, which had dozens of branches throughout Russia within a few years of its founding. The Society's mission was to make the Bible available to ordinary people. To this end, Tsar Alexander suggested that it translate the New Testament into Russian. This resulted in the publication of a Russian version of the four Gospels in 1822–23. This translation was remarkable in that it was published without a parallel Church Slavonic text, an omission that angered traditionalists.[44] Further angering them was Golitsyn's apparent indifference toward schismatics, exemplified by the fact that groups such as the Old Believers and the Molokan sect joined the Bible Society.[45] Initially, some Orthodox bishops supported the Bible Society. Metropolitan Filaret of Moscow, for instance, participated in the translation of the New Testament.[46] The Orthodox hierarchy was not entirely averse to change. But as time went on, church leaders became more and more convinced that the Bible Society was undermining the church's interests and propagating heresy.

Meanwhile, Golitsyn was endeavoring to overhaul Russian education in order to purge it of rationalist philosophy and reconstitute it on religious foundations. Helping him was Aleksandr Sturdza, whom Tsar Alexander had asked to investigate disturbances among students in German universities. Having carried out his investigation, Sturdza concluded that the disturbances were a product of German universities' autonomy and rationalism. The universities were bastions of "revolutionary spirit and atheism," Sturdza claimed.[47] The Dual Ministry, intent on

ensuring that Russian universities did not turn out the same way, earned a reputa-
tion as reactionary, oppressive, and obscurantist.

A key moment came in 1819 when the ministry sent one of its officials, Mikhail
Magnitsky, to investigate Kazan University, about 850 kilometers east of Moscow.
Magnitsky revealed what have been described as "undoubtedly scandalous defi-
ciencies, abuses, and crimes by officials" in Kazan, including theft of "significant
sums from the university budget . . . falsification of examinations, and a doubt-
ful level of qualifications of a significant part of the teachers and professors."[48]
Magnitsky went beyond these criticisms, however. He complained of a lack of
courses in religion, a prevalent "spirit of deism," and a preference for philosophy.
Shortly after writing his report, he was appointed head of the Kazan educational
district, and set about implementing reforms. In instructions issued to the rector
of Kazan University, Magnitsky stressed that the teaching of all subjects should
be founded on "the spirit of the Holy Gospels." A theology department was created, and Magnitsky directed that in the study of philosophy, "Anything that does
not agree with the reason of the Holy Scripture is an error and a lie and should
be rejected." Political science was to rest upon Moses, David, and Solomon, not
upon Plato and Aristotle. Scientists were to stress the limits of human knowledge
and point to the "wisdom of the Creator." Medical students were to be taught that
healing was inseparable from Christian love. Studies of literature were to focus
on the Bible. All students were to attend prayers and to be evaluated for their
"moral content."[49] Reason, Magnitsky said, was akin to "the diabolical spirit."[50] It
was necessary, he wrote, "to create a new science and new art, completely filled
with the spirit of Christ, replacing the false science that arose under the influence
of paganism and non-belief."[51]

In 1821, the St. Petersburg educational district also received a new chief, Dmitry
Runich, who immediately set about imposing similar reforms on St. Petersburg
Imperial University.[52] Runich had previously persuaded the government to ban
a book by Professor A. P. Kunitsyn that had argued that Russia was ready for a
constitutional form of government. The Dual Ministry had become a firm believer
in the need for censorship. Aleksandr Sturdza wrote:

> To permit people without conscience and status to write and publish without pun-
> ishment everything their mood dictates . . . means to place an immoral way of life
> under the protection of the law, to push the moods of society in a false direction
> and forever to leave them in error. . . . The law must prescribe their silence, put them
> under continual surveillance, and establish just rules of responsibility.[53]

In his history of Russian conservatism in the reign of Alexander I, Alexander
Martin refers to the religious conservatives of the Dual Ministry as Russia's

"second conservative wave"[54] (the first having consisted of men such as Shishkov and Rostopchin who had joined the Russian Party in the first decade of the century). Yet it is somewhat debatable whether the term "conservative" suits them. While some of them did put forward ideas of organic change, in other cases the religious concepts they propagated had little or nothing in common with Russian tradition. Indeed, they were in some ways quite revolutionary. At any rate, the first and second "waves" soon found themselves at loggerheads, for the former strongly objected to what they considered the anti-Orthodox line pursued by the latter. The result was a conservative backlash against the ministry.

Initially, the prime mover of the Orthodox opposition to the Dual Ministry was the rector of the St. Petersburg seminary, Archimandrite Innokenty, who argued that those who chose a Protestant form of "inner Christianity," such as that proposed by the Awakening, opened the doors for the Antichrist.[55] In his role as church censor, Innokenty refused to allow publication of a book by Jung-Stilling that Golitsyn had recommended.[56] By contrast, he permitted the publication of a book by E. I. Stanevich entitled *Conversation on a Baby's Grave about the Immortality of the Soul*, in which Stanevich sharply criticized religious mysticism and "the inner church." This constituted a direct attack on Golitsyn's policy. Golitsyn appealed to the tsar, and as a result Stanevich was expelled from Russia and Innokenty was exiled to the city of Penza, 600 kilometers south of Moscow.[57]

The banner of leadership of the Orthodox opposition now passed to one of Innokenty's former students, Archimandrite Fotii, head of the Iuryev Monastery near Novgorod (believed to be the oldest monastery in Russia). Fotii was a strong critic of the state of religious life in Russia and feared that Orthodoxy was on the verge of collapse due to foreign pressures. "The majority live like pagans," he complained, "not only don't they go to church for services, but even on important holidays . . . they occupy themselves with feasts, balls, games, theaters; they don't keep fasts and don't think anything of breaking them; pseudo–Orthodox Russians do everything impure, along with Germans who believe in different creeds." St. Petersburg was particularly degenerate in Fotii's opinion. "Love of God is scarcest in Peter," he wrote, "what can one call this town other than Babylon, Egypt, Sodom and Gomorrah?"[58]

With the help of a wealthy noblewoman, A. A. Orlova-Chesmenskaia, Fotii gradually gathered a circle of supporters among the Petersburg nobility. Thanks to them, he was able in June 1822 to obtain an audience with the tsar.[59] Fotii complained to Alexander that "the enemies of the Holy Church are getting stronger," and urged him to fight against secret societies. In 1820, Freemasons had played a prominent role in a series of revolutions in Europe, which began in the Kingdom of the Two Sicilies, then spread to Spain and Portugal. This made Alexander receptive to Fotii's message about the danger posed by secret societies. Two months after meeting Fotii, the tsar issued a decree banning Masonic lodges and other secret organizations.[60] Fotii's influence was on the rise.

This put him in a useful position when in 1824 Golitsyn finally overstepped the mark and gave the opposition an opportunity to turn the tsar against him. The pretext for action was the publication, with Golitsyn's support, of a book by a German Lutheran minister, I. E. Gossner. Gossner pointed out that the Gospels contained no discussion of church rituals, and argued that many churches were human, not holy in character. Furthermore, Gossner criticized the institution of the priesthood for standing between believers and God, and urged readers not to obey earthly authorities that were suppressing "true Christianity."[61] This amounted to a frontal assault on key Orthodox precepts.

In April 1824, Fotii sent two letters to the tsar complaining that Gossner's book was contrary to the Orthodox religion. He wrote that "this new religion is faith in the approaching Anti-Christ, the on-coming revolution, the thirst for blood-shed, fulfilling the spirit of Satan."[62] Alexander summoned Fotii for an audience, at which the archimandrite repeated his accusations. Alexander then ordered an investigation. On the basis of an analysis by Admiral Shishkov, the investigation concluded that Gossner's conclusions were "contrary to the laws of all Christian religions." Gossner was expelled from Russia, and Golitsyn's position was greatly weakened.[63]

Fotii pressed his advantage. He saw himself as fighting a "universal Masonic conspiracy,"[64] and in May 1824 he wrote again to the tsar, denouncing the "revolutionary plans" being hatched by "secret societies, whose objective is the establishment of a universal monarchy."[65] It is hard to say how seriously Alexander took these accusations. Russian historian Iu. E. Kondakov argues that the tsar regarded the priest as a holy "fool," but had to pay attention to him because he knew that Fotii was the spokesman for a larger group of influential personalities, including Shishkov and a leading member of the Holy Synod, Metropolitan Serafim.[66] According to this interpretation, Fotii "was merely the weapon" of this larger group, not the prime mover of events.[67]

Whatever the truth, Alexander had by now lost faith in Golitsyn and his policies. On May 15, 1824, he dismissed Golitsyn from his post and abolished the Dual Ministry. The Bible Society did not last much longer. Following Alexander's death in November 1825, his successor Nicholas I ordered its dissolution in April 1826.[68] The Orthodox opposition triumphed over the mystics.

POLITICAL CONSERVATISM

Like cultural conservatism, political conservatism in Russia emerged in opposition to prevailing trends, in this case Alexander I's efforts to reform Russia's political system in the decade following his accession to the throne in 1801. Alexander put his state secretary, Mikhail Speransky, in charge of the process, and in 1809 Speransky put forward a program that aimed to introduce elements of the rule of law and representative government. Some of his proposals were purely administrative in nature. For instance, to improve state administration, all public servants would have to pass examinations in order to be promoted. Other proposals went further. While they would not have dismantled the Russian autocracy, they would have been a significant first step toward the creation of a constitutional monarchy. Most important were plans to create an elected legislature, to be known as the State Duma, and an appointed State Council, which would act as a second, advisory chamber.[69]

Speransky's reforms energized the Russian Party, which saw them as threatening the status of the Russian nobility as well as being the first step on a liberal slippery slope, which could lead eventually to French-style revolution. A leading figure in the Russian Party was one of Alexander I's sisters, Grand Duchess Ekaterina Pavlovna. In 1810 she invited the historian Nikolai Karamzin to visit her in Tver, where her husband was governor. When Karamzin arrived, the grand duchess asked him to write a memorandum on the political situation in Russia. The result was one of the foundational texts of Russian political conservatism, Karamzin's *Memoir on Ancient and Modern Russia.*[70]

Many nineteenth-century Russian conservatives went through a liberal, or even radical socialist, phase in their youth. Karamzin was no exception. In 1789 and 1790, when he was in his early twenties, he traveled to Europe and watched the revolutionary leader Maximilien Robespierre speak in the National Assembly in Paris. At this point, he was still very much an Enlightenment thinker, writing that "the path of education and enlightenment is one for all people." Russia, he said, had to follow the same path as the rest of Europe.[71] Gradually, however, the experience of the French Revolution and the Napoleonic Wars pushed him away from liberalism and cosmopolitanism toward a belief that gradual, organic change was preferable to revolution and that even a bad order was better than the chaos that revolution brought. In an 1802 article, he said:

> Utopia will ever remain a dream of good minds, or at least it can never be realized but by the imperceptible effects of time, by means of the slow but certain and safe advances of the human mind, enlightenment, upbringing, and good manners. . . . But every violent upheaval is ruinous. . . . The Revolution clarified our ideas: we saw that civil order is sacred even with its local and accidental imperfections; that its authority is not tyranny, but a safeguard from tyranny; that by shattering this beneficent shield, the people suffer dreadful calamities, infinitely worse than all the customary abuses of power; that even the Turkish government is to be preferred to the anarchy which invariably follows political upheavals; . . . that the

institutions of antiquity are endowed with a magical power which no power of the intellect is capable of replacing.[72]

In *Memoir on Ancient and Modern Russia*, Karamzin argued that, historically, when state power had been weak and divided, Russia had succumbed to anarchy or foreign conquest; but when it had been strong and centralized, Russia had flourished. Karamzin concluded that "autocracy founded and resurrected Russia. Whenever her system of government has changed, she has perished."[73] It followed that Speransky's administrative and political reforms should be rejected. The tsar's subjects should tell him, "You may do everything, but you may not legally limit your power!"[74]

Like Shishkov, Karamzin argued that nations had to progress in an organic manner, in accordance with their own customs. He wrote, "Two states may stand on the same level of civil enlightenment but with different customs. A state may borrow useful information from another without copying its ways. These ways may change naturally, but to prescribe regulations for them is coercion and unlawful even for an autocratic monarch."[75] Politically, this argument implied rejecting foreign models and sticking with Russia's proven system of government—autocracy.

Karamzin saw autocracy as unbound by law but limited by custom, religion, and the innate rights of the nobility,[76] and he harshly criticized the tyrannical behavior of past rulers. He complained, for instance, that Peter the Great had resorted to "tortures and executions," while St. Petersburg was "founded on tears and corpses."[77] Similarly, wrote Karamzin, Alexander I's father, Emperor Paul, "began to rule through general terror, following no rules except his own fancy. He considered us not his subjects but his slaves."[78] Legitimate authority had bounds, wrote Karamzin, while indiscriminate punishment was despotic. In particular, the autocrat had to respect the rights of the landed nobility. "Autocracy is Russia's palladium; its integrity is necessary for its happiness," he concluded. "But from this it does not follow that the Sovereign, the sole source of power, should humiliate the nobility."[79] Autocracy was not the same as despotism. It was a form of undivided, but at the same time limited, power.

Memoir on Ancient and Modern Russia remained unpublished in Karamzin's lifetime. More immediately influential were the twelve volumes of his *History of the Russian State*, published between 1818 and 1826. The *History* repeated many of the themes developed in the *Memoir*. Karamzin claimed, for instance, that "our fatherland owes its grandeur to the happy introduction of monarchical power,"[80] but he also strongly criticized rulers such as Ivan the Terrible who had abused their position. His approach has been described as one of "Christian moralism," which maintained that monarchical authority "could be rendered fully compatible with justice and moderation."[81] Taking this line of thought a little further, in his history of Russian liberalism Victor Leontovitsch labels Karamzin's philosophy as "liberal absolutism" rather than "pure conservatism."[82] The application of the label "liberal" to Karamzin is rather contentious, but it draws attention once again to the difficulty of dividing Russian political philosophers strictly according to a liberal-conservative dichotomy. Elements of liberalism and conservatism often went hand in hand.

SOCIAL-ECONOMIC CONSERVATISM

At the start of the nineteenth century, Russian conservatives paid little attention to social and economic issues, although they did not ignore them entirely. The primary concern was the question of serfdom. At that time, the vast bulk of the Russian population consisted of peasants. About half of these were "state peasants," who were tied to the land and had obligations toward the state in the form of taxes or labor. The other half consisted of privately owned serfs, whose obligations were primarily toward the noble landowners who controlled them. Needing the nobility in order to govern the country, eighteenth-century Russian rulers had sought to strengthen noble authority. To this end they had expanded serfdom, bringing more and more peasants under its sway, and had also increased nobles' powers over their serfs. At the same time, the process of Westernization begun by Peter the Great had produced a cultural divide between the peasantry and the nobility, with the former retaining traditional Russian customs while the latter increasingly adopted Western ones. By 1800, therefore, Russia consisted of a small group of Westernized nobles ruling over a much larger group of non-Westernized peasants. The dangers inherent in such an arrangement made the future of serfdom a matter of considerable importance.

Conservatives were aware of the huge gulf dividing Russia's two main social classes. In a 1792 story entitled *Poor Liza*, Karamzin described an ill-fated romance between a nobleman and a peasant girl, ending with the suicide of the latter. "Even peasant women know how to love," Karamzin wrote. *Poor Liza* attracted considerable attention for its "motif of social inequality."[83] Nevertheless Karamzin, like most people of his class, considered this inequality to be a natural phenomenon, and denounced revolutionary concepts of equality as senseless. In 1825 he wrote,

> Liberals! What do you want? Peoples' happiness? But is there happiness where there is death, illness, vice, passion? The foundation of civil societies is unchangeable; you can put the lower classes on top, but there will always be lower classes and higher ones, freedom and lack of freedom, wealth and poverty, pleasure and suffering.[84]

Karamzin argued in favor of serfdom. Peasants, he claimed, were "lazy by nature, by experience, by ignorance of the benefits of hard work."[85] If given freedom, he claimed, "the peasants will take to drinking and villainy," and would become even poorer than they were already. According to Karamzin, "They have the experience of slaves. It seems to me that for the stability of the state it is safer to enslave men than to prematurely give them freedom, for which it is necessary to prepare them through moral improvement."[86]

This would become a common argument of Russian conservatives in the decades that followed—a rejection of various forms of political or social freedoms on the grounds that people were not morally ready for them. It followed from this that the moral improvement of the people was a necessary prerequisite for any political or social reform. What Karamzin and others were not very good at explaining was how precisely this moral improvement was to take place while people remained serfs.

Rostopchin put forward arguments similar to Karamzin's. "An agriculture of free peasants cannot prosper in Russia," he wrote, "because the Russian peasant doesn't like arable farming, and doesn't take care of it, seeing no use in it." Rostopchin predicted that if peasants gained their freedom they would soon fall into debt and effectively become slaves of a new class of rich peasants who would exploit them and force them to pay off loans they had given them.[87] To this he added a philosophical twist: freedom was in any case unnatural, "a word that imprisons our feelings with a promise of independence, and is as dangerous for mankind and society as fruits that look beautiful but contain in themselves cruel poison."[88] According to Rostopchin:

> The word "liberty" or "freedom" portrays a flattering but unnatural condition for man, for our lives are incessantly dependent on the whole. We are free in our will, but not in its execution, in front of which stand moral and physical obstacles. Social relations and connections make each person dependent on others.[89]

Shishkov similarly regarded social hierarchy to be the natural order of things. "Any connection between people, in which some of them give orders and others obey, is morally and beneficially founded," he wrote, adding that "the people is like a river flowing within its banks; but increase the amount of water, and it will burst its banks and nobody will be able to hold back its savageness. The people's prosperity consists in restraint and obligation."[90]

Not all conservatives agreed, although there was no discernible pattern in terms of who leaned which way. Aleksandr Sturdza, for instance, argued in favor of abolishing serfdom on the grounds that it damaged Russia's moral development.[91] And in 1818, Count Aleksei Arakcheev, often regarded as one of the more reactionary public servants of the era, put forward a proposal that would have allowed serfs to buy their freedom if their masters agreed.[92] Glinka also opposed serfdom, and refused an inheritance of thirty serfs, saying, "I will not take, and will never have, a person as property."[93] According to Glinka, "True Russian landowners . . . were always humane landowners. They knew and tried to imprint in the hearts of their children that *peasants are people just as they are.*"[94]

As far as economic development was concerned, conservatives tended to favor protectionist policies, with some, such as Glinka and Runich, proposing high tariffs on luxury goods for moral reasons.[95] An exemption was Karamzin, who was in favor of free trade and opposed basing the currency on either gold or silver.[96] By the standards of the time, this made him an economic liberal.

There were also some disagreements about the desirability of industrialization. Aleksandr Sturdza regarded agriculture as morally superior to trade and industry. According to Arkady Minakov, Sturdza was the first to clearly formulate the "anti-capitalist motives . . . [that] were quite characteristic of Russian conservatism."[97] By contrast, Glinka wrote that "industry is the true and inexhaustible source of wealth. What country is more suited to it than Russia? . . . Where there are factories and manufacturing, there without doubt are also established schools." Industry, said Glinka, reduced poverty, provided labor for the excess agricultural population, and strengthened the state and the army. Contrary to Sturdza, he also argued that it improved morals, due to the required ethos of hard work.[98]

CONCLUSION

The beginnings of Russian conservatism in the reign of Alexander I demonstrate many of the points made in the previous chapter. Russian conservatives were not defenders of the status quo. Indeed, they were often deeply dissatisfied with it. They sought to resist the pressures of Westernization and to create an organic national culture but very few were anti-Western per se. Indeed, many of their ideas were strongly influenced by intellectual currents in the West. Meanwhile, there was disagreement on linguistic, religious, political, and socioeconomic issues. Oppressive politics could be combined with apparently liberal stances on certain issues, such as Karamzin's economic liberalism, and Sturdza's and Glinka's opposition to serfdom. Some conservatives believed in Russia's holy mission to save Europe; others did not, and felt that Russia should worry only about defending itself.

While Russian conservatives believed in autocracy, they certainly did not identify it with unlimited power and unquestioning submission. Even the clergy resisted state policy when it threatened their interests. In fact, for most of this period, conservatives found themselves in loyal opposition to the state and its policies.

Cultural concerns dominated early Russian conservatism. Political and social-economic concerns were of secondary importance. Russian conservatives were engaged in a process of nation-building, and were deeply interested in issues of language, history, and religion. In this they had some success. Shishkov lost the battle against the new style in literature, but he helped introduce the concept of Romantic nationalism into Russian thought. Karamzin and Glinka contributed to the creation of a patriotic narrative in Russian history, while Karamzin also forged an ideology of the state. And the church conservatives ensured that Orthodoxy retained its dominant position in Russian society and so remained a central part of Russian national identity.

CHAPTER 3

OFFICIAL NATIONALITY

On December 1, 1825, Tsar Alexander I died of typhus at the early age of forty-seven. Next in line to the throne was his brother Grand Duke Konstantin Pavlovich. Konstantin, however, had made it clear that he had no intention of becoming tsar. On Alexander's death, therefore, the throne passed to the second of his three brothers, who became Tsar Nicholas I. Nicholas's thirty-year reign would witness several important developments in Russian conservatism, most notably the creation of the ideology of "Official Nationality."

Nicholas, who was twenty-nine years old when he became tsar, was not popular with the guards officer corps in St. Petersburg, some of whom were members of a secret organization known as the Northern Society, which advocated relatively liberal policies such as the abolition of serfdom, the establishment of the rule of law, and an elected legislative assembly.[1] On December 26, 1825, officers of the Northern Society led three thousand troops out onto the streets of the capital, and refused to swear allegiance to Nicholas. This "Decembrist revolt" lasted only a few hours. Nicholas ordered loyal troops to suppress the rebellion, and by the end of the day it had been crushed. Several of the Decembrists were executed, and others were exiled to Siberia.

Nicholas had secured the throne, but the threat of revolution continued to hang over his entire reign. In 1826 the new tsar created the Third Section of His Majesty's Own Chancery, which was in effect a secret service designed to root out political subversion.[2] Nicholas did not rely solely on repression, however. He was aware that the Decembrist revolt had deep roots. As W. Bruce Lincoln writes, "the entire fabric of Russian society was permeated with an arbitrariness which left subordinates at the mercy of their superiors."[3] One reason for this was the small size of the central state administration. Russia had only 1.3 state officials per thousand inhabitants, compared to 4.1 in England and 4.8 in France.[4] Nicholas therefore sought to address the country's problems through administrative means, centralizing power in the hands of the state bureaucracy. In effect, he attempted to create a modern bureaucratic state.

The emphasis on bureaucratic regulation suited Nicholas's character. He was a great lover of order, and had a high regard for the military. He said:

> Here [in the army] there is order, there is a strict unconditional legality, no imper-
> tinent claims to know all the answers, no contradiction, all things flow logically one
> from the other; no one commands before he himself has learned to obey; no one
> steps in front of anybody else without lawful reason; everything is subordinated to
> one definite goal, everything has its purpose. That is why I feel so well among these
> people, and why I shall always hold in honor the calling of a soldier. I consider the
> entire human life to be merely service, because everybody serves.[5]

Nicholas applied this principle in his own life. He worked extremely hard, perhaps too hard, showing an unwillingness to delegate. He believed that the French
Revolution had occurred as a result of Louis XVI's leniency. He was determined
"not to be soft," but to fulfill his duty to be a tough ruler.[6] At the same time, he recognized the need for reform. But he strongly believed that this had to be gradual
in nature. In a manifesto issued on the occasion of his coronation, he said:

> Not by daring and rash dreams, which are always destructive, but gradually, and
> from above, laws will be issued, defects remedied, and abuses corrected. In this man-
> ner all modest hopes for improvement, all hopes for strengthening the rule of law,
> and for the expansion of true enlightenment, and the development of industry, will
> be gradually fulfilled.[7]

Internal political dynamics also forced Nicholas to be cautious in enacting
reform. As before, the weakness of the central state meant that the tsar had to rely
on the landed nobility to maintain order in the country. He could not afford to
alienate the nobles lest he meet the same fate as his grandfather, Emperor Peter
III, and his father, Emperor Paul, both of whom had been murdered in palace
coups, in 1762 and 1801, respectively. Particularly on the matter of serfdom,
Nicholas proved unwilling to impose his will upon the nobility. The autocrat was
not all-powerful.

Perhaps to compensate for this lack of direct power, Nicholas sought to influence Russia indirectly by means of ideology. The result was the creation of the
concept of "Official Nationality." Nicholas believed that Russia's educational
system was in large part responsible for the revolutionary thinking behind the
Decembrist revolt. He also associated the revolt with foreign ideas, especially

liberalism. Nicholas complained of "alien ideology," "lack of respect for Russian culture," "foreign influences," and "a fatal indulgence in pseudo-knowledge." He sought to develop an alternative ideology that would counter Western European liberalism and emphasize Russia's distinctiveness, thereby forestalling revolution. To this end, in 1832 he appointed Count Sergei Uvarov as minister of popular enlightenment to reform the educational system and instill within it a new "national" spirit.[8] According to his biographer Cynthia Whittaker, Uvarov was a "statesman of progressive vision but cautious disposition," who sought a "middle ground" between revolution and reaction and "thought that each country achieved its goals by way of its own organic path."[9] As minister of popular enlightenment, he "set himself a two-pronged and exquisitely delicate task: to facilitate Russia's transition to maturity but to keep the country youthful until it was fully ripe for change, in other words to go forward while standing still."[10] The result was the ideology of Official Nationality, which Uvarov unveiled in 1833, and whose purpose was "to guide Russia through what is often called 'modernization' . . . while preserving social and political stability and a sense of national pride."[11]

Uvarov was in many respects a progressive minister. Previously, as director of the Petersburg educational district, he had founded St. Petersburg Imperial University. As minister of popular enlightenment, he "increased the number of educational institutions by 700, raised teachers' salaries and pensions, sponsored building programs, expanded the curricula at all levels, and encouraged the development of laboratories, collections, libraries, and scholarly organizations."[12] Under his tutelage, Russian schools and universities are considered to have become "among the best in Europe."[13]

Official Nationality was the moral counterpart of more practical reforms instituted by Uvarov. It consisted of three principles—"Orthodoxy, Autocracy, Nationality." According to Uvarov, these were "the principles which form the distinctive character of Russia, and which belong only to Russia." They were to be the basis of the moral education of Russia's youth, and "the anchor of our salvation."[14] They soon extended beyond the educational system, however, to become the ideological principles of Nicholas's Russia as a whole.

Official Nationality had the advantage of being succinct, and it accorded with the views of the majority of the educated class.[15] It was also rather vague. As a result, Russians were not in complete agreement as to what its component parts meant. For some, the focus of attention was the royal dynasty and the state; for others the Orthodox Church; and for others the Russian people. Pan-Slavism, which identified Russia with the wider Slavic community, also emerged in this period, while some conservatives eschewed Official Nationality altogether, notably the Slavophiles (who will be discussed in chapter 4).

Official Nationality was not incompatible with change, and the Russian state did undertake some reforms in the first twenty years of Nicholas's reign. Reform came to an end, however, following the revolutions that spread across Europe in 1848. Prior to that point, Nicholas had followed a foreign policy that if not strictly speaking isolationist, certainly sought to avoid foreign conflict. Nicholas wrote, "I love peace and recognize its value and necessity."[16] When in July 1830 a revolution overthrew King Charles X of France, replacing him with King Louis-Philippe, Nicholas blamed Charles for his fate and remarked that "as long as the French slaughter each other, it is no concern of Ours."[17] It was another matter when revolt broke out in Russian-controlled Poland in November 1830. After crushing the revolt, Nicholas modified Poland's constitution to eliminate its autonomy and make it an inseparable part of the Russian Empire. It was another matter too when revolution overthrew Louis-Philippe in 1848 and then spread to Hungary. At this point, the entire political order of Europe seemed to be under threat. In 1849, therefore, Nicholas ordered Russian troops into Hungary to suppress the revolution.

The last years of Nicholas's reign were associated with increasing domestic repression, as the tsar sought to stop the revolutionary virus from spreading to Russia. Russia's intervention in Hungary in 1849 and Nicholas's repressive domestic policies led the tsar to acquire the label "the gendarme of Europe." In 1853 a dispute between Russia and the Ottoman Empire escalated into war between Russia on one side and the Ottomans, England, and France on the other. The Crimean War, as it became known, ended with Russia's defeat in 1856. Nicholas had died a year earlier, in March 1855. His reign ended on a decidedly negative note.

Cultural Conservatism

It was no coincidence that Official Nationality originated in the Ministry of Popular Enlightenment. It was a cultural project, albeit one with a definite political purpose. Nationality was, however, loosely defined. There were three main strands of thinking, which to some degree overlapped but were nevertheless distinct. First, there was an Orthodox nationalism, which saw the West as the source of false doctrines, and which sought to renew Russia spiritually on the basis of the Orthodox religion. Notable figures associated with this strand of nationalism were the clergyman Ignaty Brianchaninov (1807–67) and the writer Nikolai Gogol (1809–52). Second, there was what one might term popular nationalism, which identified Russia with its people, its history, and its culture, and which also had connections with Pan-Slavism. An especially important proponent of this strand of nationalism was the historian and journalist Mikhail Pogodin (1800–1875). And finally, there was dynastic nationalism, which identified Russia with the state and in particular the Romanov dynasty. Nicholas I himself was the clearest advocate of this position.

It was also no coincidence that Orthodoxy came first in Uvarov's triad. Following the Orthodox opposition's victory over the Bible Society and the Dual Ministry, the relatively ecumenical religious vision of Alexander I's reign came to an end and Orthodoxy was confirmed as the primary religion of the Russian Empire. In Uvarov's eyes, Orthodoxy was the foundation both of autocracy and of nationality. As he wrote: "Without love for our ancestors' faith, the people, and also an individual person, must perish. The Russian who is dedicated to his fatherland can no more agree to the loss of one of the dogmas of Orthodoxy than he can to the theft of a single pearl from the crown of Monomakh [the ancient crown of the grand princes of Moscow]."[18] Autocracy, Uvarov believed, rested upon the population's belief in its holy nature. This belief was being undermined by the religious skepticism that had accompanied the Enlightenment.[19] The stress on Orthodoxy was not purely instrumental, however. Nicholas Riasanovsky notes that "Nicholas I and many of his followers believed in Orthodoxy. They understood it in a limited manner. . . . But the ideal and the profession of faith remained."[20]

The Russian Orthodox Church enjoyed a considerable revival during the reign of Nicholas I. Heather Coleman writes that in this period "the Russian church saw the development of an active pastoral care movement among priests who sought to reinvigorate their service to their flocks by complementing their liturgical role with social and educational activism."[21] One of the most notable features of the church's revival was a great expansion in monasticism. During the late nineteenth century the number of monks in Russia multiplied dramatically.[22] As Coleman says, "a great contemplative renewal . . . began in the second quarter of the [nineteenth] century."[23] Lay Orthodox believers flocked to monasteries to experience the church's "solemn liturgies, the relics of revered saints, and miraculous icons," in what has been described as "a mass phenomenon"[24] and "a massive upsurge of pilgrimage" drawing "millions of believers from all social backgrounds."[25]

At the heart of the religious renaissance was the Optina Hermitage, about 250 kilometers southwest of Moscow. This became famous as the home of holy "elders" who were visited by many of the leading conservative intellectuals of the nineteenth century, including Nikolai Gogol, Ivan Kireevsky, Konstantin and Ivan Aksakov, Fyodor Dostoevsky, and Konstantin Leontyev. One visitor was Ignaty Brianchaninov, who first came to the Optina monastery in 1828, and described how the elders "explained the proper and easy way of asceticism."[26] A nobleman who had served in the army, Brianchaninov later became abbot of the Monastery of St. Sergei, a poor monastery about 100 kilometers north of St. Petersburg, and then from 1857 to 1867 was bishop of the Caucasus and Stavropol. In 1988 he was canonized by the Russian Orthodox Church.

Brianchaninov played an important part in transforming Orthodox artistic practices. In the eighteenth century, icon painting and church music were strongly influenced by Italian examples. Brianchaninov commissioned composers such as Mikhail Glinka to develop new forms of music for the choir at St. Sergei monastery that would be more in keeping with Russian traditions. According to Irina Paert, "Brianchaninov was not a cultural purist, a champion of the return to medieval artistic idiom. He collaborated with the Academy of Arts and court musicians, who were trying to create a new style that would revive traditional art through modern cultural forms."[27] He is thus seen as a "reformer seeking to integrate the essence of Eastern Orthodoxy into a radically changing world."[28]

Brianchaninov was also the author of numerous essays voicing a conservative ideology. His writings have proven popular among Orthodox Christians in post-Soviet Russia, prompting Russian scholar Aleksandr Churkin to comment that Brianchaninov is nowadays "read by tens of thousands of believers, from the average man to the Patriarch," making him "probably the most published and read now" of all nineteenth-century ecclesiastical writers.[29] According to Churkin, "Modern Orthodox conservatives appreciate Brianchaninov's uncompromising stand against mysticism and Catholicism."[30] Brianchaninov held a deeply pessimistic view of Russia's spiritual condition. "The number of books containing false doctrine has increased," he wrote, "the number of minds that contain and teach others false doctrines has increased. The followers of Holy Truth have diminished to an absolute minimum. . . . A carnal life is preferred, the spiritual life is disappearing."[31] Brianchaninov believed that Western influence was largely to blame:

> We see the exceptional material development of Europe: in order to harmonize with Europe and to raise its status there, Russia by reason of state and political necessity must adopt European material development. But material development makes men cooler toward the Christian faith, allowing it to be practiced in only a superficial way. As our ties with Europe increase, it is inevitable that its religious teachings will intrude more and more into our Fatherland. All these teachings, from Popery to deism to atheism, are equally hostile to the Orthodox Faith.[32]

Brianchaninov advised believers to "stay away from books containing false teachings."[33] In particular, he denounced Catholic mystical texts, which at the time enjoyed some popularity among Russia's aristocracy. These, he said, led to "spiritual delusion." "Much filthy dust has been blown by western winds into the heart of the Church and into the heart of the nation, doing harm to our faith, morality, and national character," he wrote. In the place of the false Western teachings, he urged strict asceticism. He advised fellow monks:

> Let us avoid overeating and even satisfaction. Let us make our rule moderate, constant abstinence in food and drink. Let us deny ourselves the pleasures of tasty food and drink. Let us sleep sufficiently, but not excessively. Let us renounce idle talking, laughter, jokes, and scoffing.[34]

One author who shared Brianchaninov's views on the benefits of an ascetic lifestyle was the writer Nikolai Gogol, who died in 1852 of "starvation and exhaustion" following a prolonged regime of "fasting and incessant prayer."[35] In 1847, Gogol shocked many readers with the publication of what was widely considered a reactionary book, entitled *Selected Passages from Correspondence with Friends*. In it he wrote that in Homer's *Odyssey* one could see:

> how ancient man, with few instruments at his disposal, and with all the imperfection of his religion . . . through the simple fulfilment of ancient customs and rites which . . . were commanded to be passed down as sacred objects from father to son . . . acquired a harmony and beauty of action. . . . But we, with all our enormous resources and instruments . . . have been able to reach such slovenliness and disorder, both externally and internally, that we have managed to turn ourselves into something scrappy and petty . . . and, in addition to this, we have become so repulsive to one another that no one respects anyone else.[36]

Like so many other Russian conservatives, Gogol wished to change Russia, and felt that positive change depended above all upon spiritual renewal. In Gogol's eyes, such renewal derived in large part from suffering. "It is through suffering and grief that we will obtain fragments of wisdom that cannot be acquired from books," he wrote.[37] "Continually hearing that my life is hanging by a thread . . . I continually resign myself to it, and I cannot find words to thank God for my illness," he said also.[38] Spiritual renewal meant building the Russian nation on the foundations of Eastern Orthodoxy. Gogol predicted that Europe was heading toward bloody revolution, but the very fact that Russian national identity was still in the process of formation meant that Russia could avoid this fate. "Are we better than other peoples? Is our life closer to Christ than theirs?" Gogol asked, to which he replied:

> We are not better than anybody else, and our life is more unsettled and disordered than everybody else's. "We are worse than all others"—that is what we should always

say about ourselves. But there is in our nature something that prophesies to us. Our very disorderliness prophesies it to us. We are still molten metal, which has not yet been cast into its national form; we can still throw off, push away from ourselves things we do not like, and can still instill in ourselves all those things that other peoples, who have received and tempered their form, cannot. There is much in our fundamental nature, forgotten by us, that is close to the law of Christ.[39]

In particular, Gogol argued, Russia had retained "the full and all-around view of life," which contained "not only the soul and heart of man, but also his reason," unlike the "one-sided," rationalistic Western viewpoint.[40] By nurturing this full view of life, Russia could save not only itself but also the West. "You will see that Europe will come to us not to buy hemp and lard, but to purchase a wisdom that is no longer sold in European markets," Gogol predicted.[41]

The works of Brianchaninov and Gogol illustrate the close tie between Orthodoxy and nationality in the era of Nicholas I. Historian Mikhail Pogodin provided the basis for a slightly different form of Russian nationalism, which emphasized Russia's distinctiveness from the West for reasons that included but went beyond Orthodoxy. Born a serf in 1800, Pogodin rose to become professor of history at Moscow University and editor of the conservative journal *Moskvitianin* (The Muscovite). "Russia is a completely different state from the West. East is East, and West is West," he wrote,[42] adding that:

> We have a different climate from the West, a different geography, a different temperament, character, different blood, a different physiognomy, different opinions, a different way of thinking, a different faith, hopes, desires, pleasures, different relationships, different circumstances, a different History, everything is different.[43]

To explain these differences, Pogodin developed what became known as the "Norman Theory of History," which he adapted from the work of French historian Augustin Thierry on the Norman conquest of England. According to Pogodin, Western European states were formed when foreign invaders conquered territories and formed a privileged ruling class. This created a divide between the rulers, who were of one tribe, and the ruled, who were of another. Over time, through the processes of feudalism and urbanization, this divide evolved into a conflict not of tribes but of classes. By contrast, said Pogodin, "our state began not with conquest, but with invitation. Here is the source of the differences!"[44] The invitation in question was made when the early Russians invited the Viking prince Rurik to take the throne of Rus'. Consequently, said Pogodin:

> The winners and losers, subjugators and subjugated gave birth to two classes in the West, to nobility and slaves, but we had no victory, no subjugation, and so no

division between the rights of the newcomers and the indigenous people, the guests and the masters, no principle of nobility or of slavery.[45]

Russia had thereby avoided the class conflict that beset Europe, claimed Pogodin, and the foundation was provided for the creation of a harmonious order. In addition to this, Pogodin listed a number of other factors that explained Russia's distinctiveness, including the country's size, the pattern of settlement, the quality of the soil, the severe climate, the flat terrain, the system of rivers, the Slavic character, the religion, and education. "There were so many differences in the foundation of the Russian state compared to the West," Pogodin wrote.[46] It was therefore foolish to think that Russia should abandon its history and seek to emulate the West. "No!" he wrote, "The West can't be in the East, and the sun can't set where it rises."[47]

There were other reasons not to copy the West. First, Western Europe did not present just one political, social, or economic model that Russia could take as its own, but many. There were huge differences, for instance, between England, which was industrializing rapidly and had a form of constitutional government, and countries such as Austria, which were still largely rural and retained absolute monarchies. Second, the revolutionary upheavals that had shaken Europe in the previous forty years, beginning with the French Revolution and continuing through the revolutions in Spain and Portugal in 1820 and in France and Belgium in 1830, did not inspire confidence that Europe would enjoy a stable future. To Russian conservatives it seemed as if Europe was decadent and in decline. According to Pogodin, "Whoever looks dispassionately at the European states, with all due respect to their remarkable institutions . . . will agree that their time has passed, or at the very least they have seen better days."[48] Stepan Shevyryov (1806–64), who collaborated with Pogodin in editing the journal *Moskvitianin*, put this even more forcefully. He argued that Russia had to cast off the "magic spell" cast upon it by the West, and assert her own distinctiveness.[49] Shevyryov observed that "in our frank, friendly, and close relations with the West we have failed to notice that it is like a man who carries within himself a dreadful contagious disease. . . . We kiss him, embrace him . . . and allow the delights of the banquet to mask the odor of decay which he already emanates."[50]

Pogodin's solution to the problem of the decaying West was Pan-Slavism. "The future fate of the world depends on Russia," Pogodin wrote,[51] adding that "if in History, there is a succession of peoples, who one by one take their turn to serve humankind, then until now the Slavs have not had their turn; consequently, they should now step forward to start their great work for humanity."[52] Russia's first task was to liberate the Slavs who lived in the Ottoman and Austrian empires, "in whom flows the same blood as ours, who speak the same language and so, by the law of nature, sympathize with us."[53] Pogodin agitated for an aggressive objective in the Crimean War. "We must take Constantinople," he wrote.[54]

Pan-Slavism was not official policy. Indeed Nicholas I condemned it in no uncertain terms as a revolutionary idea that threatened the principle of states' territorial integrity and so undermined the foundations of the entire international order. Nicholas fulminated that

> under the guise of sympathy for the Slavic tribes supposedly suppressed in other states there is hidden the criminal thought of a union with these tribes, in spite of the fact they are subjects of neighbouring and in part allied states. And they expect to attain this goal not through the will of God, but by means of rebellious outbreaks to the detriment and destruction of Russia herself. . . . And if indeed, a combination of circumstances produces such a union [of the Slavs], this will mean the ruin of Russia.[55]

Nicholas was equally uninterested in Russifying the empire's non-Russian peoples, at one point ordering the arrest of the Slavophile Iury Samarin for statements that the tsar interpreted as an attack on the Baltic German nobility.[56] In general, Nicholas viewed Slavophilism as negatively as he did Pan-Slavism. For Nicholas, loyalty to the state and to him personally was far more important than ethnicity or national culture. Once again, therefore, it is important to draw a distinction between the nationalism of the Russian state and that of nationalist intellectuals.

POLITICAL CONSERVATISM

According to Uvarov, "Autocracy is the primary condition of Russia's existence. The Russian colossus rests on it, as the cornerstone of its greatness."[57] Russian conservatives were united in their support for the principle of autocracy. As time went on, however, some became disenchanted with its actual practice.

State policy under Nicholas I consisted of a combination of administrative and legal reform with political repression. The most important reform was the codification of Russian laws carried out by Mikhail Speransky and completed in 1833. By bringing together all of Russia's laws into a single publication, *The Digest of the Laws of the Russian Empire*, the codification at least in theory provided the basis for a law-based state by reducing the possibility of arbitrary application of the law.[58] This did not mean, however, that Russians began to enjoy more political liberty. In 1826, censorship was tightened with a new statute that prohibited "not only that which opposes the government . . . but anything which may weaken the respect it is due."[59] In 1838, censorship was relaxed, but following the revolutions in France and Hungary in 1848, political repression increased sharply and talk of reform came to an abrupt halt. The authorities restricted the teaching of law and philosophy at universities, faculty members were forbidden to travel abroad, and universities were prohibited from receiving foreign literature. The Slavophile thinker Aleksei Khomiakov complained that "censorship is an unheard-of scourge. You simply can't believe how far it goes."[60]

Nicholas I enjoyed some support among educated public opinion for his repressive measures. The revolutions of 1848 scared many among Russia's ruling class, and the "conservative mood increased as never before."[61] The poet Vasily Zhukovsky, for instance, wrote that the West was "a volcanic crater from which is pouring a destructive lava with a thunder of well-known disastrous cries: 'liberty, fraternity, equality.'" Zhukovsky concluded that only autocracy could stave off the forces of disorder and so lead the way in due course to enlightenment and freedom.[62]

Among the more devoted supporters of autocracy was Nikolai Gogol. In *Selected Passages from Correspondence with Friends*, published a year before the European revolutions of 1848, Gogol penned a long paean of praise to monarchy and the Romanov dynasty. Gogol wrote:

> Every event in our fatherland, beginning with the Tatar enslavement, visibly leads up to the concentration of power in the hands of one person. . . . Love has entered our blood; and we are all bound in a blood relationship with the tsar. And the sovereign has merged and become as one with his subjects to such an extent that we can all now see the general misfortune that would result if the sovereign forgot his subject and renounced him or if the subject forgot his sovereign and renounced him. How manifestly God's will is revealed in the choice for this task of the Romanov family and not another![63]

Not all conservatives were quite so laudatory. Brianchaninov, for instance, wrote that on the one hand, "power is linked with force, subordination is linked with suffering. So it is today; and so it always will be." On the other hand, "Our Savior gave mankind spiritual freedom, but he didn't eliminate authority. In his time of wandering on this earth he subordinated himself to the secular management of the world, saying that this was not his Kingdom."[64] The Christian was obliged to accept with a spirit of humility the suffering that came from subordination to earthly authority, and thereby emulate the suffering of Christ. According to Brianchaninov:

> The Savior of the world established His Kingdom on earth, but a spiritual Kingdom, which can exist in any human society, no matter what the civil system of this society

is called, monarchy or republic, or anything else; because the Kingdom of Christ, being not of this world, has no relation to the civil form of the state.[65]

Christians had to submit to the secular authorities, whatever form these might take, but there was nothing special about autocracy per se. Indeed Brianchaninov believed that "earthly power is nearly always connected with greater or lesser abuses, due to the fallen nature of man, his sin, and his limitations."[66] Still, mankind's inner freedom could be enjoyed under any form of government. "He who has spiritual freedom doesn't need civil freedom," Brianchaninov wrote, "whether he is in slavery, or prison, in fetters, or in the hands of the executioner, he is free. By contrast, even if he enjoys civil freedom, even if he enjoys complete prosperity, a man without spiritual freedom is a slave of sin and of his passions."[67]

Uvarov had yet another view. He produced a theory of organic, historical growth, according to which "states have their epochs of birth, infancy, youth, their actual maturity, and finally old age."[68] Different forms of government were associated with each age. Uvarov explained that this meant that "nationality doesn't consist of going backward or standing still; it doesn't demand immobility in ideas. The state system, like a human body, changes its external form according to its age."[69]

In Uvarov's scheme, when a country reached maturity it would acquire representative institutions and its citizens would enjoy full civil rights. Prior to that, it required an autocratic system of government that would gradually, and organically, develop the country and enlighten the people until such time as they reached maturity.[70] History gradually moved in the direction of freedom, but one could not leap ahead of the process and prematurely create institutions appropriate for a later stage of development.

Uvarov believed that Russia was still in the age of youth. Initially, he hoped that under the guidance of enlightened autocracy, it would reach maturity fairly rapidly. As time went on, however, he became more pessimistic. The moment for introducing representative institutions and civil rights kept being postponed.

For much of his career, Mikhail Pogodin was also an advocate for autocracy, which he viewed in a paternalistic way, writing:

> Russian history always imagines Russia as one family in which the sovereign is the father and the subjects are the children. The father retains complete power over the children, while giving them complete freedom. . . . While this union remains holy and unbroken, there is peace and happiness, but where it begins to shake, there is disorder, confusion, and alarm.[71]

The phrase "while giving them complete freedom" was important. Pogodin's view of the autocratic ideal was one that defended the people's liberty. He therefore strongly opposed the restrictions on freedom during Nicholas I's reign, and in 1848 even endeavored to enlist support among Russian intellectuals for a petition to the tsar against censorship.[72] In 1856, following Nicholas's death and Russia's defeat in the Crimean War, Pogodin wrote a scathing indictment of the repressive policies of the last years of Nicholas's rule. Russia's internal needs had been sacrificed in favor of foreign policy objectives, he said. In particular, fear of revolution and the resulting desire to maintain the existing order in Europe had induced Russia to spend vast sums of money on the military at the expense of other more valuable objectives, such as education.[73] Even worse, the Russian government had restricted access to education and suppressed any discussion of political matters. Literature was subjected to the same repressive measures as education, Pogodin complained: "It became impossible to write about any theological, philosophical, or political subject. . . . Whole periods of history were excluded . . . ancient writers were subjected to severe censorship."[74] Likewise, "the slightest sign of displeasure turned into a crime."[75] "Government is necessary and sacred, but government is weakened more by its own abuses than by free condemnation of its actions," Pogodin remarked, adding that "without openness [*glasnost'*] . . . every lie, untruth, and deceit receives the right of citizenship, proof of which we see in our official reports, according to which Russia is prospering." The silence produced by censorship "is a rotting and stinking cemetery, physically and morally. . . . No! Such an order leads not to happiness, not to glory, but to the abyss."[76]

Ministers hid the truth from the tsar, Pogodin said. Nobody was willing to tell the truth about the country's real situation. Instead they maintained a "system of paper pushing, a system of mutual deceit and mutual silence, a system of darkness, evil, and depravity, in the guise of subordination and legal order."[77] Pogodin argued that the government's repressive measures were all in vain. Their purpose was to prevent revolution, but unlike the West, Russia was a harmonious society without class divisions, he wrote. There was no possibility of revolution. There was, therefore, no need for political repression.[78]

Pogodin concluded that "the old system has had its day. . . . Russia needs a new system." He proposed the summoning of a Zemskaia Duma (which later Russian conservatives would generally call a "Zemsky sobor"), a consultative assembly representing the Russian people. "Freedom! That is the word that should resound above the autocratic Russian throne," said Pogodin. He then added more specific policy proposals: "Give the Poles a constitution"; "Declare an amnesty for all the Poles"; "Pardon our political prisoners"; "Declare our firm intention to gradually free the serfs"; "Allow anybody who wants to purchase land"; "Lighten censorship"; and in foreign affairs, "declare a system of non-interference; let every people live their lives freely."[79] Finally, Pogodin asserted, "We don't need a constitution, but we do need efficient and enlightened dictatorial government." Above all, though, what Russia required was *"glasnost'*, *glasnost'*, and *glasnost'*, education, education, and education."[80]

SOCIAL-ECONOMIC CONSERVATISM

Russia in the age of Nicholas I was a predominantly agricultural country. The largest single population group consisted of some 26 million state peasants, and the next largest of about 23 million privately owned serfs.[81] Industrial production was low by European standards, but did gradually increase. Its progress was restrained, however, by the fiscal policies pursued by Nicholas's finance minister, Count Egor Kankrin. These policies included limiting public spending in order to avoid large budget deficits, as well as stabilizing the currency and reducing inflation by linking the ruble to silver.[82] This meant that the state did not have substantial funds at its disposal to finance top-down industrialization. Kankrin opposed the building of railways, for instance, due to their large cost. Only in 1842 did Nicholas I approve Russia's first railway, a line between Moscow and St. Petersburg.[83] Industrial expansion did gradually gather pace, with the number of industrial workers in Russia doubling between 1825 and 1848,[84] but it failed to keep pace with economic growth in Western Europe, putting Russia in a weak position when the Crimean War broke out in 1853.

Serfdom is often held responsible for holding back Russia's economic progress. The central role that serfdom played in Russian society meant that its future pre-occupied Russian conservatives far more than theories of industrial development. The tsar himself wished to abolish it, but approached the issue with his normal caution. Nicholas set up a series of commissions to investigate the matter and make proposals, which resulted in some changes, such as permitting peasants to purchase their freedom if the estate on which they worked was put up for sale.[85] But Nicholas feared that massive disorder might erupt if the system of governing the countryside was changed. Moreover, he was hobbled by his belief in the sanctity of private property. If the serfs were freed without being granted land of their own, they would be impoverished. But they could not be granted land without infringing upon the property rights of the existing landowners. Nicholas never found a way to square this circle.[86] Consequently, in 1842 he told the State Council, "There is no doubt that serfdom, as it exists at present in our land, is an evil, palpable and obvious to all. But to touch it now would be a still more disastrous evil."[87] Unable to bring himself to take the final step and abolish serfdom, Nicholas instead focused on reducing the abuses associated with it. Between 1826 and 1855 he issued 108 decrees to protect serfs against landowners.[88] This, however, amounted to no more than tinkering with the system.

Nicholas and his government found themselves able to carry out a far more substantial reform of the system of state peasants. Under the guidance of the minister of state domains, P. D. Kiselyov, the government passed eight major laws on the issue between 1837 and 1840. The main thrust of the reforms was to provide safeguards for the peasants against abuses of authority by clearly defining peasants' obligations and by appointing officials of the Ministry of State Domains to supervise the system of village administration, in particular the village communes. The combination of safeguards and supervision would, it was hoped, improve the peasants' welfare, ensuring that communes distributed land fairly and that peasants were not subject to excessive taxation and work obligations.[89] In fact, due to its paternalistic and bureaucratic nature, the new system proved rather unpopular with state peasants, but their general situation did improve in the years that followed.[90]

Conservative intellectuals' views on serfdom varied. As might be expected from somebody who was born a serf, Pogodin favored abolition.[91] Uvarov, by contrast, viewed abolition as something desirable in the long term but not in the present. "It is necessary to proceed slowly," he wrote. "It is enough now to put this idea into circulation so that generations are prepared gradually to receive it."[92] But in the current circumstances, emancipation of the serfs, Uvarov said, "will lead to the dissatisfaction of the gentry class which will start looking for compensation for itself somewhere else, and there is nowhere to look except the domain of the autocracy. . . . Serfdom is a tree which has spread its roots afar; it shelters both the Church and the Throne."[93]

Uvarov at least accepted that emancipation would eventually be desirable. Gogol did not even agree with that. In his eyes, the social hierarchy was God-given. "It was not for nothing that God ordered everyone to be in that place where he now stands," he wrote.[94] Landowners were born landowners, and landowners they must stay, because, "God will call you to account if you were to change this calling for another, because everyone must serve God in his place, and not in another's."[95]

Gogol justified his position through religious language, but the Russian Orthodox Church was actually rather more nuanced in its view of serfdom. According to Gregory Freeze, because of its preference for otherworldly concerns, the church rarely addressed the issue of serfdom, but when it did, "It stressed the mutual responsibilities of squire and serf, not the mere subordination of the latter . . . clergy played no salient role in suppressing serf disorders and, indeed, were far better known for abetting than pacifying unruly peasants . . . [while] leading churchmen evinced growing disenchantment with serfdom."[96] An example was Metropolitan Filaret of Moscow, who commented that

> all those who have hereditary or conditional use of labor (and production through subordinate labor) must not be indifferent to the humble of this world. A person is

not a thing, which one may use and toward which one bears no obligation. State, moral, but especially Christian, law combines the right of power with obligation towards one's subordinates.[97]

In a missive to his parishioners in January 1859, Brianchaninov expressed his own views on the issue of the emancipation of the serfs. On the one hand, he produced several arguments against change. The conditions of peasant life in Russia were better than in Western Europe, he claimed.[98] Christ had accepted the sorrows of the world, and others should emulate him and accept them too. Many saints and upstanding Christians had been slave owners. And external and inner freedom were not the same; the latter was possible without the former.[99] On the other hand, he said:

> The church has always recognized the liberation of the serfs as a good deed, a merciful deed, a deed of brotherly, Christian love. From this teaching, the church regards current events concerning the improvement of landowners' peasants' existence and the granting to them of civil freedom as majestic, magnificent . . . the accomplishment of a great Christian act, an act of love.[100]

Conservatives also differed over the issue of education. Some opposed providing education to the mass of the population; others supported it. Among the former was Gogol. According to him:

> To teach the peasant literacy in order to give him the possibility of reading the frivolous booklets that European philanthropists publish for the people is really nonsense. The main thing is that the peasant has absolutely no time for it. . . . The village priest can say what the peasant needs much more truthfully than all these booklets.[101]

Similarly, Uvarov, while doing much as minister of popular enlightenment to improve and expand education for Russia's ruling classes, sought to restrict education among the peasants to what might be considered "useful" subjects.[102] In accordance with his theory of gradual historical development, he believed that enlightenment would trickle slowly down through the classes, and that giving too much education to the lower classes before they were ready for it would merely lead to dissatisfaction. For the same reason, Uvarov opposed the publication of cheap books and journals that the lower classes might be able to afford, and that might give them undesirable ideas. The only exception he made was for agricultural self-help books.[103]

As a man who had risen up by dint of education, Pogodin had a very different point of view. "One cannot limit the number of educated people," he said, adding that education should be open to all, "without any limitation by estate. . . . We are all children of one mother, holy Rus."[104] Under Nicholas I, university curricula focused on hard sciences at the expense of subjects such as philosophy and political science, which were considered potentially harmful.[105] Pogodin objected. Education could not be limited to supposedly useful subjects, he protested. Mechanics required natural sciences, which required mathematics, which in turn required philosophy. "The spread of education among the people has never been so necessary," Pogodin asserted.[106]

CONCLUSION

In a 1959 study of Official Nationality, Nicholas Riasanovsky concluded that "Official Nationality . . . meant an attempt, for three decades, to freeze growth and impose stagnation."[107] This is true only to the extent that Official Nationality endeavored to support the existing authority of the Russian Orthodox Church and the autocratic state. But neither the church nor the state were stagnant institutions. The church underwent a significant renewal in this period and at least until 1848 the Russian state under Nicholas I was a modernizing force, although it moved at a slow pace. In stating the principles of Official Nationality, Uvarov was not making an argument for freezing the status quo. Rather, he was establishing a system for the gradual progress of Russian society, through moral and educational improvement, and through the creation of a national identity. As noted, Uvarov carried out significant reforms in Russian education that greatly improved its quality, even if it did remain restricted mostly to the upper classes. Similarly, Kiselyov's reforms for state peasants brought change to the largest segment of Russia's population. Speransky codified Russia's laws. The Russian state began seriously to consider the future of serfdom. And even with the strict system of censorship, Nicholas's reign witnessed a "Golden Age" in Russian literature, associated with the likes of Aleksandr Pushkin.

Visions of the nation that rested upon Orthodoxy and autocracy fitted somewhat uneasily with the version of nationalism that based its description of Russia's distinctiveness on the country's people, history, and geography. The tsar disagreed with the Pan-Slavists and conservative intellectuals disagreed among themselves over serfdom, education, and the exact nature of the autocratic state. Nevertheless, there was a common thread of organic change running through all of their philosophies. Russian scholar S. V. Udalov comments that "the autocratic government declared itself to be the main creative force capable of leading the country toward progress . . . a guarantor of the peaceful and stable development of that progress."[108] This explains how conservatives such as Uvarov and Pogodin were able to combine a firm belief in autocracy with opinions that were on occasion somewhat progressive.

It is perhaps unfair to view Official Nationality solely through the lens of political repression, especially the more severely repressive measures that followed 1848. Not every conservative supported those measures, while some of those who did, did so not because they were enemies of progress but precisely because they believed that progress was impossible unless order was maintained and revolution avoided. Whatever the reality of Nicholas's rule, Official Nationality's ideal, in theory at least, was of autocracy as an enlightened state. Because of this, rather than viewing the age of Official Nationality as one of stagnation, it is perhaps better to regard it as a transitional era in which the foundations were gradually laid for the later reforms of Alexander II.

CHAPTER 4

THE SLAVOPHILES

The Slavophiles, mentioned in the previous chapter, were a small group of mostly Moscow-based intellectuals who came together in the mid-1840s after a split with the so-called "Westernizers," who included people like literary critic Vissarion Belinsky. (The Westernizers, not being conservatives, fall outside the scope of this book.) The core of the Slavophile group consisted of just four people—Aleksei Khomiakov (1804–60), Ivan Kireevsky (1806–56), Konstantin Aksakov (1817–60), and Iury Samarin (1819–76)—although some others, such as Aleksandr Koshelev (1806–83) and Konstantin Aksakov's brother Ivan (1823–86), also deserve mention. The Slavophiles were loyal to the autocratic regime, but their views on the nature of the nation and the state, as well as on specific issues such as free speech, departed from the official line. As a result, the government viewed them with definite suspicion. Iury Samarin and Ivan Aksakov were briefly arrested in 1849,[1] and in general the Slavophiles found it difficult to make their opinions heard. It was only after the death of Nicholas I that they were finally given permission to publish a journal of their own. Despite the restrictions on spreading their views, they were to have a profound impact on the future of Russian conservatism.

As young men, some of the Slavophiles studied under Mikhail Pogodin, whose opinions had a strong influence upon them; in particular, they adopted Pogodin's Norman Theory. But they parted company with Pogodin on some matters, notably what to think of Peter the Great, whom Pogodin greatly admired but the Slavophiles viewed very negatively. As was normal for Russian intellectuals of this period, they spoke foreign languages and often traveled to Western Europe. Kireevsky even attended lectures by the German philosopher Friedrich Schelling in Berlin.[2] In many respects they were thoroughly Westernized, and although they vigorously criticized Western Europe and stressed Russia's distinctive nature, it is perhaps incorrect to label them "anti-Western." Khomiakov, for instance, was something of an Anglophile, and in general the Slavophiles fully acknowledged the West's cultural, material, and technological achievements. Where they differed from the Westernizers was in their belief that Western models did not suit Russia. Khomiakov admired England, but he also felt that what worked in England would not work in Russia. As he put it:

> Every living creature has its own law of existence, its own order and harmony on which are based its very existence. . . . But that which is orderly and harmonious . . . becomes a principle of disorder and discord when it is grafted on another creature whose substance is based on a different law.[3]

At the same time, while in some respects the Slavophiles rejected Western Europe, in other respects they always considered the fates of Russia and Europe to be inextricably interconnected. Consequently, the tension between particularism and universalism is strong in Slavophile philosophy, leading one commentator to conclude that "the ideology of the Slavophiles contained sharp contradictions."[4]

Historians disagree as to how the Slavophiles should be classified—as liberals, as conservatives, as neither, or as both.[5] On the one hand, there were undoubtedly elements of their thinking that could be considered liberal, such as their belief in freedom of speech, their support for the emancipation of the serfs, and their opposition to the death penalty. On the other hand, there were aspects of their thinking that were very different from how liberalism was then understood in the West, such as their opposition to constitutional government, parliamentarianism, and free trade.[6] They were definitely conservatives according to this book's definition, in that they were firm believers in the principle of organicism.[7] Kireevsky wrote that

> the stability of customs, sanctity of tradition, or continuity of customary relationships of a society based on basic consensus cannot be corrupted without destroying the most essential conditions of society's life. In such a society, every coercive change dictated by logical conclusion would be a stab to the heart of the social organism.[8]

In the eyes of the Slavophiles, change founded on pure reason without reference to a society's traditions was dangerous. According to Ivan Aksakov, this had been the problem with the French Revolution, which was "the most tremendous example of violent application of theory to practice, this immolation of life on the altar of abstract theory . . . [that] replaced the concept of a people as an organism with a variety and freedom of functions by the concept of an agglomeration, an arithmetical sum of impersonal individuals."[9]

This did not mean, however, that the Slavophiles opposed progress. On the contrary, they very much desired it. As Konstantin Aksakov wrote:

> The Slavophiles are often accused of wanting to go backward, of not wanting to go forward. This accusation is unjust. . . . Do the Slavophiles think of going backward, do they want backward movement? No, the Slavophiles want to go, not only forward, but forward toward the truth, and, of course, never back from the truth. . . . The Slavophiles maintain only that their [the Westernizers'] path is mistaken, and that it is necessary to approach the truth by another path. Does that mean turning back? One can question and quarrel about whose path is true, but there can be no talk of a desire to turn back. But the Slavophiles think that the true path is that which Russia followed previously. Yes, they think that path is true, but do not forget that it is a *path*. Surely a path is not a state of immobility? Can one stop on a path? A path without fail goes forward somewhere, a path is endless movement. . . . Thus the Slavophiles think that one should turn not to the condition of ancient Russia (this would mean fossilization, stagnation), but toward the path of ancient Russia. . . . The Slavophiles desire not to turn back, but to go again forward on the old path, not because it is old but because it is true. Thus, there can be no talk of turning back.[10]

Similarly, Kireevsky remarked that while he wished to develop an "orientation different from the West," this was only an orientation, and that

> if ever I were to see in a dream that some long-dead external feature of our former life had suddenly been resurrected among us . . . I would not rejoice at such a vision. On the contrary, I would be frightened. For such an intrusion of the past into the new, of the dead into the living, would be tantamount to transferring a wheel from one machine into another that requires a different type and size; in such a case, either the wheel or the machine must break.[11]

Slavophilism was therefore neither backward-looking nor in favor of the status quo, but "a progressive project for social change."[12] Khomiakov expressed his ideal in a passage about the Crystal Palace built for the Great Exhibition in London in 1851:

> More than anything else, I confess, I wish could see those old, age-old trees in Hyde Park which they did not dare cut down, which sought room in the new building and for which the building was raised tens of yards. . . . In England they know how to respect the work of time. Today's invention does not berate what has been created by long centuries. The English know how to build, and what is built must respect what has grown up.[13]

Slavophilism was above all a form of cultural conservatism, rooted firmly in Orthodoxy, which gave it a distinctly religious feel. But it arose in response to a purely secular phenomenon, namely what has been a called an "identity crisis" among Russian intellectuals during the reign of Nicholas I.[14] Russia was one of the most powerful nations in Europe. In 1814, its armies had reached as far west as Paris. It had a highly educated, Westernized elite. Many members of this elite felt that, to match their country's hard power, they should have also what nowadays would be termed "soft power," including an advanced culture and political freedom. Instead, they were painfully aware that Russia had yet to produce high culture able to compare with that of the West, while politically they suffered under the repressive rule of Nicholas I. The elite felt Western, but it was acutely conscious that in some ways it was not.[15] The dilemma was famously expressed in a series of "philosophical letters" by another Moscow intellectual, Pyotr Chaadaev (1794–1856). In the first of these, he wrote:

> Looking at our situation, one might think that the general law of humanity doesn't apply to us. Recluses in the world, we haven't given anything to it, haven't taken anything from it, haven't introduced a single idea in the mass of ideas of humanity; haven't in any way contributed to the perfection of human reason. . . . Throughout the entire length of our social existence, we haven't done anything for the common good of mankind; not one useful thought has grown on our barren soil; not one great truth has arisen among us.[16]

Finding a way in which Russia could make a genuine contribution to the "common good of mankind" was a key objective of Russian intellectuals at this time. Some concluded that the only way of doing so was by deepening the process of Westernization. Others felt that Russia could never contribute original ideas to humanity if all it did was copy the West. Thus was born the split between the Westernizers and the Slavophiles. It is necessary to bear in mind, however, that the Westernizers and the Slavophiles had the same objective—to enable Russia to contribute to universal progress.[17] The fact that the Slavophiles chose to do so by emphasizing what they considered to be distinctive about Russia did not mean that they sought to isolate their country.

Slavophilism built on the ideas developed by Admiral Shishkov at the start of the nineteenth century. It owed much to two sources of inspiration: Orthodoxy and German Romanticism. The relative importance of each of these is a matter of some historical controversy. Some historians believe that native, Orthodox influences were more important, and that Slavophilism was "a distinctly Russian school of thought."[18] Others argue that "Slavophile ideology was clearly only an interesting offshoot of European conservative romanticism."[19] The two sources of inspiration were complementary rather than mutually exclusive, and it seems clear that both were important. Slavophilism drew inspiration from native, Russian ideas, but was also part of a much broader European intellectual movement.

Romantic ideas were among those discussed in an 1820s Moscow literary circle called the Lovers of Wisdom (*Liubomudry*), which was led by the writer Vladimir Odoevsky (1803–69) and whose members included Pogodin and Kireevsky. The German philosopher Schelling had a particularly strong influence on the Lovers of Wisdom. Odoevsky and his colleagues took from him the idea that a nation should be considered as an organic whole, not merely as a collection of individuals.[20] Schelling also taught that every nation embodied a different aspect of human progress and should develop those aspects of its character that were distinctly its own.[21] A nation's value was determined by its contribution to the universal good, but it could contribute to that good only by developing what was unique about its own culture. Diversity was good for humanity as a whole.[22]

It followed, then, that rather than copy the West, Russia should identify what was distinctive about itself and develop that. In this way, the particular served the universal. As Ivan Aksakov later put it, "Nations which have preserved and developed the specific qualities of their particular spirit, participate in an independent and fruitful manner in the general growth of humanity; nations which lack personality count for nothing."[23]

In 1844, Odoevsky put together several of his previously published short stories in the form of a novel/philosophical dialogue entitled *Russian Nights*. In it he expounded on many of the themes that would come to characterize Slavophilism. In one of the stories in *Russian Nights*, for instance, he described the fate of a city known as Benthamia that was founded upon the utilitarian principles of British philosopher Jeremy Bentham. Benthamia's citizens' relentless and rational pursuit of material self-interest produced a moral crisis including "deceit, forgery, intentional bankruptcy, total disdain of human dignity, idolatry of gold, satisfaction of the crudest bodily needs."[24] These moral failings led to war, starvation, environmental disaster, and ultimately the complete destruction of the city and all its inhabitants. The lesson was clear: the West had succumbed to rationalism and materialism, and in the long term the results would be disastrous. As Odoevsky wrote in the epilogue to *Russian Nights*:

> The West is perishing! Yes! It is perishing! . . . Time goes by, and time has its own life, different from the life of nations; in its flight it will soon overtake old enfeebled Europe and cover it with the same layers of immovable ashes with which it had covered the huge buildings of nations in ancient America, nations without names.[25]

The West's impending death provided Russia with a mission—to save it. According to Odoevsky, "Sometimes, during happy moments, Providence . . . nurses a nation, which will have to show the way from which mankind had deviated and which then will occupy the first place among other nations."[26] That nation, of course, was Russia. As Odoevsky concluded:

> Great is our calling, and difficult is our task! We have to revive everything. We have to enter our spirit into the history of the human mind, as our name is entered on the rolls of victory. Another, higher victory—the victory of science, art, and faith—is awaiting us on the ruins of enfeebled Europe. . . . The nineteenth century belongs to Russia![27]

The West's decay was spiritual rather than material. It followed that Russia's mission to save it was spiritual also. Russia would fulfill its universal role by restoring the religious faith that Western materialism and rationalism had undermined. The Slavophiles adopted and developed this argument, and in the process worked out a more detailed theory of what comprised Russia's distinctive contribution to humanity. They identified two main Russian characteristics that would be the core of Russia's contribution to the universal good: "wholeness of spirit" and "*sobornost*." The former was a reaction to what was seen as the "one-sided" rationalism of Western culture, and the latter a reaction to the West's supposed individualism.

Following Pogodin's Norman Theory, Konstantin Aksakov remarked that "Russia is an absolutely distinct country, not in the least comparable to the states and lands of Europe. . . . Western states were built on force, slavery, and enmity. The Russian state was built on voluntary consent, freedom, and peace."[28] Formulated this way, the sense of difference sometimes translated into a sense of hostility toward the West. Khomiakov, for instance, in an early critique of Western colonialism, wrote that

> throughout the world the ships of European nations are considered not the heralds of peace and happiness, but the heralds of war, and of the greatest misfortunes. Everyone knows what the arrogance of the Englishmen or of any German is. . . . Fatal seeds produce fatal fruits, and the hostility of the western nations . . . toward everyone gives rise to natural and just hatred of them among all nations.[29]

And yet, despite these occasional outbursts, there is a general consensus among historians that Slavophilism should not be seen as an anti-Western philosophy.[30] Kireevsky, for instance, admitted, "Yes, frankly speaking, I still love the West. I am bound to it by indissoluble sympathies. I belong to it by education, habits of life, tastes; by the questioning make-up of my mind, even by the habits of my heart."[31] Meanwhile, Konstantin Aksakov somewhat contradicted his own criticisms of the

West by writing that "our old neighbour, the West, has done much in the field of science. . . . The West hasn't buried in the earth the talents given to it by God! Russia recognizes this, as it always has. And may God prevent us from belittling the merits of another."[32] Similarly, Khomiakov wrote that "in the West, science, art, industry and many other manifestations of human activity have achieved significant development," and advised Russians: "Let us study Europe and its enlightenment."[33] He described the West as "the land of holy wonders." "How beautiful that majestic West was," he added.[34]

In an essay entitled "On the Nature of European Culture and on Its Relationship to Russian Culture," Kireevsky explained that the fundamental difference between the West and Russia was that "in the West, theology became a matter of rationalistic abstraction, whereas in the Orthodox world it retained its inner wholeness of spirit."[35] This did not amount to a rejection of reason. "What kind of religion is it that cannot stand in the light of science and conscience? What kind of faith is it that is incompatible with reason?" Kireevsky asked.[36] But "wholeness of spirit" implied that reason should be integrated with faith, feeling, imagination, and tradition into a harmonious, organic whole. As Kireevsky put it, "[Faith] is not contained in any sort of ability of cognition, does not refer to logical reason alone, or sentiments of the heart, or to suggestions of conscience; rather it embraces the totality of man, and appears only at the moment of this wholeness and in proportion to its fullness."[37] What Kireevsky called "believing thinking" consisted of "the tendency to gather all separate parts of the soul in one force, to discover that inner concentration of existence where reason, and will, and sentiment and conscience, and the beautiful, and the true, and the wondrous, and the desirable, and the just, and the merciful, and the whole realm of the mind flow together in one living unity."[38] Khomiakov noted that

> the spirit of God . . . cannot be understood by reason. This spirit is accessible only to the wholeness of the human spirit under the inspiration of grace. . . . Faith is not a purely logical and rational belief. It is much more than that. It is not an act of reason, but an act of all the powers of the mind . . . Faith is not only thought or felt; it is thought and felt at the same time. In short, faith is not knowledge alone, but knowledge and life at the same time.[39]

According to Kireevsky, this kind of knowledge had been lost in the West, but had been preserved in Russia. Having acquired Christianity from Byzantium rather than Rome, Russia avoided the one-sidedness of Western rationality. As a result, said Kireevsky, "we find in Russia . . . a predominant striving for wholeness of being."[40] "It is on this foundation and no other that we must erect the sturdy edifice of Russian culture," he concluded.[41]

Kireevsky identified another important aspect of Slavophilism—its belief that the ordinary people preserved the "primordial culture" of Russia,"[42] which had been corrupted among the elite as a result of the reforms of Peter the Great at the start of the eighteenth century. The Slavophiles somewhat idealized what Konstantin Aksakov called "the simple people [who] possess great human goods: brotherhood, wholeness of life, and . . . a common way of life."[43] The Russian peasant, Aksakov claimed, "stands . . . higher than all of us."[44] Slavophilism was thus a form of popular nationalism, in that it defined the nation in terms of the people, not the state. As Aksakov put it, "Society speaks French; the people Russian. Society wears German clothes; the people, Russian. . . . Society is temporary; the people eternal."[45]

The concept of wholeness of spirit fitted well with the Orthodox view of tradition, in which truth is found not just in reason but in the collective knowledge of a community built up over time. Kireevsky noted that "true knowledge can originate only in integral being—that is, where reason is subordinated not to the logical understanding, but to the heart. . . . Since integral being is attainable only in an organic, integral society, knowledge becomes inherently social, or interpersonal."[46] This connected with the distinction drawn in chapter 1 between the "individual" and the "person." An individual is isolated. A person exists through relationships with others. Konstantin Aksakov thus wrote that "in society, personality is not suppressed, and does not disappear . . . on the contrary . . . it receives its highest meaning, for only when personality denies itself . . . does it [become] a new phenomenon where every personality appears in loving unity with [other] personalities."[47]

This idea found expression in the second of the Slavophiles' core concepts—sobornost'. Whereas it was Kireevsky who was mostly responsible for developing the idea of wholeness of spirit, it was Khomiakov who produced the concept of sobornost'. Khomiakov had no formal theological training. Nevertheless, he was to prove a highly original religious thinker whose work would have a powerful impact on future generations of Orthodox theologians. The title of one of his most significant works, *The Church Is One*, expressed his central belief. According to Khomiakov,

> We know that those among us who fall, fall by themselves, but that no one is saved by oneself. Those who are saved are saved in the Church as her member and in unity with all her other members. . . . no one is saved in any way other than by the prayer of the entire Church in which Christ lives, knowing and hoping that, until the fulfillment of the ages, all the members of the Church, both the living and those who have fallen asleep, ceaselessly attain perfection by mutual prayer.[48]

As a body uniting the living and the dead under the leadership of Christ, the church was eternal and unchangeable[49] and rested on the principles of "freedom and unity." These principles, wrote Khomiakov, "are the two forces upon which was worthily bestowed the mystery of human freedom in Christ."[50] This combination of freedom and unity formed the basis of *sobornost'*, a term that has no obvious equivalent in the English language but that describes a form of spiritual unity in which people come freely together on the basis of a shared set of beliefs. In a letter to an English friend, William Palmer, Khomiakov described it as the opposite of the "individualism and rationalism [that] lies at the bottom of every Protestant doctrine."[51] In more detail, Khomiakov wrote:

> The union of earthly human beings and their Savior is always imperfect; it becomes perfect only in the region where they deposit their imperfection in the perfection of mutual love that unites Christians. In this region, people no longer rely on their own powers, which are only weakness. They no longer count on their own individuality; they count only on the holiness of the bond that unites them with their sisters and brothers; and their hope cannot deceive them, for this bond is Christ Himself.[52]

With *sobornost'*, the individual subordinates himself or herself to the collective. But he or she does so freely. There is no compulsion in *sobornost'*. Decisions are taken on the basis of consensus, which is possible because of the common moral bond of tradition and Christian faith uniting all the community's members.

According to Khomiakov, Catholics and Protestants were "isolated" individuals, "not members of a living organism."[53] Lacking the spirit of *sobornost'*, "the Christianity of the West has committed suicide," Khomiakov wrote.[54] Fortunately, *sobornost'* remained a fundamental characteristic of Russian Orthodoxy. Russia, therefore, could return Western Christianity to its original purity. Addressing the West, Khomiakov remarked:

> We do no more than return to you the cornerstone rejected by your ancestors, the mutual love of Christians and the divine graces attached to it. Put back the cornerstone of this building and . . . this building will rise in all the grandeur of its sublime proportions to be the salvation, happiness, and glory of all future generations.[55]

By preserving and propagating the principles of wholeness of spirit and *sobornost'*, Russia would save the West from its moral decay and thereby contribute to the universal good and finally take its place as one of the great nations of the world.

POLITICAL CONSERVATISM

Although Slavophilism was primarily a cultural movement, it had definite political implications. In particular, the Slavophiles' stress on organicism, wholeness
of spirit, and *sobornost'* militated against the Western liberal view of politics as
an arena in which competition between different interests is resolved by means
of representative institutions and majority decision making. Such a view was
incompatible with the harmonious society that the Slavophiles imagined. They
developed an idealized concept of autocracy as the system of government best
able to create harmony. At the same time, however, their conception of the people
as the heart of the nation inclined them toward a belief in limited government that
supported the people's freedom (even if freedom was often defined in a way that
was different from that of classical liberalism).

Beyond autocracy, the Slavophiles had no fixed view of the role of the state.
Samarin, for instance, has been called a "statist," because he believed that the state
had played, and would continue to play, an important role in Russia's historical
development.[56] Unlike the other Slavophiles, and possibly not coincidentally, he
had an active career as a public servant. Kireevsky, meanwhile, viewed the state
as a necessary guarantor of order against the threat of rebellion, especially after
the European revolutions of 1848.[57] By contrast, Konstantin Aksakov has been
described as believing in "a kind of conservative anarchism."[58] Khomiakov took
a position somewhere in the middle. According to Michael Hughes, his "views
about the relationship between state and civil society in Russia were always quite
variegated and fluid."[59] Khomiakov described the state as "a living organic cover
enveloping [society], fortifying and defending it from external threats, growing
with it, modifying it, broadening and adjusting itself to its growth and internal
change."[60] He recognized the need for a state, but argued against excessive state
supervision of the church.[61]

Konstantin Aksakov drew a distinction between the state and the "land" (*zem-
lia*), the latter in effect meaning the ordinary people. He and his fellow Slavophiles
believed that prior to Peter the Great, the two had coexisted in organic harmony.
Peter's reforms had supposedly artificially separated the state from the land by
placing the nobility and the bureaucracy between them, and also by creating a
cultural divide between the Westernized elite and the still-Russian people. The
state had in this way overstepped its correct boundaries.[62] What was needed was
to find a method of restoring the lost unity between state and land.

"For us," wrote Konstantin Aksakov, "the concern is that the state gives as
much space as possible to internal life and understands its own limitedness and
inadequacy."[63] Aksakov added that "freedom is the supreme good."[64] Primarily,
this meant inner freedom. However, it also meant the freedom to follow one's

own customs and traditions. Aksakov strongly opposed the Russian state's efforts from Peter the Great onward to prohibit nobles from wearing beards and traditional Russian clothes. "The Slavophiles want only one thing: *that everybody be able to dress as they want*," he wrote.[65] At the same time, *sobornost'* meant that customs and traditions were a communal matter. True inner freedom came from voluntary, free subordination to the collective will.[66] The Slavophile view of freedom was more collective than individual, but it did lend itself to a belief in local self-government. As Samarin wrote, "Every private *mir* [commune] lives and governs itself."[67]

That said, in part because of their Christian beliefs, the Slavophiles did not entirely reject the notion of basic personal rights and freedoms. Konstantin Aksakov, for instance, opposed the death penalty, calling it "legalized murder, but murder nonetheless."[68] Having suffered severe censorship under Nicholas I, the Slavophiles were also firm believers in freedom of thought and speech. Khomiakov said that the development of science required "freedom of opinion as well as freedom of doubt."[69] Konstantin Aksakov was possibly the most forthright in his defense of freedom of speech. In 1853 he wrote the following poem:

> You are the wonder of God's wonders,
> You are the lamp and the flame of thought,
> You are a ray sent to us from heaven to earth,
> You are for us the flag of humanity.
> You drive away the lie of ignorance,
> You renew eternal life,
> You lead us toward light, toward the truth,
>   Free speech![70]

The Slavophiles did not believe that formal, written law provided the best way of protecting the people's freedoms. They preferred custom. According to Khomiakov, custom "differs from law in that law is something external . . . whereas custom is an inner force penetrating the whole life of the people . . . the aim of every law . . . is to become custom."[71] He wrote further:

> Law, written and armed with compulsion, brings the differing private wills into a conditional unity. Custom, unwritten and unarmed, is the expression of the basic unity of society. . . . The broader the sphere of custom, the stronger and healthier the society, the richer and more original the development of its jurisprudence.[72]

The Slavophiles likewise rejected the idea of a formal, written constitution. They preferred an idealized concept of autocracy. Samarin, for instance, wrote:

The gentry has separated the common people from the Tsar. Standing . . . between
them, it conceals the common people from the Tsar and does not permit the people's
complaints and hopes to reach him. It hides from people the bright image of the Tsar
so that the Tsar's word does not get to the simple people, or does so in a distorted
form. But the common people love the Tsar and yearn for him, and the Tsar for his
part looks with love upon the common people. . . . And some day, reaching over the
heads of the nobles, Tsar and people will respond to one another, and reach out their
hands to one another.[73]

This theory in part explains the Slavophiles' hostility to democratic institutions that might check the sovereign's power. In the context of nineteenth-century
Russia, such institutions would have given power to the nobility, which would
have then been in a position to block reforms such as the emancipation of the
serfs. Constitutional government would have made it harder for the peasants to
reach "over the heads of the nobles." It was better to concentrate power in the
hands of the tsar.

Following the death of Nicholas I in 1855, Konstantin Aksakov wrote a memorandum to the new tsar, Alexander II. Other Slavophiles did not agree entirely
with what Aksakov wrote, but his memorandum, entitled "On the Internal State
of Russia," nevertheless provides the clearest synthesis of the Slavophiles' political
views.

Aksakov's memorandum was, above all, a plea for political reform, especially
for a relaxation of censorship. To convince Alexander that it was safe to end the
repressive measures of Nicholas's reign, Aksakov sought to demonstrate that the
tsar had nothing to fear from the Russian people. Drawing on Pogodin's Norman
Theory, he argued that just as in the ninth century Russians had invited the Viking
chieftain Rurik to rule over them, they had later invited Mikhail Romanov to
become tsar in 1613. This proved, Aksakov said, that the Russian people had no
interest in governing the country themselves. They were not interested in political
rights, and there was no history of political rebellion in Russia. Repressive measures were completely unnecessary.[74]

Next, Aksakov argued that what the Russian people did want was inner freedom,
that is to say "moral freedom, freedom of the spirit, social freedom."[75] According
to Aksakov, "The Russian people, having renounced the political element, having
given complete state authority to the government, gave itself *life*, moral-social freedom, the high purpose of which is Christian society." In line with this, there arose a
natural distinction between the state and the land. Military affairs and the defense
of the realm were the main responsibilities given to the state. However, everything

to do with "the life of the people," including their spiritual and moral life and "agriculture, industry, and trade," remained the "business of the land."[76]

Aksakov thus proposed a very limited view of the state's sphere of competence, as well as a clear division of powers. The spheres of state and land were distinct, and neither was to intrude upon the other. Aksakov wrote:

> The people does not interfere in government, in the system of administration; the state does not interfere in the life and being of the people, does not coerce the people to live according to the rules made by the state: it would be strange if the state demanded that the people got up at seven o'clock, ate at two, and so on; it would be just as strange if it demanded that the people comb their hair in a certain way, or wore a certain type of clothing. Thus, the first relationship between the government and the people is a relationship of *mutual non-interference*.[77]

"The government exists for the people, not the people for the government," Aksakov added. It followed that "the government . . . [would] never encroach upon the independence of the people's lives and spirit."[78]

Because the state and the land were independent of one another, it followed also that the state system should be a monarchy, not a democracy, and that within its sphere of competence "the state must be unlimited."[79] But, said Aksakov, "In recognizing the unlimited power of the state, he [the Russian] retains complete freedom of spirit, conscience, and thought. . . . The Russian is not a slave, but a free man. Unlimited monarchical government, in the Russian understanding, is not an enemy, nor an opponent of freedom, but its friend and defender."[80]

Unfortunately, Aksakov continued, due to its fear of revolution the Russian state had increasingly intruded into the affairs of the people. "The suppression of all opinion, of all expression of thought, has reached a point where some representatives of state authority forbid one even to express an opinion favorable to the government," Aksakov complained.[81] The only way out of the dire situation Russia found itself in was for the government to rediscover the correct relationship with the people. This required it to cease its repression of the people and also to seek out the people's opinions. This meant above all that "it is necessary to end repression of the spoken and written word. Let the government give back to the land the freedom of thought and speech that belong to it, and then the land will give back to the government what belongs to it—its trust and its strength."[82] While censorship could not yet be completely eliminated, "In time there should be complete freedom of spoken and written speech, once it is understood that free speech is indissolubly linked with unlimited monarchy."[83] Finally, Aksakov concluded:

To the government—unlimited freedom to rule, which belongs only to it; and to the
people—complete freedom of *life*, external and internal, which the government protects. *To the government—the right to act*, and consequently, law; *to the people—the
right of opinion*, and consequently, free speech. That is the Russian civil order! That
is the one true Russian civil order![84]

SOCIAL-ECONOMIC CONSERVATISM

The Slavophiles were wealthy landowners, who were able to engage in intellectual pursuits without having to earn a living.[85] They were not content to sit on
their wealth, however, but were active managers of their estates who took a great
interest in modern agricultural techniques, including new machinery, new crops,
and new patterns of crop rotation.[86] Aleksandr Koshelev was a particularly keen
student of agricultural reform, writing a book in 1852 outlining his impressions of
the Great Exhibition in London, where he spent five days examining agricultural
equipment.[87] Among the items on display in London was a steam engine invented
by Khomiakov. The Slavophiles were certainly not against economic and social
progress.

Their views on these matters reflected both their ideological beliefs and their
own personal financial interests, as can be seen in their attitude toward serfdom.
With the exception of Kireevsky, who feared peasant rebellion, the Slavophiles
supported the emancipation of the serfs. Samarin in 1854 completed a 119-
page memorandum on the subject, urging emancipation, and later played a
major role in the government commissions that led to the abolition of serfdom
in 1861. Serfdom was incompatible both with the Slavophiles' religious outlook
and with their view of the nation as being founded on the people. Koshelev, for
instance, wrote that "it is shameful and incomprehensible that we can call ourselves Christians and keep our brothers and sisters in slavery. A master cannot be
a Christian."[88] Samarin added to this an argument that free labor was more efficient than serf labor.[89] Nonetheless, Khomiakov, Samarin, and Koshelev all owned
serfs and none made any attempt to free them.[90] Their own interests perhaps also
affected their opinion on how emancipation should take place. Khomiakov and
Samarin believed that rather than receiving land from the landowners as individual private property, peasants should receive land collectively, with all land being
under the control of the peasant communes. Noble landowners and peasants were
to have very different property rights.[91]

The peasant commune played an important part in Slavophile economic and
social thinking. Rural poverty was widespread in Western Europe in the early
and mid-nineteenth century. England, for instance, contained many landless

agricultural laborers, while in other countries peasant landholdings were often extremely small. The commune provided a means for avoiding such poverty, by ensuring that all peasants were part of a larger community and received a fair share of available land. The commune was also the physical embodiment of the principle of *sobornost'*, and as such the Slavophiles believed that it represented a superior way of life to that of industrialized Western society. Konstantin Aksakov described the idea of the commune as "the principle of the Slavic tribe and especially the Russian people."[92] It was therefore of as much spiritual and cultural as economic and social significance. According to Aksakov, "The communal principle, manifesting itself on earth as separate communes within a nation . . . fuses the whole nation into one commune."[93] Commune and nation were inseparably connected. As Samarin noted, "the communal principle constitutes the foundation, base of all Russian history, past, present, and future."[94]

Samarin also saw the continuance of the commune as a means of reconciling Western capitalism and socialism.[95] For him and other Slavophiles, this was a way of ensuring economic progress without undue social unrest. On the whole, the Slavophiles supported industrialization. Khomiakov wrote in 1845 that "all or almost all are agreed on the necessity of railroads,"[96] and one of the less well-known Slavophile thinkers, Fyodor Chizhov, even became a railroad developer.[97] However, the Slavophiles were also deeply concerned about the process of proletarianization, which they believed accompanied industrial development. The commune could provide a model of collective self-help, which, they hoped, could prevent the worst consequences of industrialization, and which would be superior to the doctrine of laissez-faire economics. Khomiakov even toyed with the idea of creating "industrial communes" as a form of economic development. The idea did not get very far, however, as he was unable to find any actual examples of such an organization.[98]

It is noticeable that, for all their support of the commune, the Slavophiles never suggested that landowners such as themselves should join one. For reasons such as this, Slavophilism has been described as an attempt to reform state and society "without fundamentally assaulting the existing pattern of privilege."[99] Certainly, ideological perspectives were tempered by practical interests. Nevertheless, Slavophilism remained a project for social and economic reform, not a defense of the existing system.

CONCLUSION

The Slavophiles' spiritual frame of mind, along with their utopian view of Russia's past and their belief in the peasant commune, may make them appear somewhat at odds with modernity. Yet, they were in many ways very modern men, up to date with the latest European philosophical trends, and keen to introduce the newest agricultural techniques and machinery. Dissatisfied with the status quo, the Slavophiles sought change, above all in the sphere of culture, but also in the spheres of politics and social and economic life. In the process, they hoped to find a way for Russia to contribute to universal civilization.

The Slavophiles adopted what now seem to have been paradoxical, even contradictory positions. They were particularists, but also universalists; they saw Russia as different from the West, yet part of it; they were conservative, while also being progressive; they believed in autocracy, but also in limited government; they rejected political freedoms, yet demanded freedom of speech; and they opposed serfdom, but kept their own serfs. The history of the Slavophiles forces one to urge caution on those who would view Russian conservatism as simply being anti-Western, politically reactionary, and socially backward. Slavophilism defies simple classification.

In an 1893 lecture, the liberal Russian historian and politician Pavel Miliukov, who in 1917 briefly became foreign minister in the revolutionary Provisional Government, argued that the contradictions within Slavophilism had been too great for the philosophy to survive long after the deaths of the main Slavophiles in the late 1850s and early 1860s. In particular, Miliukov argued that the Slavophiles' particularist and universalist beliefs had proved to be incompatible with one another. Consequently, he said, Slavophilism eventually decayed into simplistic, crude nationalism.[100] This is only partially accurate. While it is indeed true that the Slavophiles' stress on Russia's distinctiveness did lead some of their successors to reject universalism, others never abandoned the attempt to reconcile the search for Russia's distinct identity with a pursuit of some universal mission. The idea that Russia served the common good by resisting Westernization was one that continued, and continues to this day, to attract many. The Slavophile quest for national purpose thus left its mark on the generations that followed.

CHAPTER 5

THE GREAT REFORMS

I n March 1855, Nicholas I died, aged fifty-eight. A year later, Russia admitted
defeat in the Crimean War (1853–56) and signed the Treaty of Paris, which
brought an end to the war. From the point of view of international politics,
the treaty's most important clause was probably the one that prohibited
Russia from stationing warships in the Black Sea. Even more significant than the
penalties imposed by the treaty, however, was the war's impact on Russia's prestige.
Russia had not lost a war for nearly fifty years. Now the aura of invincibility had
been smashed.

This loss of prestige had serious domestic ramifications. As Geoffrey Hosking
points out, "The Romanov dynasty had identified itself so completely with military power that the loss of a war . . . made autocracy for the first time seem inef-
fective. It is not an accident that within a few years political movements appeared
which rejected monarchy outright and aimed to overthrow it."[1] Shocked by their
country's defeat, those interested in preserving the Russian Empire realized that
change was necessary. This would have to include radical reforms of the country's
economic and social system. It was clear that Russia's economic infrastructure was
incapable of successfully supporting modern military operations on a large scale.
Russia's soldiers had fought bravely during the Crimean War, but their army's
logistical system was inadequate, Russian military technology had proven inferior
to that of Russia's French and British opponents, and the country's underdevel-
oped railway system made it extremely difficult to transport the vast amount of
supplies required by a modern army.[2] If the Russian state was to regain its lost
prestige, then the pace of industrialization would have to accelerate. In the eyes of
many, that was impossible as long as the economy remained rooted in the system
of serfdom. Their conclusion was that serfdom would have to be abolished. Fears
that the serfs would try to liberate themselves by revolutionary means gave an
additional urgency to this matter. Abolishing serfdom would, however, upend the

entire system of local government. To be successful, any reform program would have to be far-reaching in scale.

By forcing Russia's elite to face these realities, the Crimean War paved the way for a period of rapid transformation. The death of Nicholas I also removed a significant obstacle from the path of change. On coming to power, Nicholas's son and successor, Alexander II, almost immediately set about what became known as the Great Reforms.

Preparation for the reforms began a year after Alexander's accession to the throne, when in March of 1856 the new tsar gave a speech to the Moscow nobility in which he declared his intention to free Russia's approximately 23 million serfs.[3] Five years later, in March 1861, he put his promise into action and decreed the emancipation of the serfs. Another important element of the Great Reforms was an overhaul of the judicial system in 1864, the most notable part of which was the establishment for the first time of trial by jury. Also in 1864, Alexander introduced a system of elected local self-government, with each district and province of the country (with the exception of some districts on Russia's periphery) electing a committee known as a *zemstvo*, which was responsible for matters such as health care and education.

Reforms continued into the 1870s, the most important probably being the reorganization of the army carried out by the minister of war, Dmitry Miliutin (1816–1912), which introduced a system of general conscription. But although reform continued, from the mid-1860s onward popular enthusiasm for it began to decline, and Russia's educated elites shifted in a conservative direction. Two factors contributed to this conservative turn. The first was a revolt that broke out in Poland in 1863, which the Russian government eventually crushed in 1864. The second was an increase in radical terrorism. Especially noteworthy was an attempted assassination of the tsar in 1866 by a student who had been expelled from Moscow State University. A government committee established to examine the causes of the assassination attempt concluded that "everyone is tired out by the constant changes and is asking the government for a more peaceful and conservative era."[4]

As Alexander's reign continued, there was a growing sense in some circles that the reforms had gone too far or had been badly implemented. In early 1878 a court heard the case of Vera Zasulich, a revolutionary who had shot and wounded the governor of St. Petersburg, Fyodor Trepov. Zasulich's guilt was undoubted, but the jury were sympathetic to her intentions and declared her not guilty. This was enough to convince some that the judicial reforms of 1864 had been a terrible mistake. By the time of Alexander's death in 1881, the pro-reform sympathies that had attended his accession had largely worn themselves out.

Russian conservatives of this era were as usual far from united in their approach to issues of national identity, politics, and social and economic reform.

On matters of identity, successors to the Slavophiles branched out in a number of different directions. One road was that taken by the so-called *pochvenniki*, Apollon Grigoryev (1822–64) and Fyodor Dostoevsky (1821–81), who sought to reconcile the differences between the Russian elite and the ordinary people, and also between Russia and the West. Another route was taken by the writers Nikolai Danilevsky (1822–85) and Konstantin Leontyev (1831–91), who stressed the importance of diversity and developed a concept of the world as being divided into distinct civilizations. A third path, which to some degree crisscrossed with those of the *pochvenniki* and Danilevsky (although not Leontyev), was Pan-Slavism. This urged Russia to take a leading role in uniting the Slavic peoples of Eastern Europe.

Variations of post-Slavophilism were not the only trend among Russian conservatives of this era. As before, some conservatives regarded Russia as very much part of Western civilization; some supported the idea of Russia as a multiethnic, multiconfessional state; and some, notably the journalist Mikhail Katkov (1818–87), promoted an ethnic Russian nationalism that demanded that the interests of ethnic Russians take precedence within the Russian Empire.

In terms of foreign policy, Pan-Slavs urged an aggressive, imperialist stance. Many Russian nationalists rejected Pan-Slavism, however. Such nationalists were more isolationist, arguing that Russian foreign policy should be dictated by the interests of Russians, not those of Slavs in other countries.

The differences between conservatives were often quite profound. This could be seen in their views on domestic political and economic policy. The Great Reforms led to the creation of an "aristocratic opposition," which sought not so much to stop reform as to shape it in ways that would suit the interests of the landowning class. On occasion, this led members of the aristocratic opposition to support policies that might be termed "liberal." For instance, some of them supported various types of political reform designed to create representative institutions. Others favored abolishing the peasant commune and establishing the Russian economy on the basis of private property and free market relations. Meanwhile, so-called "liberal conservatives," such as the legal scholar Boris Chicherin (1828–1904), opposed the aristocratic opposition's political proposals and stressed the need for a strong, centralized state. The liberal conservatives felt that the state was the main propagator of liberal reform and therefore rejected surrendering any of its prerogatives. In some cases they also defended the peasant commune as a source of stability in the countryside.

Russian conservatism in the reign of Alexander II therefore consisted of a complicated medley of post-Slavophiles, Pan-Slavs, ethnic nationalists, imperialists, isolationists, aristocratic oppositionists, and liberal conservatives. As Aleksandr Kireev (1833–1910), an adjutant of Tsar Alexander II's brother Grand Duke Konstantin Nikolaevich, and a noted second-generation Slavophile thinker, put it in 1870:

Given the confusion of concepts regarding our political parties, you don't know who's a friend, who's an enemy, the conservatives are mixed up with the progressives, the reds with the whites, all has turned out so spotted, and changes day to day, that there isn't any measure that can describe what is going on among us.[5]

Cultural Conservatism

Russian conservatives in this era continued to be greatly concerned with issues of national identity and culture. Among the most significant new ideas on these subjects were those of the native soil conservatives (*pochvenniki*—named after the Russian word for soil, *pochva*). The first of the *pochvenniki* was the critic Apollon Grigoryev, who from 1850 to 1856 helped to edit Mikhail Pogodin's journal *Moskvitianin*.[6] Aware of the deep divisions in Russian society, Grigoryev sought to unite the various parts of the Russian nation into an organic whole. This marked a shift from the Slavophile perspective, which had drawn a clear distinction between Russia's Westernized elite and the peasantry. Grigoryev developed the idea that all parts of Russian society were part of the same nation, advancing together toward the realization of some national idea. He did not believe that it was only the peasants who had preserved Russian culture. In particular, he wrote, "[it is] in the middle, manufacturing and primarily merchant class that we see the old, primordial Rus."[7]

Similarly, Grigoryev advanced the idea that all the various parts of Russian history contributed to what Russia had become. Again, this contrasted with the Slavophiles, who regarded the reforms of Peter the Great as a sharp and artificial break with Russia's past. Rather than trying to restore some lost pre-Petrine path, Grigoryev looked to include all the various aspects of Russian history in a continuous narrative. In 1859 he wrote that "when we speak of the Russian essence, or of the Russian soul, we mean neither the essence of pre-Petrine nor of post-Petrine Russia, but an organic whole; we believe in Rus' as it is, as it has formed and *is forming* after clashes with other lives and other national organisms."[8]

Grigoryev's views had a strong influence on the writer Fyodor Dostoevsky, who became the most famous representative of the *pochvenniki*. In the late 1840s Dostoevsky was a member of a radical discussion group known as the Petrashevsky Circle, after its leader Mikhail Petrashevsky, a translator in the Russian Ministry of Foreign Affairs. In 1849 the members of the Petrashevsky Circle were arrested for allegedly subversive activity, and Dostoevsky spent the years from 1849 to 1854 in prison in Siberia. This experience shattered his revolutionary illusions and helped turn him into one of the foremost conservative thinkers of his time. In certain respects, Dostoevsky retained the progressive views of his youth, and he has been described as "from first to last a Christian socialist." But whereas in his youth he imagined that socialism would be achieved by institutional change, in his later years he regarded "inner spiritual regeneration of the person as the principal goal."[9] Dostoevsky wrote in later life that

> contemporary socialism in Europe, even our own, is completely separated from Christ; it is concerned almost completely with bread . . . it is better to inspire man's soul with the idea of Beauty; possessing it in their souls, all men become brothers, and then, finally, working for each other, they also become prosperous. But give them bread and from boredom they will become enemies of one another.[10]

Grigoryev's ideas appealed to Dostoevsky who, following his encounters with members of Russia's poorer classes in Siberia, sought a way to reduce Russia's class divisions. Dostoevsky wrote: "We believe that both sides must finally come to an understanding of one another. . . . Union at all costs, in spite of all sacrifices and as quickly as possible, that is our motivating idea, that is our motto."[11] This reconciliation was to be a two-way process. The elite needed to get back in touch with its native soil; but the elite also had a great deal to offer the ordinary people by way of culture and education.

"Anyone who loves Russia," wrote Dostoevsky, "has long been sick at heart at the separation of the upper layers of Russians from the lower ones, from the people and the people's lives."[12] According to Dostoevsky, the people:

> Are national and stand up for this with all their strength, but we [the educated classes] are of universalist convictions and have established universalism as our goal. . . . This is the cause of our discord and our split with the people, and I proclaim frankly: if we removed this problem . . . all our disagreements with the people would immediately cease.[13]

By restoring the connection between the educated classes and the people, Dostoevsky hoped that revolution could be forestalled. "I put my hope above all in our youth," he wrote, "having got to know the soul of the people better, they will discard the extreme fantasies that have captivated so many of them. . . . What could be more fruitful for Russia than this spiritual merging of estates?"[14] Native soil conservatism has thus been described as a form of "evolutionary conservatism," designed to provide "a weapon against the ideologies of class divisiveness."[15]

In his *Writer's Diary*, Dostoevsky recounted numerous stories of domestic assault, child abuse, murder, and other crimes. But at the same time, he argued that one should "judge the Russian people not according to the loathsome things that they so often do, but according to those great and sacred deeds for which they continuously pine."[16] Above all, Dostoevsky believed, the Russian people, despite their lack of knowledge of scripture and of formal Christian doctrine, possessed a "warm-hearted knowledge of Christ and a true understanding of him."[17] According to Dostoevsky, "The people know Christ, their God ... because for many centuries they have endured many sufferings. . . . Believe me, in this sense, even the darkest layers of our people are far more educated than you, in your cultured ignorance of them, suppose."[18]

Western liberalism had entailed a rejection of God, from which flowed nihilism and revolutionary terrorism, and which if left unchecked would eventually lead to the collapse of Western civilization. But the truth of God remained firm in the hearts of the Russian people, Dostoevsky believed. The people's capacity to suffer and their simple faith in Christ provided the key to Russia's and the world's salvation. As Dostoevsky put it,

> Doesn't the truth and salvation of the Russian people, and the future of all mankind, lie in it [Orthodoxy] alone? ... And perhaps the main, predestined purpose of the Russian people, in the fate of all mankind, consists solely of preserving this divine image of Christ in all its purity, and when the time comes, revealing this image to a world that has lost its way![19]

Like the Slavophiles, Dostoevsky believed that Russia had a universal mission. Also like the Slavophiles, he swung between praising the West and denouncing it, between proclaiming the inherent differences between peoples and proclaiming the existence of universal truths. He declared that "everything, almost everything, in our development, in our science, art, citizenship, humanity, everything, everything comes from there [Europe], from that land of holy wonders! From our earliest childhood, our entire lives are formed by the European mold."[20] And yet, he claimed, "We're not Europe at all and everything of ours is so distinct that, compared with Europe, we're almost on the moon."[21]

Dostoevsky faced the same problem as the Slavophiles—how to reconcile the universalist and particularist elements of his thinking. He dealt with the problem differently. Objecting to Konstantin Aksakov's assertion that the universal was served by the national, he reversed the equation: what was particular about the Russian nation was precisely its universality. Russians had shown a unique ability to assimilate other cultures. Russians were therefore universal in a way that other peoples were not.[22] In an 1880 speech in honor of Aleksandr Pushkin, he declared that "of all peoples, perhaps the Russian heart is the most inclined toward the universal and toward the brotherly union of all humanity."[23] What he meant, he explained, was that the Russian people "is perhaps the most capable of all peoples of accommodating within itself the idea of the union of all mankind, of brotherly love."[24] By maintaining this unique national characteristic, Russia would save the West from itself, and thus ultimately reconcile Russia and the West.

Dostoevsky explained this in an 1873 letter to the twenty-eight-year-old heir to the throne, Grand Duke Aleksandr Aleksandrovich, who would later become Tsar Alexander III. Dostoevsky wrote:

> Embarrassed and afraid that we have fallen so far behind Europe in our intellectual and scientific development, we have forgotten that we ourselves, in the depth and tasks of the Russian soul, contain in ourselves as Russians the capacity perhaps to bring new light to the world, on the condition that our development is independent. . . . Without such an arrogance concerning our importance to the world as a nation, we will never be able to be a great nation and leave behind anything distinctive for mankind's benefit. We have forgotten that all great nations displayed their great powers only to the extent that they were arrogant in their assessment of themselves, and precisely in this way they have benefited the world, and each of them has brought something into it, be it only a single ray of light, because they have remained themselves, proud and steady, arrogantly independent.[25]

In Dostoevsky's eyes, the first step in this universal mission involved freeing the Slavic peoples from the domination of other countries, notably the Ottoman Empire. In 1877 war broke out between Russia and the Ottomans. Dostoevsky fervently supported the war. "Sooner or later *Constantinople must be ours!*" he declared.[26]

This gave Dostoevsky something in common with the Pan-Slavs. Among them was another former member of the Petrashevsky Circle, Nikolai Danilevsky. In an 1867 book entitled *Russia and Europe*, Danilevsky provided a philosophical foundation for the idea that the Slavs formed, or at least could form, a distinct civilization, but he parted with the *pochvenniki* when he denied that Russia had a universal mission. Instead, he argued that every civilization—or "cultural-historical type," as he called them—was unique, and so could not be measured against other civilizations.

Danilevsky began *Russia and Europe* by asking why European states were not as outraged by Prussia's invasion of Denmark in 1864 as they had been by Russia's 1853 war against Turkey, the latter of which had led to Anglo-French intervention and the Crimean War. The cause of the double standard, he answered, was that Europeans regarded Russia as different and therefore hostile. But Europe was merely a peninsula of Asia. Russia and Europe were not geographically distinct entities. Rather, they were different cultural-historical types.

Danilevsky identified ten cultural-historical types in human history, and laid out various laws that he said applied to them. He believed that to develop, a cultural-historical type had to have "political independence," and that it only reached the peak of its development when its various ethnographic elements formed a political federation. Moreover, "The principles of civilization of one cultural-historical type are not transferable to peoples of another type."[27] Like living organisms, civilizations grew, developed, and died. One could not correctly speak of linear progress, claimed Danilevsky, nor could one say that any one civilization represented universal truth. Indeed, a universal truth of the sort imagined by the Slavophiles did not exist, Danilevsky wrote. Instead, he said:

> Progress . . . doesn't consist of everything going in the same direction (in that case it would soon stop) but of covering the entire field that constitutes mankind's historical activity, in all directions. Therefore no single civilization can take pride in being the highest point of development.[28]

Danilevsky added that "humanity's task consists . . . of the manifestation, at various times and among various tribes, of all those features and peculiar tendencies that exist virtually (in possibility, in *potentia*) in the idea of humanity."[29] He identified a type of common good in the form of diversity—the more diversity among human civilizations, the better for humanity as a whole. As Danilevsky put it: "Humanity's collective existence has no ultimate purpose, no task, other than the expression at various times and places (that is, among different tribes) of life's diverse features and tendencies."[30]

Russia's problems with Europe, Danilevsky argued, followed from the fact that many people imagined that the European ("Germanic-Roman") cultural-historical type was the one true civilization. It was not. But although Russia's cultural-historical development was "completely different" from that of Europe,[31] Russia, along with the Slavs, had yet to properly form a cultural-historical type of its own. This had to be the priority, Danilevsky wrote: "The idea of Slavdom must be the highest idea, higher than freedom, higher than science, higher than enlightenment, higher than any earthly good," because none of those things could be achieved "without a spiritually, nationally, and politically original and independent Slavdom."[32] Russia would need to lead a struggle to liberate other Slavs from Turkish and Austrian domination. This would lead to an inevitable conflict with Europe, the outcome of which would determine whether Slavs became a cultural-historical type of their own or were "predestined to the secondary importance of a vassal tribe."[33] The ultimate aim should be the creation of a federation of all the Slavic nations, whose capital would be Constantinople.[34]

Danilevsky concluded with words that continue to resonate today among Russian conservatives who want to resist the forces of globalism and what they see as Western cultural hegemony:

The danger consists not of the political domination of a single state, but of the cultural domination of one cultural-historical type . . . The issue is not whether there will be a universal state, either a republic or a monarchy, but whether one civilization, one culture, will dominate, since this would deprive humanity of one of the necessary conditions for success and perfection—the element of diversity.[35]

Alexander II was no more a fan of Pan-Slavism than his father, Nicholas I, but in 1858 he nevertheless gave permission for the formation of the Moscow Benevolent Slavic Committee, which became the center of the Pan-Slavic movement.[36] Also important for a while was the journal *Den'* (*Day*), edited by Ivan Aksakov from 1861 to 1865. Aksakov asserted that Russians should recognize that the West was inherently hostile to Russia. Given that there was nothing that could be done to appease the West, Russia should seek allies against it, and the natural place to find these was among the Slavs.[37] In 1878, though, Aksakov overstepped the mark by making a speech to the Moscow Benevolent Slavic Committee in which he accused Russian diplomats of throwing away the victories won by the Russian army in its war against the Ottoman Empire. In response, the authorities shut down the committee and banned Aksakov from Moscow.[38] Alexander II made his own dislike of Pan-Slavism clear, telling an Austrian diplomat, "I am a Russian rather than a Slav."[39]

Despite this, Alexander gave remarkable latitude to another advocate of the Pan-Slav cause, Mikhail Katkov, who was allowed to publish what he pleased, despite the fact that his opinions often angered the tsar. Initially, Katkov held liberal, progressive views,[40] and wrote that a conservative "is not an enemy of progress, of innovations, or of reforms. . . . The truly conservative direction goes hand in hand with the truly progressive."[41] Over time, however, Katkov abandoned many of his liberal opinions. A turning point was the Polish revolt of 1863, after which Katkov began to propagate nationalist and monarchist ideas as well as extremely hawkish opinions on foreign policy.

Originally a professor of philosophy at Moscow University, and strongly influenced by German thinkers such as Georg Wilhelm Friedrich Hegel and Friedrich Schelling, Katkov had turned to journalism after Nicholas I banned the teaching of philosophy in Russia's universities in the early 1850s. As editor of the journal *Russkii vestnik* (Russian messenger) and the newspaper *Moskovskie vedomosti* (Moscow gazette), he became perhaps the most prominent journalist in Russia. In this capacity he popularized the idea that ethnic Russians should play a dominant role in the Russian state.

Katkov argued that all great states were multinational in character.[42] Non-Russian nations within the empire should therefore keep their language and customs. At the same time, he insisted that they would have to acknowledge the

leading role of the Russians. As Katkov put it, "We do not want coercion or per-
secution or restraints against ethnic peculiarities . . . but we do indeed propose
that Russian government can be solely Russian throughout the whole expanse
of the possessions of the Russian power."[43] From 1863 onward, Katkov waged a
war of words against the Polish aristocracy, demanding that they be stripped of
their privileges and property as punishment for the 1863 revolt. In 1867 he also
launched a campaign against the Germans who made up much of the nobility in
the Baltic region, and demanded that German-language education be replaced
with Russian-language education. This infuriated Alexander II, but the tsar did no
more than send Katkov a "confidential signal" of his displeasure.[44]

Some conservatives shared the tsar's hostility toward ethnic Russian nationalism. The conservative newspaper *Vest'* (News), for instance, took offence at
Katkov's attacks on the Polish nobility, and accused him of wishing to harm not
the Poles but nobles as a class.[45] For *Vest'*, class solidarity was more important
than nationalism. *Vest'* also denounced Pan-Slavism, and in 1867 proclaimed
the slogan "Russia for the Russians!" This was *not* an ethno-nationalist statement
about the supremacy of the Russian nation within Russia's borders. Rather, the
slogan was primarily about foreign policy, and amounted to a reassertion of what
might be called the isolationist tendency in Russian conservatism. *Vest'* said:
"Sacrificing Russian interests for the Slavs? No, and a thousand times no! Russia
for the Russians! That is our banner."[46] The newspaper continued by asking, "Is the
Russian treasury so full, and the blood of Russians so cheap, that we can spend one
and the other on something other than Russia itself? . . . We repeat, *Russia for the
Russians!*"[47] In a later edition, *Vest'* clarified what it had it mind:

> Russia for the Russians . . . means not for the Germans, not for the Slavs, not for the
> Greeks—that is to say that valuable Russian blood should only be shed for Russia.
> But Russia for the Russians isn't a cry of hostility to humanity; it doesn't mean the
> persecution, devastation, or pursuit of foreigners. It does not mean enmity toward
> that which isn't Russian. . . . Russia for the Russians means Russia for all loyal sub-
> jects of the Russian Empire.[48]

Another person who rejected Pan-Slavism was the philosopher Konstantin
Leontyev, possibly the most original and eccentric of the conservative thinkers
of this era. Initially trained as a doctor, Leontyev became a Russian diplomat in
Turkey and then a monk. During his time in Turkey, he acquired a great admiration for the Ottoman Empire and its cultural diversity and an equally great dislike
of the Bulgarians. He rejected categorically the idea that the different Slavic nations
had anything significant in common, and declared that there was nothing quintessentially Slavic. Pan-Slavism was an "amorphous, spontaneous, and unorganic

concept," he complained.[49] "Slavdom is strong in numbers; Slavism doesn't exist, or is still very weak and unclear," he added.[50]

Despite his rejection of Pan-Slavism, Leontyev was strongly influenced by Danilevsky, sharing his desire for diversity, and adapting his theory of the life cycle of civilizations. Leontyev wrote that "the aesthetic criterion is the most trustworthy and general, for it is uniquely applicable to all societies, and to all epochs."[51] More precisely, simplicity and homogeneity were aesthetically dull, and therefore undesirable; complexity and diversity were aesthetically interesting, and therefore desirable. This led Leontyev to reject what he saw as the homogenizing effects of modern Western European culture. Describing a conversation he had had in St. Petersburg with a Russian nihilist named Piotrevsky, he wrote:

> As we spoke, we were about to cross the Anichkov bridge. On our left we could see the rose-colored Beloselsky Palace, with its stately windows and caryatids; in the background, further along the Fontanka canalside, there was the silhouette of the Troitsky Monastery, its church surrounded by a golden cupola; on our right, giving on the Fontanka Canal, were the fishermen's quarters, little yellow houses, and fishermen standing around in their red shirts. I pointed out these sights to Piotrevsky, saying: "That is a living illustration of my thesis.... But you would destroy all this, and in its place you would have nothing but little houses as alike as two peas, or six-storey barracks like those on the Nevsky Prospect!"[52]

In an 1876 book entitled *Byzantism and Slavdom*, Leontyev outlined a theory of a three-stage development in the rise and fall of civilizations. Leontyev argued that organic beings, which included human societies, began as simple and homogeneous, but gradually became more complex and colorful as they grew, until such time as they began to decay, at which point they became simpler again. Thus there were three stages of development: "primary simplicity," "flowering complexity," and "secondary simplicity."[53] In the case of human societies, the entire process took one thousand to twelve hundred years.[54]

The second period, "flowering complexity," represented the peak of a nation's progress in Leontyev's scheme. This led him to the conclusion that liberalism, with its egalitarian urges, was not progressive at all, as it promoted the simplification of society and so accelerated the onset of the third stage and society's decay. This could be seen in Europe, where liberalism and economic development had produced a leveling of the social structure through mass education, the spread of ideas of equal rights, and the like. As Leontyev wrote in another essay, in Europe, "the homogeneity of individuals, institutions, fashions, cities, and in general of cultured ideals and forms is spreading ... and the interfusion or mixing of homogenous component parts ... leads not to greater solidarity but to ruin and death."[55]

Leontyev was not anti-European. He recognized that in its time the European civilization had achieved more than any other before it. But European civilization was almost one thousand years old, and was reaching the end of its life, Leontyev argued. The various nations of Europe would gradually merge together and lose their individuality. This presented Russia with a choice. Either it followed Europe's path toward a liberal, homogeneous future, and so joined in its inevitable decline into secondary simplicity, or it could defend its independence and try to avoid Europe's fate.[56] Leontyev's preference was clear. Russia should choose the second option. However, given that it was almost as old as Europe, its only way to avoid decay was to found a new civilization, and so begin anew the thousand-year life cycle. This could perhaps be done on the basis of the kind of Slav federation proposed by Danilevsky, but the federation would have to avoid any merger between its component parts, so as to maintain "diversity in unity."[57]

For all his criticisms of Europe, Leontyev was not a Russian nationalist. He preferred multinational and multiconfessional states, urging that the Ottoman and Austro-Hungarian empires be maintained;[58] he opposed attempts to Russify the Baltic Germans; and he denounced nationalism as "liberal democratism."[59] Although they differed on many matters, Dostoevsky, Danilevsky, and Leontyev did ultimately agree on one thing: the interests of humanity as a whole demanded that Russia not copy the West, but rather defend its own distinctive culture.

POLITICAL CONSERVATISM

The struggle over political reform in the 1860s was fought both at the national level and at the local level of government. From the very beginning of Alexander II's reign, the "aristocratic opposition" began to agitate for changes to the political order to strengthen the nobility's power. An early example was a memorandum written in 1856 by the head of Russia's military educational institutions, General Ivan Rostovtsev (1803–60). In his memorandum, entitled *On the Necessity of Summoning a General Meeting of the Senate*, Rostovtsev argued that the Senate (originally created in 1712 by Peter the Great and consisting of members appointed by the tsar) should be turned into the highest legislative body in the country, and should include some members elected by the nobility as well as others elected by the more important businessmen and merchants. This modified Senate would then take command of the reform process.[60] This set the tone for superficially democratizing proposals that in reality aimed to protect certain narrow interests.

In 1857, the St. Petersburg nobility received permission to form a committee to reform local administration. The committee, chaired by Count Pyotr Shuvalov (1827–89), proposed the creation of elected local institutions, including representatives of all classes. As Russian historian I. A. Khristoforov notes, this proposal made sense "in the context of the aspiration to guarantee a dominant position in the state for the large landowners based on their predominance in local affairs."[61] Nobles were abandoning their hostility to elected institutions. At the same time, though, many were unhappy with the way that the reform process was being handled, and by 1858 members of the nobility were publishing memoranda and pamphlets denouncing the government's approach. The main theme of these publications was that reform was in the hands of a hostile bureaucracy that was intent on enacting socialist principles, such as expropriation of noble land. The nobility could defend itself only by means of a fundamental review of the system of power.[62] In a brochure addressed to the Editing Commission charged with drawing up legislation for the emancipation of the serfs, Rostovtsev and Count Vladimir Orlov-Davydov (1809–92), a large landowner in the Petersburg area, wrote that the fate of the country depended on "whether noble property owners or the bureaucracy constitute the highest order . . . one of these two estates must triumph or die."[63] Viktor Apraksin, a nobleman from the Orel region, proposed in a memorandum to the tsar that representatives be elected by the nobility from each province to participate in central state institutions.[64] These ideas found some support among ministers, particularly Pyotr Valuev (1815–90), who was minister of the interior from 1861 to 1868. In 1862, for instance, Valuev put forward a proposal for constitutional reform that would have seen the creation of a noble-dominated representative assembly, although this would have been purely consultative and would not have had legislative authority.[65]

In 1872, Pyotr Shuvalov, who in 1866 had become head of the Corps of Gendarmes and thus the person in charge of Russia's internal security, established a commission to examine proposals for reform. Shuvalov explained that he wished to include representatives of the *zemstva* (plural of *zemstvo*), elected by the *zemstva* themselves, in the legislative process. In response to an objection that this would be the beginning of the end of autocracy, Shuvalov said, "It is clear that for Russia this is the last autocratic government."[66]

Shuvalov also wished to create a second legislative chamber consisting of the provincial marshals of the nobility (who were elected by the nobles in each province). This proposal met with stiff resistance from both the tsar and ministers within the government, who believed that their reform plans required the continuation of the autocracy. By this time, as Richard Weeks says, "democracy and representative government had become antithetical concepts" in Imperial Russia.[67] Supposed conservatives in the government supported proposals for representative institutions, while supposed liberals opposed them. Faced with resistance, Shuvalov watered down his proposals, suggesting that representatives of the *zemstva* and the marshals of the nobility be invited to join a commission to examine just one specific problem—the relations between employers and employees in the rural economy. This pilot project achieved nothing, however, and in 1874 Shuvalov was dismissed as head of the Gendarmes and sent to London to serve as Russian ambassador.[68]

Members of the aristocratic opposition of this era generally accepted that all classes should be allowed to participate to some degree in elections for whatever new institutions were created, but they aimed to keep the participation of peasants largely symbolic. Their primary objective was to shape the institutions so as to maintain noble dominance.[69] The government rejected the aristocratic opposition's proposals on the assumption that the peasantry were naturally conservative and would form a basis of support for the tsarist system at the local level. The eventual decree forming the *zemstva* thus gave more representation to the peasants than the nobles had desired. This caused Count Orlov-Davydov to comment: "The thought comes to mind that the Sovereign is the sworn enemy of the nobility."[70] Orlov-Davydov was not entirely wrong. The government was seeking to expand its own bureaucratic control of Russia's provinces as much as possible and thereby to supplant the nobility with its own functionaries.[71]

Conservatives nevertheless persisted in proposing reforms of local and central government. In an 1871 book, for instance, N. A. Lobanov-Rostovsky clearly identified the introduction of an electoral element into central government as a conservative measure. He wrote:

> It is necessary to change the electoral law for the *zemstva* in a conservative sense, that is to strengthen the voice of property owners. It is necessary to create a permanent editing commission attached to the State Council, consisting of elected members, conservative people. . . . This commission will work out drafts of laws.[72]

In 1871, a new conservative newspaper, *Russkii mir* (Russian world), began publication. A year later, it published an essay by General Rostislav Fadeev (1824–83) that outlined a radically different program of reform. Fadeev argued that previous conservative programs had failed because they were not rooted in Russian tradition, due to the fact that the nobility was so thoroughly Westernized. Thus, wrote Fadeev, "our conservatism is the most imported of imported things."[73] Fadeev argued that the central government bureaucracy was incapable of properly administering the countryside. Consequently, the state apparatus should be dismantled and power should be handed over to representatives elected by the nobility.[74]

The Slavophile Iury Samarin categorized Fadeev's ideology as "revolutionary conservatism," that is to say conservative in intent, but revolutionary in method.[75] The opposite of this was liberal conservatism, which was liberal in intent, but conservative in method. Aleksandr Gradovsky (1841–89), a professor of law at St. Petersburg Imperial University, commented that the creation of some sort of noble-dominated representative institution of the type proposed by the aristocratic opposition would be dangerous.[76] By contrast, civil liberties could develop under autocracy. Therefore, Gradovsky wrote, liberalism and conservatism were not diametrically opposite concepts.[77] "Conservatism," he said, "is not preservation come what may and by all means possible. . . . The conservative preserves the old, but within the limits of the demands of the present, and the institutions that are renewed according to these demands become in his eyes a part of the historical institutions and thus worthy of being preserved."[78]

The most prominent personality among the liberal conservatives (or, as they are less commonly, but perhaps more accurately known, "conservative liberals") was Boris Chicherin, a professor of law at Moscow University until his resignation in 1868 in protest at government repression. A "right Hegelian," Chicherin defies easy classification. One view categorizes him as an important figure in the development of Russian liberalism;[79] another as profoundly conservative and not liberal at all.[80] Chicherin himself outlined his position by saying that "autocracy can lead the nation with giant steps towards citizenship and enlightenment." According to Chicherin, "the extreme development of liberty, inherent in democracy, inevitably leads to the breakdown of the state organism. To counteract this, a strong state is necessary."[81] In essence, he supported autocracy as the best means of pursuing liberal reform. As he said:

> The essence of conservative liberalism lies in reconciling the principle of freedom with the principle of power and law. In political life its slogan is: liberal measures and strong power. . . . securing the rights and personality of the citizens, securing freedom of thought and freedom of conscience . . . a strong system of power, the guardian of state unity . . . preserving order, strictly watching over the fulfilment of the law.[82]

In Chicherin's view, order was an essential prerequisite for progress. He therefore argued that "Enlightened absolutism . . . contributes much more to the development of popular welfare than do republics torn apart by factionalism."[83] Chicherin's conservatism derived not from his belief in a strong state but from his belief in gradual, organic change. As he said, "There are those who demand sudden changes and do not admit the gradualness of historical evolution. . . . History, like nature, does not make leaps."[84] Chicherin believed that political liberty would only produce positive results if people had the necessary political and legal culture to make appropriate use of their liberty. Unfortunately, the mass of the Russian population did not yet have the required culture. It would be unwise, therefore, to grant them political rights, such as the right to vote. Drawing a distinction between civil and political liberty, Chicherin proposed that the former should precede the latter. Having acquired civil liberty, the people would gradually acquire also the necessary political and legal culture, which would in due course enable them to attain political rights.

In an 1857 essay, Chicherin protested against the repressive nature of the tsarist state and demanded civil liberties, namely: "freedom of conscience" (including the ending of restrictions on Jews and schismatics); emancipation of the serfs; "freedom of speech"; "freedom of the press"; "academic freedom"; "publication of all government activities"; and "public legal proceedings."[85] But, he wrote elsewhere, political rights were different, for "the basis of the [electoral] right is not freedom but competence."[86] Politics was a difficult art, and it presupposed participants who were interested in politics and who were committed to "the rule of law, to those things benefitting the fatherland, to the family, to property."[87] According to Chicherin, "An individual person is a member of an organic entity, which introduces the individual into a community of shared values." This meant that individuals had responsibilities as well as rights. An acceptance of responsibilities toward the community was therefore a prerequisite for political rights.[88] From this it followed that the correct form of the state in any given country was dependent on the level of development of its political culture and the people's acceptance of their responsibilities. As Chicherin put it, "A form of government is the consequence of the entire evolution of national life; it is determined by the character of the people, its makeup, position, level of education."[89]

According to Chicherin, inner freedom was in any case more important than external freedom, because "the imperative of external liberty is based upon inner liberty. . . . Without internal liberty, external liberty loses its foundations and significance."[90] Meanwhile, Chicherin maintained that any state requires people to obey the law. This obedience should ideally be freely given, but this was only possible where there was "an advanced state of civic consciousness and civic spirit." Otherwise, coercion was required to maintain order.[91] Unfortunately, in Russia civic spirit was lacking. "It would be hard to find someone less capable of democratic government than the Russian peasant," wrote Chicherin.[92] But the problem went beyond the peasantry. As Chicherin complained:

> The Russian liberal, in theory, admits of no authority. He wants to obey only that law which he happens to like. The indispensable action of the government appears to him as oppression. . . . The Russian liberal travels on a few high-sounding words: freedom, openness, public opinion, merger with the people, and so on, which he interprets as having no limits. . . . Hence he regards as products of

outrageous despotism the most elementary concepts such as obedience to law [or] the need for a police or bureaucracy.[93]

Mikhail Katkov shared some of the liberal conservatives' views. For instance, as befitted a journalist, he opposed press censorship.[94] He maintained, like Chicherin, that civil and political liberties were independent of one another and that rights were connected to duties. Civil rights should be given to everybody, but political rights could only be given to people capable of fulfilling their responsibilities. In Katkov's eyes, that meant the nobility.[95] But unlike the liberal conservatives, Katkov rejected representative forms of government in principle, not just in practice. "We cannot allow any [social] contract between the people and the supreme authority," he wrote.[96] This would merely separate the two, making them distinct beings rather than one organic whole.

Foreign examples of constitutional government did not apply to Russia, Katkov argued, for "Russia, as a country called to a great historical life, has its own original type and characteristic form of development."[97] Russia, he said, should stick to the form of government that was natural to it—monarchy. "The monarchical principle is not only a fundamental principle for Russia—it is Russia," Katkov wrote.[98] Constitutions were alien to Russian culture and national identity; they also did not work very well, as seen by the endless political upheavals in Western Europe. The one stable European country, in Katkov's eyes, was England, but that was precisely because its constitution was unwritten and was the product of organic growth over many centuries.[99]

Katkov wrote that "strength doesn't grow out of weakness. Weakness leads only to more weakness."[100] In foreign policy, this attitude led Katkov to regard almost every incident as a test of Russia's resolve that required a firm response. He became an advocate of an aggressive foreign policy, earning the displeasure of both Tsar Alexander II and Tsar Alexander III. Like many conservatives in Russian history, Katkov spent his time criticizing government policy while professing his loyalty to the state in principle.[101] In domestic politics, following the Vera Zasulich trial, he called for the government to take a hard line against the radical intelligentsia. "The debilitating fear of dark forces can be conquered only by salutary fear of the legal authority," he wrote.[102] Increasingly, he viewed a strong state in the form of autocracy not only as being in keeping with Russia's traditions but also as being a necessary bulwark against revolutionary chaos. As Katkov put it, "Tear out the monarchical principle by the root . . . and you will destroy the natural aristocratic element in society, but its place won't remain empty, it will be filled by bureaucrats or demagogues or an oligarchy of the very worst sort."[103] Autocracy was all that stood between Russia and chaos, he believed.

Konstantin Leontyev likewise supported autocratic rule, although in his case without any liberal pretensions. Due to his belief in diversity, and in accordance with the idea that there were no universal standards applicable to all civilizations, he considered that no type of government was in principle superior at all times and in all places to all others. It all depended on the country in question. As he wrote:

> There are no statistics for the subjective bliss of individual people; nobody knows under what government people live better. . . . There are no statistics to determine that it's better for an individual to live in a republic than a monarchy, in a limited monarchy better than an unlimited one, in an egalitarian state better than one based on estates, in a rich one better than in a poor one. . . . To know what suits an organism, you need above all to understand the organism.[104]

In Russia's case, understanding the organism meant accepting autocracy as the correct form of government. According to Leontyev, "Our strength, discipline, and ancient enlightenment, our poetry, in other words everything about us, is organically connected to our native Monarchy. . . . If we change it . . . we will destroy Russia."[105] In any case, Leontyev did not truly believe that one type of government really was as good as another. "Democracy is always fatal," he opined.[106] Democracy accelerated the process of secondary simplification. A strong, centralized authority was needed to prevent the process of democratization and so maintain the period of flowering complexity.[107] According to Leontyev, this meant that "the state is obliged always to be terrible, and sometimes cruel and merciless . . . [the state] must strengthen itself, and think less about *good* and more about *force*. If there's force there will be some good."[108]

The *pochvenniki* shared Leontyev's and Katkov's view of the organic connection between Russia and autocracy.[109] As Dostoevsky wrote to Alexander II in 1880:

> We believe in the ancient truth, a truth that has penetrated into the soul of the Russian people: that the tsar is its father, and that his children can always approach their father without fear, so that he can lovingly hear from them their needs and their desires, that the children love their father, and that the father believes in their love, and that the relations of the Russian people towards their tsar-father are free and loving and without fear, and not deadly formalistic and based on contract.[110]

Based on this belief, the *pochvenniki* rejected Western-style constitutionalism. Nevertheless, as Wayne Dowler writes, they "looked forward to the day when a truly Russian form of constitutionalism, based on the historical tradition of the nation, would emerge."[111] In line with the Slavophiles, they imagined this to involve local self-government. Dostoevsky and Grigoryev therefore argued that the *zemstva* should be democratically elected on the basis of universal suffrage, not according to a system weighted in favor of the wealthier classes.[112] To eliminate barriers between the people and the tsar, they also rejected proposals to put local administration into the hands of the landed nobility.[113] Until it ran afoul of the censors for an article about Poland and was shut down, the journal *Vremia* (Time), published by Fyodor Dostoevsky and his brother Mikhail, was considered to be "in the camp of the progressive journals." Wayne Dowler notes that "it advocated the abolition of corporal punishment, agitated for sweeping hospital and prison reform, and recommended that Jews be granted the full rights of citizens."[114] It also supported female emancipation, and Dostoevsky argued in favor of increasing women's access to higher education.[115] Despite his denunciations of Russia's liberals, "Dostoevsky genuinely believed that *pochvennichestvo* was a progressive force."[116]

SOCIAL-ECONOMIC CONSERVATISM

The most important social-economic question facing Russian conservatives in the 1860s and 1870s was the future of the countryside following the abolition of serfdom. Once it became clear that the tsar was intent on freeing the serfs, the issue became not whether one should free them, but how to do so, and then once it had been done, how to manage the rural economy and society thereafter.

Following Alexander II's announcement in 1856 that he planned to emancipate the serfs, landowners were permitted to form provincial committees to make proposals on how to enact the reform. On two occasions, representatives from these committees convened in a joint assembly. The final decisions, however, were made not by the landowners' committees or the two joint assemblies but by three editing commissions appointed by the tsar. The noble committees were purely consultative in nature.

The tsar and his government viewed emancipation as a conservative measure, a form of change designed to prevent popular rebellion and ensure continued social and political stability. Recognizing that if the peasants were freed without any land they would soon become impoverished and possibly rebellious, the government favored giving the peasants the land they currently worked on condition that they pay for it in small instalments over a long period of time.[117] The government also favored keeping the peasant commune as a means of governing villages and so maintaining order. In this way, the reform followed the logic expressed by Chicherin in an 1856 essay entitled "On Serfdom," in which he argued that rebellion would inevitably result if the existing system was retained, but also said that if the peasants were freed and given land, they would become pillars of stability, because "property owner[s] . . . are the most conservative element that one can imagine."[118]

Members of the aristocratic opposition had a very different opinion. Their ideal was the landowning British aristocracy, and they sought to shape reform so as to recreate the British example in Russia.[119] Count Orlov-Davydov, for instance, was a great admirer of the British, having completed a law degree in Edinburgh, served in the Russian embassy in London, and become a friend of the famous novelist Walter Scott. Aristocrats such as Orlov-Davydov supported the abolition of the commune, the reorganization of landholding on the principle of private property, and laissez-faire economics. They were in some ways more liberal (in the sense of proposing greater individual freedom) and less conservative (in the sense that they adopted foreign models and rejected organic, Russian ones) than either the state or the liberal conservatives, both of whom favored keeping the commune.

In 1857 Orlov-Davydov, who was something of a modernizer on his own estates, proposed that the peasants should be emancipated without land, with the land being concentrated instead in the hands of large estate owners from whom the peasants would rent the land they needed. Inevitably, this change would leave some peasants landless, but they could then leave the villages to work in industry. Orlov-Davydov argued that this would benefit the process of industrialization.[120] Following similar reasoning, the second joint assembly of provincial nobles denounced the plans of the editing commissions in the vocabulary of laissez-faire economics, saying:

> Compulsory relations have outlived their time. Government regulation is impossible; we need to completely abolish such relations. Peasants need complete liberation, free attachment to the land, and the right to move . . . personal independence, free of the power of the commune, is needed.[121]

The aristocratic opposition lost this battle. The emancipation proclamation of 1861 retained the commune. But by 1870, there was a growing sense that Russian agriculture was in crisis, and disgruntled nobles returned to the attack. In an 1871 book, N. A. Lobanov-Rostovsky complained that communal ownership of land "prevents any individual enterprise—the basis of progress—destroys the significance of the family . . . [and] the desire to work, because property is insufficiently guaranteed."[122] Orlov-Davydov argued that the commune encouraged socialism and inhibited industrialization. Abolishing the commune would produce the proletariat needed for industry. In addition, concentrating ownership in fewer hands would increase profits and so produce the capital required for economic development.[123] Peasant farmers operating independently of the commune would also constitute a rural middle class, which would be naturally conservative in inclination, thus reinforcing social and political stability.[124] Those making these arguments often cited the works of English economists in support. Confronted by the normal conservative argument that Russia was different from other countries, they responded that the laws of economics were universally applicable.[125] This added to the confusion as to who could really be called conservative. As Khristoforov notes, "It is a paradox that the nobility, which was considered conservative and reactionary, defended ideals that were far less connected to Russian reality than the liberal reforms that they criticized as being theoretical in origin."[126]

Not every conservative supported the abolition of the commune. For instance, Mikhail Katkov's St. Petersburg agent, B. M. Markevich, wrote to Katkov that "if we abolish the commune, Russia won't last twenty-four hours. The peasant commune is the only conservative element that we have."[127] In line with his Slavophile tendencies, Dostoevsky also supported the commune.[128] So too did Leontyev. He wrote:

> Those who would destroy the *village commune*, naively imagining that everything rests in the *enrichment of the individual*, are destroying the last support, the last remnants of the former alignment, stratification, serfdom and immobility . . . at a stroke they are depriving us of our individual peculiarity, our diversity, and our unity.[129]

Leontyev wished to keep Russia a stratified society. He therefore recommended restricting education.[130] The *pochvenniki* were more egalitarian. They strongly promoted the spread of education, hoping that this would produce a country without class divisions. To this end they placed particular importance on teaching literacy to the peasants.[131] Education also garnered much attention from Katkov, who argued that nihilism was "the natural product" of the existing school system, which turned out "unfortunate, scatter-brained half-wits."[132] To correct this problem, he proposed a bifurcated school system, in which only a small number of students would receive a classical education in *gymnasiia* (academically-oriented high schools), while most would receive technical training in *realschule* (vocational high schools). This way, Russia would be able to provide itself with the skilled technicians it needed for industrial development without filling too many young people's heads with controversial ideas.[133]

In terms of economics, Katkov favored industrial growth, and promoted railroad building as a means of uniting the country. Initially an economic liberal who supported laissez-faire, he later turned into an economic nationalist and wrote articles attacking free trade. He also denounced cheap credit, believing it served foreign financial interests, and instead supported the maintenance of a tight monetary policy. At the same time, he proposed improved social welfare for industrial workers.[134]

As noted above, laissez-faire economic theory had some support among the aristocratic opposition. Chicherin also had decidedly liberal economic views, including a belief in free trade. He linked economic growth to civil liberty, saying that the former was impossible without the latter. This formed the basis of his opposition to serfdom. Chicherin wrote that, "only free labor, only activity driven by the mainspring of personal gain, only those things can significantly advance society."[135] This in turn led him to believe that material inequality was desirable, as "it is the inevitable consequence of free activity."[136]

The *pochvenniki* had a very different view. Due to their religious and anti-materialist perspective, they viewed capitalism with suspicion and favored protectionism, although they were willing to countenance industrial development in the form of cooperatives, and proposed that the government promote cottage industries by means of cheap credit.[137] In general, protectionism was more common among conservatives than belief in free trade. Danilevsky, for instance, condemned attempts by social scientists to establish universally applicable social rules, including in the realm of political economy. As he wrote:

> Political economy affirms that so-called free trade, which is the most suitable form of exchange for England . . . should without fail apply to America and Russia. In my opinion, this is like affirming that one can breathe only with gills or only with lungs, ignoring whether an animal lives in the water or on land . . . an economic or political phenomenon observed among one people, for whom it is appropriate and beneficial, can never be considered appropriate and beneficial for another.[138]

CONCLUSION

There has been a tendency to latch onto Pan-Slavism and the more anti-Western statements of writers like Dostoevsky, Danilevsky, and Leontyev, and to view Russian conservatism of the era of the Great Reforms primarily in terms of growing Russian nationalism. The reality is more complicated. Dostoevsky and Katkov still saw Russia's fate as intimately bound up with that of Europe while, for all their complaints about the West's hostility toward Russia, Danilevsky and Leontyev admitted that the West's cultural and scientific achievements were very great. Meanwhile, in drawing up their economic and political proposals, the members of the aristocratic opposition drew on British examples and sought to restructure Russia to some extent along a British model. As for Pan-Slavism, it came under attack from Leontyev and the conservatives of *Vest'*. Danilevsky's and Leontyev's particularism did not entirely separate itself from notions of the universal good. Rather it identified a universal good in the form of diversity (or flowering complexity). This in many respects continued rather than broke with the Slavophile insistence that Russia would serve humanity by maintaining and developing its own peculiarities.

Politically speaking, most conservatives continued to support the autocratic system, but they did so for varying reasons. Liberal conservatives felt that autocracy was more likely to produce liberal reform than any form of representative government in which the nobility played a leading role. They also felt that Russian political and legal culture was not sufficiently developed for democratic rule. Others believed that autocracy was the natural product of Russia's history and wanted a strong state to keep order and forestall revolution. At the same time, others still, such as Shuvalov, experimented with forms of political reform that might bring a gradual end to the autocratic order. In the ensuing confusion, it was hard, as Kireev noted, to work out who was a liberal and who a conservative.

The same could be said of conservatives' ideas on social and economic issues. Some supported the commune; others opposed it. Some supported free trade and laissez-faire economics; others did not. Some wanted a more equal society and supported expanding education to the mass of the population. Others wanted to keep society stratified, and wanted to restrict education or to divide it into classical education for the few and technical education for the many.

The reign of Alexander II is often known as the era of the Great Reforms, but it was also something of a golden age for Russian conservatism. Not only were some of the most famous writers in the history of Russian conservatism active at this time, but there was also a great expansion in the conservative press, with newspapers and journals such as *Moskovskie vedomosti*, *Russkii vestnik*, *Vest'*, and *Russkii mir* springing up. This was not as paradoxical as it seems. Rapid change produced an inevitable reaction. What it was not able to produce was unity. Different conservatives responded to the Great Reforms in different ways. The common thread was concern with managing change during a time of great social and economic upheaval. Conservatives (with the possible eccentric exception of Leontyev) accepted the necessity of the upheavals, but sought at the same time to preserve certain things they valued and also to ensure that the reform process did not unleash revolutionary forces. Once again conservatism was more about managing change than it was about stopping it.

THE ERA OF COUNTER-REFORM

I n March 1881, a member of the terrorist organization People's Will threw a bomb at Tsar Alexander II's carriage in St. Petersburg. The explosion failed to kill the tsar, but when Alexander exited his carriage to investigate, a second terrorist threw another bomb, which exploded by the tsar's feet. Badly wounded by the blast, which shattered his legs, Alexander was taken to the nearby Winter Palace where he died a few minutes later. The oldest of his five surviving sons inherited the throne, becoming Tsar Alexander III just three days short of his thirty-sixth birthday.

At the time of his death, Alexander II had been considering plans for political reform put forward by the minister of the interior, Count Mikhail Loris-Melikov (1824–88). In Loris-Melikov's scheme, legislative proposals would have been initiated in two commissions appointed by the tsar and including representatives from the *zemstva*; the proposals would then have moved up to a general commission composed of elected delegates; and after that to the State Council, expanded by the addition of some elected members; finally, the tsar would make a decision. This proposal fell well short of creating a parliamentary system of government, but would have introduced an elected element into the legislative process for the first time.[1] A committee appointed by Alexander II to study the proposal approved the reform in early 1881, and Alexander ordered Loris-Melikov to prepare a decree to bring it into effect. Before the decree could be issued, however, Alexander was assassinated.

On becoming tsar, the most important question facing Alexander III was whether to proceed with the reform. As heir to the throne, Alexander had been a member of the committee that approved Loris-Melikov's plan. Alexander ordered the Committee of Ministers to meet to consider the matter, and at first it seemed very possible that the reform would go ahead. At this point, Alexander's former tutor, Konstantin Pobedonostsev (1827–1907), who held the position of procurator of the Holy Synod (in effect, the minister in charge of church affairs), intervened.

Pobedonostsev was to become one of the leading conservative figures of the late nineteenth century. A lawyer by training, he spoke German, French, English, Latin, Italian, Czech, and Polish, traveled regularly to central Europe, "read deeply and widely in Western literature,"[2] and was something of an Anglophile. Prior to 1861 Pobedonostsev supported the emancipation of the serfs and was a harsh critic of the judicial system. He played a role in drawing up the legal reforms of 1864.[3] Soon after, however, he became thoroughly disillusioned with the reform process, and turned into a fervent opponent of further change. He believed that political concessions would only embolden revolutionaries, and that autocracy was necessary to prevent Russia from descending into chaos. For this reason, he rejected Loris-Melikov's reforms, and wrote to the new tsar telling him that it was his responsibility to accept the burden of power given to him by God and to assert his autocratic authority.[4] "Time will not wait. Either save Russia now or never," Pobedonostsev wrote.[5] Having received Pobedonostsev's letter, Alexander summoned him for a meeting. Exactly what was said is not known, but it seems that the new tsar was sympathetic to Pobedonostsev's point of view. At the meeting of the Committee of Ministers that followed, the ministers were divided. Some opposed the changes; others wished to press ahead. But Pobedonostsev had convinced the one person who truly mattered, the tsar. The reform was canceled, and in late April 1881 Alexander III issued a manifesto, drafted by Pobedonostsev, affirming his intention to retain the autocratic system.

Attempts to promote political reform continued for a while longer. Loris-Melikov resigned as minister of the interior, and was replaced by Count N. P. Ignatyev (1832–1908), who in spring 1882 proposed to the tsar that he summon an elected consultative assembly of the people, a Zemsky sobor. Alexander rejected this proposal and dismissed Ignatyev.[6] With this, the era of reform came to an end, and the era of counter-reform began. It would last throughout the thirteen-year reign of Alexander III and into that of his son, Nicholas II, who came to the throne in 1894 and was to be Russia's last tsar.

The first notable counter-reform was an 1884 regulation restricting university autonomy.[7] Next, an 1889 law amended the system of rural administration by creating "land captains," state-appointed officials to whom peasant institutions, including the communes, were subordinated. An 1890 law increased noble representation in the *zemstva*, thereby giving the nobles more control over *zemstva* affairs, although not as much control as many conservatives had hoped. An 1892 statute restricted the independence of municipal governments. And the minimum property and educational qualifications for jurors were increased, although juries were not entirely abolished as some, like Mikhail Katkov, had desired.[8] These and other counter-reforms rolled back many of the changes enacted during Alexander II's reign, although not all of them.

To a certain degree, the counter-reforms reflected not just a shift in political attitudes but also what has been termed "increasing technological capacity for control."[9] As this capacity increased, the Russian state attempted to rectify its traditional weakness and to establish the type of centralized administration that had previously been lacking. One aspect of this was "a dramatic increase in the sheer numbers of officials and bureaucrats."[10] This was not necessarily a bad thing in terms of governmental efficiency, but many conservatives resented the resulting intrusion of state officials into areas of life that had traditionally been left to various forms of local self-government. Conservatism in this era thus often acquired an anti-bureaucratic flavor.

While the state sought to strengthen its own power, it also sought to stimulate economic development, and in this way balanced political counter-reform with more positive reforms of another type. An example was the creation of the Peasant Land Bank, which helped peasants buy land. The reign of Alexander III also witnessed a huge acceleration in industrialization, promoted by policies of protectionism and state investment (particularly in railways). As the number of industrial workers increased, the state sought to improve their conditions through legislation creating commissions of factory inspectors.[11] Even during the reign of Alexander III, the Russian state remained to some degree a modernizing force. As in the past, this occasionally placed it in opposition to conservative intellectuals, as well as to elements of the church and the nobility.[12]

CULTURAL CONSERVATISM

Late nineteenth-century Russian conservatism is generally seen as having become increasingly nationalistic, chauvinistic, and anti-Semitic.[13] Whereas Alexander II had little time for proposals to Russify the empire's non-Russian peoples, his son was more sympathetic. The Baltic region was a particular target for Russification. In the 1880s, a decree replaced German with Russian as the language of local administration and as the first language in educational institutions in Russia's Baltic provinces. In 1885, the Holy Synod forbade marriages between Orthodox and non-Orthodox persons in the Baltics (where there was a large non-Orthodox population) unless the couple agreed that their children would be raised as Orthodox. Elsewhere in the empire, under the guidance of Konstantin Pobedonostsev, the Synod sought to undermine the Catholic and Uniate churches, enforcing laws that stated that marriages had to be celebrated in an Orthodox Church. Pobedonostsev also rejected proposals to translate the Bible into Ukrainian, fearing that it might strengthen Ukrainian nationalism.[14] He considered Jews to be largely responsible for the growing revolutionary movement in Russia, and in 1887 he persuaded the tsar to issue decrees imposing strict quotas on the number of Jews who could attend university.[15] Pobedonostsev was not, however, a supporter of Pan-Slavism. Having initially endorsed the Russo-Turkish war of 1877–78, he was appalled by the actual experience, and came to believe that war of any sort could lead to revolution. Consequently, he became increasingly isolationist, and in 1899 played an important role in persuading Tsar Nicholas II to establish the Hague Conference on Disarmament.[16] In this way, he followed in the footsteps of the newspaper *Vest'* (News) and its slogan "Russia for the Russians."

Russification measures were not universally popular among conservatives, and were particularly disliked by nobles of Germanic origin. The conservative German-language *St. Petersburger Zeitung* (St. Petersburg newspaper) argued forcefully against defining Russia as a nation-state. The *Zeitung*'s editor, Paul von Kügelgen, wrote that nation and state were entirely different concepts, and that the idea of the nation-state "not only violates every legal precept, but also runs contrary to the historical genesis and growth of the empire."[17] Von Kügelgen denounced "crass nationalists" and warned that "if the ethnographic principle of Russianness becomes the foundation of the state, those who are not ethnic Russians will be forced to conclude that they are aliens and not genuine Russian subjects."[18]

The Orthodox Church, meanwhile, began to embrace a third position, one that sought to reconcile the universalist and particularist trends within Russian conservatism. This was "Orthodox patriotism," a philosophy that was explicitly differentiated from ethnic Russian nationalism. Orthodox patriotism first came to the fore in 1888 on the nine hundredth anniversary of the conversion of Russia to Christianity.[19] The occasion was used by senior clerics such as Archbishop Nikanor of Kherson and Metropolitan Platon of Kiev to propose that Orthodoxy and patriotism were mutually reinforcing: Orthodoxy shaped Russian identity, while it also had a specifically national, Russian, character. In a biography of St. Vladimir written for the anniversary, Kiev historian Ivan Malyshevsky argued that "the universal Church ... though by definition not limited to a particular nationality, was nevertheless centered upon the experiences of a particular people."[20] In the philosophy of Orthodox patriotism, Russia was defined as the particular people in which the universal truth was preserved. It followed that the propagation of patriotism would help reinforce religion. Religious education began to acquire an increasingly patriotic tone on the assumption that patriotic Russians would be less likely to succumb to schismatic heresies.

According to Orthodox patriotism, Russia was the "New Israel," the land in which God's truth was preserved.[21] As the curator of the universal idea, Russia had a missionary purpose.[22] In accordance with this idea, in the late nineteenth century the Orthodox Church greatly expanded its missionary, educational, and charitable activities. Perhaps the best-known exemplar of the missionary zeal was John of Kronstadt (1829–1909). Described as "the first modern Russian religious celebrity,"[23] John was a parish priest in the town of Kronstadt on the island of Kotlin near St. Petersburg, where he introduced some radical innovations in liturgy. These included facing his parishioners at times when traditional practice required the priest to face the altar, adding his own prayers into the service, and allowing people to take communion without the normal preparation, which included days of fasting. These innovations proved immensely popular, and John's services attracted thousands of worshippers, obliging John to introduce another innovation—group confessions, with people shouting out their sins and receiving collective forgiveness.[24] John also raised large sums of money that he dispensed to charitable organizations, and he denounced government policies that he felt created poverty.

John preached, and practiced, an ascetic way of life. "Everything about our way of life is contrary to God," he complained, "the [tobogganing] hills, and the reindeer, and horse races, and the music they play there, and where are those who are concerned with saving their souls? . . . What is this short life given to us for, after all—for amusement?"[25] In the place of amusement, he celebrated the benefits of suffering. "The true Christian ought to long for outward, carnal, worldly suffering, for it strengthens his spirit," he proclaimed.[26]

John championed the ordinary people against the elite. "The uneducated man's simplicity of heart, his meekness, gentleness, humility, and unassertive patience, are dearer to God than all our knowledge,"[27] he said. He denounced the sins of the liberal intelligentsia, saying that

> because of the godlessness and impiety of many Russians, the so-called intelligentsia . . . the Russian empire is not the Kingdom of the Lord but a broad and depraved kingdom of Satan that has penetrated deeply into the hearts and minds of the "learned," the half-educated. . . . If things continue the way they do, and the godless and the mad anarchists are not subjected to righteous punishment by the law, and if Russia is not cleansed of its many weeds, it will become deserted, just like the ancient kingdoms and cities that were wiped from the face of the earth by God's justice for their godlessness and lawlessness.[28]

The assassination of Alexander II induced John to turn increasingly to politics, as a defender of the autocratic order against the forces of evil. The revolutionaries were "the seed of the Antichrist," he said. "By overthrowing the kings, they want to establish anarchy and crude tyranny, faithlessness, immorality, illegality, fear, and horror."[29] "The Tsar is the Image of the Heavenly King. God is unique and so is the Tsar," John declared.[30]

Orthodox patriotism endorsed the autocratic system, portraying the tsar as "an apostle-like leader" of Holy Rus'.[31] This did not mean that conservative clergymen were happy with the existing arrangement of church-state relations. On the contrary, they were increasingly outspoken about their dislike of the church's subordinate position. From the 1890s onward, senior clerics, including those on both the liberal wing of the church (such as Metropolitan Antony [Vadkovsky]) and the conservative wing (such as Metropolitan Antony [Khrapovitsky]) pressed for a restoration of the Patriarchate abolished by Peter the Great in 1721 and for the summoning of a church council to discuss reform. These proposals made no headway due to resistance from Pobedonostsev, who declared that "patriarchal rule was dangerous to the state."[32] As so often, conservatives' loyalty to the Russian state did not win them any concessions from those in authority.

POLITICAL CONSERVATISM

Historians' views of Pobedonostsev's political philosophy vary. His thinking has been criticized as an "eclectic hodgepodge, never systematically put together,"[33] which was characterized by a "lack of originality, system and organization."[34] He has also been described in a more positive way as "a thoughtful and critical student of Western and Russian culture."[35] But while scholars disagree on the depth and originality of Pobedonostsev's philosophy, they agree that he espoused "a consistent body of religious and political opinion,"[36] and that "at the core of his thoughts and actions lay a basically coherent political position which remained fundamentally consistent throughout his life."[37] Central to this political philosophy was profound pessimism. Change, in Pobedonostsev's eyes, was inevitable, but it needed to be gradual and organic, and it required political stability and the firm hand of a strong state to guide it. Otherwise it could all too easily lead to disaster.

Pobedonostsev was deeply critical of Western-style democracy. Universal suffrage was "a fatal error," he wrote, as with it "political power would be shattered into a small number of infinitesimal bits."[38] In Pobedonostsev's eyes, democracy was a charade. The people did not really hold power. Rather, power lay in the hands of political parties and those who funded them. According to Pobedonostsev, while "in theory, the elected candidate must be the favorite of the majority, in fact, he is the favorite of a minority, sometimes very small, but representing an organized force, while the majority, like sand, has no coherence, and is therefore incapable of resisting."[39]

Nature, Pobedonostsev said, "does not produce results quickly."[40] The key to producing a good society, he believed, was the establishment of stability, peace, and quiet. If this could be achieved, then, he said, there could be a "slow moral improvement and uplift of the soul in society."[41] Responsibility for providing this stability lay with the state, the church, and the family.[42] Church and state, there-fore, had to be firmly united, and schismatic groups that tried to drive a wedge between church and state had to be repressed.[43] Firmness was essential to stability, Pobedonostsev wrote:

> When the government stood and acted on firm principles, then society did not whirl about. Everyone knew thoroughly, without hesitation, what would be permitted by the government and what the government would not suffer in any event. Although the government was silent, everyone knew what it was necessary to expect. . . . Now, this assurance does not exist, and as a result, everything staggers along. . . . Even when they [the people] make crazy speeches, do crazy things, transgress against order, the government avoids action.[44]

Pobedonostsev told Alexander III that "the whole secret of Russian order and prosperity is found at the top, in the person of the supreme authority. . . . any weakening on your part will flood the land with weakness and indolence. . . . There is nowhere, especially here in Russia, where anything is done by itself, without the guiding hand, the supervisor's eye, the master."[45] Consequently, Pobedonostsev resisted any proposals for political reform.

Other conservatives echoed Pobedonostsev's emphasis on firmness. Historian Nikolai Liubimov, for instance, commented that "the mood of the public, however great its significance, doesn't make a revolution, and it isn't the primary danger in transitional epochs. The most important thing is the mood of the government and the manner in which it acts."[46] Writing about the French Revolution, Liubimov blamed liberals for paving the way for radicals by weakening the French monar-chy. The French example, said Liubimov, showed that revolution could never be prevented by making concessions, as these merely led to yet more concessions and eventually to total collapse.[47]

Not every conservative shared Liubimov's and Pobedonostsev's opposition to all political reform. Viacheslav von Plehve (1846–1904), who served as director of police from 1881 and as minister of the interior from 1902 to 1904, when he was assassinated by a revolutionary terrorist, sought to defeat terrorism by a combi-nation of repressive policing and economic, social, and political reform. At the same time, he was determined that any reform should be gradual, directed from above, and kept firmly under state control. The aim was to support, not supplant, autocracy. Liberal reforms in Russia had always originated with the state, Plehve told Finance Minister Sergei Witte (1849–1915), and thus, "Everyone in Russia who thirsts for reform ought to be on the side of the autocracy."[48]

Politically, Plehve's main focus was on reforming local administration by reaching out to the zemstva. He told the head of the Moscow zemstvo board, D. N.

Shipov: "I am in favor of *zemstvo* organizations, and I am convinced that no state order is possible unless society is drawn into local self-government. I believe that the broad development of local self-government is indispensable under an autocratic system."[49] Nevertheless, his idea of cooperation with the *zemstva* was limited: the *zemstva* were to work with the government, rather than separately from it, and they were to concern themselves with practical work only and refrain from political activity. In effect, Plehve viewed *zemstva* members as public servants, rather than autonomous, elected officials. His initial attempts to strike a deal with them failed to achieve any success, as the *zemstva* saw Plehve's overtures as an attempt to extend bureaucratic control.[50] Plehve persisted. In 1903 he proposed to lower the electoral qualifications for the *zemstva* to make them more democratic, and also to create an advisory Council on Local Affairs, which would centralize all matters relating to local administration and would include twelve to fifteen members appointed by the interior minister from local institutions such as the *zemstva*. This was typical of Plehve's cautious approach to reform—expanding society's role in government, but only slightly, while maintaining full bureaucratic control.[51]

A far more radical program of reform was proposed by conservative journalist Sergei Sharapov (1855–1911), who was strongly influenced by Slavophile philosophy and whose views stood in direct opposition to Plehve's bureaucratic conservatism. Sharapov declared: "Our bureaucracy has done everything possible to compromise and make hateful to all our wonderful and pure historical principle—Autocracy."[52] In keeping with Slavophile thought, Sharapov supported autocracy while simultaneously asserting his belief in freedom and local self-government. "I am a convinced advocate of freedom," he said. "Freedom could be better maintained in a monarchy, even in such imperfect one as ours, than in any republic, because the arithmetic majority [of votes] cannot warrant [freedom]."[53] At the same time, Sharapov strongly opposed parliamentarism and the creation of a written constitution. "Parliamentarism, like syphilis, is incurable," he said.[54]

To square the circle and combine political freedom with autocracy, Sharapov proposed to simultaneously centralize and decentralize state administration. This would free the tsar from having to decide on matters best decided locally. The basic level of self-government would be the parish, which was small enough for citizens to practice direct democracy without having to resort to political parties or elected institutions. The result would be a "people's monarchy."[55] Later, Sharapov suggested a system of federalism, dividing the country into larger administrative units with wide-ranging autonomy and elected institutions. Freedom of speech and of the press would ensure that these institutions functioned effectively. The model, said Sharapov, was the United States of America, but with a tsar rather than a president.[56] He wrote:

This is the combination of Autocracy and local self-government which I fancy. Could such a monarch be absolute? Undoubtedly, because, on the one hand, constitutions of the states would not hinder his power; and on the other hand he would not interfere in the self-government of the states.[57]

Another conservative opponent of the bureaucratic state was Lev Tikhomirov (1852–1923). One of the more colorful conservatives of the era, Tikhomirov had been a member of the executive committee of the People's Will terrorist organization and fled to France in 1882. In exile he reconsidered his political views, and eventually renounced his revolutionary beliefs. Pardoned by Alexander III, he returned to Russia, where he became an outspoken defender of the autocracy.

Tikhomirov distinguished between "true" and "false" conservatism. The former focused on developing a society's original culture, the latter simply on preserving existing political institutions. "True conservatism," he wrote, "completely coincides with true progress. They have one and the same task: supporting the vitality of society's foundations, preserving their freedom of development, encouraging their growth."[58] In Tikhomirov's eyes, Russian culture had taken a wrong turn that needed correcting. In his book, *Why I Stopped Being a Revolutionary*, Tikhomirov explained that the roots of Russia's revolutionary movement lay in the fact that the Russian intelligentsia thought in the wrong way; they thought in terms of abstract theories based on "foreign books," rather than in terms of practicalities and concrete facts about the actual conditions of Russian life.[59] By contrast, Tikhomirov said, "I am an enemy of theory."[60]

According to Tikhomirov, the facts demonstrated that liberal democracy and socialism were very different in practice than they were in theory. In theory, liberal democracy gave power to the people and constituted a system of government that gave expression to the "general will." In reality, this was not the case, said Tikhomirov. There was no such thing as the general will of the people, nor could there be.[61] Democracy required political parties, each of which represented the opinion of a minority. From these parties, "instead of the anticipated rule of the people, a new ruling class is born." It was the will of this ruling class that parliamentary democracy ultimately expressed.[62] However, the dishonorable methods this ruling class used to gain power in a democratic system meant that it was generally despised by the mass of the people, and so "has to govern the country with an arbitrariness that even the most popular or terrible monarch would not usually permit himself."[63] There was, said Tikhomirov, no class of people less in touch with the mass of the population than democratic politicians. Absolute monarchs could acquire a much better understanding of what the people actually wanted.[64]

Tikhomirov also poured scorn on Karl Marx's theory that socialism would lead to the "withering away" of the state and the subsequent freeing of the individual.

On the contrary, socialism was incompatible with individual rights, he said. Socialist economics stamped out independent initiative and turned people into worker ants.[65] To enact its economic policies, the socialist state would have to acquire enormous power "by way of an iron *class* dictatorship."[66] "In the face of this all-powerful state . . . the individual will be a worthless and powerless speck of dust," Tikhomirov warned.[67] State planning would require the creation of a large apparatus of managers, who would become the new ruling class. Socialism would therefore not even eliminate class differences.[68] The final product of socialism would be "an aristocratic republic with the mass of the population enserfed in a variety of ways."[69]

Whereas liberal democracy and socialism were theoretical constructs, autocracy was the concrete reality of Russian life. The fact that the revolutionaries had to resort to terrorism illustrated their lack of support, Tikhomirov argued. The mass of the people continued to support the autocratic system. "I look at the question of autocratic government in the following way," Tikhomirov wrote.

> Above all, it is the result of Russian history . . . and cannot be destroyed by anybody as long as there are tens and tens of millions of people in the country who don't know and don't want to know anything about politics. It would be impermissible not to respect the historic will of the people . . . every Russian should recognize the established government in Russia and when thinking of improvements should think of how to carry out these improvements with the autocracy, under the autocracy.[70]

Support for autocracy did not mean acceptance, or defense, of the political status quo, with which Tikhomirov was far from happy. In particular, he was extremely critical of the bureaucratic nature of the contemporary Russian state. He denounced Plehve as "to the marrow of his bones a bureaucrat [who] carried in his soul and heart that enormous evil from which Russia is perishing."[71] Bureaucracy, he complained, destroys "the free life of the nation, abolishes all the centers of social life in it, undermines moral and social authorities. In this way it demoralizes the nation, and generally mortifies everything."[72] Like other conservatives, Tikhomirov drew a distinction between autocracy and despotism. The two should not be conflated, he argued, for "in reality *any* system of government is capable of *despotism*, whether it is monarchical, aristocratic, or democratic."[73] Russia suffered from "bureaucratic usurpation," Tikhomirov argued.[74] To limit the bureaucracy, Tikhomirov, like Sharapov, proposed that the autocrat delegate some of his authority to institutions of local self-government.[75] He also argued in favor of representative institutions, although he opposed direct elections and instead wanted institutions to be organized by classes and estates, "according to the real collectivities in which [people] live."[76]

Autocracy, Tikhomirov said, was strongest when it was closest to, and restrained by, some higher ideal. The Russian ideal was provided by Orthodoxy. "Without the religious principle, autocratic power, even of the greatest genius, can only be a dictatorship, unlimited power," he wrote.[77] Tikhomirov added that the Orthodox Church could only serve as an ethical foundation for the state if it was truly independent. He therefore denounced "Caesaropapism" and argued for church reform so that the relationship of church and state could be transformed from one of subordination to one of "union."[78]

Religion did not provide the only limit on state power. According to Tikhomirov, "the person [*lichnost*'] has certain natural rights on which the state should not encroach." These included "personal freedom (for example, from illegal arrest), inviolability of the home, the right to property, freedom of labor and occupation, freedom of conscience, family rights, freedom of speech (press, teaching), freedom of assembly and union, the right to demand that one is defended by the state, and the right to oppose illegal demands by the government."[79] The state, said Tikhomirov, had an obligation "not to do anything that stifles the original, independent existence of the person."[80] In this way, autocracy and personal rights went hand in hand.

SOCIAL-ECONOMIC CONSERVATISM

Late nineteenth-century conservatives' views on social and economic issues were conditioned to a large extent by the policies of state-led industrialization pursued by the Russian government under both Alexander III and Nicholas II. To pay for industrialization, the state resorted to protectionist tariffs and, especially after Sergei Witte became finance minister in 1892, foreign loans. This was underpinned by a tight monetary policy after Witte introduced the gold standard for the Russian ruble. The result was an impressive increase in industrial output in the final two decades of the nineteenth century. The great majority of the Russian population, however, continued to live in the countryside, and agriculture failed to make as much progress as industry. Indeed, in 1891 Russia experienced a severe famine. Many conservatives opposed the state's economic policies and sought to develop alternatives. Economic policy acquired a growing importance in Russian conservative thought.

Within the state bureaucracy, there was broad support for the policy of industrialization. Even Pobedonostsev recognized the need for economic development, calling Russia "extremely undeveloped" and arguing that Russia had to be transformed into a major industrial power. His approach to industry was nationalistic, favoring government investment in railways, protection for domestic production by means of high import tariffs, and preventing foreigners from owning strategically important industries.[81]

Conservatives outside of government generally shared Pobedonostsev's nationalist approach, but were more guarded in their attitude to industrial development and often displayed a definite anti-capitalist sentiment. This reflected fears that industrialization came at the expense of the countryside and undermined Russia's independence by subordinating it to foreign capital, as well as concerns that capitalism led to the spread of liberal ideas among the elite and socialist ideas among the masses.[82] Conservative journalist Mikhail Menshikov (1859–1918), for instance, strongly rejected capitalism as a model for Russia, warning that Russia could not avoid the social tensions that accompanied capitalism in Western Europe.[83] Conservatives sought modes of development that might bring economic advances while avoiding these negative phenomena.

One of the most prominent conservative critics of government economic policy was journalist Sergei Sharapov, who argued that it promoted industrialization at the expense of the rural population. Peasants suffered from high import duties for agricultural products as well as from a lack of cheap credit. Given that 80 percent of the Russian population lived on the land, the rural population was potentially the largest market for industrial products. Government policy was suppressing demand and so undermining future growth, Sharapov said. He felt that the emphasis should be on developing agriculture in order to enrich the peasantry and so boost consumer demand. The increased demand would then drive industrial investment in a sustainable manner, using domestic resources rather than foreign capital.[84] Sharapov criticized the gold standard, complaining that it deprived agriculture of cheap credit,[85] and argued instead in favor of the introduction of paper money. Its flow into the economy would stimulate demand and also liberate Russia from having to rely on foreign loans and investment.[86] "Foreign capital," he said, "doesn't come to serve us but to lord over us."[87]

Citing the idea of *sobornost'*, Sharapov argued that the commune preserved the national spirit, which had been lost among the country's upper classes.[88] He supported maintaining the commune as the bedrock of the rural economy. Other conservatives, however, more and more favored abolishing the commune, reflecting a growing belief that it stood in the way of improvements in agriculture. Pobedonostsev, for instance, by the 1890s came to favor replacing communes with family farms. Communal landownership, he wrote, "did not provide strength and scope for enterprise and for the production of new value and new capital."[89] Pobedonostsev saw the replacement of the commune as being a slow process. So did von Plehve, who in 1903 drafted an imperial manifesto that promised to uphold existing communal institutions but also to make it somewhat easier for peasants to leave the commune and consolidate their scattered plots of land into an individual farm—a cautious compromise opening the way to gradual change.[90] A report published by the Ministry of the Interior in 1903 commented that "it is extremely important that we strive to inculcate among the peasants the notion of the right of property. . . . True conservatism consists in the proper guarding and development of this principle."[91] Many conservatives believed that a landowning peasantry would be supportive of the existing regime. Conservative economist K. F. Golovin remarked that "the presence of a numerous independent peasantry, sitting on its own land, is important not so much for guaranteeing the property of the working class as for making the peasantry serve as a bulwark of social order."[92]

Former revolutionary Lev Tikhomirov proposed another model of economic development. He argued that Russia could not skip the capitalist stage of economic development and disagreed with those who felt that Russia should focus on cottage industries, not large-scale factories. He wrote that "it is utopian to think that one can develop small-scale industry while large-scale production lags behind."[93] Tikhomirov adopted a nationalistic line, remarking that "economic independence is one of the most important and necessary elements of general independence, and so naturally, autarky should be considered a permanent objective of the country's economic policy."[94] He opposed foreign loans, which, he believed, directed economic activity toward serving the needs of the world market rather than the internal Russian market, the development of which should be the primary objective.[95] Like Sharapov, he wanted to limit inputs of foreign capital. This put him in opposition to the economic policies pursued by the government under Finance Minister Witte.[96]

Tikhomirov rejected communist economics, saying that communism would deprive people of incentives to work hard. "All we can expect from communism is an extremely despotic order coupled with weak production," he predicted.[97] But he also wrote that "contemporary industrial life, built on the principle of excessive freedom, leads to social revolution. Without doubt, what is needed is some general, national, to be precise, simply *state* reason, ordering production. The consequences of industrial anarchy are no better than communism."[98] Thus, while he rejected full-blown socialism, he advocated a type of dirigiste economic system in which the state took a leading role in allocating resources. He added that state intervention was necessary not only for economic development, but also in order to avoid the social problems that came with industrialization. In particular, Tikhomirov proposed that the state should guarantee social welfare for workers in the form of insurance, pensions, and support for families.[99]

This last point had some support within the state, most notably from von Plehve. In 1886, von Plehve played an important role in drafting legislation expanding the system of factory inspections and protecting workers' rights, for instance by requiring that wages be paid in cash without deductions for medical expenses and the use of tools, and also decreeing that compensation should be paid to workers and their families in the event of injury or death. Plehve also supported proposals for the election of workers' representatives who would convey workers' desires to employers. In 1902, despite some misgivings, he approved a scheme by the head of the Moscow secret police, Sergei Zubatov, to set up workers' self-help societies led by loyal personnel, in effect state-sponsored trade unions. Plehve, however, balanced these moves with others of a repressive nature, including increased penalties for illegal strike activity.[100] Overall, his measures failed to achieve their intended goal of persuading industrial workers that the state was their protector. The conservative ideal of industrial progress without significant social tension proved unachievable.

CONCLUSION

Although they are often seen as a period of political reaction and counter-reform, the last twenty years of the nineteenth century were a period of dramatic change in Russian society. This forced Russian conservatives to work out ideas for coping with the stresses of modernization, exploring ways not to reject it but to manage it so as to avoid serious dislocation of a political or social nature. Statist conservatives, such as Pobedonostsev and Plehve, proposed a combination of extremely gradual reform and measures to strengthen bureaucratic control over Russian society. Church conservatives sought a solution founded in a new national identity—Orthodox patriotism. And intellectual conservatives like Sharapov and Tikhomirov explored alternatives to state economic policy as well as ways of remodeling the political system. These intellectual conservatives railed against the bureaucratic system and came up with often quite imaginative, even radical proposals for political and economic reform, as well as serious critiques of the weaknesses of democratic and socialist systems. Tikhomirov's predictions about the reality of communism proved prescient, while Sharapov's model of demand-led economic development represented a legitimate alternative to that pursued by the Russian government. Russian conservatives remained true to the principles of Orthodoxy, Autocracy, and Nationality, but continued to redefine what these meant.

CHAPTER 7

BETWEEN REVOLUTIONS

I n 1898, Russia acquired a lease from China for a naval base in Port Arthur in Manchuria, thereby for the first time giving the Russian Empire a Pacific port that was ice-free all year round. To secure this strategic asset, the Russians built a railway through Manchuria, and stationed troops along the railway to protect it. This move into northern China brought Russia into conflict with Japan, which also had imperial ambitions in the area, and in February 1904 Japan declared war on Russia. The Russian army and navy suffered defeat after defeat until eventually Russia made a humiliating peace with Japan in September 1905, which obliged the Russians to abandon Manchuria and to surrender the southern half of Sakhalin Island to Japan. As the prestige of the Russian crown diminished, economic and political disorder began to spread through the Russian Empire. The 1905 Revolution, as it is generally known (even though the revolutionary turmoil continued into 1906 and 1907), for a while threatened to topple the tsarist regime. In the face of this danger, Tsar Nicholas II agreed to a major political compromise in October 1905, hoping to appease the revolutionary movement. In his October Manifesto, the tsar promised to summon an elected assembly whose assent would be required for any future legislation to come into effect. Russia acquired a national parliament, the Duma.

The first elections to the Duma in spring 1906 produced a majority of liberal and radical deputies. Under the leadership of the liberal Constitutional Democratic Party (the "Kadets"), the Duma attempted to exploit what it saw as the weakness of the autocracy. It pressed for more power and sought to make the government subordinate to the Duma. Nicholas II was unwilling to concede. He appointed a new prime minister, Pyotr Stolypin (1862–1911), who recommended that the Duma be dissolved. This happened in July 1906, after the new parliament had been in session for a mere ten weeks. Angered at the dissolution, Kadet party members decamped to the town of Vyborg near St. Petersburg, where they issued a manifesto calling on the Russian people to resist the government by refusing to pay taxes or serve in the army. This appeal failed to galvanize public opposition to the tsar and his government, but did help to confirm Nicholas II's and Stolypin's suspicions that compromise with the Kadets was impossible.

Following further elections, the Second Duma convened in February 1907. This proved no more successful than the first, prompting Prime Minister Stolypin to call on the tsar to dissolve it shortly afterward in June 1907. Stolypin then amended the electoral law to favor the wealthier segments of Russia's population. This ensured that when the Third Duma was elected in autumn 1907 it had a more conservative complexion. Thanks to this, and to the use of a combination of repression and economic and social reform, Stolypin was gradually able to restore order to Russia. His reform policies were not popular among many Russian conservatives, who did their best to frustrate them. In September 1911, Stolypin was murdered by a revolutionary terrorist during an opera performance in Kiev, and was replaced by Finance Minister Vladimir Kokovtsov (1853–1943).

At the start of the twentieth century, Russian conservatives for the first time began to organize themselves into formal political associations and parties. The earliest such association was the Russian Assembly, established in 1901 and consisting mainly of aristocratic and bureaucratic intellectuals. Originally devoted to cultural matters, from 1905 it turned increasingly political. Members of Russia's elite were also active in two organizations founded in 1905, the Union of Russian Men, led by Aleksandr Shcherbatov (1850–1915), and the Russian Monarchist Party (RMP), led by Vladimir Gringmut (1851–1907).[1] The elite nature of these organizations limited their support. Far more popular was the Union of the Russian People (URP), founded by a St. Petersburg doctor, Aleksandr Dubrovin (1855–1921?), in November 1905. The URP is often classified as "far right," rather than conservative. It was the first mass right-wing organization in Russian history, and at its peak had nearly 400,000 members,[2] mostly drawn from Russia's peasantry. But it was unable to translate its mass membership into electoral success, performing poorly in elections to the First and Second Dumas, although winning some seats in the Third Duma. Internal squabbling tore the URP apart, with one group, led by Vladimir Purishkevich (1870–1920), splitting off to form the Union of the Archangel Michael (UAM). After Dubrovin was ousted as leader of the URP in 1910 by Nikolai Markov (1866–1945), Dubrovin formed his own splinter group, the Dubrovinite URP.[3] Thanks in part to these splits, by the time the First World War began in 1914, the far right was largely a spent force.

The far right, despite its professed support for the monarchy, often stood in direct opposition to government policies. Although the government on occasion aided the far right, it also tended to view it with considerable suspicion, and relations between the two were far from always being friendly. More positive were the government's relations with the moderate nationalists in the Duma who joined together in 1908 to create the Nationalist faction, formally known as the All-Russian National Union. This was distinguished from the far-right parties by its acceptance of the parliamentary system established by the October Manifesto and by its support for Stolypin's policies.[4] The Nationalists did not, however, enjoy a majority in the Duma (no single party did). The government struggled to get its legislative agenda accepted in the face of resistance not only from the left but also from the right.

Cultural Conservatism

The 1905 revolution triggered a conservative reaction among some Russian intellectuals. A notable example was the economist and philosopher Pyotr Struve (1877–1944). Originally a Marxist, in 1898 Struve wrote the manifesto of the Russian Social Democratic Labor Party, the precursor of the Communist Party. In 1905 he joined the liberal democratic Kadets, and during the 1905 Revolution he at first supported efforts to strip the tsar of his autocratic powers and to create a constitutional monarchy. However, he opposed the Kadets' Vyborg Manifesto of 1906, and following the dissolution of the Second Duma he became thoroughly disenchanted with the revolutionary movement and the liberal opposition. The liberal intelligentsia had made a great mistake, he believed, in refusing to cooperate with the tsarist state after the creation of the Duma and in attempting to push the revolution even further in alliance with socialist radicals.[5] Struve denounced the Russian intelligentsia for its political "nihilism" and "incapacity for compromise," and for having "no sense of statehood."[6] Russia's problem, he now decided, was fundamentally a cultural one. Its people lacked the culture required to operate a liberal democratic order. "No political progress is possible without cultural progress," he asserted. "To reduce everything to a critique of the government would mean infinitely to exaggerate the importance of a given government and of authority in general. The source of the failures, disappointments, and defeats which have afflicted Russia lies much deeper."[7]

In 1909, Struve teamed up with various other notable Russian intellectuals to produce a collection of essays entitled *Vekhi* (Landmarks). Although none of the *Vekhi* authors could previously have been described as conservative, their collective work was a distinctively conservative product, and indeed can be seen as one of the seminal texts in Russian conservative philosophy.

In a preface to the book, literary scholar Mikhail Gershenzon laid out its central thesis as follows:

The people who have come together here for this common task . . . share a common
platform—recognition of the theoretical and practical primacy of spiritual life over
the external forms of community, in the sense that the inner life of the person is
the only creative force of human existence . . . the contributors consider the Russian
intelligentsia's ideology, which rests entirely on the opposite principle—on recognition of the unconditional primacy of social forms—to be intrinsically mistaken.[8]

Philosopher Nikolai Berdiaev (1874–1948) provided the first essay in *Vekhi*.
In it he complained of the "exclusive and despotic dominance of the utilitarian
criterion."[9] The Russian intelligentsia's atheism and its hatred of the ruling regime
had led it to stop caring about the truth; instead, it was willing to accept any philosophy that would justify revolution, regardless of its validity. Berdiaev wrote:

The intelligentsia's basic moral outlook can be summarized by the formula: "May the
truth perish if its death will give the people a better life . . . down with the truth if it
stands in the way of the cherished call 'Down with autocracy.'"[10]

Berdiaev demanded a new way of thinking. He concluded:

The intelligentsia . . . chose to idolize man and by so doing perverted its own soul
and destroyed its instinct for truth. . . . We will free ourselves from this external
oppression only when we free ourselves from internal slavery; that is, when we take
responsibility upon ourselves and stop blaming everything on external forces.[11]

Former Marxist-turned-Orthodox theologian Sergei Bulgakov (1871–1944)
continued along the same lines in *Vekhi*'s second chapter. According to Bulgakov,
"After the political crisis [of 1905] there ensued a spiritual crisis, demanding
deep, concentrated meditation."[12] The 1905 Revolution had been the fault of the
intelligentsia, which had provided the ideology that directed the masses, claimed
Bulgakov. It followed that Russia could not recover from its present crisis without first changing the intelligentsia's culture.[13] Bulgakov identified several failings
of this culture: its atheism; its superficial aping of Western ideas; its dogmatic,
abstract rationalism, which tended to drive it toward maximalist positions and
which led to a rejection of the complexity of reality in favor of theoretical principles; and its consequent aversion to history and tradition. The intelligentsia, complained Bulgakov, "has been torn away from the organic way of life."[14]

Other *Vekhi* contributors advanced similar theses. Mikhail Gershenzon
argued that the average Russian intellectual learned from youth to focus on
things "outside himself,"[15] that is to say on improving society. In the process,
intellectuals neglected their own personal spiritual development, forgot God,

and ended up with "crippled souls."[16] The intelligentsia believed that "with our reason we can comprehend the laws of life on earth." This was a "monstrous error."[17] "We will have no freedom until we become spiritually healthy," Gershenzon concluded.[18]

In another chapter, lawyer Bogdan Kistiakovsky (1863–1920) complained that the intelligentsia had a poorly developed legal consciousness, and a consequent lack of respect for the law. In pursuit of revolutionary goals, it was willing entirely to ignore legal principles. In order to be restored to health, the intelligentsia needed to "thoroughly examine itself" and reconsider its attitude to law, Kistiakovsky said.[19]

Next, Pyotr Struve attacked the intelligentsia for its "alienation from the state and hostility to it," as well as for its "irreligiosity."[20] According to Struve,

> The irreligious rejection of the state that is characteristic of the Russian intelligentsia's worldview has brought about its moral frivolity and political incompetence. . . . the intelligentsia must reconsider its entire worldview. . . . In particular, the intelligentsia needs to change the way it views "politics." Politics must cease to be isolated and independent from the rest of spiritual life, as it has been to date. For at the foundation of politics lies the idea not of the external organization of social life but of man's inner perfection.[21]

Finally, philosopher Semyon Frank (1877–1950) denounced the intelligentsia's "nihilistic utilitarianism" and "mechanical-rationalistic theory of happiness," which, he said, had led to the "religion of socialism."[22] In pursuit of utopia in the far-distant future, the intelligentsia devoted itself to destruction in the present. Thus, concluded Frank,

> The most tragic and, from an external point of view, unexpected fact about recent cultural history is that the subjectively pure, disinterested, and selfless servants of the social faith have turned out to be in the same party and the same spiritual family as robbers, mercenary murderers, hooligans, and unbridled lovers of sexual depravity.[23]

The *Vekhi* authors demanded that the intelligentsia reject atheism and accept faith and tradition alongside reason. Berdiaev stated that "tradition must be opposed to our rapidly changing passion for fashionable European teachings," and he wrote of the need for a "synthesis of knowledge and faith . . . an organic union of theory and practice."[24] And according to Bulgakov:

> Our intelligentsia has fed, and is still feeding itself, with many savory dishes from the table of Western civilization, in the end upsetting its already spoiled stomach. Isn't

it time to remember the simple, crude, but undoubtedly healthy and nutritious food of Moses's ancient Ten Commandments, and then go on to the New Testament?[25]

The far right adopted a very different form of cultural conservatism. In some cases, this took the form of ethnic nationalism, which often went hand in hand with blaming national minorities for Russia's problems. Anti-Semitism was prevalent. Vladimir Gringmut of the Russian Monarchist Party remarked that "Jews . . . as greedy parasites, desire not only one part of Russia but the whole of the vast territory of the Russian Empire, in order to suck the blood out of its entire population."[26] Likewise the URP's second leader, Nikolai Markov, said in a speech in the Duma in 1911 that "from the creation of the world, Jews were always antihuman."[27]

Many Russian conservatives supported Russification measures and discriminatory policies against minorities (especially Jews). These had some support at high levels in the Russian state, most notably from Prime Minister Stolypin. In 1908, Stolypin appointed a new education minister, A. N. Schwartz, who almost immediately introduced stricter quotas for Jews in Russian universities.[28] Stolypin sought to incorporate the Polish province of Kholm into Russia and also undertook measures to restrict the autonomy of the Grand Duchy of Finland, which until then had been a largely self-governing region within the Russian Empire.[29]

But while it is true that ethno-nationalism, racist attitudes, and support for Russification became more common in this era, outside of the far right, Russian conservatives generally still adhered to a non-racial definition of Russian nationality, and identified Russia with Orthodoxy and autocracy.[30] The conservative newspaper *Grazhdanin* (Citizen), for instance, promoted an imperial, state-oriented version of nationalism.[31] *Grazhdanin*'s editor, Vladimir Meshchersky (1839–1914), denounced Stolypin's policy on Finland as "Finlandophobia."[32] Similarly, journalist Sergei Sharapov wrote that "any success of Russification [in Finland] is dangerous. . . . One shouldn't be making efforts for union [with the Finns], but for *Russia's isolation*."[33] "Our motto is not 'Russia for the Russians,' but 'Holy Rus,'" Sharapov said.[34]

The far right received some support from Orthodox clergymen, most notably John of Kronstadt, who accepted honorary membership in the URP. Metropolitan Antony (Khrapovitsky) of Volhynia (1863–1936) provided the far right with support within his diocese through the auspices of the Pochaevsky Monastery, which published a conservative newssheet, *Pochaevskie izvestiia* (Pochaev news).[35] This featured critical remarks about Poles and Jews, both of whom formed a significant portion of the population in Volhynia. But on the whole, the Orthodox Church remained wedded to a religious rather than an ethnic interpretation of Russian national identity, and groups such as Poles and Jews were targeted more for their religion than for their ethnicity. As Metropolitan Antony said,

Russia is identified properly as an organism, as a people, as a powerful idea flowing through history. But what is our people, its history, and in our present circumstances? Is it an ethnic community? Is it first of all a community dedicated to state
defense? No. Russians define themselves before all as a religious community . . .
which includes even Georgians and Greeks who are unable even to speak the Russian language.[36]

Speaking to a meeting of the Union of the Archangel Michael in 1909, Antony
lamented that the lack of a fully developed sense of nationhood had allowed
Russia "to come under the influence of liberal and cosmopolitan ideas." Antony
argued that Russia should not copy Western nationalism, as it was both pagan and
political. "Russian self-consciousness," he said, "is not a self-consciousness that is
racial or tribal, but religious and ecclesiastical."[37] Historian John Strickland argues
that the church's participation in far-right groups was aimed not so much at supporting them as at redirecting them from ethnic to religious nationalism, in order
to promote what Antony termed "universal ecclesial patriotism."[38]

Clergymen across the political spectrum supported reform of church institutions, including the reestablishment of the Patriarchate, the summoning of a
church council, and the guaranteeing of places for the clergy in any future Zemsky
sobor.[39] To promote such reforms, a pre-council committee convened in 1906 and
proposed the restoration of the Patriarchate. Among those attending was the rev-
olutionary-turned-conservative intellectual Lev Tikhomirov, who proposed turning parishes into independent legal institutions in an effort to revive the parish as
the basis of the church.[40] Prime Minister Stolypin opposed the proposals, and the
tsar rejected them.[41]

The state remained unwilling to cede its control over church affairs. It did,
however, cave in to pressure from church conservatives on some matters. As part
of the liberalizing reforms that followed the October Manifesto, the tsar had
issued a decree affirming toleration of non-Orthodox confessions and religions.
When Stolypin attempted to put the tsar's decree into practice by means of a bill
in the Duma that, among other things, would have extended the right to prosely-
tize and would have permitted marriages between Orthodox and non-Orthodox
believers, he met with stiff opposition from the Orthodox Church and its supporters on the political right. One notable conservative priest, Ioann Vostorgov
(1864–1918), wrote: "the Duma project will produce not freedom of faith and
conscience but the destruction of Orthodoxy in Russia."[42] In the face of this
opposition, Stolypin backed down and withdrew his bill.[43] In the decade prior to
the First World War, the Orthodox Church was becoming increasingly independent and assertive.

POLITICAL CONSERVATISM

As prime minister from 1906 to 1911, Pyotr Stolypin sought to pursue a form of liberal conservatism, combining a strong state with reform. Rightists opposed his policies and found themselves increasingly alienated from the state that they professed to support.

Vekhi represented the liberal conservative end of the conservative spectrum. Its authors retained their core belief in individual freedom, but no longer believed that this could be achieved by revolutionary methods, which were likely only to bring further chaos.[44] Evolutionary methods were preferred. As one *Vekhi* author, Semyon Frank, noted of a second, Pyotr Struve,

> P. B. [Struve]'s conservatism consisted of the conviction that tradition, historical succession, organic growth of the new from the old is a necessary condition of genuine freedom and that, on the contrary, any arbitrary "revolutionism" and forceful or radical breaking of the social order, every unbridling of the revolutionary passions leads only to despotism and slavery.[45]

Struve came to represent what Richard Pipes calls a "conservative liberalism that stressed strong authority, social reform, legality, and a vigorous foreign policy."[46] In many respects this echoed the line taken by Boris Chicherin several decades earlier.[47] Apart from the "vigorous foreign policy," it also fitted fairly well with the line pursued by Stolypin. The Russian prime minister laid out his philosophy in a speech to the Duma in May 1907 about agrarian reform. In it he said:

> It is impossible to solve this question all at once; it must be solved over a period of time. This has required decades in Western countries. We propose to you a moderate path, but a true one. Those who oppose our state system prefer the path of radicalism, a path of emancipation from Russia's historic path and from its cultural traditions. They want great upheavals—we want a great Russia![48]

A devout supporter of Russia's traditional system of government—monarchy—Stolypin sought to strengthen the tsarist state, but at the same time to reform it gradually. As his biographer, Abraham Ascher, notes:

> At an early stage of his life ... he [Stolypin] had concluded that if Russia was to be a strong and prosperous country it would have to be thoroughly modernized.... Stolypin can best be described as an authoritarian reformer, or as a pragmatic conservative.... He recognized that unless the masses were transformed into full citizens ... the fire of revolution would not be put out.[49]

Stolypin described himself as a "constitutionalist," not a "parliamentarist."[50] He tried to make the constitutional system established after October 1905 work, and therefore sought to work with the Duma wherever possible. At the same time, he continued to believe that ultimate authority should lie with the tsar. In a speech in November 1907, he declared:

> There are words which have caused the hearts of Russians to beat for centuries past, and such words and sentiments must be kneaded into the mind, and must be reflected in the acts of the government. These words are: undeviating loyalty to Russian historical traditions. These words form a counterpoise to socialism, and magnify the country in opposition to those who desire its disruption, and finally they express loyalty to the death to the Tsar, who personifies Russia.[51]

In 1906 Stolypin issued a decree establishing field courts martial, which circumvented normal legal procedure. In the following eight months over one thousand people were executed.[52] Stolypin was clear, however, that repression on its own would not be sufficient to save Russia. He wrote:

> Reform at a time of revolution is necessary since revolution is caused by defects of the internal structure. If we concern ourselves exclusively with the struggle against the revolution, then at best we will eliminate the consequences but not the causes. . . . The State Duma has been created, and it is impossible to turn back. That would be a fatal mistake—where governments vanquished revolutions, they succeeded not by resorting exclusively to physical force but by relying on strength, taking the lead in instituting reform.[53]

Accordingly, in August 1906 Stolypin introduced a plan of sweeping reform, including "freedom of religion; inviolability of the person; civil equality; improvements in peasant land ownership and in the condition of workers, including a system of state insurance," expansion of the *zemstvo* system into the Baltic region and Poland, and reform of local courts and of the educational system.[54]

One of the conservatives who supported Stolypin's policies was Lev Tikhomirov, who wrote in 1909 that "if our reaction . . . begins to turn into a restoration of what was being destroyed of its own accord before the revolution . . . it will just be a pause between two revolutions."[55] Most conservatives, however, opposed Stolypin's reform program. His efforts to reform local administration were stymied by resistance from the nobility; his attempt to introduce universal primary education ran into the objections of the Orthodox Church, which complained that it made no provision for church schools; his bill to introduce an insurance scheme for workers was opposed by industrialists and passed through the Duma only in June 1912, after he had been assassinated;[56] and, as previously noted, his effort to expand religious freedom floundered in the face of resistance from the Orthodox Church. Stolypin's form of liberal conservatism proved to be far too liberal for most conservatives of the era.

One of the most persistent opponents of Stolypin's reform program was Pyotr Durnovo (1845–1915), who served as minister of the interior from 1905 to 1906 and who thereafter was a member of the State Council. Durnovo described his political views in the following terms:

> Everyone considers me an inveterate monarchist, reactionary, defender of autocracy, incorrigible obscurantist . . . and doesn't realize that in my views I am the most convinced of republicans. In fact I consider best for a people the situation where the people can have at the head of the administration as president the most worthy citizen chosen by themselves. For some countries, such an ideal, through one fortunate circumstance or another, is becoming a possibility. But this it is by no means possible to say about our immense and very varied Russian Empire, where because of purely practical considerations the machinery of administration and the Empire's unity demand the existence of the Imperial banner woven by history. If it goes, Russia will disintegrate. That is the immutable law of nature in Russia's political history.[57]

Durnovo had an extremely negative view of the Russian people's ability to govern itself. He felt that strong power was necessary to keep the people in check. Radical reform would weaken the state, would do nothing to assuage the revolutionary mood, and would merely make things worse. What Russia needed, in Durnovo's eyes, was enlightened autocracy, which would guide the country slowly forward.[58] According to Durnovo:

> The content and sense of national policy consists of persistent and careful movement along the straightest possible line toward a definite, carefully thought-out and previously planned goal. . . . One can deviate from this path only because of the demands of caution, but there are limits and boundaries to the demands of caution, consisting of the fact that one must remember that the further one deviates from the straight path, the worse it is, and the quicker one returns to the straight path, the better.[59]

Conservatives of all stripes remained committed to autocracy. Ioann Vostorgov, for instance, declared that Christ had never urged resistance to secular authority. "Do not offend Christ the Lord by betraying his teachings," Vostorgov preached. "Do not make your situation worse by agitating and striking. Do not obstruct the Tsar and government from caring for you and acting on your behalf."[60] But support for the principle of autocracy took many forms: some accepted the new constitutional order established by the October Manifesto; others rejected it and wanted a return to the status quo ante; while others still favored a different type of order, including in some cases the summoning of a Zemsky sobor, in which all the people of Russia would be represented but according to a system of estates rather than direct election.

Among those who accepted the new order was the Nationalist faction in the Duma, which supported Stolypin and his program.[61] A Nationalist document produced during the Third Duma declared that "only the legislative power of representative institutions can defend Russia from bureaucratic government."[62] In other cases, support for representative institutions was more reluctant, but nonetheless present. For instance, the editor of the conservative newspaper *Grazhdanin*, Vladimir Meshchersky, wrote that Russia had its own distinct path of development, which "requires strict limitation on representatives and on government."[63] The reference to "limitation" did contain a grudging acceptance that some form of representation was there to stay. Meshchersky therefore argued merely for reform of the Duma, not its abolition.[64]

The URP's position was somewhat unclear. On the one hand, it initially supported the creation of the Duma and participated actively in Duma elections;[65] on the other hand, it insisted on the unchanged nature of the autocracy, arguing that the new order was not a constitutional system, as the tsar retained the power to abolish the new Fundamental Laws should he choose to do so. Following the split in the URP, the Dubrovinite faction came out firmly against the Duma and argued in favor of its abolition.[66]

The Russian Monarchist Party (RMP) also opposed the new constitutional order.[67] The RMP's leader, Vladimir Gringmut, wrote:

> No person and no institution can stand higher than the Tsar or level with him. All Supreme Power is concentrated in his hands. . . . In Russia there can be no representatives of the people other than the Sovereign Emperor, for nobody other than Him can combine in himself the aggregate of *all* the state, estate, and class interests of the Russian people.[68]

Gringmut shared the general suspicion of the bureaucracy. The only way to make it accountable, he argued, was through a strong power operating above it, in other words through the tsar. Like Sergei Sharapov and Lev Tikhomirov before him, Gringmut proposed strengthening the tsar's power by delegating authority for local administration, thereby freeing the monarch from having to deal with minor, purely local issues. Gringmut also advocated the creation of consultative assemblies operating at all levels of government, from local administration right up to state ministries and the State Council.[69]

The idea of such assemblies was popular among conservatives who sought an alternative to directly elected representative institutions. A favored option was a Zemsky sobor. Neo-Slavophile courtier Aleksandr Kireev was among those who supported such a body. He denounced what he called "our decrepit Polizei Staat [police state],"[70] but also opposed constitutional government. According to Kireev, "Only people who doubt the creative forces of the Russian people advise the adoption of the constitutional structure that was worked out abroad. Our Zemsky sobor is a resurrection of the old structure, worked out by *our* history."[71] He added: "We were always in favor of the reestablishment of the order that governed Russia in the seventeenth century, when there wasn't any bureaucratic barrier between the Tsar and the people, but a living link in the form of the members of the Zemsky sobor. This . . . is our contemporary ideal."[72] Kireev opposed the October Manifesto and the new order that emerged from it. "Why have we failed?" he asked in April 1906. The answer was that

> many of us conservatives . . . have been careless and associated conservatism, devotion to the autocratic monarch, and defense of his rights, with a defense of the rights of a very dubious government and bureaucracy. . . . Conservatives have failed adequately to distinguish the concepts of *Russian* and contemporary *bureaucratic* autocracy.[73]

Overall, their anti-bureaucratic views and their rejection of the new political order put conservatives in an awkward position: on the one hand, they professed their allegiance to the monarchy; on the other hand, they rejected the system into which the monarchy had evolved. Moreover, the radical methods used by the far right, including vigilante violence, inevitably ran afoul of a system devoted to maintaining order. Whatever the far right's theoretical position, in practice it found itself in continual opposition to the government, and thus to monarchy as it actually was. More and more it began to see the government as the enemy.[74] Many conservatives blamed the monarch himself for this. Nicholas II disappointed them; they felt that he was weak and unwilling to fight for his own autocratic privileges.[75] The disappointment was such that when revolution broke out in 1917, the tsar found that he had few supporters left even among conservatives.

The 1917 revolution was in large part a product of the First World War, a war that some conservatives had warned the government against becoming involved in. Generally, conservatives of this era favored a policy of peace, avoiding foreign entanglements in order to allow Russia to recover from the 1905 Revolution. As Stolypin said in 1911, "We need peace; war in the course of the next few years would be fatal for Russia and the dynasty. On the other hand, every year of peace strengthens Russia."[76] This was a widely held view. The experience of the Russo-Japanese War had made many fearful that any future war would lead to another revolution. Thus a monarchist appeal during elections to the Fourth Duma declared, "Don't elect the left, which wants to drag us into an even more terrible war. They see the possibility of creating a second bloody disturbance . . . and make a new attempt to seize power."[77]

In the Reinsurance Treaty of 1887, Russia and Germany had agreed to remain neutral if the other became involved in a war with another European power, but in 1890 Kaiser Wilhelm II of Germany refused to renew the treaty. This left Russia diplomatically isolated. Forced to look elsewhere, Russia agreed to a formal military alliance with France. This was to last until the First World War. Conservatives for the most part agreed with Stolypin about the need for peace, and considered the alliance with France a mistake, fearing that it could drag Russia into a war with Germany. Ideological considerations contributed to this attitude: Germany was viewed as a bastion of conservatism and monarchy, and so a more natural friend than Republican France.[78]

The most famous exponent of this point of view was Pyotr Durnovo, who in February 1914 wrote a memorandum to Tsar Nicholas II warning him of the dire consequences that would follow any war with Germany. Taking the opportunity of the dismissal of Vladimir Kokovtsov, Stolypin's successor as prime minister, Durnovo argued in favor of a fundamental rethinking of Russian foreign policy, a rethinking that in Durnovo's eyes would also have important implications for domestic policy.[79] He argued that

> a struggle between Germany and Russia, regardless of issue, is profoundly undesirable to both sides, as undoubtedly involving the weakening of the conservative principle in the world of which the above-named two great powers are the only reliable bulwarks. . . . There must inevitably break out in the defeated country a social revolution which, by the very nature of things, will spread to the country of the victor.[80]

The result of war between Russia and Germany, predicted Durnovo, would be that "Russia will be flung into hopeless anarchy, the outcome of which will be hard to foresee."[81] This did not mean that Durnovo was anti-war per se, let alone anti-military. On the contrary, he considered strengthening the armed forces to be a top priority.[82] As Nikolai Markov put it, conservatives' policy was to avoid a quarrel with Germany, but at the same time, just in case, "to arm ourselves to the teeth."[83]

SOCIAL-ECONOMIC CONSERVATISM

Probably the most important social and economic legislation in this period was a decree issued by Stolypin in 1906 enacting agrarian reform. This made it possible for peasants to leave the commune and set themselves up as individual farmers whose land was their own private property. Although this promised to radically transform the Russian countryside, Stolypin viewed it as a largely conservative measure. As he told the tsar, "Private peasant ownership is a guarantee of order, because each small owner represents the nucleus on which rests the stability of the state."[84]

Russian conservatives were divided in their views of Stolypin's agrarian reforms. The Nationalist faction, URP leader Markov, UAM leader Purishkevich, and also Lev Tikhomirov supported the reforms.[85] Others, such as Sergei Sharapov, opposed them. Sharapov argued that the result would be speculation in land, which in turn would lead to peasants becoming landless and flooding into the cities, threatening social stability.[86] Sharapov said that the reforms would lead to a social revolution in the countryside, "which strives to overthrow everything: the understanding of property; family life; the life of the commune; everything that the Russian people has lived for a thousand years and that the state has never previously touched."[87] Kireev also opposed Stolypin's policies. "I'm against a gradual and voluntary transfer of communal land into private hands . . . I fear that these plots of land will pass into the hands of kulaks and Yids," he said.[88]

Anti-Semitic opinions contributed to anti-capitalist sentiment on the political right, with Jews being portrayed as having undue financial power.[89] Right-wing parties such as the URP propagated an anti-capitalist message, and the URP's manifesto for elections to the Second Duma included a demand for key industries to be nationalized.[90] In general, conservatives opposed the government's economic policy, largely for the same reasons as in the decade before the 1905 revolution. In particular, conservatives continued to dislike the role played by foreign capital in Russia's industrial development,[91] and there was a widespread feeling that government policy favored industry at the expense of the countryside. Vladimir Gurko (1862–1927), a leading agricultural expert within the state bureaucracy and also a member of the Russian Assembly, put it this way: "Our successes in the realm of factory industry were achieved not through the natural growth of the country's productivity and consequently the prosperity of its population, but at the expense of the fundamental wealth of the rural masses."[92]

As in the previous decade, conservatives felt that economic development was best served by boosting demand among the mass of the population that lived in the countryside. This meant that priority should be given to agricultural interests. As Tikhomirov wrote: "the placing of peasant farming on a sound footing represents the basic way to help the peasants build up their savings and to assure the purchasing capacity of the countryside, which will then provide the factories with a market incomparably broader and more durable than those abroad."[93] Similarly, Lev Polovtsov (1867–1936), a Nationalist deputy in the Duma, declared:

Our industry has flourished and begun to manufacture a huge number of products, but we forget one thing, that we don't have an internal market in which to distribute these products, we lack consumers, because in promoting factory industry we simultaneously attacked agriculture, attacked the large number of consumers who were the main consumers of our industry's products.[94]

To boost consumer demand, conservatives proposed measures to support the agricultural economy, such as cheap state credit for farmers and cottage industries;[95] abolition of the gold standard; the printing of paper money;[96] development of infrastructure in the countryside, including the construction of public grain elevators; a reduction in the role of middlemen (often believed to be Jews) in the rural economy;[97] state purchase of land to resell to peasants at affordable prices; and state support to peasants for resettlement.[98]

Conservatives of this era, therefore, sought an alternative model of economic development to that being pursued by the state.[99] As one URP member put it, "To be a conservative in this time [means to be] a radical."[100] This was reflected in right-wing parties' policies vis-à-vis workers' rights. In their attempts to attract mass support, these parties tried hard to present themselves as defending the interests of labor against capital,[101] while simultaneously attempting to combat the influence of socialism by proposing measures that they hoped would reduce tensions between workers and employers.[102] The URP, for instance, proposed a reduction in the working day, the creation of a State Industrial Bank to provide funds to workers' cooperatives, and the introduction of state insurance for death, illness, and old age.[103]

Overall, these policies made the far-right parties strong supporters of state intervention in the economy. Aristocratic conservatives, meanwhile, tended to believe more strongly in the sanctity of private property and consequently minimal state interference. Gurko, for instance, argued that "economic freedom must be the slogan of our time.... The state should strive not to expand its economic activity, but rather to reduce it everywhere."[104] And Durnovo firmly opposed the extension of workers' rights, regarding this as a surrender to socialism.[105] The conservatism of the elites therefore differed substantially from that of those who sought to appeal to a mass audience.

Conclusion

During this period, autocracy came under increasing pressure, and many conservatives either positively or grudgingly accepted the need for representative

institutions or at least consultative ones, such as a Zemsky sobor. Anti-bureaucratic sentiment continued to grow and many conservatives pursued apparently
paradoxical goals of strengthening autocracy while simultaneously limiting it.
Meanwhile, the idea of the Russian nation remained very strongly associated with
Orthodoxy, but a strand of conservatism that rested on ethno-nationalism, xeno-
phobia, and anti-Semitism gained ground.

Divisions among conservatives limited their political effectiveness. Aleksandr
Kireev complained in his diary in April 1905: "We, in particular Russian conservatives, are absolutely unable to organize ourselves."[106] Kireev had a point. The
defeat of the 1905 Revolution left liberalism and socialism in retreat. There was
an opportunity for conservatives to take the lead and direct Russia along a new
path, but they proved unable to unite around common projects. Stolypin's liberal conservatism proved unpalatable to bureaucratic conservatives, to church
conservatives, and to conservatives in the parties of the far right, who combined
to thwart much of his reform program. But Stolypin's opponents were unable to
enact their own alternative proposals for reform, in large part because they lacked
power, and the state proved unwilling to countenance their ideas—be it the restoration of the Patriarchate and the calling of a church council, abandoning the
new constitutional order created in 1905, or changing the direction of economic
and social policy. Conservatives of nearly all stripes realized that change of some
sort was necessary, but they could not agree on what this change should be. The
result was political paralysis. Had the tsarist system had more time to find a way
to resolve its pressing internal problems, it might have survived. Unfortunately,
time was not on its side.

CHAPTER 8

EMIGRATION

I n March 1917, revolution erupted in Russia, overthrowing Tsar Nicholas II and replacing him with a Provisional Government that professed its commitment to democratic ideals. The country descended rapidly into chaos over the next eight months, until in November 1917 the Provisional Government fell to a coup that put the Bolshevik (later known as Communist) Party into power. Before long, civil war resulted, with a large number of factions raising armies to fight the Bolsheviks and each another. The most powerful of these were the White armies (so-called to distinguish them from the Bolshevik "Reds"), led by Admiral Aleksandr Kolchak in Siberia, General Nikolai Iudenich in the Baltic region, and first General Anton Denikin, then later General Pyotr Wrangel in southern Russia. Bit by bit, the Bolsheviks overcame the Whites and their other opponents. In November 1920, Wrangel's White army abandoned Crimea and was evacuated by boat to Turkey. With this, the Russian Civil War largely came to an end.

The revolutions and civil war produced a flood of refugees, with hundreds of thousands of Russians who opposed communism fleeing abroad. The largest single group of émigrés was Wrangel's army, which dispersed throughout Europe but maintained an informal structure in the form of a veterans' organization known as the Russian General Military Union (Russky Obshche-Voinsky Soiuz—ROVS). At first, Wrangel hoped that his army could provide the focus for uniting émigrés around a single political center, but the emigration was too deeply divided to rally behind it. By 1923, hopes for unity were transferred to the person of a cousin of Tsar Alexander III, Grand Duke Nikolai Nikolaevich (1856–1929). In 1926, an Émigré Congress was held in Paris in the hope of uniting the overwhelming majority of émigré organizations under the grand duke's leadership. This too failed when the congress produced two competing unity organizations. Subsequently, the emigration split into an ever-increasing number of small groups.[1]

Historians have contrasted the political weakness of the Russian emigration with its vibrant artistic and intellectual life. In 1922, the Bolsheviks expelled 220 of Russia's leading intellectuals on the so-called "philosophers' steamer." They and other émigrés made important contributions to a large range of subjects, including philosophy and history, while émigré communities produced hundreds of journals and newspapers. In the post-Soviet era, as Russian politicians and intellectuals have sought non-communist sources of inspiration, many have turned to émigré writings. Important political figures such as President Vladimir Putin and Foreign Minister Sergei Lavrov have cited émigré thinkers in their speeches. Although it was cut off from the vitally important developments taking place in the Soviet Union, the emigration is an integral part of Russian history.

CULTURAL CONSERVATISM

The Russian emigration included people with a wide variety of political opinions, ranging from Mensheviks and Socialist Revolutionaries on the far left through to monarchists and fascists on the far right. The divisions were particularly marked among émigré intellectuals. Intellectuals were, however, only a small portion of the overall emigration, and in any case the majority of émigrés were too busy with the daily struggle for existence to be deeply involved in politics. For the most part, they resisted assimilation into their host communities, waiting vainly for the day when communism would collapse and they could return home. This tendency gave the emigration a culturally conservative bent, in the sense that émigrés sought to retain their Russian identities and to preserve Russian culture abroad. In the eyes of many émigrés, communism was more than just a political and economic enemy; through its internationalism and atheism it posed an existential threat to Russian culture. The longer that the communists remained in power, the more likely it was that Russian culture as previously understood would vanish. Many émigrés felt that it was their duty to maintain that culture in exile so that they could restore it to Russia when the country was finally liberated from the communist yoke.

What constituted Russian culture was a matter of debate. For some its core was Orthodoxy, but this was complicated by the fact that the Orthodox Church abroad had split into competing factions.[2] For others, particularly liberal intellectuals, it was about art and philosophy. For the large number of military personnel in the emigration it meant something different still: the preservation of Russian traditions, including that of service to the state; values such as honor and duty; the traditions of their regiments; and the memory of Russian military victories.

One issue on which there was broad agreement was that the causes of the Russian revolution were as much spiritual as material, and that the emigration had to lead the way in promoting a spiritual renewal. Nikolai Berdiaev, who was among the philosophers expelled from the Soviet Union in 1922, wrote that

> the way to improve Russia's spiritual health must be found in the inner exposure of the revolution's false holiness, and in liberation from its charm. Revolutionary holiness isn't a true holiness, it is false holiness . . . godless holiness. . . . Revolutionary morality, revolutionary holiness is deeply contrary to Christianity.[3]

In his book *Philosophy of Inequality*, Berdiaev denounced revolutions. "Every revolution has aroused the dark and evil element in man," he wrote.[4] *Philosophy of Inequality* was possibly Berdiaev's most conservative work, and as such perhaps does not accurately represent the philosopher's thinking in general. Nevertheless, it is an important work in the history of Russian conservatism.[5] Published in 1923, but written for the most part in 1918, it very much reflected the moment of its writing—the period immediately after the Russian revolutions of 1917 and the Bolshevik seizure of power. In *Philosophy of Inequality*, Berdiaev condemned the revolutionaries for, among other things, favoring the abstract and rational and ignoring the importance of the historical. Addressing the revolutionaries, Berdiaev said,

> Truly historical activity is a living concrete reality, a distinctive reality, different from other levels of being, living according to its own law, knowing its own good and evil, incommensurate with rational criteria of good and evil. You rejected this historical activity, didn't see any inner, organic life within it, and replaced it with sociological abstractions.[6]

Berdiaev applied this organic view, and this stress on the importance of history, to his understanding of what constituted a nation. According to Berdiaev:

> A nation is a mystical organism. . . . In the nation speak not only the living, but also the dead, the great past and the enigmatic future. In a nation enter not only human generations, but also the stones of churches, palaces, and estates, gravestones, old manuscripts, and books. In order to catch the will of the people one has to listen to these stones, read the rotting pages. But with your revolutionary-democratic noise you want to drown the voices of the dead, of past generations, you want to kill the feeling of the past.[7]

Berdiaev argued in favor of what he called a "true conservatism," which he said "supports the connection across time, does not permit a final severing of this connection, unites the future with the past." True conservatism, he wrote, "is the struggle of eternity against time, the opposition of incorruptibility to decay. It contains the energy not only of preservation but also of transformation."[8] Properly understood, conservatism was "a free, organic principle. It consists of a healthy reaction to violations of organic nature. . . . The conservative principle is not by itself opposed to development, it merely demands that development be organic, that the future not destroy the past, but continue to develop it."[9]

Although he rejected the revolution, Berdiaev nevertheless believed that some good could come of it, as a sort of cathartic spiritual experience. He wrote: "The spiritual consequences of the revolution will be enormous. These consequences will be positive as well as negative. We are passing to a different dimension of being."[10] "Russian sins were eliminated in the Russian revolution," he wrote elsewhere, "The path to rebirth lies through repentance, through recognition of one's sins, through a cleansing of the people's minds from diabolical spirits."[11] Berdiaev rejected the idea of continuing the struggle against Bolshevism by political or military means. Émigrés instead should focus on the inner process of spiritual renewal. Thus, he wrote to Pyotr Struve that

> Russia is gravely ill and can be saved only by means of a spiritual healing and strengthening, and not by external politics. Russia's political recovery will come only by means of spiritual sources. Bolshevism is a secondary phenomenon, of the reflexes, and only a symptom of the spiritual illness of the people.[12]

This put Berdiaev seriously at odds with the veterans of the White armies and their supporters, such as Struve, who believed that continued political and military struggle against Bolshevism was essential. The Whites denied that there was any positive side to the revolution. ROVS propagated the spirit of "irreconcilability," in other words a refusal ever to reconcile with communist rule. The attitude was well expressed in a pamphlet entitled *Why We Are Irreconcilable*, written by General Evgeny Miller, who was head of ROVS from 1930 until he was kidnapped by Soviet secret agents in 1937, taken back to Russia, and eventually executed. Miller wrote:

> I cannot reconcile myself with the existing situation in Russia because I was brought up by my parents as a believing Christian to respect human individuals. . . . Orthodox faith, the motherland, family—these are the three foundations on which the Russian people built its life, its state. And the Soviet regime has declared merciless war on them.[13]

Among the irreconcilables was Struve, who had played an active role in the White movement during the Russian Civil War, becoming foreign minister in Wrangel's White government in Crimea in 1920. For Struve, the emigration's tasks were not only political, but also cultural, above all instilling a proper sense of nationalism into the next generation of Russians. He wrote:

> We tell every young Russian: Russia doesn't care if you believe in socialism, a republic, or the commune, but it does matter to it that you honor the grandeur of its past and expect and demand greatness for its future, that the piety of Sergei of Radonezh, the audacity of Metropolitan Philip, the patriotism of Peter the Great, the heroism of [Aleksandr] Suvorov, the poetry of Pushkin, Gogol, and [Lev] Tolstoy . . . are sacred things to you. . . . Only through their spirit and power can we resurrect Russia. In this sense, Russia's past, and it alone, is the guarantee of Russia's future.[14]

Even more than in Struve, the spirit of irreconcilability found its philosopher in the shape of another of the intellectuals expelled from the Soviet Union in 1922 on the philosophers' steamship, Ivan Ilyin (1883–1954). A fervent opponent of Bolshevism, once in exile Ilyin made his way to Berlin and contacted veterans of Wrangel's army, whom he greatly admired. Ilyin in due course became the unofficial ideologue of the White movement.

In the post-Soviet era numerous Russian politicians, including President Vladimir Putin, have taken to citing Ilyin in their speeches. This has turned the émigré philosopher into an extremely controversial figure. Various authors have accused Ilyin of having been a fascist.[15] Most notably, American historian Timothy Snyder has claimed that Ilyin provided the "metaphysical and moral justification for political totalitarianism, which he expressed in practical outlines for a fascist state."[16] According to Snyder, Ilyin despised individualism and propagated a "totalitarian" vision of the state, in which "lawlessness [was] a patriotic virtue," and freedom was reinterpreted in terms of subjugation to a leader.[17]

These claims represent a very lopsided view of Ilyin's work. While it is true that Ilyin did express support for authoritarian forms of government, he was also firm in his denunciations of totalitarianism. Asked by the Nazi authorities to engage in anti-Semitic propaganda, he refused. As a result, in 1934 he was dismissed from his job teaching at the Russian Institute in Berlin. After twice being summoned by the Gestapo for questioning due to "dozens, if not hundreds, of denunciations . . . by members of the so-called Russian National Socialist Movement," in 1938 Ilyin fled Nazi Germany and lived the rest of his life in Switzerland.[18]

Contrary to Snyder's claims, Ilyin was a fervent advocate of the rule of law and of personal dignity and freedom. This has led Russian commentators to label him as a "liberal conservative,"[19] a supporter of "the liberal political model of society and the state"[20] and of "moderate conservative liberalism,"[21] and as "belonging to the school of classical liberalism."[22] "Liberal conservative" is possibly the best description but it is far from perfect. The complexities and apparent paradoxes in Ilyin's thought, in which authoritarian and liberal elements exist side by side, make him extremely difficult to classify.

In 1925 Ilyin caused something of a storm in émigré philosophical circles with the publication of a book entitled *On Resistance to Evil by Force*,[23] in which he argued that the use of force against evil was not only justifiable but on occasion mandatory.[24] For Ilyin, communism was an absolute evil that needed to be fought. But Ilyin's belief in the necessity of armed struggle did not mean that he disagreed with Berdiaev about the spiritual roots of the Russian revolution. Indeed, he made it very clear that "physical coercion never was and never will be a self-sufficient means . . . [but] is a secondary and subordinate means in the general system of spiritual influence."[25] Although he differed from Berdiaev about what needed to be done, he agreed that the Russian Revolution was primarily a spiritual problem, stemming among other things from a loss of religious faith, a lack of patriotism, and a poorly developed legal consciousness.[26] In his view, "Revolution is a *mass spiritual illness*—a weakening and collapse of *spiritual foundations*."[27] He wrote:

> The political and economic reasons leading to this catastrophe are unquestionable, but its essence is deeper than politics and economics; it is spiritual. It is a crisis of Russian religiosity; a crisis of Russian legal consciousness; a crisis of military loyalty and firmness; a crisis of Russian honor and conscience. A crisis of the Russian national character; a crisis of the Russian family. It is a great and deep crisis of all Russian culture.[28]

According to Ilyin, it was necessary both to get rid of the Bolsheviks and to address Bolshevism's roots.[29] The first problem required political and military struggle; the second required an effort "to instill in the people a new Russian spiritual character."[30] In a 1926 pamphlet targeted at ROVS members, Ilyin argued that their primary task was spiritual—to preserve the values of the White movement, namely honor, service, and loyalty. "First of all," he wrote, "we must preserve the spirit of honor, for *Russia perished from a lack of honor*. . . . Second, we must preserve in ourselves the spirit of service, for *Russia perished from indifference and self-interest*. . . . Third, we must preserve in ourselves the spirit of loyalty, for *Russia perished from mental confusion, duplicity, and treachery*."[31] Emigration, said Ilyin, "was given to us so that we could strengthen our spiritual character."[32] This was the emigration's main task because the struggle with Bolshevism "*is above all a matter of religion, spirit, and patriotism*."[33]

The last of these—patriotism—played an important role in Ilyin's thought, although he also often used the word "nationalism." He wrote that "what is important is to be Russian, to love Russia, to fight for it honestly and formidably."[34] To Ilyin, each nation had its own God-given soul. As he wrote:

> Every people has its own national instinct, given to it by nature . . . And each people and spirit lives in its own way and creates valuable peculiarity. . . . For every national peculiarity in its own way manifests the Holy Spirit and in its own way glorifies God. . . . In a word, each people has its own, special mental makeup . . . And this is good. This is beautiful. The grasses and the flowers in the field are diverse. The trees and the clouds are diverse. God's garden is rich and beautiful; it has abundant forms, and glitters with colors and views.[35]

From this, Ilyin concluded that "nationalism is the confident and strong feeling that my people has also received the gifts of the Holy Spirit,"[36] and so "Russian nationalism is . . . faith in our vocation and the strength given to us."[37] In Ilyin's view, nationalism was a creative force, which propelled people to love their country and to seek to develop the distinct tasks given to them by God. It was a purely positive phenomenon, and could not in any way be associated with hatred or denigration of other nations. As Ilyin put it:

> A true patriot loves *the spirit* of his people, and takes pride in it, and sees in it the source of greatness and glory precisely because it is *Spirit* . . . shining on *all* people and *all* peoples. . . . Every true spiritual achievement . . . is the property of *all mankind*. . . . He who is able to love the spirit knows its supernatural, universal essence; therefore, *he cannot hate and despise other peoples*. . . . The true patriot not only is not blind to the spiritual achievements of other peoples, but he seeks to comprehend and assimilate them, to introduce them into the spiritual life of his own motherland, in order to enrich it.[38]

In this way, Ilyin continued the Romantic-Slavophile tradition that sought to reconcile the particular with the universal by seeing the universal good as dependent on the flowering of a diversity of national forms. Like the Slavophiles, he had a somewhat complicated relationship with the West. Ilyin's mother was German, he spoke fluent German, and he possessed an excellent knowledge of Western philosophy. He was not anti-Western, but he did feel that Russia was distinct from the West, and also that the West was innately anti-Russian. In this he was far from alone. Russian émigrés did not find their host nations particularly welcoming. European states were unsympathetic to the Whites' efforts to reignite the civil war, and émigrés felt misunderstood and isolated. Furthermore, once the Great Depression began, many European states openly discriminated against Russian émigrés, who were seen as taking jobs from native citizens. As Ilyin put it, "We live as aliens among alien peoples. These peoples don't know Russia, don't respect it, don't like it. They are used to fearing its size and its power. . . . When we bear witness to the truth about Russia, they don't believe us and begin to treat us with suspicion."[39]

Life in Europe made many Russian émigrés aware of how they differed from Europeans. Ilyin was no exception. "All our culture is different," he wrote, "because we have a different, particular spiritual makeup. We have completely different churches, different church services, different goodness, different bravery, different family life; we have a completely different literature, different music, theater, art, dance."[40] From this it followed that Russia was not bound to follow Western ways. Ilyin concluded that

> There is no single "Western culture" that is mandatory for everybody, compared to which everything else is "darkness" or "barbarianism." The West is neither obligatory nor a prison for us. Its culture is not the ideal of perfection. . . . The West has its own errors, its own ailments, weaknesses, and dangers. We will not be saved by Westernism. We have our own paths and our own tasks.[41]

Ilyin was far from the only émigré to speak of Russia's distinctive nature, but one group took the logic in a completely new direction. These were the Eurasianists, who rose to prominence following the publication in Sofia in 1921 of a collection of essays entitled *Exodus to the East*. The introduction to *Exodus to the East* laid out its primary thesis: "Russians and peoples of the 'Russian world' are neither Europeans nor Asians. Merging with the native element of culture and life surrounding us, we are not ashamed to identify ourselves as Eurasians."[42]

Eurasianism had deep roots in Russian thought. From the second half of the nineteenth century onward, Russian artists and intellectuals had increasingly stressed the Asian roots of much of Russian culture. For instance, the historian and art critic Vladimir Stasov (1824–1906) wrote a series of articles in 1868 arguing that Russian medieval epics (*byliny*) were modeled on Persian and Indian equivalents. Stasov later went on to claim that Asian influences could be found in all aspects of Russian culture, including language, clothing, architecture, and music.[43] In the decade before the revolution, various conservative thinkers such as Prince Esper Ukhtomsky (1861–1921) and Sergei Syromiatnikov (1862–1933) put forward the idea that Russia's future lay in the east, and proposed an alliance of eastern states against the West.[44]

Eurasianism built on these foundations, which were strengthened by the tumultuous events that shook Europe from 1914 onward. The First World War and the revolutions and civil strife that followed shattered many people's faith in European civilization. This included Russian émigrés. In 1920, one of these, Nikolai Trubetskoi (1890–1938), at the time working at the University of Sofia, published a short book entitled *Europe and Mankind*. In it, Trubetskoi argued that Europeans' claims that their civilization was superior to others were false and egocentric.[45] Attempts by other cultures to imitate Western civilization invariably produced negative results. Peoples subjected to European colonialism were becoming aware of this and were beginning to rise up and demand national liberation, Trubetskoi said. He argued that Russia should put itself at the head of this process and lead the struggle against colonialism.[46]

A natural retort against Trubetskoi's thesis might have been to protest that Russia too was a colonial power, which ought therefore to be broken up. Eurasianism provided a response to this objection: the Russian Empire was not a colonial construct, but a "harmonious, symphonic, organic association of peoples which constituted a higher historical and cultural unity."[47] Eurasianists could lambast the West for its colonialism while justifying the existence of a large Russian Empire.

A year after *Europe and Mankind*, Trubetskoi laid out in *Exodus to the East* some of the arguments justifying his claim that the territories within the former Russian Empire, and now within the Soviet Union, were a natural entity. For instance, Russian folk songs differed from both Romano-German and Asian songs in being polyphonic; Russian dances were similar to the dances of the Finns, Turkic peoples, and Mongols; Russian ornamentation had "its own original style . . . connected with the Balkans and through the Ugro-Finns with the East"; Russian folk literature had nothing in common with that of the Romano-Germans or the Slavs, but resembled that of the Turks and Caucasian peoples; and so on. Thus, said Trubetskoi, "in ethnographic terms, the Russian people are not exclusively Slavic. The Russians, together with the Ugro-Finns and the Volga Turks, constitute a special cultural zone that is connected both with Slavdom and with the Turanian East."[48] Other Eurasianists later added arguments based on research in other disciplines, such as linguistics, botany, and geography, reinforcing the point that Eurasia formed an organic whole. As another leading Eurasianist, Pyotr Savitsky (1895–1968), said, "Russia is not only the 'West,' but also the 'East,' not only 'Europe,' but also 'Asia,' and even not Europe at all, but 'Eurasia.'"[49]

In Eurasian thought, Russia was very clearly opposed to Western Europe. Trubetskoi remarked: "We must get used to the fact that the Romano-German world, with its culture, is our greatest enemy."[50] It followed that it was necessary to reject the idea that Western civilization constituted "universal human civilization." As Trubetskoi put it:

The only genuine national culture is a completely original one. . . . Thus, the culture of every people must be different. . . . A universal human culture, identical for all peoples, is impossible. . . . Thus, the aspiration to create a universal human culture must be rejected. On the contrary, the aspiration of each people to create its own peculiar national culture is completely morally justified. Any cultural cosmopolitanism or internationalism deserves to be resolutely condemned.[51]

The Eurasianists had no doubt that the days of Romano-German universalism were numbered. In Eurasianist thought, Western Europe was in terminal decline. Another of the essayists in *Exodus to the East*, Georgy Florovsky (1893–1979), wrote: "this is the only 'law' of life: the *young* incessantly force out the *old*. . . . 'The land of the children' . . . will replace 'the land of the fathers.'"[52] The "old" was Europe; the "young" was Russia and America. Savitsky argued that the cultural center of world power had shifted over time from warmer to colder regions. In due course cultural power would shift to North America and to Russia.[53] "We know that a historical spasm separating one epoch of world history from another has already begun," said the introduction to *Exodus to the East*. "We do not doubt that the replacement of the Western European world will come from the East."[54]

For the Eurasianists, the coming decline of the West and rise of the East had deep religious significance. The Eurasianists rejected communism, but at the same time claimed that the revolution had had a positive outcome in terms of "the rejection of socialism and the affirmation of the church."[55] Through "its immeasurable sufferings and deprivations," said Savitsky, "Russia took upon herself the burden of searching for truth, for all and on behalf of all."[56] In due course, communism would collapse, wrote another contributor to *Exodus to the East*, musicologist Pyotr Suvchinsky (1892–1985). At that point, "Russia's great ordinance, its prophetic secret, will be realized: a wise and calm people and an intelligentsia that has recovered its sight will be reconciled and united under the one great and all-deciding dome of the Orthodox Church."[57] According to Suvchinsky,

> Perhaps the Russian Revolution, its results, are fated to redeem all the blind, cruel, and self-satisfied actions and deeds, all the unrepentant sins of the European war. . . . The burning Russian flame has been raised over the whole world . . . every Russian, without exception, is infecting peoples and lands with his inflammability . . . and preparing unprecedented glory for Russia in the coming epoch.[58]

In this way, the Eurasianists combined denunciations of the idea of universal human civilization and an insistence on Russia's particularity with a messianic vision of Russia saving the world.

In the immediate aftermath of the overthrow of Nicholas II, Russian conservatives were generally willing to engage with the new Provisional Government, and very few sought a restoration of the monarchy. As 1917 progressed and the situation in Russia deteriorated, calls for the establishment of a military dictatorship to restore order grew louder. Few people, though, were willing to act.[59] Only when the Bolsheviks seized power in November 1917 did serious opposition to the revolution begin, and even then counterrevolution did not equate to a desire to restore tsarism. The White armies stuck strictly to a policy of "non-predetermination," which stipulated that they would not predetermine Russia's future political system. The Whites' aim was first and foremost to defeat the Bolsheviks. What was to replace Bolshevism was to be left to the people to decide through some unspecified mechanism at some future point in time. Meanwhile, potentially divisive political issues were to be put to one side so that everybody could concentrate on the business of fighting the civil war.

Once the civil war was over, this logic no longer applied, and some émigrés began to argue that the Whites' lack of a definite political ideology had proven to be a serious weakness. In particular, some monarchists no longer felt obliged to abide by the constraints of non-predetermination and began to press the case for a restoration of the monarchy. On May 29, 1921, twenty-four monarchist groups met for a congress at Bad Reichenhall in Germany. Congress delegates established a Supreme Monarchist Council to promote their cause, headed by former URP leader Nikolai Markov, who during the Russian Civil War had fought with General Iudenich in the Baltic region.[60]

Most émigrés were probably monarchists at heart, albeit along a broad spectrum of opinion from those wishing to restore the pre-1905 autocracy to democratic, constitutional monarchists. Despite this, the Supreme Monarchist Council and other monarchist groups had little success in émigré politics. There were a number of reasons for this. One was that émigré military organizations, especially Wrangel's army and later ROVS, held firm to non-predetermination, in large part out of a fear that if members were allowed to engage in politics it would tear what was left of the White armies apart. Although Wrangel was a monarchist himself, he regarded émigré monarchist groups as extremely dangerous. In large part to prevent them from acquiring excessive influence, in 1923 he issued an order prohibiting members of his army (and thus also later of ROVS) from participating in politics in any way.[61] This cut the monarchist groups off from probably their largest potential source of support—military officers.

Another problem for monarchists was the lack of a clear candidate for the post of tsar. Nicholas II and his immediate family, including his wife, his children, and his brother, had all been murdered by the Bolsheviks. Going strictly according to the line of succession, the Romanov with the best claim to the throne was Nicholas II's cousin, Grand Duke Kirill Vladimirovich (1876–1938), a former naval officer who in 1904 was one of the few survivors of the battleship *Petropavlovsk* when it was sunk by the Japanese at Port Arthur. But some émigrés cast doubt on Kirill's right to the throne because his German mother had not converted to Orthodoxy at the time he was born. More importantly, Kirill was unpopular because he was believed to have shown undue haste in recognizing the revolution of March 1917, marching his unit of marines to pledge allegiance to the Provisional Government while sporting a red armband. When in 1924 Kirill declared himself emperor of Russia, very few émigrés agreed to support him, and his declaration was roundly denounced by some other surviving members of the Russian royal family.

Most émigrés preferred Grand Duke Nikolai Nikolaevich, who had been supreme commander of the Russian army during the First World War. The grand duke reluctantly agreed to help try to unite the emigration politically, but affirmed the principle of non-predetermination. In April 1924, the grand duke gave an interview to the Associated Press, in which he laid out his views. He said:

> We must not here, abroad, predetermine for the Russian people questions of the state structure. They can be restored only on Russian soil in accordance with the aspirations of the Russian people. . . . Now a party rules Russia in the name of class and international interests. It must be replaced by a national power, above classes and parties. This power must be firm and strong, but at the same time, just and enlightened.[62]

In a June 1925 interview with Pyotr Struve, the grand duke emphasized that "nobody should dream that it is possible to turn back the wheel of history. Our task is not to re-create the old order but to build a new Russia." He then repeated that "we must not here, abroad, determine for the Russian people the fundamental forms of the state structure."[63]

If monarchism proved unsuccessful among émigrés, so too did both liberal democracy and fascism. Russia's brief experience with what purported to be a liberal democratic order, under the rule of the Provisional Government in 1917, had been a disastrous failure. This experience, combined with the troubles faced by many European countries in the 1920s and 1930s and the establishment of dictatorial governments in countries such as Italy, Spain, and Germany, fatally discredited democracy in the eyes of many. Nikolai Berdiaev summed up the prevailing mood in his book *The Philosophy of Inequality*, when he wrote that "the triumph of democracy is always illusory and short-lived. . . . Always, always a small number rule." There were, said Berdiaev, only two options: aristocracy or "mob rule," in other words it was "the rule of the best or the rule of the worst."[64] Berdiaev complained that

> democracy is a departure from the organic condition, breaking up the unity of the people. . . . Democracy cannot be an expression of the people's spirit, for the people's spirit can be expressed only in an organism, but democracy is a mechanism. . . . Universal suffrage is an unsuitable way of expressing qualities in the people's life. A minority can better and more perfectly express the will of the people as an organic whole possessing the spirit of *sobornost'*. . . . The people perish under popular sovereignty, it drowns in mechanistic quantity, and cannot express its organic spirit, whole and indivisible.[65]

What mattered to Berdiaev was inner freedom. He distinguished between "cosmos,"[66] which was aristocratic and hierarchical, and "chaos," which was not. He wrote:

> Liberation of the chaotic element isn't the liberation of man, it is the source of enslavement. . . . The liberation of man, of the human individual, is liberation from the captivity of the chaotic element. . . . Unbundling the elemental passions enslaves, makes one a slave. When a man is in the power of chaos, he is a slave, his personality is atomized by his passions, weakened by his sins.[67]

In Berdiaev's eyes, democracy represented chaos, not cosmos. Thus, he concluded, it was "deeply hostile to the spirit of freedom."[68]

Most other émigrés shared Berdiaev's suspicions of democracy, even if they did not express their reservations in quite such mystical language. Their rejection of democracy did not, however, make them amenable to fascism. Only in Manchuria did Russian fascist organizations attract any significant support.[69] ROVS's leader in the 1930s, General Miller, instructed members to study fascism because, "we, members of ROVS, are natural fascists," but it is noteworthy that some of his most senior subordinates refused to pass this instruction onto members, while Miller himself regarded the Russian fascist party in Germany, the Russian National Socialist Movement, as a Nazi puppet organization and denounced those who joined it as suffering from "pure hysterics and a loss of sense not only of proportion but also of personal virtue." ROVS leaders exerted considerable effort to prevent members from joining fascist organizations.[70] Attempts to provide ROVS with a political ideology in the mid-1930s failed to gain any traction after senior officers strongly resisted the idea and reaffirmed non-predetermination. In this sense, émigré officers espoused a conservatism that was quite deliberately and consciously non-ideological.[71]

Political philosophers who were close to the Whites exhibited an occasional sympathy with fascism, but ultimately condemned it and headed in another direction. Struve, for instance, was attracted by European dictators such as Marshal Jozef Pilsudski in Poland, seeing them as bulwarks against the spread of communism. Struve was initially even supportive of Adolf Hitler, praising his "personal stature as a statesman." By 1938, however, he had changed his mind, denouncing Hitler as a "psychopathic leader" and calling upon France and Britain to take a strong stance against him.[72] Ilyin, likewise, said in a 1926 pamphlet that the White armies were in the "vanguard" of a worldwide movement, as seen in countries such as fascist Italy, Hungary, Spain, and Bulgaria.[73] But, as previously noted, in the 1930s he fell afoul of the Nazi authorities and had to flee Germany.[74] Later Ilyin maintained that fascism had contained some positive elements, but that overall it had "committed a whole series of deep and serious mistakes," including "a hostile attitude to Christianity . . . the creation of right-wing totalitarianism . . . the establishment of a party monopoly . . . [and] extreme nationalism and military chauvinism."[75] "The totalitarian state is godless," he wrote.[76]

Like Wrangel, Ilyin was a monarchist but also a strong supporter of non-predetermination. In a speech to the 1926 Émigré Congress, Ilyin declared that "Russia was built and flourished with a monarchical spirit and . . . collapsed due to the establishment of a republican spirit." But, he added, "We have to know how to have a tsar. We lost Russia because we forgot how to have one, and we won't have one until we learn it again."[77] This reflected his belief that the form of the state had to reflect the culture of the people. It also typified the apparently paradoxical nature of many of his views: monarchism combined with non-predetermination; liberalism paired with a belief in dictatorship; and Slavophilism side by side with a powerful defense of law.[78]

One of Ilyin's most original contributions to Russian conservative thought was his stress on that last point—the importance of law and "legal consciousness" (*pravosoznanie*). His book *On the Essence of Legal Consciousness* has been described as "perhaps the most impassioned defense of the rule of law ever penned by a Russian legal theorist."[79] For Ilyin, the fundamental task of politics was creating among the people an appropriate legal consciousness, by which he meant not just knowledge of law, and obedience of it through fear of punishment, but "recognition" of law "from conscience, and not from blind habit, but from sighted, reasoned *conviction*." A proper legal consciousness, he wrote, is "*a free recognition of law*."[80] In a society with such a legal consciousness, he thought, people would automatically respect one another's dignity, and the state would automatically respect the dignity of the individual.[81]

According to Ilyin, "every person is distinctive and singular in his own way."[82] It followed from this, that *freedom of the will* is necessary . . . in the sense of an absence of external, alien commands and prohibitions. . . . The fundamental dignity of the human consists in living a spiritual life *independently* of any heterogeneous encroachment and pressure. . . . *Free self-determination* in spirit is the deepest law of this life.[83]

This precept formed the basis of natural law. Ilyin believed that "law is above all the human right to be an independent spirit, the right to being, and the right to freedom."[84] A state was nothing other than a group of people who had come together for the "realization of the natural law," which was the state's "single, objective, and highest goal."[85] It followed that the purpose of the state was to secure the rights mentioned above. Ilyin affirmed that the state's mission

> consists of the *protection and organization of the lives of the people belonging to a given political union.* The protection of the spirit consists of guaranteeing to *all the people and each individual* [*individuum*] their natural right to determine their life in their own way, that is, the right to *life* and, moreover, to *a worthy* life, externally free and internally independent.[86]

Ilyin's use of the word "individual" (*individuum*), rather than the word "person" (*lichnost'*), is quite striking. "An individual [*individuum*] can be limited . . . only for his own benefit," he continued.[87] Statements like this not only give the lie to Timothy Snyder's claim that Ilyin despised the individual, but also explain why many Russian commentators consider Ilyin to have been a liberal. However, he was certainly not a liberal democrat, as he did not consider democracy the best way of securing individuals' rights. According to Ilyin, the state had to be governed by the "best people,"[88] that is to say the people with the most highly developed legal consciousness. The key issue in designing a state was finding a way of selecting the best people. That in turn depended upon the level of legal maturity of the population as a whole. Democracy might produce leaders with an advanced legal consciousness if the people themselves were spiritually mature, but would certainly not if they were not. In short, the form of the state depended upon the condition of popular legal consciousness.[89] This would vary from country to country, and from era to era. Ilyin concluded: "There is not, and cannot be, a single political form that is the most expedient at all times and for all peoples. . . . For each given nation in each given epoch the most expedient political form is that which best takes into account the maturity and firmness of the political will."[90]

Ilyin was convinced that the level of legal consciousness of the Russian people was already low and was sinking even lower all the time due to the arbitrary forms of government practiced by the communists. As a result, Ilyin argued, Russia after the fall of communism would not be morally capable of supporting a democratic order.[91] Introducing such an order would in fact be thoroughly counterproductive. He wrote:

> After its [communism's] fall, the long-standing moral debauchery will be overcome slowly. . . . And until such time as the spiritual renewal is completed, we must foresee that any attempt to introduce a democratic order will lead either to mob rule (that is the masses, morally unbridled and deprived of any sense of self-worth, having no sense of responsibility, or of freely given loyalty), or to a new right-wing totalitarian tyranny. Democrats who don't think about this and can't foresee it, don't understand the essence of either democracy or totalitarianism.[92]

It would take years of developing Russia's legal consciousness before it would be ready for elections, Ilyin assessed. In the meantime, Russia would need "a national, patriotic, authoritarian but far from totalitarian, educational and vivifying dictatorship."[93] This would be "a dictatorship, but not a totalitarian one, not internationalist, not communist; a dictatorship organizing a new informal democracy, and so a democratic dictatorship."[94]

By dictatorship, Ilyin meant in part that state power should be single and undivided. He wrote that state authority "must be one,"[95] and "at the head of the state there must stand *a single will*."[96] He therefore was a strong opponent of federalism. But he also emphasized that state power was "limited,"[97] and that

> strong government is not at all the same as totalitarian government. . . . For a strong state depends not on the bayonet, not on terror, but on the government's authority; not on threats and punishments, but on the free loyalty of the people. Therefore, when speaking about a strong government in the future Russia, I have in mind above all its spiritual authority.[98]

External freedoms in Ilyin's scheme were secondary to inner freedom, but he recognized that the latter depended to some degree upon the former. Ilyin therefore argued that the state, even in its dictatorial form, must grant certain freedoms to its citizens. They were to enjoy "freedom of belief"; were to be "equal before the law"; were to have freedom of movement inside and outside the country; were not to be arrested, prosecuted, or punished by the courts except in precise accordance with published law; homes and property were to be inviolable; and citizens were to have the right of association, including the right to form political parties.[99] Ilyin's views fitted well within the Russian conservative tradition of supporting autocracy as an undivided, but decidedly limited form of government, which far from undermining peoples' freedoms was the best guarantee of them against the forces of chaos and, in the twentieth century, of totalitarianism.

Ilyin exemplified the White spirit of irreconcilability. Some other conservative philosophers sought ways to either reconcile Red and White, or move on from the differences between them in an attempt to find new answers to Russia's problems. An example of the latter was Ivan Solonevich (1891–1953), who in 1934, along with his brother Boris, escaped from a concentration camp in the Soviet Union and crossed the Soviet border into Finland. From Finland, Ivan moved on to Bulgaria, and then to Germany, before finally settling in Argentina, where in 1951 he penned his best-known work, entitled *Popular Monarchy*.

Strongly influenced by Slavophile thought, Ivan Solonevich argued that every nation was different and so should follow its own, unique path of development.[100] Rejecting Eurasianism, he remarked that "Russia isn't Europe, but isn't Asia, or even Eurasia. It's simply Russia."[101] For him, Russia's problems derived from the fact that since Peter the Great it had built up political structures that were not Russian, and had no roots among the Russian people. Solonevich applied this criticism not just to prerevolutionary Russia, but also to the revolution and civil war, to the Reds and to the Whites. "The Russian masses fought against both the Reds and the Whites," he said,[102] a position that put him in opposition to that part of the Russian emigration that remained loyal to the memory of the White armies. According to Solonevich, after the fall of communism, Russia would need a form of government based not upon foreign philosophy but on the historical life of the Russian people. This implied a monarchical system of government combined with a form of popular representation, based upon historical Russian models. Thus, wrote Solonevich, "We return to Aksakov's formula: 'To the people—the power of opinion; to the tsar—the power of government.'"[103] Under such a system, Solonevich said, the tsar would be above the law, but "public opinion will have incomparably more weight than in a usually constructed republic as it will not be falsified by any 'dark forces.'"[104]

Solonevich's Slavophilism was quite archaic, looking back to the period before Peter the Great as its ideal, and seemingly dismissing recent history out of hand. A very different approach, which accepted recent history, and tried to reconcile its various strands, came in the form of the *Smena vekh* movement. This took its name from a collection of essays published in 1921 and edited by Nikolai Ustrialov (1890–1937), who during the Russian Civil War had served as a minister in Admiral Kolchak's White government in Siberia. The title of the book, *Smena vekh* (Changing landmarks), was a deliberate reference to the 1909 publication *Vekhi*, and indicated the authors' desire for a change of political direction following the Whites' defeat. Ustrialov and his fellow authors firmly believed in the need for a strong state. They were also nationalists. Ustrialov argued that Bolshevism was abandoning its internationalist credo and instead becoming nationalist in form, reuniting the old Russian Empire in the process. When in 1921 the communist leader Vladimir Lenin introduced a New Economic Policy, which permitted limited forms of private economic enterprise, Ustrialov interpreted this as evidence that Bolshevism was evolving in other directions as well.

The Smena vekh movement's members soon became known as "National Bolsheviks." A National Bolshevik activist in Bulgaria expressed their viewpoint clearly, writing, "All the sins of the Soviet system are temporary. In due course this system ... will be gradually transformed into a genuine national étatist power."[105] Accordingly, the National Bolsheviks urged fellow émigrés to return to Russia in order to work within the system to accelerate this process of evolution by means of "internal, organic transformation."[106] In retrospect, Smena vekh looks rather naïve and reliant on much wishful thinking. It did not prove popular among émigrés, most of whom remained firmly anti-Bolshevik. The idea of reconciling communism and nationalism did, however, gain some support in the Soviet Union, and the idea of National Bolshevism has been resurrected in Russia in the post-Soviet era.

Eurasianists also sought to move beyond the Red-White dichotomy of the Russian Civil War. Like most émigrés, the Eurasianists overwhelmingly rejected Western-style democracy. Instead, they proposed an "ideocracy," in other words "the reign of an idea, implemented by a ruling party representing the idea."[107] This meant maintaining the political system founded by the Bolsheviks but replacing the Communist Party of the Soviet Union with a different party, governed by a different idea—in essence, Bolshevism without the Bolsheviks, or as one of the leading Eurasianist political ideologists, Lev Karsavin (1882–1952), put it: "to replace the communist ideology while at the same time keeping the regime."[108]

In Karsavin's eyes, culture and the state were intertwined. Any given national culture could only be realized through the state, and the purpose of the state was not to promote material prosperity but rather to carry out this realization of national culture.[109] Karsavin believed that Bolshevism was closer to Russian culture than were Western individualism and democracy. As he wrote, "Bolshevism is a personification of some elemental aspirations of the Russian nation."[110] By contrast, Karsavin was scathing in his criticisms of Western democracy, calling human rights "abstract, doctrinaire phraseology," and denouncing the separation of powers as "a fiction ... [that] generates absurd and debilitating bureaucratization.... Elections do not ensure a permanent contact between electors and their representatives, but result in depriving people of political rights."[111] He wrote that "in the sphere that is distinctly its own, government is absolute; otherwise it would not be government."[112] Such views made Karsavin somewhat sympathetic to fascism,[113] and have led some historians to view Eurasianism as "totalitarian" in essence,[114] although it is worth noting that the Eurasianists were far from united in their political views and Karsavin's opinions were not universally held.

Furthermore, Eurasianism's ambivalence toward the Soviet Union discredited it in the eyes of the majority of émigrés. Like National Bolshevism, in this era its influence remained largely limited to a narrow circle of intellectuals.

SOCIAL-ECONOMIC CONSERVATISM

Compared with matters of culture and politics, socioeconomic issues occupied Russian émigrés very little, probably for the obvious reason that exile removed them entirely from the Russian economy. In their social thinking, émigré conservatives strongly supported the concept of hierarchy and firmly rejected egalitarianism of the sort associated with both liberalism and communism. Ilyin, for instance, considered the idea of "rank" to be of great importance,[115] while Berdiaev commented that

> inequality is religiously justified by the unrepeatable individual fate of the human person in eternity. This doesn't, of course, mean that one shouldn't alleviate and improve man's earthly lot. . . . But it means that it is impossible to rebel against the first principle of the divine order. . . . Inequality is the foundation of entire cosmic order and harmony, it justifies the very existence of the human person and is the source of all creative movement in the world. Man was born from inequality. Absolute equality would leave existence in an unrevealed state, in indifference, that is in non-being. The demand for absolute equality is a demand to return to the original chaotic and dark condition . . . a demand for non-being.[116]

Berdiaev concluded that "the dream of a harmonious combination of freedom and equality is unachievable rationalist utopia. . . . The thirst for equality will always be the most terrible danger for human freedom. Freedom is above all the right to inequality."[117]

Just as they rejected socialist ideas of equality, émigré conservatives also rejected socialist economics. Insofar as they discussed economics, it was generally to stress the importance of private property and free enterprise. Ilyin, for instance, claimed that it was private property that inspired the creative instinct. Because socialism undermined this instinct, it was doomed to economic failure, he argued.[118] Solonevich similarly stated that the most important freedom was that of economic activity. He expressed his support for property rights, which should be restricted only in extreme circumstances.[119] In his 1924 interview with the Associated Press, Grand Duke Nikolai Nikolaevich expressed the view that the post-communist order "must stand for the defense . . . of holy personal rights of private property. . . . Our industry . . . can be restored only on the basis of an unshakeable right to private property."[120] B. N. Sokolov, who gave a report on Russia's future economic system to the 1926 Émigré Congress, agreed. The future economy, he said, "will be founded on recognition of the right to private property and guaranteeing personal freedom and creative initiative in economic activity." Sokolov added that this meant the "denationalization and demunicipalization" of industry.[121]

Despite their belief in private property, with only a few exceptions émigrés rejected the idea of restoring land seized from landowners by peasants during the revolution and civil war. Political as much as economic calculation determined this: émigrés realized that there was no hope of overthrowing the Bolsheviks if the peasants thought that it would mean a return to the status quo ante. Delivering a report to the 1926 Émigré Congress on the land question, Vladimir Gurko argued that following the collapse of communism, "All the land that is actually being economically exploited, whether by land societies or individual landowners . . . must be assigned to them with full rights of private property."[122] The congress then voted unanimously in favor of a resolution saying that "the land that the peasants are using must not be taken from them and to recover from the peasants that which was lost or plundered during the revolution is impossible."[123]

Some of the Eurasianists provided a rather different approach to economic questions. In *Exodus to the East*, Savitsky pointed out that ocean transport was much cheaper than land transport, placing those parts of the world that were far from the ocean at a disadvantage in a global economy based upon international trade. Russia's geography put it in a particularly weak position in this regard. The solution, Savitsky argued, was for Russia to break away from the world market and instead develop a continental market, selling its produce to places that were close by, rather than trying to compete globally.[124] Thus, wrote Savitsky, "Russia's economic future lies not in aping the 'oceanic' policy of others, which is in many ways inapplicable to Russia, but in recognizing its 'continental' nature and adapting to it."[125]

Savitsky also came up with the idea of "Masterocracy" to provide a third way between capitalism and communism. Whereas the entrepreneur was concerned with making a profit for himself, the "master," filled with an Orthodox spirit, "pursued a holistic approach to the economy," caring for the environment and his employees, and if necessary suffering material loss to help them.[126] Viewed this way, economics was as much a religious as a material subject, and through Orthodoxy Russia would be able to transform the world by a form of "harmonious economic modernization."[127] Most Eurasianists, however, rejected these ideas. Eurasianist economic thinking was no more unified than its political thinking,[128] although in general the Eurasianists opposed economic liberalism and proposed an economy with a mixture of state planning and private enterprise.[129]

CONCLUSION

In his cultural history of the Russian emigration, Marc Raeff comments that "the conservative and reactionary monarchists thought only in terms of a restoration, whatever its specific form."[130] This was not the case. Most ordinary Russian émigrés were of a conservative inclination, but the restorationist wing of the emigration, as exemplified by the Supreme Monarchist Council, enjoyed little support. Conservative monarchists more commonly stuck to the principle of non-predetermination, and as the debates about the economy and land during the Émigré Congress show, they also repudiated a restoration of the prerevolutionary social and economic order. Moreover, conservative philosophers regarded the roots of Russia's problems as primarily spiritual in nature, believing that Imperial Russia had collapsed because of its moral failings. Restoring the old order was not a desirable objective, as it would mean restoring those failings as well. Instead, émigré conservatives sought a spiritual renewal. Ilyin, for instance, saw the root of the Russian crisis as lying in its immature legal consciousness, and the task of the future as being to develop a new type of legal consciousness in place of the old. This was a philosophy of change, not of restoration.

Émigré conservatives disagreed on many things, but they agreed on the principle that change should not involve blind copying of Western models and should be founded on principles that accorded with Russian national culture and tradition. Whites, Eurasianists, National Bolsheviks, and others accepted Orthodoxy, a strong state, and nationalism as the core principles involved. People differed in their interpretations of these principles, taking them in often very different directions. But the underlying idea that Russia was distinct from the West, and that change must be organic in nature was common to all.

In political terms, this led conservatives of all stripes to reject liberal democracy and favor authoritarian models of government. For the Eurasianists, this meant adopting much of the communist system while rejecting its ideology, but that was far from the only model. As can be seen in the writings of Ilyin, authoritarianism could also accompany assertions of the importance of individual freedom, natural rights, and law. Just as in the nineteenth century, the ideal was a centralized but limited form of government.

CHAPTER 9

THE SOVIET UNION UNDER STALIN

Thé Russian revolutions of 1917 swept away the foundations of conservatism within the boundaries of the former Russian Empire, in what became the Soviet Union. Communism was atheistic and actively hostile to religion. Consequently, the first element of Uvarov's triad—"Orthodoxy, Autocracy, Nationality"—suffered greatly under communist rule. Between 1917 and 1940, the number of churches operating within Russia fell from 39,530 to 950.[1] Although religious belief remained alive underground, Orthodoxy almost ceased to exist as a formal institution. Meanwhile, the second element of Uvarov's formula, autocracy, entirely vanished, at least in the form in which it was originally understood. Communist rule in reality retained many autocratic elements, but was much broader in its scope than was autocracy as traditionally understood by Russian conservatives. Finally, nationality too came under threat as the communists preached a philosophy of internationalism. Orthodoxy, Autocracy, and Nationality seemingly had no place in the communist political order.

The communist revolution extended also into social and economic life. Following the death of the Soviet Union's first leader, Vladimir Lenin, in 1924, a bitter power struggle divided the leadership of the Communist Party. By 1928, Josef Stalin had emerged as the unchallenged leader, and that year the Soviets embarked upon a massive campaign of industrialization accompanied by the collectivization of agriculture. The communist economic system abolished private enterprise, radically revised the social structure of the countryside, and led to a flood of peasants into the cities, resulting in massive urbanization as well as rapidly expanding literacy. The speed of change was remarkable.

It would be wrong to speak of conservatism as such in the Soviet Union in this period. There was nobody being published in the Soviet Union whom one could properly call a conservative philosopher; nor did the Soviet Union under Stalin make any original contributions to conservative thought. Nevertheless, from the early 1930s onward, what might be considered conservative ideas, such as nationalism and religious and family values, reemerged and began to play a growing role in determining certain aspects of state policy. These ideas contributed to the development of a more intellectual form of conservatism following Stalin's death in 1953. For that reason, the Stalin era can be seen as a time in which a sort of proto-conservatism began to reappear in the Soviet Union. This was to provide the foundation on which later Soviet conservatism was to be built.

Sustaining revolutionary momentum over a long time is difficult. It is perhaps natural that people, including the leaders of a revolution, will tire of continual change, wish to consolidate the original gains of their revolution, and start valuing order and stability. In Russia's case, the upheavals of revolution, civil war, collectivization, and industrialization came at a very heavy cost. By the early 1930s, the Soviet Union was suffering from "massive amounts of thefts of state property, an epidemic of political murders, train derailments and robberies, widespread black market activities and a dramatic increase in numbers of homeless and hooligan children's gangs. Armed and mounted bandit units roamed the countryside."[2] By 1933, in large part as a result of collectivization, there were over half a million homeless children in the Soviet Union, a fact that led to "a soaring child crime rate."[3] Once the Nazis came to power in Germany in 1933, the Soviets also faced a deteriorating international situation and an increasing threat of war.

In the face of these problems, the Soviet regime sought ways of stabilizing society while continuing its modernizing agenda. To this end, in the 1930s it turned to what might be called "traditional" values and institutions—the nation, the family, law, education, and finally even religion.

Historian Nicholas Timasheff termed the resultant shift in policy the "Great Retreat."[4] His use of the term "retreat" is controversial. Some historians support Timasheff's general thesis. Robert Daniels, for instance, writes of a return to "traditionalist policy norms . . . [and] conservative models," including an "embrace of Russian nationalism."[5] According to Daniels, "Stalin swept away practically everything in the realm of social experiment and cultural innovation that had been attempted in the name of the revolution for the previous fifteen years."[6] Others, however, have advanced different interpretations. Soviet architectural historian Vladimir Paperny has offered the thesis that the shift in state policy was just one more example of a perpetual cycling of Russian culture between two variants: "culture one" and "culture two," the former being horizontal and egalitarian, the latter vertical and hierarchical.[7] And American historian David Hoffmann points out that the Soviet regime at no point in the 1930s abandoned its commitment to communist ideology, while it continued to press ahead with policies of radical social and economic transformation.[8] Although elements within the Soviet regime had indeed attacked traditional institutions such as the nation, the family, and the law, others had not, and so it is possible to view the change in policy as merely a shift of the balance of power within the existing system rather than a retreat.[9] Hoffmann concludes that the "retreat" was in fact "the selective use of traditional institutions and culture for mobilizational purposes";[10] in other words, tradition was used instrumentally to support the Soviet program of modernization and the building of socialism.

Hoffmann's analysis represents a good way of looking at the processes underway in the Soviet Union in the 1930s and 1940s. But however instrumental the Soviet appeal to traditional values may have been, it subtly altered the direction of the country's progress. Conservatism may be seen as a path, that is to say as a route along which a society progresses while retaining connections to its past. By reframing his revolutionary policies to include reference to Russia's traditions, Stalin did not "retreat" back along the existing path, but he did alter the Soviet Union's heading from one path to another. Initially, the divergence between the new and the old paths was not great. But over time, the new path would come to diverge more and more from the old one, until in the decades after Stalin the Soviet Union could be seen to be heading somewhere very different from where it had been heading at the start of the 1930s.

Cultural Conservatism

In communist theory, nations were a product of the capitalist stage of economic development. As communism replaced capitalism, divisions between nations would naturally disappear. Communist theory also suggested that revolution was a product of the social contradictions that emerged in advanced capitalist societies. However, Russia in 1917 was not an advanced capitalist society; the vast mass of the population still worked in the countryside. This led to doubts as to whether communism could be built in Russia. The future of communism seemed to depend on exporting revolution to countries with a sufficiently large working class, above all Germany. These two factors gave early Soviet ideology an internationalist flavor, strongly opposed to all manifestations of Russian nationalism. By the early 1920s, however, it had become clear that revolution was unlikely to spread in the short to medium term. In 1924, Stalin proclaimed the idea of "socialism in one country."[11] Exporting revolution and propagating internationalist ideas now took second place to nation-building within the Soviet Union.

History provided one mechanism for advancing the nation-building policy. The leading historian in the Soviet Union in the 1920s was Mikhail Pokrovsky (1868–1932), who followed a strict Marxist line in seeing economics as the driving force in history and in downplaying the role of great men. His views dominated the Soviet study of history until his death in 1932. Thereafter, matters changed. In 1934 the Central Committee of the Communist Party denounced Soviet historians for teaching "abstract definitions of social and economic formulations, which replace the consecutive exposition of history with abstract sociological schemes." In place of this, the Central Committee demanded a return to narrative history, filled with "sketches of historical personages." Consequently, historians abandoned economic determinism and began instead to stress the importance of great men in historical development.[12] This meant praising figures from Russia's imperial past, including tsars and generals.[13] Thus in April 1939, the Soviet newspaper *Izvestiia* declared: "In this struggle we ought to be inspired by the images of our glorious ancestors, Alexander Nevsky, Dmitry Donskoi, [Kuzma] Minin and [Dmitry] Pozharsky, Suvorov, [Mikhail] Kutuzov . . . The cosmopolitanism of the nineteenth century is a thing of the past."[14]

The rising political tensions in Europe provided an additional incentive to rehabilitate Russia's past and promote Russian nationalism. As the 1930s progressed, war with Nazi Germany became increasingly likely. Communist ideology did not provide a sufficiently compelling basis for rallying the Soviet people against the external threat. Nationalism did. Not all nationalisms were the same, however. Russian nationalism, because of its historically multiethnic nature, and because it represented the largest population group within the Soviet Union (ethnic Russians), could play a useful role, and therefore became an increasingly common theme in Soviet propaganda. A notable example was the 1938 film *Alexander Nevsky*, which portrayed medieval Russia's victory against the German Teutonic Knights.

By contrast, the nationalism of minority groups was potentially dangerous. Non-Russian nationalities were in many cases seen as potential fifth columns that might subvert the Soviet authorities in time of war. In the 1920s the Soviet Union had pursued a policy of "indigenization" (*korenizatsiia*), through which it promoted local languages, culture, and cadres.[15] In the 1930s, perhaps out of a lack of confidence in the loyalty of minority peoples, the Communist Party reversed course and began to encourage instead a form of Great Russian nationalism. Following a series of denunciations of "bourgeois nationalists," in 1938 the Russian language became compulsory in all schools throughout the Soviet Union. The Soviet government also directed that the Cyrillic alphabet would be used instead of the Latin alphabet to write the languages of the Soviet Union's Muslim peoples.[16] The promotion of regional cultures was downplayed and many leaders of the non-Russian areas of the country were arrested and executed in 1937 and 1938 during the period known as the "Great Terror."

Another important aspect of the Soviet Union's increasing cultural conservatism was the suppression of the experimental and avant-garde forms of painting, literature, music, and architecture that had flourished in the immediate aftermath of the revolution. In 1932, the Russian Association of Proletarian Writers was dissolved,[17] and from 1934 onward "socialist realism" became the approved form that Soviet literature and arts were to follow. According to Andrei Zhdanov (1896–1948), at the time a member of the Central Committee of the Communist Party, socialist realism meant "knowing life so as to be able to depict it truthfully in works of art, not to depict it in a dead scholastic way, not simply as 'objective reality,' but to depict reality in its revolutionary development."[18] Following the precepts of socialist realism, in the 1930s the arts largely abandoned the experimentalism of the 1920s. Writers and artists of the imperial period regained an honored status. Most notably, in 1935, study of the works of the great Russian poet Aleksandr Pushkin became compulsory in Soviet schools. Henceforth, the supposed "dictatorship of the proletariat" preferred not proletarian culture, but aristocratic "masters of the past."[19]

The German invasion of the Soviet Union in 1941 gave added impetus to the revival of Russian nationalism. Military units that distinguished themselves in battle acquired the title "Guards." Epaulettes were reintroduced to adorn military uniforms. Orders of military merit introduced during the war bore the names of great leaders of Russia's past: Aleksandr Nevsky, Suvorov, and Kutuzov.[20] More remarkable still was Stalin's decision to relax the repression of the Russian Orthodox Church. The publication of anti-religious literature ceased, anti-religious museums closed, and taxes on the church were reduced. The church had not been permitted for many years to elect a new patriarch, having instead only an acting patriarch, Metropolitan Sergei of Nizhny Novgorod. But in September 1943 Stalin met with Sergei, as well as Metropolitan Aleksei of Leningrad and Metropolitan Nicholas of Kiev, and gave his permission for the election of a patriarch. Sergei was duly elected a week later.[21] In December 1943, a theological academy opened in Moscow, the training of priests resumed, and churches began to reopen.[22] The church certainly did not regain its former position, but it was granted an unlikely reprieve.

POLITICAL CONSERVATISM

Communist theory claimed that the state was the means by which the ruling class wielded power over other classes. In the aftermath of capitalism's overthrow, a socialist state, the "dictatorship of the proletariat," would be necessary to enable the working class to secure its power over the previous capitalist rulers. In time, as socialism developed into full-fledged communism, all class divisions within society would disappear. Consequently, the state would no longer be necessary, and would "wither away." Yet, as the Soviet Union developed, far from withering away, the state became more and more pervasive and more and more repressive. On the ideological level, Stalin explained this by claiming that the closer the Soviet Union came to true communism, the more its enemies resisted, and so the stronger the state needed to be in order to fight them.

On a purely practical level, the rising tide of crime made the Soviet state reconsider its attitude toward law. This too was meant to wither away as the remnants of the old, capitalist order disappeared. But in the 1930s, the Soviet state turned back to a traditional understanding of law, as a tool in its search for stability and order. Initially, in accordance with the idea that law would eventually disappear, the Soviet regime had done very little to prepare a new generation of lawyers. Legal training almost entirely ceased, so that in 1933 the entire Soviet Union graduated only 180 new lawyers. As of 1935, almost 85 percent of judges in the People's Courts, the lowest rung of the legal system, had only an elementary school education.[23] In the eyes of many communist officials, "revolutionary expediency" was far more important than law or legal procedure. At the Fifteenth Party Congress of the Communist Party in 1927, various speakers argued that rather than following the letter of the law, they should follow their "revolutionary instinct" in determining specific cases.[24] The deputy commissar [minister] of justice, Nikolai Krylenko (1885–1938), set about simplifying legal procedure to eliminate rules that gave accused people "resources that might save an enemy of the revolution from punishment." Rules were to be "guidelines" only, Krylenko argued.[25]

The campaign of collectivization against the peasants from 1929 to 1933 caused an almost total collapse in legal procedure in the Soviet Union, as "legal officials all but abandoned procedural norms and standards of evidence," sentencing peasants without hearing any witnesses or allowing any evidence from the defense.[26] From 1934 onward, however, in the face of the growing lawlessness in Soviet society, the communist state shifted direction. In 1936, Stalin denounced the theory that law would wither away under communism. "Revolutionary legality" was now redefined to mean "strict observance of the law."[27] Some within the Soviet legal community, the most prominent of whom was Andrei Vyshinsky (1883–1954), had always defended a more traditional view of the legal system. This view now gained Stalin's support, and in 1935 Vyshinsky became the Soviet Union's procurator general (the top legal official). Vyshinsky declared that "law is the complex of rules of human behavior established by state power. . . . Law in such a conception is possible also in socialist society: the dictatorship of the proletariat does not exclude law and legality as one of the forms of legal expression."[28]

Historian Peter Solomon notes that under Vyshinsky, the Soviet Union "witnessed the start of a return to traditional legal order," including "key aspects of Tsarist justice." As part of what Solomon terms the "return to tradition," simplified procedures were rejected, and legal training recommenced.[29] New law schools opened, with the annual intake of students rising to 3,550 by 1940.[30] At the same time, the legal system increasingly focused on punishing criminals rather than reforming or rehabilitating them, and punishments became more and more severe.[31]

As with other aspects of the Great Retreat, the shift in legal thinking was only partial. The Soviet Union's rulers continued to make use of decidedly arbitrary methods of government when it suited them to do so, most notably in 1937 and 1938, when hundreds of thousands of supposed "enemies of the people" were arrested and in many cases executed during the Great Terror. Nevertheless, an important change had taken place, and the groundwork was laid for the return of a more traditional view of the state.

SOCIAL-ECONOMIC CONSERVATISM

Perhaps the most striking feature of the Great Retreat was the change in Soviet social policy, with the 1930s seeing a revival of what are often called "traditional family values." According to the founders of communist ideology, Karl Marx and Friedrich Engels, the family assumed different forms at different stages of economic development. Marx and Engels envisioned that under communism much of what characterized the family would disappear, since tasks such as education and child-rearing would be handed over to society as a whole.[32] They viewed the family as a property-holding institution, and as such undesirable. In the Soviet Union, the authorities had an additional reason for viewing the family with suspicion: it provided a focus of loyalty other than the Communist Party, and provided a means by which non-communist values might be propagated from generation to generation.[33] As Aleksandra Kollontai (1872–1952), the most prominent woman in the Soviet government in the 1920s, put it, "the family deprives the workers of revolutionary consciousness."[34] That said, attitudes toward the family varied among Soviet leaders. Lenin never supported the destruction of the traditional family.[35] Others, though, looked confidently toward a future in which the family, as previously understood, would vanish.[36] The commissar for education, Anatoly Lunacharsky (1875–1933), remarked: "Our problem is now to do away with the household and to free women from the care of children. . . . There is no doubt that the terms 'my parents,' 'my children,' will gradually fade out of usage."[37] Similarly, in a 1929 book entitled *The Sociology of Marriage*, Professor S. Y. Volfson predicted that the family would lose many of its existing characteristics. For instance, child-rearing would take place collectively, through state-run kindergartens; people would no longer eat meals as families, but communally; and care of the aged would pass from families to state institutions. "Deprived of its social content, the family will die out," Volfson concluded.[38]

The young Soviet state set about turning this rhetoric into reality. According to the terms of a December 1917 law, divorce was granted almost automatically on demand. Next, adultery was decriminalized, and then abortion was permitted under a decree issued in 1920.[39] In January 1927, a new family code came into effect. This put common-law marriages on the same legal footing as registered ones.[40] Soviet propaganda emphasized that loyalty to the state took precedence over loyalty to the family. The most notorious example was that of thirteen-year-old Pavlik Morozov, who in 1932 supposedly reported his father to the authorities for selling forged documents and was then killed by angry villagers. Morozov became the object of an official cult, and was portrayed as a role model for young Soviet citizens.

Accompanying the attack on the family was a move in favor of sexual liberation. Again, this did not have universal support within the Communist Party. Lenin, for instance, "held rather Victorian notions about morality," and declared that promiscuity was "a sign of degeneration."[41] In general, though, the initial view of the Soviet authorities was that individuals' sex lives were not the business of the state.[42] In December 1917, the Soviet state decriminalized homosexuality.

By the early 1930s, urbanization, the breakdown of traditional family units, and easy access to abortion together had produced a dramatic fall in the birth rate. In 1928 there were 42.2 births per thousand people in the Soviet Union. In 1932, there were only 31, a decline of 25 percent in just four years.[43] In Moscow in 1934 there were 154,600 abortions but only 57,000 births.[44] The number of unmarried mothers was increasing.[45] To combat this demographic crisis, the Soviet government changed direction and began to tout "family values." *Sotsialisticheskaia zakonnost'* (Socialist legality), the official journal of the Ministry of Justice, declared that

> the state cannot exist without the family. Marriage is a positive value for the socialist Soviet state only if the partners see in it a lifelong union. So-called free love is a bourgeois invention and has nothing in common with the principles of conduct of a Soviet citizen. Moreover, marriage receives its full value for the state only if there is progeny.[46]

In the 1930s the Soviet authorities revised family law to reflect the changing attitude. In particular, it became harder to get a divorce. Legal fees for divorces rose dramatically, with the amount getting larger for each successive divorce. From the mid-1930s onward the Soviet state increasingly condemned sexual promiscuity, and in 1934 homosexuality once again became illegal.[47] And in an effort to tackle the declining birthrate, in 1936 the Soviet state banned abortion, except in cases where pregnancy threatened the life or health of the mother or there was a danger of some hereditary disease.[48] The state also introduced positive measures to encourage births. These included increased maternity grants and the expansion of the system of state nurseries.[49]

As part of the drive to strengthen the family, the Soviet press began to propagate the idea that children should respect their parents. The journal *Sovetskaia iustitsiia* (Soviet justice), for instance, declared that "sound moral ideas must be inculcated into the minds of young persons. They must know that lack of care for their parents is found only among savages and that in every civilized society such conduct is considered dishonest and base."[50] A key figure in the new policy was the educator Anton Makarenko (1888–1939), who from 1920 to 1935 worked with homeless children and concluded that children needed firm authority in order to develop successfully. In his 1937 *A Book for Parents*, Makarenko portrayed the family as requiring order, strictness, and discipline.[51] Correspondingly, state policy now sought both to reinforce parental authority and to make parents responsible for their children. Thus in 1934 a new law made parents criminally responsible for actions committed by their children.[52]

The idea of strictness made a return in the educational system as well. In the 1920s, Soviet schools had experimented with what nowadays would be called "child-centered learning." In 1931, the government reversed direction, and ordered a restoration of school discipline and the authority of teachers.[53] Experimental forms of education were condemned, traditional methods of pedagogy were restored, and school uniforms were reintroduced. The school system was divided into two streams: an academic stream for the elite, and a vocational stream for everyone else that focused on the teaching of practical skills.[54] In 1943 the Soviet Union abolished coeducation in secondary schools and began what was to prove to be an unsuccessful eleven-year experiment with single-sex education.

It is noticeable that Soviet propaganda continued to promote the idea of women working outside the home, rather than portraying women first and foremost as wives and mothers. The turn toward traditional family values was only partial. Nevertheless, the catastrophic loss of life during the Second World War impelled the Soviet state to take measures to try to increase the birthrate. These included the creation in 1944 of the Order of Maternal Glory, which was awarded to mothers with seven or more children. In an effort to encourage paternity, a 1944 decree reintroduced the legal notion of illegitimate children and freed fathers of such children from any obligation to make support payments.[55] The decree also abolished the concept of unregistered marriages and obliged courts to attempt to reconcile couples seeking a divorce.[56]

The Soviet press now praised female chastity outside of marriage, describing it as a matter of "honor."[57] This word was not accidental, as ideas of honor were

making a comeback. In 1947, the Soviet government even went so far as to create a system of Courts of Honor within the state bureaucracy, the Communist
Party, and the military. This was "geared towards the internalization of a Soviet
version of honorable behaviour" within those institutions, and was modeled on
similar courts that had operated within the Imperial Russian military prior to the
revolution.[58]

The value placed on honor was also manifested in the growing number of
medals, orders, and titles created by the Soviet government, such as the Order of
Lenin (first awarded in 1930); Hero of the Soviet Union (1934); Hero of Socialist
Labor (1939); Order of the Badge of Honor (1935); Order of Aleksandr Nevsky
(1942); Order of Suvorov (1942); Order of Kutuzov (1942); and so on. These
honors restored what are normally seen as conservative ideas of social rank and
distinction.

A similar process can be observed in the economic sphere. In general, Soviet
economic policy was far from conservative, as it involved a massive and sudden
transformation of the economy. Theoretically speaking, communism was egalitarian, and in accordance with this, the Soviet system initially sought to equal-
ize wages across the economy. The stresses of rapid industrialization, however,
made Soviet planners realize the benefits of financial incentives. Accordingly, in
the early 1930s, a new wage system allowed for a degree of differentiation, paying
more productive workers and managers more. The so-called "party maximum"
provided a limit on what members of the Communist Party could earn, but in due
course even this was abolished.[59] Although the Soviet Union remained theoretically committed to equality, in practice it began to recreate a system of social and
economic hierarchy. Finally, in 1935, faced with a catastrophic decline in agricultural production following collectivization, the government permitted peasants
within collective farms to have their own private allotments of land on which they
could grow food to sell in a private market.[60] This represented only a very minor
part of the overall economy. Nevertheless, the idea of private property returned in
at least a small way.

CONCLUSION

The central question that has always faced Russian conservatives has been how to
modernize Russia without ceasing to be authentically Russian, and without causing so much disruption to the social and political order that the country falls into
chaos. In the 1930s, the very speed of the Soviet Union's transformation almost
inevitably generated a conservative backlash, as it produced serious social dislocation that obliged the regime to turn to traditional institutions in order to maintain

stability. The result was not a "retreat." Newly revived institutions took on new forms. For instance, the influx of women into the urban workplace ensured that the family promoted by the Soviets from the mid-1930s onward was not the same as the family of the prerevolutionary peasantry.[61] The country continued to move forward. But by the late 1930s it was moving forward along a slightly different path, one in which tradition played a more important part. The Russian Orthodox Church received an unexpected deathbed reprieve. And Russian nationalism once again became an important force. The conservative turn was not, of course, the only process taking place in the Soviet Union at this time, and it was overshadowed by the dramatic changes wrought by industrialization, collectivization, and the Great Terror. Nonetheless, bit by bit, a new conservatism took shape in the Soviet Union, creating the conditions for an even stronger revival in the decades after the Second World War.

LATE SOVIET CONSERVATISM

I n 1953 Josef Stalin died after suffering a brain hemorrhage. After a brief
power struggle, Nikita Khrushchev (1894–1971) emerged as the new leader
of the Soviet Union. Some of the policies mentioned in the previous chapter did not survive long under his rule. For instance, in 1955 abortion was
re-legalized; from 1959 to 1964, the Soviet state again embarked on an anti-religious campaign, closing many of the churches that had reopened during and after
the Second World War;[1] and the Communist Party returned to the concept of
"indigenization" in its nationalities policy.

In 1956, Khrushchev denounced Stalin in a speech to the Twentieth Congress
of the Communist Party. A political thaw followed, in which slightly freer expression was permitted. The Khrushchev era was also marked by experimentation in
economic policy, most famously an attempt to develop agriculture in the so-called
"Virgin Lands" of southern Russia and northern Kazakhstan, an experiment that
ended in failure. Another important feature of the era was rising tensions between
the Soviet Union and the West, culminating in the Cuban Missile Crisis of 1962.
Khrushchev did not survive long in power, however. Exasperated by what was
seen as Khrushchev's erratic behavior, in 1964 the Communist Party leadership
ousted him and installed Leonid Brezhnev (1906–82) in his place.

By the mid-1960s, the Soviet regime had been in place long enough for it
to have developed historical, political, and economic traditions of its own. This
enabled the creation of a type of Soviet conservatism dedicated to preserving the
existing system. Many Soviets resisted the idea of any further radical upheavals
and wanted instead to enjoy the benefits of stability. To this end, Brezhnev stopped
the repeated shuffling and purging of officials that had characterized the past, and
instituted the policy of "stability of cadres." This provided officials with a degree of
job security that they had never previously enjoyed. Meanwhile, various attempts
to carry out major reforms of the economy, most notably the so-called "Kosygin

reforms" of the mid- to late 1960s, came to naught. The government chose instead to merely tinker with the existing system.

Under Brezhnev, the political thaw came to an end, as the state clamped down on views considered threatening to the authority of the Communist Party. That said, political repression under Brezhnev never reached anything like the scale of that experienced under Stalin. There remained a certain amount of leeway for the expression of conservative opinions, both officially and unofficially. Russian nationalism in particular found an official outlet in journals such as *Molodaia gvardiia* (Young guard). There was also a growing volume of unofficial literature (known as samizdat) being printed privately and circulated underground, including what might be described as conservative literature. Critics of the Soviet system—"dissidents"—became increasingly vocal, despite regular arrests. One of the most famous of these dissidents was Aleksandr Solzhenitsyn (1918–2008), who in 1974 was expelled from the Soviet Union.

In a 1979 article, American Sovietologist Stephen Cohen described the "profoundly conservative attitudes" that existed "among ordinary [Soviet] citizens and officials alike."[2] Conservatism, wrote Cohen, was "an artifice not of the regime but a reflection of deep currents in Soviet officialdom and society," making the Soviet Union "arguably . . . one of the most conservative countries in the world."[3] This conservatism took various forms: first, what one might call official conservatism, which sought to protect the existing system; second, semi-official conservatism, which was tolerated by the Communist Party but not formally endorsed by it, and which accepted Soviet authority but pressed for change along ideologically conservative, and especially nationalist, lines; and third, unofficial, dissident conservatism, which rejected communism and embraced Orthodoxy.

Underpinning official conservatism was a kind of unwritten social contract, according to which the Soviet people accepted the Communist Party's rule, but in return the Party gave them an ever-improving standard of living. For some time under Brezhnev, the Party was able to deliver its part of the bargain. Throughout the 1960s and most of the 1970s, the Soviet economy grew considerably. By the late 1970s, however, severe problems were beginning to emerge. Growth rates declined, and the country faced an increasing number of social problems, for instance growing alcoholism among Soviet men and a fall in life expectancy. By the early 1980s, it was clear that the Soviet system was in trouble. The Soviet Union was not just failing to catch up with the economic performance of the West, it was falling further behind. Aware of the country's problems, many now put their hopes in radical reform as a way of rescuing the situation.

The result was the promotion of Mikhail Gorbachev to the leadership of the Soviet Union in 1985. Gorbachev's efforts to reform the Soviet system politically and economically through the policies of glasnost (openness) and perestroika (restructuring) failed. In the late 1980s, the situation in the Soviet Union continued to deteriorate. Political opposition to communism grew rapidly, especially among some of the country's non-Russian national minorities. The three Baltic republics (Estonia, Latvia, and Lithuania) demanded independence. The Soviet Union teetered closer to the brink of collapse, triggering a conservative backlash among those wanting to preserve what they could of the existing order. This reached its culmination in August 1991 in a failed coup d'état against Gorbachev. Following this, the communist system disintegrated extremely quickly, and on December 25, 1991, the Soviet Union officially ceased to exist.

CULTURAL CONSERVATISM

The revival of Russian nationalism under Stalin carried forward into the Brezhnev era and formed an important part of semi-official and unofficial conservatism. One of the earliest manifestations of this was the "village prose" movement, the best-known member of which was the writer Valentin Rasputin (1937–2015). Rasputin held a quintessentially conservative worldview, writing that

> each nation differs from others in its historical and ethnic features and in the spirit
> of the land that gives its people birth. . . . There are no misfortunes on earth that a
> people cannot overcome if they are properly organized and directed in accordance
> with the whole flow of their historical progression and their spiritual commonality.
> And only the following can have extremely serious, even irreparable, consequences
> for any people: the complacency of a generation or several generations, oblivious-
> ness to their roots, and a conscious or unconscious break with the centuries-old
> experience of the past, all of which lead, through subsequent phases, to the loss of
> national feeling and historical memory, to fragmentation, depersonalization, and
> homelessness.[4]

Rasputin and other village prose authors saw the historical locus of Russian national identity as lying in the village, which they believed was being destroyed by the march of industrial progress, beginning with collectivization in the early 1930s and continuing through to their own time. In their stories, the village authors described the fate of people caught up in the process of modernization.[5] Rasputin's 1979 novel *Return to Matyora*, for instance, depicted a village about to be flooded as a result of the construction of a dam.[6] Village prose lamented the loss of Russia's heritage in the form of "destruction of the natural environment[,] . . . ancient buildings and monuments," as well as the destruction of traditional ways of life, and pleaded to save what remained of Russia's national identity before it was too late.[7] It played an important role in the development of Russian conservatism, moving it beyond the nationalism of the Stalin era, with its focus on the great heroes of Russia's past, and reconnecting it with the natural environment, the ordinary people, and traditional values. It perhaps also contributed to the long-term undermining of communist ideology. For while they never attacked the communist system as such, the village authors clearly regretted much of what communism had to done to Russia's heritage and sought to recreate Russia on a different basis, more in harmony with its pre-Soviet past.[8]

The desire to preserve Russian heritage extended beyond literary circles, and from the 1960s onward acquired the nature of a mass movement enjoying some official support. Perhaps the most notable manifestation of this was the creation in 1965 of the All-Russian Society for the Preservation of Historical and Cultural Monuments, which by 1972 was said to have had 7 million members,[9] and by 1982 over 14 million members.[10] The journal *Molodaia gvardiia* provided intellectual support for this cultural trend, beginning with a 1965 appeal to Soviet youth by sculptor Sergei Konenkov (1874–1971), artist Pavel Korin (1892–1967), and writer Leonid Leonov (1899–1994), entitled "Guard Our Sacred Objects!" They denounced Khrushchev's anti-religious campaign and the resultant destruction of Russian churches. "Our descendants will never forgive the destruction of monuments of Russian national culture," the three wrote. "Every Russian calls out, with heart and soul, 'Stop! Guard our sacred objects!'"[11] The following year, *Molodaia gvardiia* published a provocative article by one of the village writers, Vladimir Soloukhin (1924–1997), entitled "Letters from the Russian Museum." Soloukhin began his essay by lamenting the destruction of historical monuments, especially churches, in Moscow. Four hundred churches had been destroyed in Moscow since the revolution, Soloukhin said, including the huge Cathedral of Christ the Savior, which afterward became the site of an outdoor swimming pool. "There are no less than fifty such pools in Budapest alone, for which they didn't ruin a single architectural monument," complained Soloukhin, adding, "when we destroy old things, we always tear up our roots."[12]

Soloukhin complained also about the Soviet habit of renaming towns, streets, and institutions after communist heroes. "We will never in a thousand generations forget the old names," he said. "The best thing would be to restore all [the old names] either gradually or immediately (immediately would be better in my opinion), without exception."[13] Next, Soloukhin praised Russian religious painting—icons and frescoes. It was shocking, he said, that an exhibition of American architecture in Leningrad had been widely advertised, but an exhibition of ancient Russian frescoes had not been graced with even a single advertising poster. "Why do we allow organized and well-thought-out propaganda for architectural styles that are alien to us, but are afraid of popularizing ancient Russian art by even a thousandth of the amount?" he asked.[14] He commented that wonderful examples of Russian art still existed in old churches in remote corners of the country but were rotting away. It was time to save them, Soloukhin said.[15]

Praising prerevolutionary (especially religious) heritage and rejecting the heritage of the Soviet era was extremely bold at that date. It was also popular. Soloukhin's article resulted in a great increase in subscriptions to *Molodaia gvardiia*.[16] It, and similar articles by other authors, tapped into a growing cultural conservatism among Soviet Russians. This challenged Soviet policies in a number of ways. For instance, Soviet ideology officially opposed nationalism and put forward the idea that the various peoples of the Soviet Union would eventually merge into one Soviet nation. Russian nationalists, including some Russian members of the Communist Party, were uncomfortable with this, and felt that the Party's affirmative action policies discriminated against ethnic Russians. The Central Asian population of the Soviet Union was rapidly expanding and, if existing trends continued, Russians might soon find themselves a minority within the Union. This made Russians receptive to the kind of nationalism espoused by *Molodaia gvardiia*.[17]

Molodaia gvardiia was for a while able to get away with its subversive form of conservatism. Eventually, however, in 1970 the Party's top institution, the Politburo, condemned *Molodaia gvardiia*'s editorial policy. On the instructions of Brezhnev and the Communist Party's chief ideologist, Mikhail Suslov (1902–82), the journal's editor was fired, and thereafter *Molodaia gvardiia* had to toe a more moderate line.[18] A general crackdown on Russian nationalism followed. The Party's victory was only temporary, however. The genie of Russian traditionalism had been let out of the bottle, and could not be stuffed back in. When the nationalist, monarchist, and Orthodox painter Ilya Glazunov (1930–2017) staged exhibitions in 1978, about half a million people lined up to view his work in Moscow and perhaps a million in Leningrad.[19] Cultural conservatism had deep roots in the Russian people.

Another semi-tolerated, but very different, challenge to the official Soviet view of nationality came from the historian and ethnographer Lev Gumilyov (1912–92). The son of poets Anna Akhmatova (1889–1966) and Nikolai Gumilyov (1886–1921), Gumilyov was twice imprisoned during Stalin's rule. Subsequently, he had a complex relationship with Soviet officialdom. While some Soviet officials tried to prevent him from publishing his work, he also enjoyed a certain amount of support in high places. This included a protector in the Central Committee of the Communist Party, Anatoly Lukianov.[20] From the 1960s onward, Gumilyov worked in the Geography Institute in Leningrad and devoted himself to a study of the nomadic peoples of the Eurasian steppes. In the process, he developed esoteric ideas about the origins and importance of ethnic groups, and became a conduit through which the ideas of émigré Eurasianists infiltrated the Soviet Union. He was to have an important influence on the development of Russian conservative thought in the post-Soviet era.

Gumilyov opposed the Soviet concept of the merging of the nations. He asked, "Why should we try to squeeze the behaviour of an Abkhazian and a Chukot, a Lithuanian and a Moldavian all into a single frame?" Instead he praised the value of diversity and the multinational nature of the Soviet Union, stating: "If everyone merges and becomes the same, then there will be no movement, no cultural development, and life will simply cease to exist."[21]

Gumilyov argued that ethnic groups (*ethnoi*) were an inherent part of human existence, calling them "phenomena of nature ... not a social phenomenon."[22] Ethnicity, according to Gumilyov, was not racially determined, rather it was a matter of a group of people sharing a "behavioral stereotype." "The phenomenon of an *ethnos*," wrote Gumilyov, "is not in peoples' bodies, but in their acts and relationships. Consequently no one is outside an ethnos, except the newborn baby. Everybody must behave in some way, and it is the character of his behavior that defines his ethnic affiliation."[23]

In Gumilyov's view, the development of each ethnic group's behavioral stereotype was shaped by the natural environment in which the group found itself. The "decisive factor" in the creation of *ethnoi*, he said, was "the territorial one."[24] Each ethnos was suited to its own natural environment, which differed from that of other *ethnoi*. This meant that *ethnoi* could not be compared with one another. None could be said to be better or worse than any other, and none therefore had the right to impose its way of life upon others. In particular, this meant that the West had no right to claim that its own civilization was superior to that of Russia. As he wrote:

> With such an approach to the subject of research, the Eurocentric idea of the superiority of technical civilization over the development of other types falls away. . . . Undertaking research into the global norms of ethnic history, one has to immediately reject the principle of Eurocentrism.[25]

Gumilyov regarded Western Europe as Russia's enemy.[26] In opposition to Western-style universalism, he proposed a separation of sovereign peoples, writing that "the best way to maintain peaceful cooperation between peoples consists in guaranteeing to each of them a territory that each people has the right to administer in its own way, and in which it is permitted to develop itself culturally as it sees fit."[27]

Although Gumilyov said that every ethnos was different, he also argued that some enjoyed a certain "complementarity" that enabled them to coexist within the same borders. In this case, they could form what he called a "*superethnos*," which he defined as "a group of *ethnoi* arising simultaneously in a specific region, mutually connected by economic, ideological, and political intercourse."[28] In Gumilyov's scheme, *superethnoi* could not come together to form even higher units. Rather, "a *superethnos* . . . opposes itself to all other *superethnoi*."[29] In Gumilyov's opinion, the peoples of the Soviet Union were such a *superethnos*, and they stood in opposition to the *superethnos* that was Europe. Consequently, in the 1980s when Soviet leader Mikhail Gorbachev sought to end the Cold War and proposed the idea of a "common European home," of which Russia would be an integral part, Gumilyov vehemently opposed it. He wrote:

> It would be a great error to think that the construction of a "common European home" will be the mutual victory of common human values. The entry into a foreign *superethnos* always involves a rejection of one's own ethnic *dominanty* [dominant ideals] in exchange for the system of the new *superethnos*. It is highly unlikely that this will be any different in our case. The price for joining civilization [i.e., the West] will be the domination of West European behavioral norms and psychology . . . [resulting in] the total rejection of our national traditions.[30]

The idea of the *superethnos* provided the basis on which Gumilyov constructed an updated version of Eurasianism, which he had become acquainted with during the 1950s (including meeting and corresponding with one of the leading interwar émigré Eurasianists, Pyotr Savitsky). Just as the Eurasianists viewed the peoples of the former Russian Empire as forming part of a natural, organic whole, Gumilyov claimed that ethnic Russians and the steppe peoples, such as the Mongols, Kazakhs, and Kyrgyz, were bound together through long-standing complementarities. To prove his point, Gumilyov set about rewriting Russian history. Especially controversial was his reinterpretation of the Battle of Kulikovo in 1380. At this battle, the forces of the grand prince of Moscow, Dmitry Donskoi, defeated the army of the Mongol commander Mamai. In the traditional telling of Russian history, this was a first step in liberating Russia from the Mongol yoke. Gumilyov described it very differently, as a battle pitting an alliance of Mamai and Western European Catholic powers against an alliance of Moscow and Mamai's chief Mongol rival, Tokhtamysh.[31] Seen this way, the Russians and the steppe peoples were actually allies at Kulikovo, not enemies. Gumilyov then extended the theory further, and painted the Mongols not as having conquered and oppressed the Russians, but rather as having played a positive role in Russian history, by supporting the Russian Orthodox Church, protecting Russia against Western aggression, and engaging in "intensive ethnic intermixing."[32] Thereafter, he claimed, Russia and the steppe peoples had created a common civilization.

Gumilyov's interpretation of history and of the nature of the Eurasian *supereth-nos* reflected his own personal admiration of the steppe peoples. He believed in the need to respect the culture of non-Russian nationalities within the Soviet Union, and opposed any efforts to prioritize the interests of ethnic Russians.[33] This put him at odds with Russian nationalists of the *Molodaia gvardiia* variety, some of whom denounced him as a "Tatar lover."[34] These two strands of conservative thought mirrored similar strands that had existed prior to the revolution: one that promoted the idea of "Russia for the Russians" and of national, distinctively Russian traditions; and another that stressed the importance of diversity, the incommensurability of different civilizations, and the multinational nature of the Russian Empire. Both of these strands continue to influence Russian conservatives to this day and to push them in different directions.

A third strand appeared in underground samizdat publications. This empha-sized Russian Orthodoxy. Particularly noteworthy was the samizdat journal *Veche*, which appeared between January 1971 and December 1973 and then was suppressed. *Veche's* editor, Vladimir Osipov, was influenced by the dissident Orthodox priest Dmitry Dudko (1922–2004), who called him his "spiritual son."[35] Father Dmitry combined Russian nationalism with fervent denunciations of declining morality in the Soviet Union, especially alcoholism.[36] *Veche* pursued similar themes. The introduction to its first edition proclaimed:

> Our moral state leaves much to be desired. We are witness to the following: an epi-demic of alcoholism; the breakup of the family; a striking growth in rudeness and vulgarity; the loss of an even elementary concept of beauty; uninhibited cursing, the symbol of the brotherhood and equality of the pigsty; envy and denunciation; a devil-may-care attitude toward work; stealing; the cult of bribery; double-dealing in social interaction. . . . We must revive and preserve our national culture, the moral and intellectual capital of our ancestors. We must continue along the path laid down by the Slavophiles and Dostoevsky.[37]

Veche reintroduced Soviet readers to the writings of the Slavophiles and of other Russian conservatives of the imperial era such as Dostoevsky, Leontyev, Danilevsky, and *Vekhi*. It also proclaimed the central importance of Orthodoxy to Russian national identity.[38] "Nationalism is inconceivable outside of Christianity," wrote Osipov and his fellow contributor V. S. Rodionov.[39] "Russia is saved by Orthodoxy," declared another *Veche* article, adding that "Orthodoxy is indestruc-tible. It is God's work, and Russia can only be Orthodox."[40]

Veche attacked cosmopolitanism as "spiritual slavery." In the journal's view, religion and national identity were mutually reinforcing. Just as nationalism depended upon Orthodoxy, so did Orthodoxy depend on nationalism. An article in the second edition declared that "religion must be preserved through national feelings, then it will be an organic phenomenon,"[41] while another article denounced "distrust and doubt relating to all spiritual and national values, cosmopolitanism, the spreading of debauchery and drunkenness, the extreme proliferation of abortions, forgetting and neglecting the fulfilment of family, parental and patriotic duty, hypocrisy, betrayal, falsehood, money-grubbing and other vices."[42]

Veche revealed the religious element slowly reemerging in Russian conservatism. As faith in communist ideology declined, Russians began to look elsewhere for moral inspiration, and some found it in Orthodoxy. In October 1974 one of Dmitry Dudko's disciples, Aleksandr Ogorodnikov, began a series of religious-philosophical seminars in Moscow. These continued until Ogorodnikov's arrest in 1979. Meanwhile, a similar seminar series began in Leningrad in 1975.[43]

The importance of religion could also be seen in Russia's first dissident feminist group, Mariia, which was named after the Virgin Mary. Communism had officially liberated women, who had become firmly integrated into the Soviet labor market. But while women had jobs, and therefore incomes of their own, they also continued to bear a disproportionate share of domestic chores, giving rise to what was called "the double burden." Soviet women's disillusionment with their lot resulted in the unofficial publication in Leningrad in 1979 of what is considered the first feminist journal in the Soviet Union, entitled *An Almanac: Women and Russia*.

The main contributors to the *Almanac* were Tatiana Goricheva, Nataliia Malakhovskaia, Tatiana Mamonova, and Iuliia Vosnesenskaia. The group soon split. Mamonova supported a form of feminism resembling that popular in the West. The others rejected this and formed Mariia in order to promote a more Russian kind of feminism founded on Christianity. Vosnesenskaia explained their attitude, writing: "Christianity attracts us primarily because of its moral principles. We are tired of hearing that the only good is what which serves the [Communist] Party. We long for eternal, absolute values—of justice, love, goodness."[44] The fact that the great majority of Orthodox parishioners were women was an additional attraction. As Goricheva put it, the church was "the only place where women can talk about all their problems. No men come."[45] Goricheva criticized Western feminists' "ideology of emancipation, condemning it for blurring the distinctions between the sexes."[46] She and other Mariia members "emphasized a woman's right to family life and stressed the responsibilities she has as wife and mother."[47] They condemned abortion and supported the institution of marriage, while also criticizing Soviet men for being inadequate husbands. As another Mariia member, Galina Khamova, wrote, Soviet women wanted to rid themselves of the double burden. Instead, "We want to be mothers, wives, housewives, women at last!"[48]

The writings of Mariia members won the approval of Russia's most famous conservative dissident, Aleksandr Solzhenitsyn, who shared the group's Christian

outlook. Like émigré writers such as Ilyin and Berdiaev, Solzhenitsyn saw Russia's
problems as being fundamentally spiritual in nature, and Russia as needing a spiritual rebirth, founded on Christianity.[49] In a 1974 letter to the Soviet leaders, he
declared, "I see Christianity as the only living force capable of undertaking Russia's
spiritual healing."[50] Empire, in the form of the Soviet Union and of the Soviet
Union's communist allies in Eastern Europe, stood in the way of this rebirth,
Solzhenitsyn believed. In 1974 he contributed to a volume entitled *From under
the Rubble*, which was deliberately modeled on, and designed to update, the 1909
collection *Vekhi*.[51] In it he wrote that the mark of a nation was its "inner development." This meant that "the Russian air, and Russian soil, can only be purified by
means of repentance." Russians would have to "acknowledge our *external* sins"
against other peoples.[52] He continued:

> Just as a family, in which there has been a great misfortune and shame, tries to isolate
> itself from everybody for a bit, and to work out its grief on its own, so too must the
> Russian people be alone with itself, without neighbors and guests; concentrating on
> its inner tasks: on healing its soul, educating its children, and sorting out its own
> house.[53]

In a 1990 essay entitled "How Can We Rebuild Russia?," written just before
the collapse of the Soviet Union, Solzhenitsyn described in concrete terms what
this meant. The Soviet Union consisted of fifteen national republics. Solzhenitsyn
argued that it would be best for twelve of them to secede from the union, leaving
just a Slavic core of Russia, Belarus, and Ukraine, plus perhaps the northern half of
Kazakhstan. Even Ukraine could secede, Solzhenitsyn added, although not all of it:
which parts left, and which stayed with Russia, should be decided on a local basis.
"We do not have the strength for an empire, we don't need it," Solzhenitsyn wrote.
"By separating twelve republics . . . Russia will liberate itself for a precious *inner*
development."[54] Solzhenitsyn's ideal was decidedly anti-imperial and involved a
much smaller Russia than had existed theretofore.

Solzhenitsyn's status as a prominent dissident made him something of a hero
in the West. In 1974, he was expelled from the Soviet Union, after which he went
to live in America. He was not enamored by what he saw there. The West, he felt,
had become overly materialistic, and consequently weak-willed. The late 1970s
were the period of détente, during which the West and the Soviet Union tried to
improve relations. In this context, Solzhenitsyn feared that the West lacked the
willpower to confront communism. In a 1978 speech at Harvard University he
lambasted the West, declaring, "A decline in courage may be the most striking
thing to an outside observer in the West today."[55] "The West finally asserted human

rights, even to excess, but consciousness of man's sense of responsibility to God and society has grown dimmer,"[56] he said, and added:

> If I was to be asked whether I would propose the contemporary West as a model for my own country, I would frankly have to answer: no, I could not recommend it as an ideal for our transformation. . . . The Western system, in its current, spiritually exhausted form is not tempting. . . . It is an undoubted fact that the human character has become weaker in the West and stronger in the East.[57]

The problems of the twentieth century were due to the fact that "men have forgotten God," Solzhenitsyn said in another lecture five years later, "the entire twentieth century is being drawn into a whirlpool of atheism and self-destruction." "The West is irreversibly slipping into the abyss," he concluded.[58]

It would nevertheless be wrong to view Solzhenitsyn as entirely anti-Western. As with so many Russians in the Slavophile tradition, his relationship with the West was far more complex—part admiration, and part dislike of the West's supposed degeneration. "I am not a critic of the West," Solzhenitsyn said, "I am a critic of Western weakness."[59]

In reality, in the 1980s it was the Soviet Union that was slipping into the abyss. As the situation within the country deteriorated, Russian conservatives for the most part reacted with alarm, particularly as separatist sentiments grew in the non-Russian republics and it looked more and more likely that the union would fall apart. Few shared Solzhenitsyn's belief that the dissolution of the union would be a good idea. However, conservatives' reactions to the problem were somewhat contradictory. Some, such as Patriarch Aleksei of the Orthodox Church, journalist Aleksandr Prokhanov, and writer Iury Bondarev, signed a letter in September 1990 to the newspaper *Sovetskaia Rossiia* (Soviet Russia) calling on Gorbachev to clamp down on separatism. But conservatives also promoted a sort of Russian separatism by demanding the creation of distinctly Russian institutions. Most notably, although there had always been national branches of the Communist Party in all fourteen of the non-Russian republics of the Soviet Union, there had never been an equivalent for the Russian republic (the Russian Soviet Federative Socialist Republic, RSFSR). In summer 1990, a Communist Party of the RSFSR came into being, dominated by conservative forces dedicated to maintaining the union.[60] Appalled by Gorbachev's plan for a "Union Treaty" that would have devolved substantial autonomy to the fifteen republics, in July 1991 Prokhanov, Bondarev, Rasputin, and other conservatives issued an appeal to the Soviet army to intervene to restore order.[61] The coup that followed a month later was a disastrous failure, and the Soviet Union fell apart soon afterward.

POLITICAL CONSERVATISM

Conservatives in the Brezhnev era focused on cultural issues for the simple reason that the Communist Party was willing to accept a certain amount of cultural
debate whereas challenges to the political system were forbidden. Russian conservatives of this period generally accepted Soviet rule. Russian author Aleksandr
Tsipko, who was acquainted with many of the Russian nationalists of the Brezhnev era, notes that the "Russian party," as he calls it, "not only didn't have any plans
to loosen or weaken the Soviet system, but on the contrary counted on preserving
the principles of the political system created by Stalin."[62] In this sense they were
Soviet rather than Russian conservatives.

At least until the final months of the Soviet Union, it was therefore left to dissidents to develop alternative political principles. While the conservative dissidents
rejected communism, they nonetheless were strongly influenced by Soviet norms.
In particular, they opposed liberal democracy, which was strongly associated with
the negative aspects of capitalism, and retained a belief in an autocratic system of
government.

Veche, for instance, supported liberal concepts such as freedom of speech, but
at the same time opposed democracy. Contributor Gennady Shimanov criticized
Solzhenitsyn for merely saying that Russia was not ready for democracy, rather
than rejecting democracy outright. According to Shimanov, democracy would
result in Russia becoming subordinated to Western capital, would stand in the way
of a religious revival, and would incite nationalism in the non-Russian regions of
the union.[63] Shimanov urged *Veche* readers to remain loyal to the Soviet state, but
at the same time he predicted that the Communist Party would in due course be
transformed into a "Orthodox Party of the Soviet Union," leading to a "Christian
transformation of Soviet power." This would inspire a spiritual rebirth of the
Russian people and thereafter a spiritual rebirth of the world as a whole.[64]

This messianic vision had much in common with émigré Eurasianism. Initially,
its appeal was very limited, but as the Soviet Union began to fall apart, various
Soviet politicians and thinkers turned to this view in a paradoxical effort to save
communism by combining it with Christianity. Two examples were Gennady
Ziuganov, who later became head of the post-Soviet Communist Party of the
Russian Federation, and who argued for an "evolutionary-organic path of development of Soviet society,"[65] and theater director Sergei Kurginian, who became
politically active in the Communist Party in the late 1980s and in 1990 co-pub-
lished an ideological pamphlet entitled *Post-Perestroika*. In this, Kurginian and
his fellow authors argued against the establishment of a liberal democracy and
free-market economy in Russia, saying that if this happened, "the country, having
set out on the path of imitation [of the West], will get not bureaucratic capitalism

(the lesser of two evils) but precisely the establishment of unlimited rule by the criminal bourgeoisie . . . the so-called statization of the mafia."[66] The authors of *Post-Perestroika* wrote that "we see communism precisely as a neo-Christian religion," and proposed transforming communism into a "red religion" governed by a technocratic elite who were to be the "knights and priests of the Red Faith."[67] This elite would govern by dictatorial means and pursue a policy of state-driven "forced modernization."[68]

A slightly different tack was taken by journalist Aleksandr Prokhanov, who in the late 1980s became one of the most prominent figures among Russian conservatives, a position that he has retained to this day. Prokhanov differed from Kurginian in that he rejected communism and the Russian Revolution. But however awful communist rule was, he feared that its collapse was paving the way for something even worse, namely the rule of the "criminal bourgeoisie."[69] Prokhanov blamed the growing impoverishment and political instability of the Soviet Union on "commercial people" who had taken control of the mass media and used it "to corrupt the people, to seduce it, to elicit its dark instincts and then exploit these instincts through pornography, sex, hallucinogenic programs, and narcotics." He urged those in authority to stop the rot before it was too late.[70] To this end, he proposed a new order based on three elements. The first would be the Communist Party of the RSFSR established in 1990, which he described as "a party of Russian people." The second he described as "everything which is connected with prerevolutionary ideology: national-Orthodoxy, and national-monarchism." And the third was the models of the prerevolutionary *zemstva* and communes.[71] The result was an eclectic mix of statism, communism, monarchism, Orthodoxy, and local self-government. This represented an attempt to fuse all the elements of Russia's past into one organic whole.

By the late Soviet period, the decades of communism had made it difficult for conservatives to determine exactly what was "organic" in Russia's case. One approach was that of Prokhanov and Kurginian: to take all of Russia's history, communist and pre-communist, and try to synthesize it. Another was to reject the entirety of communism as an alien ideology imposed upon Russia, and to view only that which came before communism as truly Russian. This was the direction taken by Aleksandr Solzhenitsyn.

In Solzhenitsyn's eyes, although the Soviet regime became less oppressive under Khrushchev and Brezhnev than it had been under Stalin, its basic nature remained unchanged. As he wrote in his study of the Soviet prison camps, *The Gulag Archipelago*:

> Rulers change, the Archipelago remains. It remains because *that particular* political regime could not survive without it. . . . The same treacherous secrecy, the same fog

of injustice, still hangs over our air, worse than the smoke of city chimneys. For half a century and more the enormous state has towered over us, girded by hoops of steel. The hoops are still there. There is no law.[72]

In *The Gulag Archipelago* Solzhenitsyn condemned not only the lawlessness but also the lack of freedom in the Soviet Union. Change would be impossible unless people could tell the truth, he argued. "The prolonged absence of any free exchange of information within a country opens up a gulf of incomprehension between whole groups of the population, between millions and millions," he wrote.[73] But while Solzhenitsyn valued external freedom, like many other Russian conservatives he considered inner freedom even more important. He therefore criticized the tendency of Russian intellectuals to view their country's salvation as lying in the external freedoms offered by Western-style democracy. He asked:

> Can external freedom by itself be the goal of consciously living human beings? Or is it only a mold for the accomplishment of other, higher tasks? We are born as beings with inner freedom, freedom of will, freedom of choice, the main part of freedom is given to us at birth. External freedom, social freedom, is very desirable for the sake of our undistorted development, but is no more than a condition, a medium, and to consider it the *object* of our existence is senseless. We can firmly assert our inner freedom even in an environment that is externally unfree.[74]

According to Solzhenitsyn, inner freedom was possible even in a prison camp. In the Soviet camps, he wrote:

> No one tries to persuade you to *apply* for Party membership. No one comes around to squeeze membership dues out of you in *voluntary* societies. There is no trade union. . . . You cannot be elected to any position. You cannot be appointed some kind of delegate. And the really important thing is that . . . they cannot compel you to be a propagandist. . . . And there is one more freedom. No one can deprive you of your family and property—you have already been deprived of them. What does not exist—not even God can take away. And this is a basic freedom.[75]

In line with this logic, inner freedom was quite possible under an authoritarian regime. Past authoritarian regimes had been limited, led by autocrats who "felt themselves responsible before God and their own consciences," Solzhenitsyn claimed. Therefore, he concluded, "perhaps we should recognize that the most natural, smoothest, and least painful path of evolutionary development for our country will be from one authoritarian form to another."[76] In his 1974 letter to the Soviet leaders, Solzhenitsyn noted that "everything depends upon what sort of authoritarian order awaits us in the future."[77] In his 1990 essay, "How Can We Rebuild Russia?," Solzhenitsyn wrote that "together with a strong central power, we must patiently and persistently expand the rights of *local* life."[78] Democracy was "very necessary," but had to be "built from the bottom up, gradually, patiently, and durably, not just loudly and impetuously proclaimed from above."[79] Political parties would be permitted, but elections would not be fought on "party tickets," "individuals, not parties, would stand for election."[80] The initial focus would be on building democracy at the local level where it could be "unmediated" by parties. Solzhenitsyn proposed direct elections to local *zemstva*, and then indirect elections to three higher levels of *zemstva* after that. A president would be elected directly from candidates nominated by the All-Union Zemstvo, and there would also be a consultative assembly modeled on the Zemsky sobor, to provide advice alongside the All-Union Zemstvo.[81]

This proposal bore a certain similarity to the ideas of prerevolutionary Russian conservatives such as Sergei Sharapov and Lev Tikhomirov. It was autocratic in nature, but not without liberal elements. Commentators have reacted differently to this combination of authoritarianism and liberalism. Some have emphasized the authoritarianism, calling Solzhenitsyn's support for democracy "limited and grudging" and saying that there was a "good reason to be apprehensive about the prospect of living in Solzhenitsyn's ideal Russia."[82] Others, though, have claimed that "Solzhenitsyn's political ideas are fundamentally misunderstood in the West . . . Solzhenitsyn . . . [was] an eloquent and principled defender of liberty and human dignity,"[83] and have declared that the description of Solzhenitsyn as "anti-democratic . . . reactionary, chauvinistic" is "false at every point."[84] The differing perspectives are rather similar to those about Ivan Ilyin—whom some view as a fascist, and others as a liberal. This is no coincidence. Both men, like others discussed in this book, belong to a Russian conservative tradition that believes firmly in the concept of inner freedom while supporting autocracy within strict limits.

SOCIAL-ECONOMIC CONSERVATISM

There were two main tendencies in late Soviet social-economic conservatism. Both were anti-capitalist, reflecting not only long-standing conservative preferences but also the influence of several decades of communism. They differed in their attitudes to economic growth and modernization, one favoring them, and the other being far more skeptical.

In the 1980s, Mikhail Gorbachev referred to the 1960s and 1970s as the "era of stagnation." This was not entirely fair. The Soviet economy grew substantially in this period, although the rate of growth declined as time went on. Where

Gorbachev's criticism had some validity was in the fact that the Soviet government failed to undertake substantial reform of the economic system as it began to slow down. There were various reasons for this. First, there were substantial risks in reforming a centrally planned economy by, for instance, relaxing central controls. The severe problems that the economy faced once Gorbachev began reform suggest that there were perhaps some good reasons for leaving things alone. Second, reform threatened the power of economic managers and Party officials, who therefore allied against it. And third, after several decades the Soviet economic model had become in effect part of the country's heritage. Anti-capitalism was well entrenched in the Soviet population. Nevertheless, it is worth noting that for all its conservatism in wishing to preserve the existing system, the Soviet state remained theoretically committed to rapid economic growth.

This was true also of many Soviet conservatives, who took pride in the Soviet Union's industrial achievements and wished to repeat the great leaps forward that the country was believed to have made under Stalin. Kurginian and the other authors of *Post-Perestroika* argued for what they called "forced modernization," writing that the aim was "to overcome in the shortest possible historical term the lagging behind of the productive forces of our society from those of the most developed states of the East and the West."[85]

At the same time, many conservatives wished to isolate Russia from what they saw as the negative influences of the world economy. Prokhanov, for instance, warned against the "world economic system" and "world money."[86] In this way, anti-capitalism morphed into anti-globalization.

Not all conservatives shared the fascination with rapid economic transformation. For the village prose authors, such transformation threatened Russia's physical and cultural heritage. It also threatened the natural environment. This last concern led conservatives to take the lead in promoting Soviet environmentalism. Perhaps the most prominent person in this regard was Valentin Rasputin, who devoted years of his life to protecting Lake Baikal in Siberia from industrial development and pollution. Baikal, he wrote, "was created as the crowning glory and mystery of nature not for industrial requirements but so that we might drink from it to our heart's content. . . . It has never refused to help human beings, but only so long as its waters remained pure, its beauty unsullied, its air unpolluted, and the life in and around it unspoiled."[87] In general, wrote Rasputin:

> Rational utilization, comprehensive development, responsible treatment of Siberia's treasures small and large—now is the time for these principles of theoretical economics to finally become the law of life and action. *Sturm und Drang* in Siberia's development is no longer acceptable. . . . Its properties of self-preservation . . . these intrinsic recuperative powers at the sites of massive industrial intervention are no

longer coping with the heavy tread of humanity. . . . Siberia is large, but we cannot allow a single meter of ground to be treated carelessly, and we cannot permit another tree in its forests to be felled without urgent need. . . . We will deserve credit if we preserve nature's primordial grandeur side by side with the grandeur of our own deeds.[88]

Lev Gumilyov was similarly interested in environmental matters. "Scarcely a single person can be found in our time who would prefer to see piles of waste and concreted squares in place of forests and steppes," he wrote.[89] Various samizdat authors also endorsed environmentalism, and took it one step further, challenging the very idea of endless economic growth. For instance, in the collection *Under the Rubble*, Mikhail Agursky argued that, "if the growth in consumption doesn't stop, mankind will soon run up against a critical shortage of resources."[90] Agursky said further that "the aim of the future should not be the growth of productivity, not continual growth of production and consumption, but maintaining an optimal level of productivity, production, and consumption, based on the limitations imposed by the interests of society and the real resources."[91] Writing in the same book, Solzhenitsyn proposed that mankind should turn "from *outward* to *inward* development." This meant "a complete restructuring of all our ideas and goals: moving from uninterrupted progress to a stable economy with no growth in terms of territory, parameters, and tempo."[92] Solzhenitsyn repeated this in his 1974 letter to the Soviet leaders, demanding "a stable economy" instead of an ever-growing one. "*Economic growth is not only unnecessary but ruinous*," he said.[93] Solzhenitsyn's attitude to the economy was, therefore, very different from that of conservative modernizers such as Prokhanov and Kurginian.

CONCLUSION

Russian conservatives in the Brezhnev and Gorbachev eras bore the imprint of the Soviet experience. It drove them to accentuate certain aspects of conservative thought that had, however, been present even before the revolution, such as anti-Westernism, anti-capitalism, and suspicion of liberal democracy. Some conservatives rejected communism entirely. Others accepted Soviet rule, but sought cultural and social change. Regardless, they repudiated Western models, and stressed that all countries, including Russia, should follow their own path of development. While they differed on exactly what that path should be for Russia, they agreed that it should be distinctively Russian.

Russians began to show increasing concern for their national heritage, embodied not only in arts and architecture but also in the Orthodox religion. Intellectuals began to reconnect with the conservative thinkers of the prerevolutionary past, and at the same time the ideas of the Russian emigration, in particular Eurasianism, seeped slowly into the Soviet Union. Conservative concerns about pollution and resource depletion also contributed to the development of an environmental movement. All of this led conservatism to become a movement with broad appeal. Samizdat, Dmitry Dudko's sermons, Ilya Glazunov's paintings, the articles in *Molodaia gvardiia*, Aleksandr Prokhanov's journalism, and so on, all attracted large audiences. After several decades of Soviet rule, communist ideology had largely lost its ability to mobilize the Russian public. The "official" conservatism of communist leaders in the Brezhnev period also held little appeal. A new form of unofficial Russian conservatism stepped into the void. Little by little, it challenged the existing system. Russian conservatism thereby had a profound effect on the final years of the Soviet Union.

POST-SOVIET RUSSIA

At the time of writing, in May 2018, Vladimir Putin is just beginning his fourth term as Russian president. His previous presidential term (2012–18) was marked by what has been called a "conservative turn" in Russian politics and society. This was associated with a revival of the Russian Orthodox Church, centralization of political authority, growing Russian nationalism, increased tensions between Russia and the Western world, and socially conservative legislation. These phenomena have made Russian conservatism a matter of considerable contemporary importance.

The conservative turn in Russian politics and society did not happen overnight, but was the product of twenty years of experience following the formal end of the Soviet Union on December 25, 1991. On that date, the Soviet Union's territory split into fifteen independent national republics, the largest of which was the Russian Federation. Under Boris Yeltsin, the Russian Federation embarked on a series of rapid economic and political reforms, known as "shock therapy." The socialist system of economics was dismantled: controls on prices were removed; private enterprise was legalized; and state-owned industries were sold off, often at rock-bottom prices. The result was a cataclysmic economic collapse, with hyperinflation, a massive decline in production and incomes, and disintegration of social services such as health care. Accompanying this were widespread criminality, a huge increase in alcohol and drug abuse, sharply declining life expectancy, a rapid fall in the number of births, and a consequent demographic crisis as deaths far exceeded births. There were some positive developments in the years that followed the end of the Soviet Union—the institutional bases for a free-market order were gradually established, for instance—but for most Russians these were overshadowed by the chaos.

Politically, Russia became much freer than it had been under the communists. But the federation was far from stable. From 1992 to 1993, power was shared between President Yeltsin and the Supreme Soviet, a legislative body left over from Soviet times. The Supreme Soviet wished to slow down the pace of reform. This led to a violent confrontation in 1993 when Yeltsin ordered the Soviet's dissolution and sent tanks to blast it into submission, shelling the parliament building until the deputies surrendered. Yeltsin then introduced a new constitution that replaced the Supreme Soviet with a new parliament known as the State Duma while simultaneously centralizing power in the hands of the president.

For many Russians, the Yeltsin years were a humiliating period of extreme poverty, state weakness, and rampant corruption. Since Yeltsin claimed to be building a liberal democratic order modeled on that of Western states, both liberalism and democracy were badly tainted in Russian eyes by the end of the 1990s. Many Russians now hoped to restore a strong central state authority, able to bring order and curb criminality. At the same time, social problems such as the growing demographic crisis made a return to "family values" increasingly attractive. In 1992, many Russians had viewed the West as the model to emulate: the West was rich and free, so if Russia would just adopt Western institutions, it would surely become rich and free too. The negative consequences of Yeltsin's reforms undermined this narrative. The idea that Russia should not blindly copy the West but should find native solutions to its problems acquired more and more support.

In the early 1990s, desperate for financial assistance, Yeltsin had followed a decidedly pro-Western line in his foreign policy. By the mid-1990s, the Russian government was beginning to chafe at having to subordinate its interests to those of foreign powers, and it gradually became more assertive. When the North Atlantic Treaty Organization (NATO) waged war against Yugoslavia in 1999, Russian attitudes toward the West shifted in an even more negative direction.

In 2000, Vladimir Putin succeeded Boris Yeltsin as president of the Russian Federation. This coincided with a turnaround in Russia's economic fortunes. For the next eight years the country enjoyed rapid growth. At the same time, Putin took a number of steps to restore the authority of the Russian state: he curbed the powers of regional governments; retook control of some of the most important oil and gas companies, providing the state with much needed revenue; and reined in the power of the so-called "oligarchs," who had amassed huge fortunes in the previous decade. The last step involved removing key elements of the mass media from the oligarchs' control and bringing them back under the control of the state. In the eyes of critics, these measures constituted a restoration of authoritarian government in Russia and the end of the liberal democratic system supposedly established under Yeltsin.

In the first two decades of the twenty-first century, actions by Western powers, including the Anglo-American invasion of Iraq in 2003, NATO's expansion into Eastern Europe, NATO's bombing campaign against Libya in 2011, and Western support for the 2014 revolution in Ukraine, cemented the idea that the West was bent on an aggressive foreign policy that was destabilizing the world and was innately hostile to Russia. Tensions between Russia and the West rose until by 2014 relations had become extremely sour. The Russian annexation of Crimea in 2014 and the war that broke out shortly afterward in Ukraine made matters even worse. The deteriorating international situation contributed to an increase in Russian nationalism and anti-Western sentiment.

All told, these developments have facilitated a rise in conservatism. Underlying this is a feeling of considerable dissatisfaction with the order established in Russia following the collapse of the Soviet Union as well as with the international system that came into existence at the end of the Cold War. In some cases, this dissatisfaction takes the form of a sense of "approaching catastrophe,"[1] both domestic and international. Demographic decline, mass immigration from Central Asian countries, and the pervasive influence of Western culture and economic power are seen as evidence that Russia's future existence is under threat. In 2015 the Russian Ministry of Culture warned of "the lowering of society's intellectual and cultural level; the devaluation of generally accepted values . . . ; the growth of aggression and intolerance . . . ; the deformation of historical memory . . . ; the atomization of society, the disruption of social ties (friends, family, neighbors), the growth of individualism, disregard of the rights of others."[2] Concerns about such social problems lead Russian conservatives to complain that "Russian society more and more resembles a broken mirror that needs to be put back together,"[3] and that their "society is disintegrating and has been disintegrating for such a long time and so steadily that one can no longer consider this a temporary 'transitional' phenomenon."[4]

Boris Mezhuev, formerly deputy editor of the newspaper *Izvestiia* and manager of the conservative website Russian Idea, notes that these processes have led to the emergence of two types of conservatism in modern Russia. The first wishes to conserve and strengthen the system created after the collapse of communism. Somewhat critically, Mezhuev comments that the preferences of this type of conservative include:

> preserving the state's functions in the economy, strengthening the market system, preserving budget expenditures, and preserving a high level of social inequality and high flow of migration. They [these conservatives] subscribe to the global economy, the international division of labor, and consider that they are willing to sacrifice some components of national sovereignty in order to stay in this system.[5]

The second type of conservative, says Mezhuev, is "against the status quo, and appeals to national traditions, national values, and recognizes the supreme value of state sovereignty."[6] This second type of conservatism is on the whole an oppositional phenomenon, and expresses the feeling of dissatisfaction mentioned above. Conservatives of this sort share their nineteenth- and early twentieth-century counterparts' suspicion of the state bureaucracy, regularly denouncing the ruling elite for its "moral irresponsibility," and calling it "criminal and corrupt."[7] Pro-Western, anti-Russian forces are suspected of controlling "the corporations, companies, trade networks, and banks. . . . They work in all the structures [of government], even in the army, even in the security services . . . and they are not like us."[8] While they do not seek to overthrow the state, conservatives of this sort seek fundamental changes in its policies.

The first type of conservatism bears a certain similarity to the official state conservatism of previous generations, in that its primary concern is conserving and strengthening the existing political and economic system. Given that the Russian economy is, albeit very imperfectly, market-oriented and integrated into the world economy via institutions such as the World Trade Organization, this form of official conservatism overlaps to some degree with a modern-day version of nineteenth-century liberal conservatism. It seeks a strong state as the protector and enactor of liberal reforms (often interpreted in economic terms). It also assigns a high value to stability in both domestic and international affairs and prefers good relations with the West, although its concern for state sovereignty means that it will not avoid confrontation with the West if important interests are at stake. This type of conservatism generally eschews the more exaggerated claims of Russia's cultural distinctiveness, but does see value in national traditions as a source of social stability and political legitimacy.

The second type of conservatism divides into two main subtypes. The first consists of what have been called the "conservative democrats."[9] Notable figures include Boris Mezhuev and Mikhail Remizov, president of a think tank entitled the Institute of National Strategy. The conservative democrats regard modern liberalism as authoritarian in nature, and contend that democracy is dependent upon conservatism, in other words upon a respect for national traditions and national sovereignty. They also tend toward Russian nationalism of the "Russia for the Russians" variety, and so toward a relatively isolationist view of foreign and economic policy. They are somewhat anti-American and hostile to globalization, but also anti-imperialist and opposed to the idea that Russia has some sort of universal mission.

The second subtype is what one might call the "radical" conservatives. They were at one point concentrated in the Institute of Dynamic Conservatism, which in 2005 issued a thousand-page conservative manifesto entitled the *Russian Doctrine*. In 2012, the Institute of Dynamic Conservatism merged with various other groups to form the Izborsky Club, headed by Aleksandr Prokhanov. The

Izborsky Club's relationship with the government has been described as one of "latent tension."[10] Working together under the umbrella of the Izborsky Club, the radical conservatives include an eclectic mix of Orthodox conservatives, "left conservatives," and Eurasianists. Noteworthy figures include Aleksandr Dugin, Nataliia Narochnitskaia, and Sergei Glazyev.

Orthodox conservatives tend to focus on opposing what they see as morally dangerous ideas coming from the liberal West, such as same-sex marriage. Orthodox conservatism rejects Russia's communist heritage, and politically can have a monarchist tinge. This separates it from is what is often called left conservatism, with which it otherwise has much in common. In particular, both groups share a belief that the economic system should be oriented more toward social justice. Left conservatives take some pride in Soviet achievements, and try to bring together elements of socialism, Orthodoxy, and Russian nationalism. They share the Orthodox dislike of Western liberalism, and are strongly opposed to globalization. This leads them to emphasize Russia's distinctiveness from the West. This last idea finds strong expression in the works of Eurasianist conservatives, who in many cases see Russia as locked into inevitable conflict with the West. Eurasianism often (although not always) goes hand in hand with an imperialistic and messianic worldview.

What all these groups have in common is support for a strong centralized state and belief in the need for Russia to protect its sovereignty and develop in an organic fashion, befitting its national traditions. Despite all the differences, as in previous eras, Orthodoxy, a belief in a strong central authority, and variations of nationalism remain at the core of Russian conservatism.

Cultural Conservatism

Perhaps the main force driving contemporary Russian cultural conservatism is a fear that "if nothing is done, the R[ussian] F[ederation] will disappear off the map of the world."[11] Beset by a combination of Russia's own internal problems and the pressures of globalization, Russian conservatives seek a way of ensuring the continued existence of their national culture and identity.

Two difficulties conservatives face are determining the nature of that identity, and deciding whether it includes both the Soviet and the imperial heritage. Liberal conservatives and some monarchists reject the Soviet Union in its entirety, saying that "there can be no spiritual rebirth of Russia, resting on its sacred heritage, without a consistent decommunization."[12] Left conservatives often have a far more positive view of the Soviet era. Among the Soviet nostalgists is Aleksandr Prokhanov, who writes:

Our people haven't forgotten the grandiose Soviet experiment. The opening up of the Virgin Lands. The creation of an "oil civilization." The space race. Rivalry with the USA. The dash into the future. . . . Stalin . . . created scientists of genius, incomparable pilots, tireless builders, inspired artists . . . united the people around a "common cause" . . . created a brilliant elite of Stakhanovites, marshals, cosmonauts. He built an unprecedented state of labor and creativity.[13]

The Orthodox Church unequivocally describes the Soviet era as "seventy years of Satanic theomachism."[14] In between the church and the Soviet nostalgists lies what is probably the majority view. This rejects communism but takes some pride in what are seen as its positive accomplishments, such as victory in the Second World War and putting the first man and first woman in space. In general, just as the nineteenth-century *pochvenniki* tried to reconcile the periods before and after Peter the Great, most conservatives seek what Foreign Minister Sergei Lavrov calls "a synthesis of all the positive traditions and historical experience"[15] of the imperial and Soviet eras, taking what they consider good from both periods while rejecting the rest. According to Prokhanov, Russians need to create a "metahistory," synthesizing all the parts of Russian history, in a way that will "unite severed Russian history into one continuous stream."[16] As he says:

Metahistory is the mother's womb from which in turn came Kievan Rus', Muscovy, the Petersburg empire, the Soviet red state. . . . All these periods are her children. We, living at an epochal turning point, do not prefer any one of these already vanished periods, but feel toward our Motherland's history a filial feeling, a holy gratitude.[17]

Similarly, the Institute of Dynamic Conservatism's manifesto, the *Russian Doctrine*, argues: "Until we outline a single scheme of our history from A to Z, it will be simply impossible to carry out the Russian national project in any decent form."[18]

Another problem facing conservatives is defining who qualifies as Russian. The collapse of the Soviet Union left millions of ethnic Russians outside the Russian Federation in countries such as Ukraine, Kazakhstan, Latvia, and Estonia. At the same time, it left large numbers of non-ethnic Russians within the Russian Federation, and these numbers have become even larger due to a relatively open immigration policy designed to attract workers from former Soviet states, particularly those of Central Asia. An idea of Russia based upon ethnic identity would include parts of other countries within the so-called "Russian World," but exclude many Russian citizens. An idea of Russia based purely upon citizenship would include many non-Russians but exclude Russians abroad.

Despite occasional nods in the direction of the "Russian World," the Russian state has to date preferred the second option. Vladimir Putin, for instance, has regularly stressed the multiethnic identity of the Russian Federation, and made it clear that "we will not support any Russian nationalism, nor do we intend to resurrect the empire."[19] On another occasion, he remarked:

> It is precisely the state-civilization model that has shaped our state polity. It has always sought to flexibly accommodate the ethnic and religious specificity of particular territories, ensuring diversity in unity. Christianity, Islam, Buddhism, Judaism and other religions are an integral part of Russia's identity, its historical heritage and the present-day lives of its citizens. The main task of the state, as enshrined in the Constitution, is to ensure equal rights for members of traditional religions and atheists, and the right to freedom of conscience for all citizens.[20]

The stress on the state as the basis of Russian nationality is in line with the practice of past Russian rulers such as Nicholas I, Alexander II, and the Soviets. In this sense, it is the traditional view of Russia's rulers. It is also far from popular with conservative Russian nationalists, who fear that it undermines Russian national identity and will lead to ethnic Russians becoming lost in a sea of Muslim immigrants from Central Asia.

One notable nationalist critic of state policy is the Institute of National Strategy's Mikhail Remizov, who complains that Russia is suffering from "reverse colonization" by peoples from the periphery of the former Soviet Union.[21] Mass immigration from Central Asia into Russia is a "project of the Russian elites," who want cheap labor, says Remizov. It constitutes "a model for the gradual changing of the R[ussian] F[ederation]'s ethnic composition."[22] Immigration rarely works well when the immigrants come from a very different culture, he argues; while there are success stories, such as the USA and Canada, the European example is very unsuccessful and has led to "multiple social problems."[23] These include the costs of providing welfare to immigrants, organized crime, disease, a failure by immigrants to assimilate, and the creation of ethnic ghettoes.[24] Instead of relying on Central Asian immigrants to solve Russia's demographic problems, Remizov urges the government to encourage Russians living in other states of the former Soviet Union to move to the Russian Federation, for instance by making it easier for them to get citizenship.[25] Instead of an expansionist, imperial nationalism, this amounts to a gathering in of the Russian people, drawing them back into the Russian "island."

Remizov rejects the idea that Russia has a universal mission. "One can say that this country gave the best years of its life to 'mankind' (i.e., the realization of a definite conception of the global community), and not to itself. This must never happen again," he writes.[26] Instead of trying to save the world, Russia should focus on the internal task of creating a genuine nation-state. Remizov strongly criticizes the Russian government's efforts to promote a civic rather than a Russian nationalism. This policy, he says, does not allow Russians "to realize ourselves as a nation."[27] Remizov complains also that official government documents contain "no objective connected with the national development of the Russian people, the preservation of the ethnic balance and the preservation of Russia as a country in which Russian culture has a predominant influence. . . . The state considers the Russian nation as just one of the 180 ethnic groups of the country."[28] Yet Russians constitute 85 percent of the population of the Russian Federation. The state's policy is undemocratic, Remizov believes. This means that "after centuries of national history we as a people don't have a state about which we can say, 'the state is us.'"[29]

Underlying this attitude is a deep suspicion of the country's rulers, who are seen as willing to betray Russia's national interests in their desire for access to cheap labor and offshore accounts. They are felt to lack "national *loyalty*." According to Remizov, Russian nationalism provides the solution to this problem, as it can integrate the elites with society through a sense of belonging to the same community and having shared historical traditions.[30] Remizov argues that "in the modern era, the national and democratic principles of the foundation of government go hand in hand. . . . at the local level you can have self-government without a nation, but not at the larger level. Thus the principle of a multinational state that we inherited from the USSR is a barrier to democratization."[31] By adopting nationalist policies Russia can at last build a democratic order, he claims.

Remizov states that Russia should consider the "inherited Christian identity of the European peoples as the foundation of a culture of human rights."[32] For him and others, Russian Orthodoxy has once again become a central element of Russian conservatism. Orthodoxy's recovery from the repression it suffered under communism has been quite remarkable. Between 1992 and 2016 the number of parishes in the Russian Orthodox Church increased from 7,000 to 33,000, and the number of monasteries from fewer than 30 to over 800. Between 70 and 80 percent of Russians now identify themselves as Orthodox.[33] This does not mean that most Russians actually go to church on a regular basis; perhaps only 5 percent do so. Orthodoxy is rather a mark of national identity.[34] Nonetheless, this is a significant development: for a majority of Russians, being Russian now means being Orthodox.

The church is seeking to gradually change the culture of Russian society so that religion becomes something more than just identity and Russians develop a spiritual as well as a material worldview. Its strategy has been to build churches, surround Russians with Orthodox symbols, and popularize rituals such as swims in icy rivers on the day of Epiphany. The idea is that Orthodox customs will become part of everyday life, and this will eventually encourage Russians to learn more about the religion's teachings. The church has also done much to advance

Christian culture through education, establishing what has been called a substantial "infrastructure of schools, universities, seminaries, publishing houses, and mass media."[35] Notably, after a long struggle, it eventually persuaded the Russian government to introduce religious education in state schools, although the government resisted making studies in Orthodoxy compulsory: instead, pupils are given a choice of doing one of six courses and studying the foundations of Orthodoxy, Judaism, Islam, Buddhism, world religions, or secular ethics. The last of these has proven to be the most popular.[36]

Where Orthodoxy has probably had the most impact is in the sphere of what are often called "traditional" or "family" values, as seen by demands for "the immediate adoption of norms defending society from the spread of pornography, obscenity, the destruction of traditional religiosity, traditional norms of morals."[37] For some conservatives, such issues are *the* point of division between Russian and Western civilization.[38] Vladimir Putin put it the following way:

> We see that many Euro-Atlantic countries have to all intents and purposes rejected their roots, including Christian values that constitute the foundation of Western civilization. They reject moral principles and any traditional identity: national, cultural, religious, and even sexual. They pursue a policy that places a family with many children on the same level as a single-sex partnership, a belief in God on the same level as belief in Satan. . . . And they are aggressively trying to impose this model on everybody, on the entire world. . . . Without the values embedded in Christianity and other world religions, with the moral norms formed over thousands of years, people naturally lose their human dignity. And we consider it natural and right to defend these values.[39]

Many conservatives link Russia's demographic difficulties to abortion as well as to the decline of the traditional family. For instance, Elena Mizulina, head of the Duma committee on women, children, and families, argues that Russia must "tighten up certain moral values. . . . This is vital for the birth rate to rise."[40] The *Russian Doctrine* proposes banning abortion, claiming that

> from the 1960s onwards, of every three to four Russians who were conceived only one was born, and two to three were aborted. An evaluation shows that 2.5 million more Russians were lost from abortions in the second half of the twentieth century than from the German [First World] War, the Civil War, the anti-kulak campaign of the 1930s and the Great Patriotic [Second World] War put together.[41]

The Russian Orthodox Church opposes abortion, as well as surrogate motherhood and fertility treatment involving the "conservation and purposeful destruction of 'spare' embryos."[42] In 2011, Patriarch Kirill suggested that provisions for abortion in health insurance schemes be removed, and proposed a compulsory two-week waiting period for any woman requesting an abortion.[43] And in July 2016 the Russian Orthodox Church signed an agreement with the Russian Ministry of Health to create "crisis pregnancy centers" in hospitals, at which psychologists and representatives of the church would advise women considering having abortions.[44]

Even more than abortion, it is the issue of gay rights that has really mobilized contemporary Russian conservatives. The church's view is that homosexuality is a sin,[45] but that it is not necessarily the job of the state to prohibit sin. Without therefore calling for the legal prohibition of homosexuality, the church has opposed gay pride parades and supported a 2013 law prohibiting what was termed "propaganda of non-traditional sexual relations to minors."[46] Western pressure on Russia to enhance gay rights has led to a strong backlash among Russian conservatives, who are especially opposed to the idea of same-sex marriage. Egor Kholmogorov, who appears regularly on the conservative Orthodox television station Tsargrad, says that "America is being turned in front of our eyes into an aggressive LGBT caliphate, in no fundamental way different from the Islamic caliphate."[47] According to Kholmogorov,

> Gay marriage is not simply the establishment of equal rights for gays, but the destruction of the institution of the family as such, because at the basis of marriage is a fundamental law of life and not sexual preference. . . . The family is a naturally arising social union on the basis of the marriage of a man and a woman, intended for the reproduction of human life, the birth and raising of children.[48]

Similar sentiments are common among Russian conservatives, many of whom see demands for equal rights for gay people as a sign of Western cultural imperialism.

To fight this cultural imperialism, the Russian Orthodox Church has actively promoted Russian nationalism. In a recent study of the church, American theologian John Burgess notes that the it "has offered Russians . . . a compelling narrative of national greatness and uniqueness. . . . It has told Russians that their worldview is fundamentally different from the West's."[49] At the same time, Orthodoxy, due to its claims to universality, gives Russia a national mission, and thus a messianic purpose. As Burgess notes,

> [The church] has come to the following conclusion: because Russia, often in spite of itself, has preserved Orthodoxy through the ages, the nation and its Church now have a special responsibility to demonstrate what is good and true not only

for Russians but also humanity as a whole. Russia's greatness lies in preserving this vision of heaven on earth and offering it to the world.[50]

Orthodoxy today, as in the past, attempts to reconcile the universal and the particular. The church itself states in one of its key documents, *Foundations of the Russian Orthodox Church's Conception of Society*, that "the universal nature of the Church does not mean that Christians should have no right to national identity and national self-expression. On the contrary, the Church unites in herself the universal with the national."[51]

The idea that Russia has a global mission finds expression in the concept of *katechon*, which has acquired some popularity in radical conservative circles.[52] Originally a biblical term, the *katechon* is that which holds back the Antichrist and protects the world from the forces of evil. Egor Kholmogorov describes it as follows:

> This is how the Byzantine idea of *Katechon* is refracted in our imperial conscious-ness, the idea of withholding the world. That which stands on the bridge between the Antichrist and the world and which does not let the Antichrist into the world. Now it is not a bridge but rather a manhole, the lid of which is removed from time to time, and some vampires or werewolves or murderers come out of this hole. The Russian tarpaulin [army] boot stamps on that lid, and restores the silence for some time.[53]

Russia saved Europe from the forces of Satan during the Second World War, the theory goes; now its task is to save Europe in a cultural sense, from the forces of globalism, liberalism, and postmodernism. In effect, Russia is Europe's *kate-chon*. As the *Russian Doctrine* puts it:

> The defense of civilization from barbarism, its assimilation, this is the first func-tion of the *katechon*. . . . The *katechon* as an Orthodox kingdom defends Christians against forces hostile to the salvation of the soul. . . . It is clear that the crisis of the Western project inevitably gives rise to the question of a new world leader. The inte-grationist potential of Russian civilization, which Dostoevsky spoke about in his speech on Pushkin, is once again demanded by history.[54]

Connected to this idea is another: that Russia, and the Russian Orthodox Church in particular, will lead an international movement dedicated to the defense of traditional values. Russian conservatives are often seen as anti-Western. This is true to the extent that they regard Western liberalism as inimical to Russia, and also often see the West as bent on confrontation with Russia. But the principle of *katechon* actually defines Russia's mission in terms of defending the West. There is general agreement among Russian conservatives that Russia is under attack from a culture emanating from the West. However, many of them see the West as also being a victim of this attack and consider that they have a common cause with Westerners who are resisting the cultural assault. Mikhail Remizov, for instance, says that he is for the West as it was until its original values were undermined by postmodernist philosophy. He claims, therefore, that he is anti-postmodern, not anti-Western.[55] Russian conservatives are defending true European values on which Europeans are turning their backs. Russia and Europe are "in the same boat," fighting a common cultural enemy.[56] One-time Duma deputy and current Izborsky Club member Nataliia Narochnitskaia similarly remarks that "the main dilemma is 'conservative Europe versus postmodern Europe,' and Russia is on the side of conservative Europe."[57] "Russia's future is Europe's future," Narochnitskaia asserts.[58]

For conservatives such as Remizov and Narochnitskaia, Russian civilization is historically tied to that of Europe through a common Christian heritage, even if Europe in the postmodern era has begun to move in a different direction.[59] Eurasianist thinkers, most notably Aleksandr Panarin (1940–2003) and Aleksandr Dugin, hold a different view. A central element of contemporary Eurasianism is the concept that the world is divided up into distinct civilizations. According to this train of thought, Russia is a separate civilization from Europe. At the same time, Eurasianists support the claim that Russia has a universal mission, and have attempted to overcome the resulting tension between the particular and the universal in much the same way as many nineteenth-century Russian conservatives did, by identifying the universal good with cultural diversity.

A professor at Moscow State University, Panarin initially supported Gorbachev's perestroika and the introduction of a liberal democratic order in Russia, but by the mid-1990s he had become thoroughly disenchanted with the results and thereafter sought alternatives.[60] Panarin asked:

> Is it possible . . . for humanity as a whole to advance into the future not on the basis of cultural disarmament and depersonalization, but preserving mankind's cultural-civilizational diversity? We can answer this question positively if we can find a civilization that has no pretensions to solve problems separately. . . . Doesn't Russian civilization meet this criterion? Being distinct from the West, and being aware of its distinctiveness . . . it has nevertheless never revealed any tendency to separate arrangements, let alone to discard its responsibility for the fate of the world.[61]

To Panarin, Western civilization was universalistic and wished to spread throughout the world, turning everybody into a copy of the West, whereas Russian civilization was built upon recognition of the value of diversity and was content to let others be. Russia, then, could help create a world civilization based upon "poly-culturalism."[62] Panarin stressed the need for Russia to preserve its distinctiveness from the West, which meant also preserving its own internal diversity.[63] At the same time, he declared Orthodoxy a "universal project," writing that

> by Orthodox civilization we do not mean a specific cultural and historical entity juxtaposed to other such entities and doomed to clash with them because of its specificity. . . . When we speak about the Orthodox civilization we mean a historical project whose mission is . . . to prepare for the complete replacement of contemporary parasitical civilization.[64]

Panarin drew inspiration from the European "New Right," notably French philosopher Alain de Benoist.[65] The New Right originally emerged in France in the late 1960s and argued in favor of the "right to difference" of local cultures, and against the homogenizing forces of modernity and globalization. Benoist, for instance, wrote in 1986 that "on the international level the major contradiction is no longer between right and left, liberalism and socialism, fascism and communism, 'totalitarianism' and 'democracy,' it is between those who want the world to be one dimensional and those who support a plural world grounded in the diversity of cultures."[66]

The New Right also influenced Aleksandr Dugin,[67] who outside of Russia is probably the best known Russian conservative thinker. In the 1990s, Dugin played a prominent role in the short-lived National Bolshevik Party, in which he sought to merge elements of socialism with nationalism and Orthodoxy in a manner reminiscent of the émigré Smena vekh movement. Dugin's intellectual inspirations are eclectic, and include the writings of European, Persian, and Indian philosophers.[68] "In Russia," says Dugin, "there are elements of Iranian culture, and Indian, although to a lesser degree, and also Mongolian and Turkish, which have brought colossal positive benefits into our history."[69] Because of this, he views Russia as a multiethnic, Eurasian civilization, and opposes racial or narrowly ethnic definitions,[70] declaring that "civilizations are cultural and religious communities, not ethnic-national ones."[71] He regards Western, especially American, culture as innately racist, because it asserts that it represents universal truth. As he says,

> The Westerner never allows himself to think that he might be fundamentally wrong, and that, for instance, the African, the Russian, the Muslim, the Japanese, the Chinese, or the communist might be cleverer or more right than he. So where are we? We are in a racist model, which is becoming more and more intolerant.[72]

Dugin is extremely critical of modern Western society, and has written that "the entirety of Russian history is a dialectical argument with the West and against Western culture, the struggle for upholding our own (often only intuitively grasped) *Russian* truth."[73] But he also says:

> I am not anti-Western. I am anti-liberal. In fact, I love the West. . . . Until a certain moment when this liberal, globalist ideology triumphed, the West was a jewel. The West produced daring thought, beautiful thought, sunny thought. It had everything. Until the 1980s. What happened in the West in the 80s affected universities, art, mass media, all of society. I consider that contemporary Europe is an anti-Europe. I simply cannot accept the West in its current condition, at the end of modernity. . . . The West is my spiritual, intellectual motherland. That's not to mention Western European culture, which I admire. . . . I'm not some evil Russian peasant who hates the West. I know European languages quite well. I know the West, I live my life through it. One can even say that I love the West. But I am deeply offended by its current condition, because it's sincere pain for a close friend. It's a systemic pain. Not accidentally, something malfunctioned, something went wrong. And I am trying to understand what it was.[74]

Dugin distinguishes between "the West as America" and "the West as Europe." It is the former (in the form of "Atlanticism") that Russia must oppose; the latter could be an ally.[75] For Dugin, the Anglo-Saxon-dominated Atlantic world is a great danger, as it is the source of globalizing trends that threaten to homogenize the planet. He complains that "spiritually, globalization is the creation of a grand parody, the kingdom of the Antichrist. . . . American values pretend to be 'universal' ones. In reality, they are a new form of ideological aggression against the multiplicity of cultures and traditions still existing in the rest of the world."[76] This "ethnocentric attitude is precisely the crime of globalization and westernization," says Dugin.

In Dugin's opinion, Russia's mission is to oppose American-led globalization and forge an alliance with other cultures to defend a polycultural world respecting a diversity of civilizations. This alliance should include "Muslims and Christians, Russians and Chinese, both leftists and rightists, the Hindus and the Jews."[77] In this way, Dugin says, Russian universalism is entirely different from Western universalism.[78] The latter tries to homogenize everybody, whereas "the Eurasian project . . . proceeds from the necessity of preserving and developing the identity of peoples and cultures."[79]

A central element of contemporary Eurasianism is the concept that the world is divided up into civilizations. This idea, which can be seen as having roots in the work of Nikolai Danilevsky, also has adherents among conservatives who are not

Eurasianists. Talk of Russia as an "independent civilization" or "original civilization" is common in modern Russian political circles.[80] However, Russian nationalists of the "Russia for the Russians" variety disagree with the Eurasianists on
many points. Egor Kholmogorov, for instance, writes that Russia would be better
described as "Euroarctic" than "Eurasia,"[81] adding that "Russia isn't Asia and it isn't
in Asia. . . . We deceive ourselves if we think that Asia will welcome us in Asia."[82]
To Kholmogorov, the ideal is the nineteenth-century Europe of sovereign states.
"Let's be honest," he writes, "both our government and most of our society want to
be part of Europe. But not the Europe of Merkel and Hollande, but the Europe of
Bismarck and Alexander III."[83] As so often in the past, conservatives are divided in
their understanding of Russian national identity.

POLITICAL CONSERVATISM

Boris Mezhuev notes that the current Russian government understands conservatism in terms of maintaining the existing system. This leads it to emphasize three
things: "territorial integrity, state sovereignty, and stability."[84] Underlying this is an
assumption that "postcommunist Russia . . . has already generated enough that is
worth conserving."[85]

The desire for stability and strong government appears often in the speeches
of Russia's president Vladimir Putin.[86] Putin means by this a presidential system
of government, with the president standing above party conflicts as the representative of the entire people. This, he says, is required due to Russia's situation as
a country with imperfect political institutions, an often-obstructive bureaucracy,
and a poorly developed system of political parties. "In the medium term Russia
will need a strong presidential power," he said in September 2007, adding that "no
other form of democratic leadership, democratic I wish to underline, is possible
other than strong presidential power."[87]

Putin has combined his desire for a strong state with repeated rejections of
authoritarianism and totalitarianism. To this end, he has quoted Ivan Ilyin to
make the point that "state power has its limits."[88] And in 2012 he said, "Attempts
by the state to intrude into the sphere of personal convictions and opinions are
without doubt manifestations of totalitarianism. This is completely unacceptable
for us. We will not be going down this path."[89]

Putin stresses the connection between democracy and stability. "I consider it
very important to instill in our country democratic principles and institutions and
respect for the law and constitution. This is in reality the deep foundation of stability in the country," he has said.[90] Speaking to the Federal Assembly in December
2012, he also noted that "Russia has no political option other than democracy. I

would also like to underline that we share the universal democratic principles accepted by the whole world." On the same occasion, however, he remarked that "Russian democracy means power precisely for the Russian people with its own traditions of national self-governance, and not at all the implementation of standards imposed on us from outside."[91]

Other members of the ruling United Russia Party have engaged in similar rhetoric. For instance, Oleg Morozov, deputy chairman from 2005 to 2011 of the lower chamber of Russia's parliament, the State Duma, remarked in 2011 that

> the tasks of Russia's modernization can be effectively decided only through social-conservative ideology. . . . Social conservatism shares the common world democratic values. . . . Russia's agenda includes strengthening and developing the fundamental institutions of democracy: civil society and independent mass media, local self-government and parliamentarism, and a professional and independent judicial authority.[92]

This does not, however, imply blind copying of Western democratic models. Valentina Matvienko, the chairwoman of the upper chamber of Russia's parliament, the Federation Council, has said that

> any national legal system is only stable and effective when the principles and fundamental norms are a legalization of the constituent political, economic, social, cultural, and spiritual-moral values of a concrete country or nation. We should always remember this truth both when we are adopting laws and when we amend them.[93]

Liberal conservatism enjoys some support within the ruling United Russia Party,[94] and among intellectuals. There is a belief in certain circles that "a synthesis of liberalism and conservatism is possible and even necessary."[95] Referencing the examples of Pyotr Struve and Nikolai Berdiaev, political philosopher Aleksandr Tsipko calls liberal conservatism "the ideology of Russia's salvation, it has everything or almost everything . . . the conservative accent on the continuity of Russian development, and recognition of a national, sovereign state as the highest moral and spiritual value; and a recognition that Russia is part of European legal civilization." Tsipko defines liberal conservatism as an ideology combining individual freedom, a strong state, and "a developed national feeling, religious feeling."[96]

In the rhetoric of liberal conservatism, one can see a commitment to universal norms of democracy and to distinct national traditions combined. This has something in common with the more moderate version of oppositional conservatism, except that the oppositional conservatives cast doubt on the democratic nature of the Russian state, viewing it instead as "liberal authoritarianism."[97]

Moderate oppositional conservatives express their support for the principle of democratic government, hence the label "conservative democrats." Mikhail Remizov, for instance, says, "personally I am an unconditional supporter of democracy . . . in contemporary society there is no alternative."[98] But this group rejects liberalism as it has evolved in the West in recent decades and as it is seen as having been imposed on Russia in the 1990s. Remizov and other conservative democrats complain that modern Western liberalism is in fact anti-democratic, as it tramples on national traditions and subordinates national authorities to international ones and to the impersonal forces of globalization. Conservatism, resting on national traditions and national sovereignty, is a necessary prerequisite for genuine democratic order.[99]

Boris Mezhuev comments that "conservatism and liberalism . . . are not direct ideological rivals. Conservatives in general . . . have not spoken against 'freedom.'"[100] But liberals have adopted authoritarian methods to impose policies upon Russia that the people do not want, and that have created an order in which the people do not control their government. As Mezhuev puts it:

> Our authoritarian tendencies are not derived from conservatism but, as is well known, from liberalism. Our authoritarian Constitution was adopted in 1993 under the influence of ultraliberal ideas and the desire to rapidly modernize the country. . . . In opposing liberal modernizing authoritarianism, conservatism arouses and rests upon democratic forces. . . . The primary cause of the authoritarian turn in Russia is the idea (beginning with Peter the Great) of dragging Russia out of backwardness by authoritarian means, an idea that is in no way connected with conservatism.[101]

According to Mezhuev, contemporary liberalism is associated with globalization, which strips power away from nation-states and transfers it to other states and global corporations. Liberalism has therefore become profoundly undemocratic.[102] By contrast, conservatism protects democracy by preserving links with a people's history and protecting national independence. Consequently, Mezhuev concludes that "the opposition of conservative democracy to liberal authoritarianism is the fundamental conflict of the contemporary world."[103] Another author on the conservative Russian Idea website, Oleg Barabanov, comments that

> the linking of conservatism and democracy . . . isn't anything unnatural. Under the influence of the globalist elites and their mainstream ideological schools, we have gotten used to understanding democracy in a strictly procedural sense, exclusively as the Western electoral system and nothing else. But if you understand democracy not as an electoral procedure for producing the ruling elite, but as deriving from the

term's original semantic, as power of the people, then the contradictions between conservatism and democracy disappear.[104]

The "conservative democrats" are extremely critical of the existing order in Russia due to its alleged authoritarian liberal tendencies, including its economic and immigration policies. At the same time, however, they share official conservatism's desire for stability, stating that "conservatism today . . . is order against chaos,"[105] and that "the sense of conservatism consists of valuing the present because there is a threat of chaos."[106] Prominent TV talk-show host Vladimir Solovyov expresses the prevailing sentiment well, writing that "in a country like ours, any sign of weakness leads to civil war . . . when you destroy the building of statehood . . . the consequence is always chaos, anarchy, and violence."[107] For this reason, conservatives of this sort do not directly challenge the existing system, even if they dislike much of it. Theirs is a loyal opposition, and there are few specific proposals for what sort of democratic constitution should replace the current one.

Instead of advocating changes to formal institutions, the more moderate oppositional conservatives tend to emphasize the importance of informal ones. This reflects a view of the state in which legitimacy derives not from force, or even from democratic process in a purely mechanistic, quantitative sense, but from the state being in touch with national tradition. Mezhuev, for instance, considers that Russian rulers have always depended on "charismatic legitimacy," according to which a ruler's legitimacy is based solely on perceptions of whether he or she is successful. When Russia has had unsuccessful rulers, such as Nicholas II and Mikhail Gorbachev, the legitimacy of the entire system has come into question, leading to regime collapse. Mezhuev argues that rulers must draw their legitimacy from a source other than perceptions of success:

> I am convinced that a republic can arise in Russia only as the result of a restoration, or more precisely, some sort of restoration or renewal of traditional monarchical legitimacy. Whether a monarch is restored or not isn't important. What's important is that people recognize that the power of tradition is more important than the power of force.[108]

In terms of foreign policy, the nationalist tendencies of the moderate, democratic conservatives push them toward isolationist positions. Western studies of modern Russian geopolitical thought have tended to focus on the writings of Aleksandr Dugin, but the less well-known works of the late Vadim Tsymbursky (1957–2009) are probably more influential among Russian conservatives of this type.

Tsymbursky rejected the aggressive geopolitical ideas of the Eurasianists, and instead proposed the idea of "Island Russia." In Tsymbursky's view, Russia would not benefit from challenging the US-dominated world order, as the disintegration of that order would bring chaos in its wake. Instead Russia should focus on being a regional power, and ensure peace with the West by means of a buffer zone in the form of "limitrophe states," such as Ukraine. Island Russia could then focus on its internal development, which in Tsymbursky's view should move eastward, concentrating on Siberia. In extreme circumstances, such as the collapse of one of the limitrophe states, it might be desirable for Russia to annex territories to which it had particularly close ties, but this was generally undesirable. Russia's security would best be served by the West and Russia recognizing each other as distinct civilizations, defined in the sense of political centers toward which other states gravitate. Russia should seek to preserve what he called a "one-and-a-half polar world," in which the United States constituted the only large civilization but there were also several smaller regional ones, including Russia.[109]

This constitutes the basis of what Tsymbursky called "geopolitical conservatism."[110] It has found support in the works of a number of prominent Russian conservative intellectuals, such as Mezhuev, Remizov, and Kholmogorov. Mezhuev, for instance, argues in favor of a "civilizational realism" based on Tsymbursky's concepts.[111] Remizov writes that "we simply do not have the resources to legitimize an imperial/super-national power," adding that "we have no need to either dispute or lighten the USA's hegemonic burden, turning it into a sparring partner in the global ring."[112] He cites Tsymbursky as saying that Russia's objective should be "a pre-imperial cultural geographic core with a stable and absolute predomination of Russians."[113] Kholmogorov, meanwhile, concurs that "Russia is an island" and praises Tsymbursky for "showing the necessity of Russian isolationism."[114] Kholmogorov qualifies this, however, by arguing that Russia should be extending its borders westward to incorporate the part of Eastern Ukraine that has rebelled against the Kiev government since 2014. He concludes that "offensive isolationism is now the best strategy for Russia."[115]

The radical wing of the oppositional conservatives disagrees with Tsymbursky's isolationism, and argues that Russia should be leading a coalition to destroy the hegemony of the Atlantic powers. The most prominent exponent of this point of view is Aleksandr Dugin, whose foreign policy ideas derive in part from his sharp anti-liberalism. In his book, *The Fourth Political Theory*, he argues that "we must strike the individual, abolish him, and cast him into the periphery of political consideration. . . . Man is anything but an individual. . . . Liberalism must be defeated and destroyed, and the individual must be thrown off his pedestal."[116] He continues:

The term "liberalism" should be equated with the terms fascism and communism. Liberalism is responsible for no fewer crimes than fascism (Auschwitz) and communism (the Gulag); it is responsible for slavery, the destruction of the Americans in the United States, for Hiroshima and Nagasaki, for the aggression in Serbia, Iraq, and Afghanistan, for the economic exploitation of millions of people on the planet.[117]

Liberalism, says Dugin, "tempts man to an insurrection against God, against traditional values, against the moral and spiritual foundations of his people and culture."[118] In the place of liberalism, he proposes a theory based on "social justice, national sovereignty, and traditional values."[119] To oppose liberalism, he has suggested the creation of a "new empire." According to Dugin, "The New Empire must be Eurasian, continental, and in the long-term global."[120] Dugin writes of Russia expanding to include the northern Balkans, Moldova, eastern and southern Ukraine, the Caucasus, the eastern and northern shores of the Caspian Sea in Kazakhstan and Turkmenistan, Central Asia, and Mongolia, all of which "should be seen as bases for further geopolitical expansion to the south."[121] The choice facing the world, says Dugin, is "either integration into one Great Space under the leadership of the Atlanticists, or the organization of a new Great Space capable of countering the last superpower."[122] It is

> either a planetary "new world order" under the USA's leadership, where every state and people will be impersonal and obedient "screws" of the worldwide technocratic, atheistic, small-trading "Disneyland" cosmopolitan model—or the rapid creation of a geopolitical opposition to Atlanticism and globalization, and the organization of anti-globalistic, traditional, grounded peoples and states in an alternative bloc.[123]

Dugin admits that Russia lacks the power to enact this plan. Nevertheless, he argues that it is worth pursuing, saying:

> Nothing is ever impossible for Russians. We are a magical, fantastical people, and when it seems that all is lost, that we have no more resources, we somehow win. Napoleon came, considered that we were nobodies, and then ran away. Hitler's powerful army, which was much stronger than ours, came. This was a worthy opponent. But they lost everything. In the 90s Eurasianism . . . was considered pure nonsense. Then Putin proclaimed the Eurasian Union. We began to move forward a little; we pushed back a bit. Crimea is ours. Donetsk is ours. South Ossetia is ours. Abkhazia is ours. Soon, still more will be ours. Yes, of course, the maps I draw are absurd. But the path to the ideal project is long. You have to have a lofty goal. You must remember that any of our achievements, expansions, are nothing compared with what we must do. We must carry the light of Eurasian polycentric civilization. . . . This is our mission. Whether we can do it or not, nobody knows, but we are trying.[124]

Aleksandr Prokhanov propounds a similarly ambitious imperial mission, writing that the United States and Europe will eventually collapse, and "there will be a new repartition of the world, an upheaval of the centers of power. . . . And the great Russian expanses will band together into a magnificent church, between three oceans, where the Eurasian peoples, each with its own God, beauty, and understanding of the world, will serve the imperial mass."[125] Unlike Dugin, however, Prokhanov believes that Russia does not need to "rush to reconstruct the imperial expanses. It waits patiently" for the United States to lose control.[126]

Dugin regards democracy as only suitable for societies that are reasonably homogenous culturally, writing that "the more heterogeneous and composite a society the further it must depart from democracy and strive for authoritarian power." Western liberal democracy is based upon purely "quantitative methods of rule," while the mass of the people do not in reality participate in decision-making, which is left to the elites.[127] Other radical conservatives share his skepticism about democracy, but do not dismiss it out of hand, and seek to combine elements of representative democracy with elements of more traditional Russian forms of statehood. Journalist Vitaly Tretiakov, for instance, writes of "the deep *crisis of party representation*. Multiparty democracy isn't working . . . *why impose on Russia something that has already stopped working in Western Europe?*"[128] Tretiakov proposes moving away from a party-based model of democracy to one in which people would be represented in parliament through what he calls "estate-professional groups."[129] The radical conservatives' 2005 manifesto, the *Russian Doctrine*, takes a similar line, stating that

> if you look at "democracy" as an external instrument for influencing Russian politics, if you see it as a means of simplifying and primitivizing Russian political tradition, then such "democracy" should be thrown straight out. But if you construct an original Russian democracy without harming the national organic chemistry, without damaging the vitally important fabric of the state organism, then such a construction can only be welcomed.[130]

The *Doctrine* condemns Russia's existing constitutional order, saying that "there is nothing Russian in the Yeltsin constitution,"[131] and it expounds a detailed model of its authors' ideal state. First, "state power must be strong, effective, and accountable."[132] Second, an organic state should follow the principle of *sobornost'*.[133] Third, "Russian national government must be a combination of three state principles—democracy, competent aristocracy, and unified leadership [*edinonachalie*]."[134] For the first of these principles, the *Doctrine* proposes the creation of posts equivalent to those of tribunes in the Roman Republic, that is to say representatives of the people whose job it is to defend their interests; for the second, it proposes a senate consisting of well-qualified representatives of the military, the priesthood, and academia; and for the third, it supports the principle of concentrating power in the hands of a single person.[135] The *Doctrine* also proposes regular referenda as part of the political system's democratic element,[136] and remarks that a plan for the reestablishment of the monarchy will be developed later.[137] The *Russian Doctrine* categorically rejects some of the principles of modern Western liberal democracy, most notably the ideas of the separation of powers and of the supremacy of human rights. The former, says the *Doctrine*, is "harmful to Russia," while the latter undermines Russia's sovereignty, subordinating it to international institutions.[138] Finally, the *Doctrine* sees an important role for the Russian Orthodox Church in Russia's future political order, citing the principle of "symphony"[139] and saying that

> the union of the state with the Church is an undoubted condition for Russia's future rebirth and strengthening. . . . The state should consider any public mockery of Orthodoxy not as an insult to religious feelings but as a political crime, an attack on the state's foundations and its traditions.[140]

The *Doctrine*'s mention of monarchy points to the undoubted sympathy for the monarchical principle that exists among Russian conservatives. Modern monarchists, however, face the same problem as Russian émigrés before them, namely the lack of a credible candidate for tsar. Some monarchists believe that the crown should go to one of the heirs of Grand Duke Kirill Vladimirovich (the *Kirillovichi*); others believe that there should be a Zemsky sobor to elect a new tsar. Most, recognizing the problems inherent in the lack of a legitimate successor, and aware of the absence of mass popular support for a restoration of the monarchy, choose, like the *Russian Doctrine*, simply to put the matter to one side for later consideration. The prevailing sentiment is a modern version of non-predetermination.[141]

Among the more prominent monarchists in post-Soviet Russia have been the artist Ilya Glazunov,[142] the millionaire Konstantin Malofeev, who founded the conservative religious TV channel Tsargrad, and Duma deputy Nataliia Poklonskaia. Poklonskaia, who was born in Ukraine, fled Kiev in February 2014 after the overthrow of Ukrainian president Viktor Yanukovich. She then became chief procurator of Crimea, before eventually being elected to the Russian State Duma. Poklonskaia has become famous for her expressions of monarchist sentiment, which include claiming that a bust of Nicholas II was emitting myrrh, and spearheading a campaign to ban a film depicting the love affair between ballerina Matilda Kshesinskaia and the future Nicholas II. Another notable monarchist is Aleksandr Prokhanov. In a 2017 article he wrote of the requirements for the future tsar, saying:

It must be a special person; some kind of sign, some sort of sacrament, must be upon him. Vladimir Putin is such a person. . . . And the Crimea, restored to Russia by Putin, has brought this holiness into the very center of Putin's power, Putin's statehood. That is why by this act [the annexation of Crimea], in some undefinable and undogmatic way, Putin carried the icon lamp of mysterious, mystical light into Russia, into the Kremlin, into his office, into his own mansion. He was chosen for this. He confirmed this choice. And in a very conditional way he was anointed, not by the patriarch, not in the Uspensky Cathedral, his coronation was accomplished without the presence of the bishops. It was accomplished in a mysterious, mystical manner, when the lamp of Crimean Khersones [a former Greek colony in Crimea, where Vladimir the Great supposedly converted to Orthodoxy] returned in his hands to Russia. And he stood with this lamp, having lit it up with a mysterious light. Thus, in circles close to the patriarch, in circles dreaming of monarchy, recognizing all the difficulties of restoring monarchy in Russia, more and more often one hears the name of Vladimir Vladimirovich Putin as a possible first monarch in the Putin dynasty.[143]

Some leading members of the Russian Orthodox Church have also expressed a preference for a monarchical system of government. In 2017, for instance, Metropolitan Ilarion, the head of the department of external relations of the Russian Orthodox Church, stated:

It is my opinion that [government by] a person who is anointed to reign by priests, a person who receives not merely a mandate from electors to rule for a defined period, but receives sanction for his rule from God through the Church, and remains such for life until he passes power to his successor, is, of course, a form of government that is positively recommended by history and has many advantages compared with any electoral form of government.[144]

Despite such statements, the church as a body does not endorse this option. The *Foundations of the Russian Orthodox Church's Conception of Society* reiterates a 1994 decision of the Bishops' Council of the Russian Orthodox Church that "the church does not give preference to any social system or any of the existing political doctrines." The form of government, it says, "is conditioned in many ways by the spiritual and moral condition of society. Aware of this, the church accepts the people's choice or does not resist it at least. . . . the church does not believe it possible for her to become an initiator of any change in the form of government."[145]

The Russian Orthodox Church provided more details of its official position on the nature of the state in *The Foundations of the Russian Orthodox Church's Conception of Society*. It describes the state as "an essential element of life in the world distorted by sin," and so calls on believers to obey it. At the same time, it notes that state authority is limited and that the state "has no right to make itself absolute by extending its limits up to complete autonomy from God."[146] The document adds:

> If the authority forces Orthodox believers to apostatize from Christ and his church and to commit sinful and spiritually harmful actions, the church should refuse to obey the state. The Christian, following the will of his conscience, can refuse to fulfil the commands of a state forcing him into a grave sin. . . . The Christian . . . must speak out lawfully against an indisputable violation committed by society or state against the statutes and commandments of God. If this lawful action is impossible or ineffective, he must take up the position of civil disobedience.[147]

The Foundations of the Russian Orthodox Church's Conception of Society makes it clear that church and state have different spheres of competence: "the goal of the church is the eternal salvation of people, while the goal of state is their well-being on earth." The basis of their relationship should be "non-interference in each other's affairs. . . . The church may request or urge the government to exercise power in particular cases, yet the decision rests with the state." The document states that the ideal is "symphony," defined as "cooperation, mutual support, and mutual responsibility without one side intruding into the exclusive domain of the other."[148]

Much has been written in recent years about the close relationship between the Russian state and the Russian Orthodox Church. In reality, the church's attitude to the state is far from one of unquestioning subordination, as shown by its support for the idea of civil disobedience. Patriarch Kirill has described the church's attitude in these terms: "We have chosen the following path: we have clearly designated, on the one hand, our distance from state power and, on the other hand, our full loyalty to the state."[149] Although church leaders have argued in favor of a privileged status for Orthodoxy, they have also made it repeatedly clear that they do not want Orthodoxy to become the country's state religion.[150] In practice the church is also rather "ambivalent" about the idea of symphony, seeking "both cooperation with and distance from the state."[151]

It is necessary to draw a clear distinction between the Orthodox Church as an institution and what is sometimes called "political Orthodoxy." Radical conservative politicians who make reference to Orthodoxy are often out of step with the church establishment, which is much more moderate in its pronouncements.[152] An example was a debate that erupted in 1999 when the government introduced compulsory taxpayer identification numbers. Following intense lobbying by Orthodox activists, who denounced the numbers as the "mark of the Antichrist," the government eventually relented and said that it would not force individuals to accept a number and would permit them to pay taxes without one. The church itself took no part in the lobbying campaign, saying that the issue was "of no religious significance."[153]

The official church's relative moderation leads one commentator to conclude that "the church is not at all, as is often assumed, a conservative or even reactionary institution."[154] In fact, the first label—conservative—seems accurate, but the second—"reactionary"—less so. A case in point is the church's views on the question of human rights, as laid out in a 2008 document entitled *The Russian Orthodox Church's Basic Teachings on Human Dignity, Freedom, and Rights*.[155]

This document states that human rights are founded on the notion of human dignity, which in its turn is inextricably linked to morality, a dignified life being a moral life.[156] The requirement for morality means that "human rights cannot be superior to the values of the spiritual world. . . . It is inadmissible to interpret human rights as the ultimate and universal foundation of societal life to which religious views and practice should be subjected."[157] Human rights need to be in accordance with morality and so should not justify "vices such as sexual lechery and perversions . . . abortion, euthanasia, use of embryos in medicine, experiments changing a person's nature" and "degradation of the natural environment."[158] Instead, the church proposes defining rights from "the perspective of their possible role in creating favorable external conditions for the improvement of a personality on its way to salvation."[159]

This undoubtedly distinguishes the Orthodox Church's view of human rights from that of Western liberals, but it does not mean that the church rejects the entire concept of inherent rights. On the contrary, the *Basic Teachings* states clearly that its definition implies a whole series of human rights and freedoms: "the right to life," "freedom of conscience," "freedom of expression," "freedom of creative work," "the right to education," "civil and political rights" including the "right to elect and be elected," and protection of private life and information; "socio-economic rights," including "the right to property, the right to employment, the right to protection against an employer's arbitrary treatment," and so on; and "collective rights," notably for families.[160] The *Basic Teachings* concludes by calling for action to promote human rights, including "defending human rights to the free confession of faith," "opposing crimes on the grounds of national and religious enmity," "safeguarding the individual against the arbitrary actions of those in power and employers," "protecting life," "giving pastoral care to soldiers," and actions to respect "the dignity and rights of those who are placed in social institutions and penitentiaries with special attention given to the disabled, orphans, the elderly, and other powerless people."[161]

The church has put these principles into practice by investing considerable resources into social outreach. John Burgess notes that since the collapse of communism, the Church has developed an impressive number and range of social ministries. Orthodox hospitals, hospices, orphanages, feeding and housing programs, and drug and alcohol rehabilitation centers—in these and other initiatives, the Church has taken a leading role in caring for Russia's poor and needy.[162]

According to Burgess, this has enabled the Russian Orthodox Church to "make an extraordinarily positive contribution" to Russia.[163] While others might challenge this judgment, there can be little doubt that the church has become an important conservative actor in contemporary Russia.

SOCIAL-ECONOMIC CONSERVATISM

In the 1990s, Russian economic policy followed a clear line: rapid liberalization, often without excessive concern for the niceties. Since Vladimir Putin came to power, it has been harder to identify a clear economic doctrine, beyond a sort of pragmatic conservatism that preserves the system created in the 1990s and slowly tinkers with it. Stability and continuity have been the order of the day.

There have been some significant economic changes under Putin, but they do not follow any obvious pattern. The state's role in the economy has grown substantially, as it has regained control of key industries, especially in the oil and gas sector. The government has also shown some interest in state-driven modernization, including large investments in infrastructure and key industries, such as aviation.[164] At the same time, macroeconomic policy has followed a line that might be called "neoliberal," with a tight monetary policy designed to keep inflation low, accompanied by efforts to more fully integrate Russia into the world economy. The latter culminated in Russia's accession to the World Trade Organization in 2012 and a decision to make the Russian ruble fully convertible, with a floating exchange rate.

French scholar Marlene Laruelle identifies two schools of economic thought within the ruling party. The first are the "liberal conservatives," centered on a group of Duma deputies from St. Petersburg, including Viktor Pleskashevsky, president of the Duma Committee for Property. They believe that "individual freedom, the possibility to choose freely one's destiny . . . is the ideal that orientates the liberal conservative approach," and they advocate market solutions to social problems, including the privatization of social services. The second are the "social conservatives." This group is "social" in the sense of believing in the state's social responsibilities, and "advocates adapting the socialist system to the conditions of the market economy."[165]

Putin's public statements put him somewhere between the two. On the one hand, he has spoken of the state's social responsibilities, putting him in the social conservative camp. On the other hand he has consistently supported the need to foster private enterprise and reduce the bureaucratic burden faced by small businesses. For instance, on December 4, 2014, he said:

> The most important thing now is to give the people an opportunity for self-ful-fillment. Freedom for development in the economic and social spheres, for public initiatives, is the best possible response both to any external restrictions and to our domestic problems. . . . Conscientious work, private property, the freedom of enter-prise—these are the same kind of fundamental conservative values as patriotism and respect for the history, traditions, and culture of one's country.[166]

Rhetoric of this sort shows that Putin has a foot in the liberal conservative camp as well. He has even used the words "liberal" and "liberalization" to describe his economic views, speaking in 2012, for instance, of his wish to promote the "liberalizing of the world economy."[167] This last phrase reveals an important aspect of Russian economic policy under Putin: he aims to make Russia an integral part of the world economy. Following the 2008 world financial crisis, Putin rejected the idea that Russia would do better by isolating itself. That policy "made the Soviet economy totally uncompetitive," he said. "This lesson cost us dear. I am sure that nobody wants to see it repeated."[168] Both liberal and social conservatives in the ruling party share this opinion. For example, Oleg Morozov, formerly deputy chairman of the State Duma, remarked in a speech promoting social conservatism that "Russia must occupy the largest possible position in the international division of labor."[169] The imposition of sanctions on Russia following the annexation of Crimea and the war in Donbass has slightly dented the Russian elite's support for globalization, but the preference remains.

Perhaps more than any other issue, it is this that divides official from opposition conservatism, with both the more moderate and the more radical opposition conservatives being firmly anti-globalization. Mikhail Remizov, for instance, considers globalization to be "a conspiracy of elites" combined with a "conspiracy of minorities" (sexual, gender, and ethnic), which together transfer power away from the national level.[170] He proposes an ideology of "right-wing anti-globalization,"[171] promoting a policy of "large politico-regional blocs."[172] He therefore favors economic integration with the Eurasian Customs Union,[173] established in 2010 and consisting of Russia, Belarus, Kazakhstan, Armenia, and Kyrgyzstan (although, because of his dislike of immigration from Central Asia, Remizov would prefer to exclude Kyrgyzstan). Aleksandr Dugin has similarly written of the need for the "economic autarky of large spaces."[174] In conservatives' eyes, regionalization provides an alternative to globalization.

There is disagreement among conservatives over the desirability of economic growth. The view of the Russian Orthodox Church is that "wealth cannot make man happy."[175] The church speaks of a growing ecological crisis, which is the result of "an unprecedented and unjustified growth of public consumption,"[176] and which "compels us to review our relations with the environment."[177] Meanwhile Aleksandr Dugin follows Aleksandr Solzhenitsyn in declaring that

> instead of always looking for modernization and growth, we should orient ourselves in the direction of balance, adaptability, and harmony. Instead of desiring to move upward and forward, we must adapt to that which exists, to understand where we are. . . . Instead of the ideology of development, we must place our bets on the ideology of conservatism and conservation. . . . No stability will ever come from a new round of unidirectional growth derived from energy prices, real estate, stocks, and so on, nor from the growth of the global economy as a whole.[178]

In contrast, many other conservatives favor rapid modernization, with a particular emphasis on high technology. Aleksandr Prokhanov, for instance, displays a decided nostalgia for the technological achievements of Soviet industry, and talks of moving to "a full-value high technology economy."[179] Similarly, the *Russian Doctrine* says that "Russia must consciously enter the new world. Russia must become a world center for producing the technology of the future . . . [it] must be turned into the epicenter of the global technological revolution."[180]

In general, the conservative modernizers' economic policies are what in the West would be considered "left-wing," including a large role for the state in economic planning, a tendency toward economic autarky, and a belief in the importance of social justice and state welfare. Supporters of these policies are sometimes referred to as "left conservatives."[181] To a certain degree, left conservatism can be seen as a product of the Soviet experience, and so conservative in the sense of continuing the Soviet heritage. Not coincidentally, the most extreme example of this left conservatism is the Communist Party of the Russian Federation (the successor to the Communist Party of the Soviet Union), which has developed a modern version of National Bolshevism. This combines socialist economics with Russian nationalism and Orthodoxy. The Communist Party has proclaimed that "the Russian Idea is deeply socialistic."[182] Party leader Gennady Ziuganov's philosophy is firmly anti-capitalist and anti-globalization, and regards socialism as an organic product of Russian history, developing naturally out of the peasant commune.[183] He claims that "capitalism does not go organically into the flesh and blood, the daily life, the customs and psychology of our society."[184]

Other left conservatives are not so deeply opposed to capitalism, and propose some form of mixed economy, but they share the communists' hostility to globalization. In some cases they also argue for social conservatism, including a fairer distribution of resources. For instance, Aleksandr Shchipkov, deputy president of the Russian Orthodox Church's media relations department, contends that "in Russia . . . the left idea is conservative," and links conservatism with the idea of social justice and the Slavophiles' concept of *sobornost*'.[185] Similarly, Nataliia Narochnitskaia calls for "a mixed economy; market, but with the strong participation of the state," taking the form of a "social state with a Christian attitude to life and to mankind."[186]

The *Russian Doctrine* denounces neoliberalism, saying that Russia's experience in the 1990s showed "the danger of liberal economic reforms."[187] According to the *Doctrine*, neoliberalism leads to a flow of resources from poor to rich countries, slowing growth in the former.[188] Rather than adopting a neoliberal model, the *Doctrine* says that Russia should adopt "one or other variant of the mixed, regulated economy, such as the economies of France or Italy in the 1960s and 1970s, South Korea and Taiwan in the 80s, or China as it was around 2000."[189] In a similar manner to late nineteenth- and early twentieth-century conservatives such as Sergei Sharapov, the authors of the *Russian Doctrine* feel that Russia's economy should be reoriented toward the domestic market, aided by cheap credit, as it is domestic demand that ultimately fuels growth.[190] To reorient production in this way, Russia needs to reestablish its economic sovereignty, they say.[191] The *Doctrine* therefore proposes a ban on companies registered in offshore zones, restrictions on the flow of capital out of the country,[192] and what it calls a "quasi-autarkic economy."[193] The *Doctrine* concludes that "this does not mean rejecting all external economic links or advantageous participation in world trade or the international division of labor, but it does place definite limits on the scale of this participation."[194]

The *Russian Doctrine* notes also that past failures to satisfy the desire for social justice have led to revolution.[195] It therefore states that "the center of the future economic paradigm should be not *homo economicus* but the 'moral person.'"[196] This theme appears also in the work of the most prominent conservative critic of existing policy, the economist Sergei Glazyev. Minister of foreign economic relations in the early 1990s, Glazyev resigned in protest at Yeltsin's decisions to dissolve and then attack the Supreme Soviet in 1993. He is now one of the key figures in the Stolypin Club, a group of self-described "market realists"[197] that lobbies the Russian government for significant changes in economic policy.

Drawing on Orthodox thought, Glazyev argues that "at the foundation of our traditional worldview lies the imperative of social justice" associated with "collectivism and *sobornost*'."[198] Unfortunately, says Glazyev, "For twenty years we have been living on the basis of the ideology of radical liberalism, which is cardinally opposed to these values. The ideology of radical liberalism is in essence the cult of the 'Golden Calf.'"[199] He adds that "our economy has turned into a cannibalistic mechanism of production, with the offshore business-aristocracy taking money out of the country without paying taxes."[200] He concludes that Russia needs to reintroduce "moral norms" into economic policy.[201]

Glazyev is a harsh critic of the economic system created under Yeltsin and maintained under Putin. The Russian economy, he says, is currently characterized by "oligopoly" and "external dependence."[202] The incomes of the mass of the population are falling, while economic inequality is rising.[203] Glazyev says that Russia needs a new model of development, founded on "a social-conservative synthesis, uniting the system of values of world religions with the achievements of the social state and the scientific paradigm of steady development."[204]

According to Glazyev, the existing economic system is unable either to promote sustainable growth or to reduce inequality because of the "policy of the financial authorities to serve the interests of international capital."[205] This leads him to propose measures for a looser monetary policy that would allow easier access to cheap credit and would also reduce Russia's ties to international financial markets. Underlying these policy proposals is a very negative view of the United States of America. Looking at the chaos that has ensued in the wake of American regime change efforts in countries such as Iraq, Libya, Syria, and Ukraine, Glazyev concludes that America is waging "world chaotic war."[206] By this he means that the United States is deliberately promoting chaos throughout the world: "The USA's strategy can be reduced to . . . creating a widening crater of chaos and force on Russia's border with the aim of politically destabilizing Russia."[207] As America's financial hegemony gradually declines, Glazyev says:

> The pyramids of derivatives, debt, and inequality are becoming ever higher, threatening a catastrophic collapse. This makes their owner [the United States] more and more aggressive, requiring them to seize more new resources, more and more of them, in order to preserve the financial pyramids from self-destruction. Russia, as a country that is very rich in resources but has a small population and many nations, is top of the list for removal of its resources. And this means that the war being waged against us has the aim of destroying Russia as a sovereign state.[208]

Faced by this threat, Russia must seek to isolate itself as much as practically possible from American financial dominance, Glazyev says. He therefore argues for tight control on the movement of capital, "the creation of a system of exchanging information between banks, analogous to SWIFT but independent of the USA and EU," and the establishment of "our own rating agencies." He proposes the conversion of currency reserves from dollars to gold and other currencies, pricing exported goods in rubles rather than dollars, and further Eurasian economic integration.[209] Other measures include a return to "strategic planning" to stimulate technological innovation, and the replacement of the existing flat income tax with a socially fairer progressive tax. The objective is a "restoration of the balance between individualism and collectivism . . . restoration of the balance between freedom and justice . . . [and] harmonization of relations between labor and capital."[210]

In the face of an economic recession principally caused by declining oil prices and the sanctions imposed on Russia by Western powers following the annexation of Crimea in 2014, the Russian government commissioned various groups to submit reports proposing changes in economic policy. One report, submitted by Sergei Glazyev, proposed fundamental reforms along the lines described above. Another, authored by former finance minister Aleksei Kudrin, suggested reforms of a more liberal kind. To date, the Russian state has avoided going in either direction, preferring a gradual evolution in policy rather than radical change. At present, the state is in practice perhaps more conservative than the conservatives.

CONCLUSION

Assessing the impact of conservatism in contemporary Russia is difficult. Orthodoxy has enjoyed a remarkable revival, but studies of the Russian Orthodox Church's relationship with the state suggest that the "rapprochement between church and state falls a long way short of the Tsarist 'symphonic ideal'";[211] that "Orthodoxy . . . is more limited in social and political influence than we might expect";[212] that the state pays "lip service" to Orthodoxy";[213] and that "in lobbying the state . . . the ROC has been singularly unsuccessful,"[214] as can be seen in the field of education, where the church did manage to get the state to agree to include religious education in schools, but only as one option among many.

Similarly, nationalists' proposals to reshape Russian identity reflect an understanding that the government is unsympathetic to nationalist demands. State officials, including Vladimir Putin, have occasionally talked about Russia as a distinct civilization, an idea that has nowadays become commonplace in Russian political discourse, but most analysts agree that the influence of Eurasianism on public policy is limited.[215] The annexation of Crimea notwithstanding, the Russian government has shown no interest in grand geopolitical schemes such as those proposed by Aleksandr Dugin. The creation of the Eurasian Union represents a step toward some sort of regional integration, but is just one of many Russian international initiatives, and the government has never specifically asserted a Eurasian identity. On the contrary, Putin has regularly spoken of Russian culture as European. In October 2017, for instance, he told participants at the Nineteenth World Festival of Youth and Students: "You have said Russia is a vast territory and it is indeed so—from its western to eastern borders, it is a Eurasian space. But as regards culture, even language, language group and history, this is all undoubtedly a European space as it is inhabited by people of this culture."[216]

Meanwhile, in the economic realm, the Russian government has for the most part stuck to the model established under Yeltsin. The majority of contemporary Russian conservatives oppose their government's economic policies, but their efforts to persuade the government to change direction have to date been almost entirely unsuccessful. Conservative anti-globalization has met firm resistance from the Russian state.

This does not mean that the state and its rulers are not conservative in any way, nor that any conservative rhetoric they may use is entirely instrumental, as some critics have claimed.[217] Rather, official conservatism, as so often in Russia's past, remains somewhat distant from religious and intellectual conservatism. Putin describes himself as a "pragmatist with a conservative perspective."[218] Despite being rooted in appeals to tradition, many of the changes demanded by conservative writers are actually quite radical. Putin's pragmatism renders him far more cautious, and so more moderate; conservative, but in a different way.

Conservative intellectual Leonid Poliakov notes that "Putin does not attach himself to ideological conservatives, and rightly so."[219] Nevertheless, Poliakov believes that the Russian leader is in touch with the conservative instincts of the mass of the Russian population, and is at one with them in valuing Russian history and tradition. Poliakov therefore argues that

> for the first time in Russian history a chance is opening up for us to unite the government and the people on the basis of a single set of values. . . . the Russian government was always authoritarian, right up until Yeltsin. The government today is democratic, because it is supported by the majority of the population. This is a unique situation in Russian history.[220]

In the Western world, liberalism and democracy are often considered to go together. But if Poliakov is right, a more democratic Russia would not necessarily be a more liberal Russia. It might be a more conservative one.

CONCLUSION

Russian conservatism is a response to the pressures of modernization and Westernization and, more recently, globalization. For the past two centuries conservatives have sought to adapt to these pressures while preserving national identity and political and social stability. Although the specific policies being proposed have changed over time, conservatism's approach to change has remained consistent. In this way, Russian conservatism today evinces a clear continuity with Russian conservatism of the past. In particular, Russian conservatives have continually proposed forms of cultural, political, and economic development that are seen as building on existing traditions, identity, and forms of government and economic and social life, rather than being imposed on the basis of abstract theory and foreign models.

Each generation of Russian conservatism has drawn on and developed the ideas of previous generations, modifying these ideas and generating new ones to fit the specific conditions of their time. Twenty-first-century conservatives consciously draw inspiration from their predecessors. Thus, while conservatism in Russia shares some roots with its counterparts in Western European countries, it has its own history that continues to shape its present.

Given Russia's historically multinational composition, conservatives have found it hard to agree on what Russian identity is. Russian conservatism has, therefore, been as much about exploring and developing that identity as about protecting it. One strand of conservatism, running from Mikhail Pogodin's Norman Theory through the Slavophiles, the *pochvenniki*, Pan-Slavism, the civilizational theories of Danilevsky and Leontyev, and into Eurasianism, has stressed Russia's distinct nature, separate from the West. But many Russian conservatives, such as the liberal conservatives and the aristocratic opposition in the era of the Great Reforms, have seen themselves very much as part of Western civilization. Moreover, these two strands of conservative thought have not been mutually exclusive. The Slavophiles greatly admired European achievements and believed that Russia's historical mission was precisely to save Europe. Even as aggressive a modern thinker as Aleksandr Dugin still proclaims his love of the West (or at least of the West as it used to be). At the same time, conservatives who have regarded Russia as part of Western civilization have nonetheless seen it as distinct in certain ways and rejected the idea that Russia can blindly copy Western models. Russian conservatism is the product of a complex dialectic between pro- and anti-Western views.

Russian conservatives have strongly asserted the right of different peoples to be different. At the same time, they have tended to think that Russia has a message (often associated with Orthodoxy) for the rest of the world. Conservatives therefore reject universalism while also often believing that Russia bears a universal truth. The struggle to overcome this apparent paradox has been an important feature of Russian conservatism from its beginning through to today. The preferred solution has to been to stress the universal value of diversity, or as Leontyev put it, "flowering complexity."

More universalist Russian conservatives have tended toward a messianic vision of Russia's position in the world and in many cases also toward an imperialist outlook, as seen in the writings of the Pan-Slavs and nowadays of the Eurasianists. But there is also an isolationist strand in Russian conservatism, visible from the time Admiral Shishkov opposed pursuing Russia's war against Napoleon beyond Russia's borders, through the newspaper *Vest*'s slogan "Russia for the Russians," the Durnovo Memorandum, Aleksandr Solzhenitsyn's support of the breakup of the Soviet Union, and as far as the geopolitical theories of Vadim Tsymbursky. Russian conservatism is not inherently imperialist.

Nor is it inherently anti-liberal, depending, of course, on the definition of liberalism, a subject far beyond the scope of this book. If one takes liberalism to be a philosophy focused on the freedom, rights, and dignity of the individual, then one can see that there have certainly been Russian conservatives who have advocated the primacy of state interests over individual rights. Konstantin Pobedonostsev would be a case in point. But there have also been others who have cared greatly about human dignity and personal freedom. The Slavophiles' opposition in principle to serfdom stands out as a clear example. Where Russian conservatism has consistently differed from Western secular liberalism is in its focus on inner freedom and its emphasis on the person (connected to a wider community and sense of values) rather than on the supposedly isolated individual. Nevertheless, a recognition that inner freedom is to some degree dependent on external freedom has led conservative thinkers such as Boris Chicherin, Lev Tikhomirov, Ivan Ilyin, and Aleksandr Solzhenitsyn to declare the existence of certain natural rights of the person that the state has an obligation to respect.

Another point on which nearly all Russian conservatives have agreed during the past two hundred years is the need to concentrate power in the hands of a single leader. However, for conservatives autocracy has never meant absolutism, let alone totalitarianism. State power has always been seen as limited by custom and religion, and in more recent times by law, as well as being restricted in terms of its competencies, that is to say those things over which it has authority.

There has been less constancy on social and economic matters. The conservative tent has sheltered economic liberals, supporters of state intervention, and thinkers who have been rather hostile to the idea of economic development. Mostly, though, Russian conservatives' views on economic affairs have been shaped by a dislike of top-down policies of rapid modernization promoted by the Russian state and by suspicion of the state bureaucracy. In the late nineteenth century this led to ideas such as those of Sergei Sharapov and Lev Tikhomirov, who argued that Russia should focus on developing its internal market rather than on products for export. These ideas were combined with support for protectionism and a loose monetary policy, and with suggestions that Russia reduce its dependence on foreign capital. The economic proposals of modern left conservatives, who in the name of social justice argue in favor of a fairer distribution of resources, are in some ways similar.

Conservatism is an important part of Russia's political and intellectual landscape. Indeed, given the accelerating pace of globalization and modernization, it is possible that the current conservative reaction will grow stronger rather than weaker as time goes on. The ideas discussed in this book, therefore, are of more than just historical interest; they will help to shape Russia's future, for better or for worse, in the years to come.

NOTES

NOTES TO INTRODUCTION

1. Lesley Chamberlain, *Motherland: A Philosophical History of Russia* (New York: Rookery, 2007), xvii.
2. Ibid., xi.
3. Gary M. Hamburg, "The Revival of Russian Conservatism," *Kritika: Explorations in Russian and Eurasian History* 6, no. 1 (2005): 107–8.
4. Marc Raeff, *Russia Abroad: A Cultural History of the Russian Emigration, 1919–1939* (Oxford: Oxford University Press, 1990), 10.
5. Hamburg, "The Revival of Russian Conservatism," 126.
6. Alexander M. Martin, *Romantics, Reformers, Reactionaries: Russian Conservative Thought and Politics in the Reign of Alexander I* (De Kalb: Northern Illinois University Press, 1997), 206.
7. A. Iu. Minakov, "Rozhdenie russkogo konservatizma: Uroki proshlogo," *Tetradi po konservatizmu* 3 (2014): 22.
8. For instance, Andrey Makarychev and Alexandra Yatsyk, "A New Russian Conservatism: Domestic Roots and Repercussions for Europe," *Notes Internacionals CIDOB* 93 (2014): 2; Alfred Evans, "Ideological Change under Vladimir Putin in the Perspective of Social Identity Theory," *Demokratizatsiya: The Journal of Post-Soviet Democratization* 23, no. 4 (2015): 401–2.
9. For instance, Owen Matthews, "Putin to Russia: We Will Bury Ourselves," *Newsweek*, June 12, 2014, http://www.newsweek.com/2014/06/20/putins-paranoia-card-254513.html.
10. Melik Kaylan, "Kremlin Values: Putin's Strategic Conservatism," *World Affairs* 177, no. 1 (May–June 2014): 10.
11. Oksana Drozdova and Paul Robinson, "In Others' Words: Quotations and Recontextualization in Putin's Speeches," *Russian Politics* 2, no. 2 (2017): 227–53.
12. For instance: Sergei Lavrov, "Russia's Foreign Policy: Historical Background," *Russia in Global Affairs*, March 3, 2016, http://www.mid.ru/en/foreign_policy/news/-/asset_publisher/cKNonkJE02Bw/content/id/2124391. See also: Nikolas Gvozdev, "Russia's Future," *Orbis* 53, no. 2 (2009): 347–59.
13. See, for instance, the bibliography of Ministerstvo Kul'tury Rossiiskoi Federatsii, *Osnovy gosurdarstvennoi kul'turnoi politiki*, 2015, https://www.mkrf.ru/upload/mediali-brary/3aa/3aa5ed08e6cfbb1c982fee8618c4fa09.pdf.
14. Andrei P. Tsygankov, "In the Shadow of Nikolai Danilevskii: Universalism, Particularism, and Russian Geopolitical Theory," *Europe-Asia Studies* 69, no. 4 (2017): 584–85.
15. A. V. Repnikov, *Konservativnye modeli Rossiiskogo gosudarstvennosti* (Moscow: Rosspen, 2014), 22.

16. For a summary of post-Soviet Russian writings on conservatism, see: A. Iu. Minakov, "Russian Conservatism in Contemporary Russian Historiography: New Approaches and Research Trends," *Russian Studies in History* 48, no. 2 (2009): 8–28; A. V. Repnikov, "The Contemporary Historiography of Russian Conservatism," *Russian Studies in History* 48, no. 2 (2009): 29–55.

17. Minakov, "Russian Conservatism," 11.

18. For instance: V. Ia. Grosul, ed., *Russkii konservatizm XIX stoletiia: Ideologiia i praktika* (Moscow: Progress-Traditsiia, 2000); I. A. Khristoforov, *"Aristokraticheskaia" oppozitsiia Velikim reformam: Konets 1850–seredina 1870-kh gg.* (Moscow: Russkoe slovo, 2002); Iu. I. Kir'ianov, *Pravye partii v Rossii, 1911–1917 gg.* (Moscow: Rosspen, 2001); Mikhail Luk'ianov, *Russkii konservatizm i reforma, 1907–1914* (Stuttgart: Ibidem-Verlag, 2006); A. Iu. Minakov, *Russkii konservatizm v pervoi chetverti XIX veka* (Voronezh: Izdatel'stvo Voronezhskogo gosudarstvennogo universiteta, 2011); and Repnikov, *Konservativnye modeli*.

19. V. A. Gusev, *Russkii konservatizm: Osnovnye napravleniia i etapy razvitiia* (Tver: Tverskoi gosudarstvennyi universitet, 2001).

20. Most notably, John B. Dunlop, *The Faces of Contemporary Russian Nationalism* (Princeton, NJ: Princeton University Press, 1983), and *The New Russian Nationalism* (New York: Praeger, 1985).

21. For instance, the works of Marlene Laruelle, including: *In the Name of the Nation: Nationalism and Politics in Contemporary Russia* (New York: Palgrave MacMillan, 2009), and *Russian Eurasianism: An Ideology of Empire* (Washington, DC: Woodrow Wilson Center Press, 2008). Other related works include: Peter Duncan, *Russian Messianism: Third Rome, Revolution, Communism, and After* (London: Routledge, 2000); Mark Bassin, *The Gumilev Mystique: Biopolitics, Eurasianism, and the Construction of Community in Modern Russia* (Ithaca, NY: Cornell University Press, 2016); and Charles Clover, *Black Wind, White Snow: The Rise of Russia's New Nationalism* (New Haven, CT: Yale University Press, 2016).

22. John P. Burgess, *Holy Rus': The Rebirth of Orthodoxy in the New Russia* (New Haven, CT: Yale University Press, 2017); Wallace L. Daniel, *The Orthodox Church and Civil Society in Russia* (College Station: Texas A&M University Press, 2006); Irina Papkova, *The Orthodox Church and Russian Politics* (Washington, DC: Woodrow Wilson Center Press, 2011).

23. Martin, *Romantics, Reformers, Reactionaries*; George Gilbert, *The Radical Right in Late Imperial Russia: Dreams of a True Fatherland?* (London: Routledge, 2016); Don C. Rawson, *Russian Rightists and the Revolution of 1905* (Cambridge: Cambridge University Press, 1995).

24. Abraham Ascher, *P. A. Stolypin: The Search for Stability in Late Imperial Russia* (Stanford, CA: Stanford University Press, 2001); Richard Avramenko and Lee Trepanier, eds., *Dostoevsky's Political Thought* (Lanham, MD: Lexington Books, 2013); Edward H. Judge, *Plehve: Repression and Reform in Imperial Russia, 1902–1904* (Syracuse, NY: Syracuse University Press, 1983); Stephen M. Woodburn, "The Origins of Russian Intellectual Conservatism, 1825–1881: Danilevsky, Dostoevsky, Katkov, and the Legacy of Nicholas I" (PhD diss., University of Miami, 2001).

25. Richard Pipes, *Russian Conservatism and Its Critics: A Study in Political Culture* (New Haven, CT: Yale University Press, 2005).

Notes to Chapter 1

1. For instance, Jan-Werner Müller lists four different types of conservatism. See Jan-Werner Müller, "Comprehending Conservatism: A New Framework for Analysis," *Journal of Political Ideologies* 11, no. 3 (2006): 363.

2. A. A. Gorokhov, "Konservatizm v Rossii i osobennosti russko konservativnoi sotsial'no-politicheskoi mysli pervoi poloviny XIX veka," *Tetradi po konservatizmu* 2 (2016): 127–50.

3. John Kekes, *A Case for Conservatism* (Ithaca, NY: Cornell University Press, 1998), 5.

4. For an exposition of this distinction, see Samuel Huntington, "Conservatism as an Ideology," *American Political Science Review* 51, no. 2 (1957): 455. See also the distinction drawn by Karl Mannheim between traditionalism and conservatism, as discussed in Levente Nagy, "The Meanings of a Concept: Conservatism," in *Reflections on Conservatism*, ed. Doğancan Öszel (Newcastle upon Tyne: Cambridge Scholars Publishing, 2011), 27–30.

5. Huntington, *"Conservatism as an Ideology,"* 461. For a similar definition, see Charles W. Dunn and J. David Woodard, *The Conservative Tradition in America* (Lanham, MD: Rowman & Littlefield, 1996), 41.

6. Michael Oakeshott, "On Being Conservative," in *Rationalism in Politics and Other Essays* (London: Methuen, 1962), 168, 169, 172.

7. Cited in N. V. Chestneishin, "Konservatizm i liberalizm: Tozhdestvo i razlichie," *Polis: Politicheskie issledovaniia* 4 (2006): 168.

8. Michael Freeden, *Ideologies and Political Theory: A Conceptual Approach* (Oxford: Clarendon Press, 1996), 10.

9. Kieron O'Hara, *Conservatism* (London: Reaktion Books, 2011), 91.

10. Nagy, "The Meaning of a Concept," 21.

11. O'Hara, *Conservatism*, 17, 20.

12. Freeden, *Ideologies*, 332.

13. Nagy, "The Meaning of a Concept," 21–25.

14. E. A. Popov, *Russkii konservatizm: Ideologiia i sotsial'no-politicheskaia praktika* (Rostov-on-Don: Izdatel'stvo Rostovskogo universiteta, 2005), 17.

15. See, for instance, Nataliia Narochnitskaia, "Sredi zapadnykh konservatorov meniaetsia otnoshenie k Rossii," *Tetradi po konservatizmu* 1 (2014): 74.

16. V. A. Gusev, *Russkii konservatizm: Osnovnye napravleniia i etapy razvitiia* (Tver: Tverskoi gosudarstvennyi universitet, 2001), 55.

17. Nikolai Berdiaev, *Filosofiia neravenstva: Pis'ma k nedrugam po sotsial'noi filosofii* (Berlin: Obelisk, 1923), 100.

18. Noel O'Sullivan, *Conservatism* (London: J. M Dent & Sons, 1976), 9. For similar statements, see: Nagy, "The Meaning of a Concept," 14; Gusev, *Russkii konservatizm*, 7.

19. Freeden, *Ideologies*, 333–34.

20. For instance: Huntington, *Conservatism as an Ideology*, 456; Russell Kirk, *The Conservative Mind from Burke to Santayana* (Chicago: Henry Regnery Company, 1953), 7–8; Kekes, *A Case for Conservatism*, 22; Dunn and Woodard, *The Conservative Tradition*, 48; Gusev, *Russkii konservatizm*, 32–34; O. A. Matveichev, "Klassifikatsiia vidov konservatizma: Novaia versiia," *Tetradi po konservatizmu* 2, no. 2 (2014): 75.

21. Freeden, *Ideologies*, 332.

22. O'Sullivan, *Conservatism*, 14.

23. Paul Grenier, "The Varieties of Russian Conservatism," *The American Conservative*, June 19, 2015, http://www.theamericanconservative.com/articles/the-varieties-of-russian-conservatism/.

24. A.V. Shchipkov, "Tipologiia napravlenii konservativnoi mysli v sovremennoi Rossii," *Tetradi po konservatizmu* 2, no. 1 (2014): 114–17.

25. Alexander Fedulov et al., "The Phenomenon of 'Russian Soul' as a Reflection of Traditional Conservatism: New Theoretical and Methodological Approaches and Ordinary Perception of Conservatism," *Mediterranean Journal of Social Sciences* 6, no. 6 (2015): 113–21.

26. Paul Valliere, "Vladimir Soloviev (1853–1900)," in *The Teachings of Modern Orthodox Christianity on Law, Politics, and Human Nature*, ed. John Witte and Frank S. Alexander (New York: Columbia University Press, 2005), 41.

27. For instance, see Vladimir Solovyov, *The Justification of the Good: An Essay on Moral Philosophy* (Grand Rapids, MI: William B. Eerdmans, 2005), 361.

28. A. V. Repnikov, *Konservativnye modeli Rossiiskogo gosudarstvennosti* (Moscow: Rosspen, 2014), 19.

29. Gusev, *Russkii konservatizm*, 40, 45, 70.

30. Repnikov, *Konservativnye modeli*, 21.

31. For a debate on these matters, see the discussion at the end of A. Iu. Minakov, "Rozhdenie russkogo konservatizma: Uroki proshlogo," *Tetradi po konservatizmu* 3 (2014): 27–31. Also: A. Iu. Minakov, *Russkii konservatizm v pervoi chetverti XIX veka* (Voronezh: Izdatel'stvo Voronezhskogo gosudarstvennogo universiteta, 2011), 58. There is also a third view on the matter, namely that conservatism is a product of the "disintegration of the traditional Christian society." See, for instance, the comments of Mikhail Remizov in Paul Grenier, "Definitions and Dialogue: Reflection of a Reluctant Conservative on Russian and American Conservatism," unpublished manuscript, and also Popov, *Russkii konservatizm*, 41–43.

32. Elena Chebankova, "Contemporary Russian Conservatism," *Post-Soviet Affairs* 32, no. 1 (2016): 38.

33. Ibid., 34.

34. A. E. Kotov, "'Sovremennaia nefeodal'naia monarkhiia': Russkaia konservativnaia pechat' kontsa XIX veka v poiskakh natsional'noi ideologii," *Tetradi po konservatizmu* 4 (2015): 130.

35. A. Iu. Minakov, "Rozhdenie russkogo konservatizma," *Tetradi po konservatizmu* 3 (2014): 27.

36. For a discussion of this, see S. V. Perevezentsev, "Ideinye istoki russkogo konservatizma," *Voprosy istorii konservatizma* 1 (2015): 11–32. Also, John Anthony McGuckin, *The Orthodox Church: An Introduction to Its History, Doctrine, and Spiritual Culture* (Oxford: Blackwell, 2008), 381–95.

37. Carl S. Tyneh, *Orthodox Christianity: Overview and Bibliography* (New York: Nova Science, 2003), xvii, 98.

38. Paul Evdokimov, *Orthodoxy: The Cosmos Transfigured* (Hyde Park, NY: New City Press, 2011), 19.

39. Sergius Bulgakov, *The Orthodox Church* (Crestwood, NY: St. Vladimir's Seminary Press, 1988), 10.

40. McGuckin, *The Orthodox Church*, 92.

41. Ibid., 102.

42. For comments to this end, see: Metropolitan Hilarion Alfeyev, *Orthodox Christianity: The History and Canonical Structure of the Orthodox Church* (Yonkers, NY: St. Vladimir's Seminary Press, 2011), 68; and Evdokimov, *Orthodoxy*, 25–26.

43. W. Jardine Grisbrooke, ed., *Spiritual Counsels of Father John of Kronstadt* (London: James Clarke, 1967), 210, 212.

44. Cited in Alfeyev, *Orthodoxy Christianity*, 252.

45. Metropolitan Hierotheos of Nafpaktos, "Personalism and Person," *Discerning Thoughts*, September 21, 2017, https://thoughtsintrusive.wordpress.com/2017/09/21/personalism-and-person/.

46. Pavel Florensky, *The Pillar and Ground of the Truth* (Princeton, NJ: Princeton University Press, 2004), 68.

47. George P. Fedotov, *The Russian Religious Mind: Kievan Christianity, the Tenth to the Thirteenth Centuries* (New York: Harper Torchbooks, 1946), 99, 109. For examples of kenotic statements by a Russian conservative, see: Ignatius Brianchaninov, *The Field: Cultivating Salvation* (Jordanville, NY: Holy Trinity Publications, 2016), 93, 245, 248.

48. Daniel Rancour-Laferriere, *The Slave Soul of Russia: Moral Masochism and the Cult of Suffering* (New York: New York University Press, 1995), 2.

49. Richard Pipes, *Russian Conservatism and Its Critics: A Study in Political Culture* (New Haven, CT: Yale University Press, 2005), 32–33.

50. Gregory L. Freeze, "The Orthodox Church and Serfdom in Prereform Russia," *Slavic Review* 48, no. 3 (1989): 373.

51. Argyrios K. Pisiotis, "Orthodoxy versus Autocracy: The Orthodox Church and Clerical Political Dissent in Late Imperial Russia, 1905–1914" (PhD diss., Georgetown University, 2000), 92.

52. See, for instance, Heather Coleman, ed., *Orthodox Christianity in Imperial Russia: A Source Book on Lived Religion* (Bloomington: Indiana University Press, 2014); Freeze, "The Orthodox Church," 361–87; and Wallace L. Daniel, *The Orthodox Church and Civil Society in Russia* (College Station: Texas A&M University Press, 2006), 20.

53. Gregory L. Freeze, "Handmaiden of the State? The Church in Imperial Russia Reconsidered," *Journal of Ecclesiastical History* 36, no. 1 (1985): 82–102.

54. Pisiotis, "Orthodoxy versus Autocracy," 88.

55. McGuckin, *The Orthodox Church*, 382.

56. Bulgakov, *The Orthodox Church*, 157.

57. Zoe Knox, "The Symphonic Ideal: The Moscow Patriarchate's Post-Soviet Leadership," *Europe-Asia Studies* 55, no. 4 (2003): 576.

58. Cited in Aristotle Papanikolaou, *The Mystical as Political: Democracy and Non-Radical Orthodoxy* (Notre Dame, IN: University of Notre Dame Press, 2012), 37.

59. John P. Burgess, *Holy Rus': The Rebirth of Orthodoxy in the New Russia* (New Haven: Yale University Press, 2017), 38.

60. Brianchaninov, *The Field*, 259.

61. Gusev, *Russkii konservatizm*, 43.

62. Sergei Lavrov, "Russia's Foreign Policy: Historical Background," *Russia in Global Affairs*, March 3, 2016, http://www.mid.ru/en/foreign_policy/news/-/asset_publisher/cKNonkJE02Bw/content/id/2124391.

63. For comments to this effect, see: Peter Duncan, *Russian Messianism: Third Rome, Revolution, Communism, and After* (London: Routledge, 2000), 14; Edward C. Thaden,

Conservative Nationalism in Nineteenth-Century Russia (Seattle: University of Washington Press, 1964), 16.

64. Pipes, *Russian Conservatism*, xii, 1.

65. Ibid., 9–10; Perevezentsev, "Ideinye istoki," 12, 14.

66. Pipes, *Russian Conservatism*, 11–19.

67. Ibid., 24.

68. For an examination of this thesis in a contemporary context, see Marie Mendras, *Russian Politics: The Paradox of a Weak State* (New York: Columbia University Press, 2012).

69. S. Frederick Starr, *Decentralization and Self-Government in Russia, 1830–1870* (Princeton, NJ: Princeton University Press, 1972), 47.

70. Andrzej Walicki, *A History of Russian Thought from the Enlightenment to Marxism* (Stanford, CA: Stanford University Press, 1979), 27.

71. A. Lentin, Introduction to *On the Corruption of Morals in Russia, by M. M. Shcherbatov* (Cambridge: Cambridge University Press, 1969), 46–49. See also: Marc Raeff, "State and Nobility in the Ideology of M. M. Shcherbatov," *American Slavic and East European Review* 19, no. 3 (1960): 363–79.

72. See I. A. Khristoforov, *"Aristokraticheskaia" oppozitsiia Velikim reformam: Konets 1850–seredina 1870-kh gg. (*Moscow: Russkoe slovo, 2002).

73. For a statement to this effect, see W. Bruce Lincoln, *Nicholas I: Emperor and Autocrat of All the Russias* (Bloomington: Indiana University Press, 1978), 182.

74. Gusev, *Russkii konservatizm*, 83.

75. Bruce Lincoln, cited in Stephen M. Woodburn, "The Origins of Russian Intellectual Conservatism, 1825–1881: Danilevsky, Dostoevsky, Katkov, and the Legacy of Nicholas I" (PhD diss., Miami University, 2001), 32.

76. Ivan Il'in, *Nashi zadachi* (Paris: Izdanie Russkogo Obshche-Voinskogo Soiuza, 1956), 2:551. See also, Repnikov, *Konservativnye modeli*, 151.

77. Liubov' Ul'ianova, "Pochemu Rossii ne nuzhna modernizatsii," *Russkaia!dea*, August 12, 2016, http://politconservatism.ru/articles/pochemu-rossii-ne-nuzhna-modernizatsiya.

78. Leonid Poliakov, "Shans ob"edineniia vlasti i naroda na odnoi tsennostnoi osnove," *Tetradi po konservatizmu* 1 (2014): 46.

79. A. V. Shchipkov, "Tipologiia napravlenii konservativnoi mysli v sovremennoi Rossii," *Tetradi po konservatizmu* 2, no. 1 (2014): 114.

80. Poliakov, "Shans ob"edineniia," 46.

81. See, for instance, Stefan Hedlund, *Russian Path Dependence: A People with a Troubled History* (London: Routledge, 2005).

82. *Russkaia doktrina: Gosudarstvennaia ideologiia epokhi Putina* (Moscow: Institut russkoi tsivilizatsii, 2016), 718.

83. See, for instance, A. V. Shchipkov, "Levyi konservatizm," in *Po-drugomu: Sbornik statei o traditsii i smene ideologicheskogo diskursa*, ed. A. V. Shchipkov (Moscow: Abris, 2017), 43–64.

Notes to Chapter 2

1. Kees Boterbloem, *A History of Russia and Its Empire: From Mikhail Romanov to Vladimir Putin* (Lanham. MD: Rowman & Littlefield, 2014), 58.

2. Ibid., 58.

3. For Catherine's view of law, see: Geoffrey Hosking, *Russia and the Russians: A History* (Cambridge, MA: Belknap Press of Harvard University Press, 2001), 214–15.

4. Ibid., 245.

5. For a discussion of Alexander's reform plans after the war against Napoleon, see Marie-Pierre Rey, *Alexander I: The Tsar Who Defeated Napoleon* (DeKalb: Northern Illinois University Press, 2012), 310–18.

6. Gary Hamburg, *Russia's Path toward Enlightenment: Faith, Politics, and Reason, 1500–1801* (New Haven, CT: Yale University Press, 2016), 726.

7. Ibid., 15.

8. Ibid., 742.

9. Ibid.

10. K. Papmehl, "Pososhkov as a Thinker," *Slavic and East European Studies* 6, no. 1 (1961): 81. For more on Pososhkov, see Hamburg, *Russia's Path*, 283–309.

11. A. V. Cherniaev, "U istokov russkogo konservatizma: Ivan Pososhkov," *Tetradi po konservatizmu* 3 (2014): 32.

12. Hans Rogger, "The 'Nationalism' of Ivan Nikitič Boltin," in *For Roman Jakobson: Essays on the Occasion of His Sixtieth Birthday, October 11, 1956*, ed. Halle Morris et al. (The Hague: Mouton, 1956), 425.

13. M. M. Shcherbatov, *On the Corruption of Morals in Russia*, ed., trans., intro., and notes by A. Lentin (London: Cambridge University Press, 1969), 155.

14. D. I. Fonvizin, "Pis'ma iz vtorogo zagranichnogo puteshestviia (1777–1778)," in Fonvizin, *Sobranie sochinenii*, 2:449.

15. Repnikov, *Konservativnye modeli*, 19. For a similar statement, see Minakov, "Rozhdenie russkogo konservatizma," 12.

16. Minakov, *Russkii konservatizm*, 109–10.

17. Martin, *Romantics, Reformers, Reactionaries*, 18.

18. Hosking, *Russia and the Russians*, 421–24.

19. V. Ia. Grosul, "Zarozhdenie rossiiskogo politicheskogo konservatizma," in *Russkii konservatizm XIX stoletiia: Ideologiia i praktika*, ed. V. Ia. Grosul (Moscow: Progress-Traditsiia, 2000), 55–64.

20. Martin, *Romantics, Reformers, Reactionaries*, 16–17, 21.

21. Ibid., 30.

22. A. S. Shishkov, *Rassuzhdenie o starom i novom sloge rossiiskogo iazyka* (St. Petersburg: Imperatorskaia tipografiia, 1803), 13.

23. Ibid., 5.

24. Ibid., 92.

25. A. A. Ivanov, "Lozung 'Rossiia dlia russkikh' v konservativnoi mysli vtoroi poloviny XIX veka," *Tetradi po konservatizmu* 4 (2015), 45; Minakov, *Russkii konservatizm*, 368–69.

26. A. Iu. Minakov, "Russkie konservatory v poiskakh 'russkoi formuly,'" *Voprosy istorii konservatizma* 1 (2015): 34.

27. Martin, *Romantics, Reformers, Reactionaries*, 64.

28. Minakov, *Russkii konservatizm*, 113.

29. N. N. Lupareva, "'Zabytyi patriot 1812 goda': Obshchestvenno-politicheskaia deiatel'nost' Sergeia Nikolaevicha Glinki," *Voprosy istorii konservatizma* 1 (2015): 47.

30. Franklin A. Walker, "Reaction and Radicalism in the Russia of Tsar Alexander I: The Case of the Brothers Glinka," *Canadian Slavonic Papers* 21, no. 4 (1979): 494.

31. Martin, *Romantics, Reformers, Reactionaries*, 80; Minakov, *Russkii konservatizm*, 118–19.

32. Walker, "Reaction and Radicalism," 501.

33. Minakov, *Russkii konservatizm*, 180.

34. Martin, *Romantics, Reformers, Reactionaries*, 131.

35. Minakov, *Russkii konservatizm*, 185.

36. Martin, *Romantics, Reformers, Reactionaries*, 139.

37. Ibid., 157.

38. Ibid., 146.

39. Minakov, *Russkii konservatizm*, 231.

40. Martin, *Romantics, Reformers, Reactionaries*, 173.

41. Ibid., 174.

42. Judith Cohen Zacek, "The Russian Bible Society and the Russian Orthodox Church," *Church History* 35, no. 4 (1966): 419.

43. Minakov, *Russkii konservatizm*, 223.

44. Zacek, "The Russian Bible Society," 417.

45. Ibid., 420.

46. Ibid., 421.

47. Minakov, *Russkii konservatizm*, 236.

48. Ibid., 242.

49. Ibid., 248–49, 253–54.

50. Walker, "Reaction and Radicalism," 500.

51. Minakov, *Russkii konservatizm*, 433.

52. Ibid., 258–61.

53. Ibid., 445.

54. Martin, *Romantics, Reformers, Reactionaries*, 144.

55. Iu. E. Kondakov, "Fotii (P. N. Spaskii): Filosofsko-religioznye vzgliady, obshchestvenno-politicheskaia i tserkovnaia deiatel'nost'," *Voprosy istorii konservatizma* 1 (2015): 70–71.

56. Iu. E. Kondakov, "Krizis gosudarstvenno-tserkovnykh otnoshenii i tserkovnyi konservatizm v pervoi polovine XIX veka," *Tetradi po konservatizmu* 4 (2015): 63.

57. Kondakov, "Fotii," 76–77.

58. Minakov, *Russkii konservatizm*, 346–48.

59. Kondakov, "Fotii," 85.

60. Minakov, *Russkii konservatizm*, 302–4.

61. Ibid., 306; Kondakov, "Fotii," 97.

62. Zacek, "The Russian Bible Society," 430.

63. Ibid., 431–32.

64. Kondakov, "Fotii," 107.

65. Ibid., 104.

66. Ibid.

67. Ibid., 108.

68. Zacek, "The Russian Bible Society," 436.

69. For a discussion of Speransky's intentions, see David Christian, "The Political Ideals of Mikhail Speransky," *The Slavonic and East European Review* 54, no. 2 (1976): 192–213.

70. Richard Pipes, "The Background and Growth of Karamzin's Political Ideas to 1810," in *Karamzin's Memoir on Ancient and Modern Russia: A Translation and Analysis*, by Richard Pipes (New York: Atheneum, 1966), 68–74.

71. Minakov, *Russkii konservatizm*, 81–82.

72. Pipes, "Background and Growth," 46.

73. N. M. Karamzin, *Zapiska o drevnei i novoi Rossii v ee politicheskom i grazhdanskom otnosheniiakh* (Moscow: Nauka, 1991), 48.

74. Ibid., 48.

75. Ibid., 33.

76. For comments to this effect, see: Pipes, *Russian Conservatism*, 88; William Leatherbarrow, "Conservatism in the Age of Alexander I and Nicholas I," in Leatherbarrow and Offord, *A History of Russian Thought*, 101; Walicki, *A History of Russian Thought*, 55–56; Martin, *Romantics, Reformers, Reactionaries*, 86.

77. Karamzin, *Zapiska*, 35, 37.

78. Ibid., 45.

79. Ibid., 105.

80. Natalya Kochetkova, *Nikolai Karamzin* (Boston: Twayne, 1975), 123.

81. Hamburg, *Russia's Path*, 722, 726.

82. Victor Leontovitsch, *The History of Liberalism in Russia* (Pittsburgh, PA: University of Pittsburgh Press, 2012), 55.

83. Kochetkova, *Nikolai Karamzin*, 40.

84. Minakov, *Russkii konservatizm*, 217.

85. Ibid., 398.

86. Karamzin, *Zapiska*, 73–74.

87. Minakov, *Russkii konservatizm*, 406–7.

88. Ibid., 406.

89. Ibid., 390.

90. Ibid., 414.

91. Martin, *Romantics, Reformers, Reactionaries*, 172.

92. Minakov, *Russkii konservatizm*, 414.

93. Lupareva, "'Zabytyi patriot,'" 53.

94. Ibid., 53.

95. Minakov, *Russkii konservatizm*, 424.

96. Karamzin, *Zapiska*, 77–78, 86–87.

97. Minakov, *Russkii konservatizm*, 415–16.

98. Ibid., 418–19.

NOTES TO CHAPTER 3

1. Hosking, *Russia and the Russians*, 262–63.

2. Lincoln, *Nicholas I*, 88.

3. Ibid., 76.

4. Ibid.

5. Nicholas V. Riasanovsky, *Nicholas I and Official Nationality in Russia, 1825–1855* (Berkeley: University of California Press, 1959), 1.

6. Ibid., 11–12.

7. Lincoln, *Nicholas I*, 73.

8. Cynthia H. Whittaker, *The Origins of Modern Russian Education: An Intellectual Biography of Count Sergei Uvarov, 1786–1855* (DeKalb: Northern Illinois University Press, 1984), 128.

9. Ibid., 1–2.

10. Ibid., 90.

11. Ibid., 4.

12. Cynthia H. Whittaker, "The Ideology of Sergei Uvarov: An Interpretative Essay," *The Russian Review* 37, no. 2 (1978): 169.

13. Ibid., 170.

14. Leatherbarrow, "Conservatism," 104.

15. Lincoln, *Nicholas I*, 242.

16. Ibid., 111.

17. Ibid., 132.

18. Ol'ga Vasil'eva, "Ob istokakh rossiiskogo konservatizma," *Tetradi po konservatizmu* 1 (2014): 31.

19. R. G. Eimontova, "V novom oblichii (1825–1855)," in Grosul, *Russkii konservatizm*, 124.

20. Riasanovsky, *Nicholas I*, 96.

21. Heather Coleman, "Introduction: Faith and Story in Imperial Russia," in Coleman, *Orthodox Christianity*, 9.

22. P. N. Zyrianov, *Russkie monastyri i monashestvo v xix i nachale xx veka* (Moscow: Russkoe slovo, 1999), 19. Scott M. Kenworthy, *The Heart of Russia: Trinity-Sergius, Monasticism, and Society after 1825* (Washington DC: Woodrow Wilson Center Press, 2010), 2.

23. Coleman, "Introduction," 7.

24. Kenworthy, *The Heart of Russia*, 6.

25. Ibid., 3.

26. Brianchaninov, *The Field*, 276–77.

27. Irina Paert, "The Unmercenary Bishop: St. Ignatii (Brianchaninov) (1807–1867) and the Making of Modern Russian Orthodoxy," *Slavonica* 9, no. 2 (2003): 106–7.

28. Allan Armstrong, Foreword to *On the Prayer of Jesus, by* Ignatius Brianchaninov (Berwick, ME: Ibis, 2006), xii.

29. Aleksandr Churkin, "St. Ignatius Brianchaninov and the Russian Religious Conservatism," unpublished conference paper, Fifteenth Annual Aleksanteri Conference, University of Helsinki, October 21–3, 2015.

30. Ibid.

31. Brianchaninov, *The Field*, 73.

32. Ignatii Brianchaninov, "Arkhipastyrskye vozzvaniia po voprosu osvobozhdeniia krest'ian ot krepostnoi zavisimosti," in *Polnoe sobranie tvorenii* (Moscow: Palomnik, 2001), 2:430.

33. Alfeyev, *Orthodox Christianity*, 199.

34. Brianchaninov, *On the Prayer of Jesus*, 97–98.

35. Rancour-Laferriere, *The Slave Soul of Russia*, 27–28.

36. N. V. Gogol', *Vybrannye mesta iz perepiski s druz'iami* (Moscow: Patriot, 1993), 51–52.

37. Ibid., 91.

38. Ibid., 35.

39. Ibid., 225.

40. Ibid., 94.

41. Ibid., 154.

42. Mikhail Pogodin, *Istoriko-politicheskie pis'ma i zapiski v prodolzhenii krymskoi voiny 1853–1856* (Moscow: Tipografiia V. M. Frish, 1874), 202.

43. Ibid., 254.

44. Mikhail Pogodin, "Parallel' russkoi istorii s istoriei zapadnykh evropeiskikh gosudarstv, otnositel'no nachala," in *Izbrannye trudy* (Moscow: Rossiiskaia politicheskaia entsiklopediia, 2010), 252.

45. Ibid., 256.

46. Ibid., 263.

47. Ibid., 264.

48. Pogodin, *Istoriko-politicheskie pis'ma*, 11.

49. Riasanovsky, *Nicholas I*, 76.

50. Andrzej Walicki, *The Slavophile Controversy: History of a Conservative Utopia in Nineteenth-Century Russian Thought* (Oxford: Clarendon Press, 1975), 51.

51. Pogodin, *Istoriko-politicheskie pis'ma*, 11.

52. Ibid., 13.

53. Ibid., 2.

54. Ibid., 186.

55. Lincoln, *Nicholas I*, 164.

56. Peter K. Christoff, *An Introduction to Nineteenth-Century Slavophilism: Iu. F. Samarin* (Boulder: Westview, 1991), 139–43.

57. Vasil'eva, "Ob istokakh rossiiskogo konservatizma," 31.

58. Lincoln, *Nicholas I*, 100–103.

59. Ibid., 237.

60. Eimontova, "V novom oblichii," 70–71.

61. Ibid., 174.

62. Ibid., 174–75.

63. Gogol', *Vybrannye mesta*, 66.

64. Brianchaninov, "Arkhipastyrskye vozzvaniia," 400.

65. Ibid., 409–10.

66. Ibid., 412.

67. Ibid., 416.

68. Whittaker, *The Origins*, 38.

69. S. V. Udalov, "Imperiia na iakore: Konservativnaia ideologiia v Rossii vtoroi chetverti XIX veka," *Tetradi po konservatizmu* 4 (2015): 82.

70. Whittaker, *The Origins*, 47–50.

71. Minakov, *Russkii konservatizm*, 331–32.

72. Peter K. Christoff, *An Introduction to Nineteenth-Century Russian Slavophilism: I. V. Kireevskij* (The Hague: Mouton, 1972), 122.

73. Pogodin, *Istoriko-politicheskie pis'ma*, 246–48.

74. Ibid., 257.

75. Ibid., 258.

76. Ibid., 259.

77. Ibid., 260.
78. Ibid., 261–63.
79. Ibid., 316–17, 336–39.
80. Ibid., 357.
81. Leontovitsch, *The History of Liberalism*, 91.
82. Lincoln, *Nicholas I*, 183–85.
83. Ibid., 186.
84. Ibid., 270–71.
85. Ibid., 188.
86. Leontovitsch, *The History of Liberalism*, 80.
87. Riasanovsky, *Nicholas I*, 210.
88. Leontovitsch, *The History of Liberalism*, 81–82.
89. Ibid., 92–97. Lincoln, *Nicholas I*, 188–94.
90. Leontovitsch, *The History of Liberalism*, 96–97.
91. Pogodin, *Istoriko-politicheskie pis'ma*, 338.
92. Whittaker, *The Origins*, 103.
93. Riasanovsky, *Nicholas I*, 140–41.
94. Gogol', *Vybrannye mesta*, 30.
95. Ibid., 130.
96. Gregory Freeze, "The Orthodox Church," 362.
97. Ibid., 370.
98. Brianchaninov, "Arkhipastyrskye vozzvaniia," 404.
99. Ibid., 407–16.
100. Ibid., 417.
101. Gogol', *Vybrannye mesta*, 133.
102. Riasanovsky, *Nicholas I*, 217.
103. Whittaker, *The Origins*, 117–18.
104. Pogodin, *Istoriko-politicheskie pis'ma*, 218.
105. Eimontova, "V novom oblichii, " 120–22.
106. Pogodin, *Istoriko-politicheskie pis'ma*, 248.
107. Riasanovsky, *Nicholas I*, 270.
108. Udalov, "Imperiia na iakore," 83.

NOTES TO CHAPTER 4

1. Eimontova, "V novom oblichii," 169.
2. Christoff, *I. V. Kireevskij*, 39–43.
3. Peter F. Christoff, *An Introduction to Nineteenth-Century Russian Slavophilism: A. S. Xomjakov* (The Hague: Mouton, 1961), 258.
4. A. A. Popov, "N. A. Berdiaev o konservatizme slavianofilov," *Tetradi po konservatizmu* 3 (2014): 55.
5. For discussions of this, see I. A. Khristoforov, "Nineteenth-Century Russian Conservatism: Problems and Contradictions," *Russian Studies in History* 48, no. 2 (2009): 61–62; Eimontova, "B novom oblichii," 164; Gusev, *Russkii konservatizm*, 70, 85–86; Susanna Rabow-Edling, *Slavophile Thought and the Politics of Cultural Nationalism* (Albany: State University of New York Press, 2006), 129–37; Peter K. Christoff, *K. S. Aksakov: A Study in Ideas* (Princeton, NJ: Princeton University Press, 1982): 266–67; Christoff, *Iu. F. Samarin*,

78; A. A. Teslia, "Slavianofil'skii 'konservatizm': Mezhdu natsionalizmom i liberalizmom?" *Tetradi po konservatizmu* 4 (2015): 30–32.

6. Walicki, *The Slavophile Controversy*, 256; Christoff, *Iu. F. Samarin*, 257, 332.

7. Rabow-Edling, *Slavophile Thought*, 37–39.

8. Ivan Kireevsky, "On the Nature of European Culture and on Its Relationship to Russian Culture," in *On Spiritual Unity: A Slavophile Reader*, by Aleksei Khomiakov and Ivan Kireevsky, trans. and ed. Boris Jakim and Robert Bird (Hudson, NY: Lindisfarne, 1998), 220.

9. N. V. Riasanovsky, *Russia and the West in the Teaching of the Slavophiles: A Study of Romantic Ideology* (Gloucester, MA: Peter Smith, 1965), 107–8.

10. K. S. Aksakov, "Stat'i K. Aksakova iz 'Mol'vy,'" in *Rannye slavianofily: A. S. Khomiakov, I. V. Kireevskii, K. S. i I. S. Aksakovy*, ed. N. L. Brodskii (Moscow: Tipografiia T-va I. D. Sytina, 1910), 111–12.

11. Kireevsky, "On the Nature of European Culture," 232.

12. Rabow-Edling, *Slavophile Thought*, 130.

13. Christoff, *A. S. Xomjakov*, 100.

14. Rabow-Edling, *Slavophile Thought*, 26.

15. Peter Christoff describes the recognition of Russia's cultural inferiority as "psychologically devastating to a generation raised on the glories of Russia's military skill." Christoff, *K. S. Aksakov*, 26.

16. Petr Chaadaev, *Filosofskie pis'ma* (Kazan: Tipografiia D. M. Gran, 1906), 11.

17. For comments to this effect, see: Rabow-Edling, *Slavophile Thought*, 46, 55, 91; Riasanovsky, *Russia and the West*, 180–81; N. L. Brodskii, "Slavnianofily i ikh uchenie," in Brodskii, *Rannye slavianofily*, xlii; Christoff, *A. S. Xomjakov*, 198.

18. Christoff, *K. S. Aksakov*, 426. See also Henry Lanz, "The Philosophy of Ivan Kireevsky," *The Slavonic Review* 4, no. 12 (1926): 594–604.

19. Walicki, *A History of Russian Thought*, 106. See also: Riasanovsky, *Russia and the West*, 165–66, 176–77; and Rabow-Edling, *Slavophile Thought*, 8.

20. Riasanovsky, *Russia and the West*, 15–18.

21. Brodskii, "Slavianofiliy i ikh uchenie," xxxv.

22. For a statement by Konstantin Aksakov to this effect, see Christoff, *K. S. Aksakov*, 350.

23. Rabow-Edling, *Slavophile Thought*, 164.

24. Vladimir Fedorovich Odoevsky, *Russian Nights* (Evanston, IL: Northwestern University Press, 1997), 111.

25. Ibid., 209.

26. Ibid.

27. Ibid., 211–12.

28. Walicki, *The Slavophile Controversy*, 242–43.

29. A. S. Khomiakov, "To the Serbians: A Message from Moscow," in Christoff, *A. S. Xomjakov*, 250.

30. For instance, Rabow-Edling, *Slavophile Thought*, 7, 22, 42; Christoff, *I. V. Kireevskij*, 321.

31. Christoff, *I. V. Kireevskij*, 84.

32. Aksakov, "Stat'i K. Aksakova," 115–16.

33. Christoff, *Iu. F. Samarin*, 163.

34. A. S. Khomiakov, "Mechta," in Brodskii, *Rannye slavianofily*, 146.

35. Kireevsky, "On the Nature of European Culture," 228.

36. Christoff, *K. S. Aksakov*, 430.

37. Christoff, *I. V. Kireevskij*, 165.

38. Ibid., 165–66.

39. A. S. Khomiakov, "Some Remarks by an Orthodox Christian concerning the Western Communions, on the Occasion of a Brochure by Mr. Laurentie," in Khomiakov and Kireevsky, *On Spiritual Unity*, 58, 60–61.

40. Kireevsky, "On the Nature of European Culture," 228.

41. Ibid., 231.

42. Ivan Kireevsky, "Fragments," in Khomiakov and Kireevsky, *On Spiritual Unity*, 277.

43. Aksakov, "Stat'i K. Aksakova," 113.

44. Christoff, *K. S. Aksakov*, 125.

45. Ibid., 168.

46. Robert Bird, General Introduction to Khomiakov and Kireevsky, *On Spiritual Unity*, 21.

47. Christoff, *K. S. Aksakov*, 258.

48. Aleksei Khomiakov, "The Church Is One," in Khomiakov and Kireevsky, *On Spiritual Unity*, 48–49.

49. Christoff, *A. S. Xomjakov*, 139.

50. Aleksei Khomiakov, "Some More Remarks by an Orthodox Christian concerning the Western Communions, on the Occasion of Several Latin and Protestant Publications," in Khomiakov and Kireevsky, *On Spiritual Unity*, 134.

51. Christoff, *A. S. Xomjakov*, 142.

52. Khomiakov, "Some More Remarks," 121.

53. Khomiakov, "Some Remarks," 80, 81.

54. Ibid., 102.

55. Ibid., 115.

56. A. A. Popov, "Istoriia russkogo konservatizma i slavianofily," *Tetradi po konservatizmu* 2, no. 1 (2014): 23. Also, Richard Wortman, "Koshelev, Samarin, and Cherkassky and the Fate of Liberal Slavophilism," *Slavic Review* 21, no. 2 (1962): 264.

57. Michael Hughes, "State and Society in the Political Thought of the Moscow Slavophiles," *Studies in East European Thought* 52, no. 3 (2000): 169–70.

58. Walicki, *The Slavophile Controversy*, 260.

59. Hughes, "State and Society," 167.

60. Ibid., 167.

61. Aleksei Khomiakov, "Fifth Letter to William Palmer," in Khomiakov and Kireevsky, *On Spiritual Unity*, 157. See also Riasanovsky, *Russia and the West*, 130.

62. Rabow-Edling, *Slavophile Thought*, 127; Riasanovsky, *Russia and the West*, 79.

63. Brodskii, "Slavianofily i ikh uchenie," lv.

64. Christoff, *K. S. Aksakov*, 263.

65. K. Aksakov, "O sochineniiakh Zhukovskogo," in Brodskii, *Rannye slavianofily*, 120.

66. Walicki, *The Slavophile Controversy*, 446–47; Rancour-Laferriere, *The Slave Soul of Russia*, 38–42.

67. Christoff, *Iu. F. Samarin*, 416.

68. Aksakov, "O sochineniiakh Zhukovskogo," 117.

69. Christoff, *A. S. Xomjakov*,187.

70. K. Aksakov, "Svobodnoe slovo," in Brodskii, *Rannye slavianofily*, 177.

71. Christoff, *A. S. Xomjakov*, 201. For similar views by Konstantin Aksakov, see: Walicki, *The Slavophile Controversy*, 259.

72. Rabow-Edling, *Slavophile Thought*, 118.

73. Christoff, *Iu. F. Samarin*, 182.

74. "Zapiska K. S. Aksakova 'o vnutrennem sostoianii Rossii,' predstavlennaia Gosudariu Imperatoru Aleksandru II v 1855 g.," in Brodskii, *Rannye slavianofily*, 69–72.

75. Ibid., 73.

76. Ibid., 74.

77. Ibid., 80.

78. Ibid., 81.

79. Ibid., 77.

80. Ibid., 78.

81. Ibid., 90.

82. Ibid., 95.

83. Ibid., 96.

84. Ibid.

85. Michael Hughes, "Independent Gentlemen: The Social Position of the Moscow Slavophiles and Its Impact on their Political Thought," *The Slavonic and East European Review* 71, no. 1 (1993): 72–73.

86. Ibid., 77.

87. Christoff, *Iu. F. Samarin*, 159–60.

88. Brodskii, "Slavianofily i ikh uchenie," xlix.

89. Christoff, *Iu. F. Samarin*, 308.

90. Hughes, "Independent Gentlemen," 77.

91. Christoff, *A. S. Xomjakov*, 96–97.

92. Aksakov, "Stat'i K. Aksakova," 106.

93. Christoff, *K. S. Aksakov*, 257.

94. Christoff, *Iu. F. Samarin*, 128.

95. Ibid., 179.

96. Ibid., 165–66.

97. Laura Engelstein, *Slavophile Empire: Imperial Russia's Illiberal Path* (Ithaca, NY: Cornell University Press, 2009), 128.

98. Christoff, *A. S. Xomjakov*, 97, 229, 232.

99. Hughes, "Independent Gentlemen," 85.

100. Pavel Miliukov, *Razlozhenie slavianofil'stva: Danilevskii, Leont'ev, Vl. Solov'ev* (Moscow: Tipo-lit. Vysochaishe utver. T-va I. N. Kushnerev, 1893).

NOTES TO CHAPTER 5

1. Hosking, *Russia and the Russians*, 286.

2. Ibid., 285–86.

3. Terence Emmons, *The Russian Landed Gentry and the Peasant Emancipation of 1861* (Cambridge: Cambridge University Press, 1968), 7.

4. Khristoforov, *"Aristokraticheskaia" oppozitsiia*, 198.

5. Ibid., 22.

6. Wayne Dowler, "The 'Young Editors' of *Moskvityanin* and the Origins of Intelligentsia Conservatism in Russia," *Slavonic and Eastern European Review* 55, no. 3 (1977): 310–27.

7. Christoff, *Iu. F. Samarin*, 400.

8. Wayne Dowler, *Dostoevsky, Grigor'ev, and Native Soil Conservatism* (Toronto: University of Toronto Press, 1982), 59. See also: Wayne Dowler, "Herder in Russia: A. A. Grigor'ev and 'Progressivist-Traditionalism,'" *Canadian Slavonic Papers* 19, no. 2 (1977): 167–80.

9. David Walsh, "Dostoevsky's Discovery of the Christian Foundations of Politics," in *Dostoevsky's Political Thought*, ed. Richard Avramenko and Lee Trepanier (Lanham, MD: Lexington, 2013), 24.

10. Ethan Alexander-Davey, "Ugliness, Emptiness, and Boredom: Dostoevsky on the Secular Humanist Social Religion," in Avramenko and Trepanier, *Dostoevsky's Political Thought*, 118.

11. Dowler, *Dostoevsky, Grigor'ev*, 91.

12. F. M. Dostoevskii, *Dnevnik pisatelia*, September 1876, in *Polnoe sobranie sochinenii v tridtsati tomakh* (Leningrad: Nauka, 1981), 23:121.

13. Dostoevskii, *Dnevnik pisatelia*, January 1877, in *Polnoe sobranie sochinenii*, 25:17.

14. Dostoevskii, *Dnevnik pisatelia*, January 1881, in *Polnoe sobranie sochinenii*, 27:24–25.

15. Dowler, *Dostoevsky, Grigor'ev*, 93.

16. Dostoevskii, *Dnevnik pisatelia*, February 1876, in *Polnoe sobranie sochinenii*, 22:43.

17. Dostoevskii, *Dnevnik pisatelia*, 1873 ("Vlas"), in *Polnoe sobranie sochinenii*, 21:38.

18. Dostoevskii, *Dnevnik pisatelia*, April 1876, in *Polnoe sobranie sochinenii*, 22:114.

19. Dostoevskii, *Dnevnik pisatelia*, 1873 ("Smiatennyi vid"), in *Polnoe sobranie sochinenii*, 21:59.

20. F. M. Dostoevskii, *Zimnie zametki o letnikh vpechatleniiakh*, in *Polnoe sobranie sochinenii*, 5:51.

21. Dostoevskii, *Dnevnik pisatelia*, January 1881, in *Polnoe sobranie sochinenii*, 27:8–9.

22. Christoff, *K. S. Aksakov*, 350.

23. F. M. Dostoevskii, "Pushkin," in *Polnoe sobranie sochinenii*, 26:148.

24. F. M. Dostoevskii, "Ob"iasnitel'noe slovo po povodu pechataemoi nizhe rechi o Pushkine," in *Polnoe sobranie sochinenii*, 26:131.

25. F. M. Dostoevskii, "A. A. Romanovu (nasledniku)," in *Polnoe sobranie sochinenii*, 29:1:260.

26. Dostoevskii, *Dnevnik pisatelia*, March 1877, in *Polnoe sobranie sochinenii*, 25:74.

27. N. Ia. Danilevskii, *Rossiia i Evropa: Vzgliad na kul'turnye i politicheskie otnosheniia slavianskogo mira k germano-romanskomu* (Moscow: Blagoslovenie, 2011), 113.

28. Ibid., 135.

29. Ibid., 141–42.

30. Ibid., 144.

31. Ibid., 229.

32. Ibid., 154–55.

33. Ibid., 393.

34. Ibid., 447, 461.

35. Ibid., 510, 512.

36. Karel Durman, *The Time of the Thunderer: Mikhail Katkov, Russian Nationalist Extremism and the Failure of the Bismarckian System, 1871–1887* (Boulder, CO: East European Monographs, 1988), 28.

37. Riasanovsky, *Russia and the West*, 83–85.

38. Durman, *The Time of the Thunderer*, 246.

39. Ibid., 83.

40. Eugene Pyziur, "Mikhail N. Katkov: Advocate of English Liberalism in Russia, 1856–1863," *The Slavonic and Eastern European Review* 45, no. 105 (1967): 439–56.

41. O. K. Avdeev, "Konservatizm kak faktor miagkoi sily Rossii," *Tetradi po konservatizmu* 2, no. 1 (2014), 74.

42. M. Katkov, "Chto nam delat' s Pol'shei?" *Russkii vestnik* 44 (March 1863): 474.

43. Durman, *The Time of the Thunderer*, 62.

44. Ibid., 74–76.

45. Khristoforov, *"Aristokraticheskaia" oppozitsiia*, 223.

46. Ivanov, "Lozung 'Rossiia dlia russkikh,'" 34.

47. Ibid., 34.

48. Ibid., 36.

49. Konstantin Leont'ev, *Vizantizm i slavianstvo* (Moscow: Izdanie obshchestva istorii i drevnosti rossiskikh pri Moskovskom universitete, 1876), 1

50. Ibid., 50.

51. Constantine Leontyev, "The Average European as an Ideal and Instrument of Universal Destruction," in *Russian Philosophy*, ed. James M. Edie, James P. Scanlan, and Mary-Barbara Zeldin (Chicago: Quandrangle, 1965), 2:279.

52. Cited in Sidney Monas, "Leontiev: A Meditation," *The Journal of Modern History* 43, no. 3 (1971): 488.

53. Leont'ev, *Vizantizm*, 72–73.

54. Ibid., 100–101.

55. Leontyev, "The Average European," 280.

56. Leont'ev, *Vizantizm*, 125.

57. Ibid., 127–29.

58. Ibid., 129.

59. Ibid., 30.

60. Khristoforov, *"Aristokraticheskaia" oppozitsiia*, 39.

61. Ibid., 42.

62. Ibid., 70.

63. Ibid., 82.

64. Ibid., 83–84.

65. V. Ia. Grosul, "V epokhu reform 1861 goda (1856–1866 gg.)," in Grosul, *Russkii konservatizm*, 219–20.

66. Richard Weeks, "The Attempted Reforms of Peter Andreevich Shuvalov, 1871–1874," *The Historian* 51, no. 1 (1988): 69.

67. Ibid., 70.

68. Ibid., 73–75.

69. Khristoforov, *"Aristokraticheskaia" oppozitsiia*, 152–53.

70. Ibid., 173.

71. Emmons, *The Russian Landed Gentry*, 224.

72. Khristoforov, *"Aristokraticheskaia" oppozitsiia*, 248.

73. Ibid., 296.

74. Ibid., 297.

75. B. S. Itenberg, "Ot 4 aprelia 1866 do 1 marta 1881 goda," in Grosul, *Russkii konservatizm*, 245.

76. T. E. Pliashchenko, "Konservativnyi liberalizm v poreformennoi Rossii: Istoriia odnoi neudachi," *Tetradi po konservatizmu* 4 (2015): 124.

77. L. V. Poliakov, "Vechnoe i prekhodiashchee v russkom konservatizme," *Tetradi po konservatizmu* 4 (2015): 224–25.

78. Gorokhov, "Konservatizm v Rossii," 129.

79. G. M. Hamburg, "Introduction. An Eccentric Vision: The Political Philosophy of B. N. Chicherin," in *Liberty, Equality, and the Market*, by B. N. Chicherin, ed. and trans. G. M. Hamburg (New Haven, CT: Yale University Press, 1998), 1–60.

80. Aileen Kelly, "'What Is Real Is Rational': The Political Philosophy of B. N. Chicherin," *Cahiers du monde russe et soviétique* 18, no. 3 (1977): 195–222.

81. Pipes, *Russian Conservatism*, 161.

82. Cited in Philip Boobbyer, "Russian Liberal Conservatism," in *Russian Nationalism Past and Present*, ed. Geoffrey Hosking and Robert Service (Basingstoke: MacMillan, 1998), 37.

83. B. N. Chicherin, "Excerpts from On Popular Representation," in Chicherin, *Liberty, Equality, and the Market*, 182.

84. Boobbyer, "Russian Liberal Conservatism," 40.

85. B. N. Chicherin, "Contemporary Tasks in Russian Life," in Chicherin, *Liberty, Equality, and the Market*, 134–39.

86. Chicherin, "Excerpts from On Popular Representation," 158.

87. Ibid., 160.

88. Ibid., 177–78.

89. Ibid., 165.

90. B. N. Chicherin, "Excerpts from Property and State," in Chicherin, *Liberty, Equality, and the Market*, 356, 365.

91. Ibid., 369.

92. B. N. Chicherin, "On Serfdom," in Chicherin, *Liberty, Equality, and the Market*, 102.

93. Pipes, *Russian Conservatism*, 160.

94. Gusev, *Russkii konservatizm*, 59.

95. Martin Katz, *Mikhail N. Katkov: A Political Biography 1818–1887* (The Hague: Mouton, 1966), 87–89.

96. Katkov, "Chto nam delat'?" 496.

97. Ibid., 486.

98. Ibid., 494.

99. Ibid., 488.

100. Ibid., 477.

101. See Durman, *The Time of the Thunderer*, for Katkov's foreign policy statements.

102. Ibid., 262.

103. Vasil'eva, "Ob istokakh rossiiskogo konservatizma," 34.

104. Leont'ev, *Vizantizm*, 81.

105. Ibid., 29.

106. Ibid., 101.

107. Ibid., 102.

108. Aleksandr Repnikov, "Razmyshleniia o konservatizme," *Svobodnaia mysl'* 11–12 (2012): 111.

109. Thaden, *Conservative Nationalism*, 80.

110. F. M. Dostoevskii, "Adres Aleksandru II napisannyi Dostoevskim ot imeni Slavianskogo blagotvoritel'nogo obshchestva," in *Polnoe sobranie sochinenii*, 30:2:48.

111. Dowler, *Dostoevsky, Grigor'ev*, 106.

112. Ibid., 104.

113. Ibid., 109, 145.

114. Ibid., 96.

115. Dostoevskii, *Dnevnik pisatelia*, June 1876, in *Polnoe sobranie sochinenii*, 23:53.

116. Dowler, *Dostoevsky, Grigor'ev*, 96.

117. Emmons, *The Russian Landed Gentry*, 49–55.

118. Chicherin, "On Serfdom," 102.

119. Emmons, *The Russian Landed Gentry*, 226.

120. Khristoforov, *"Aristokraticheskaia" oppozitsiia*, 43.

121. Ibid., 112.

122. Ibid., 245.

123. Ibid.

124. Ibid., 249.

125. Ibid., 250.

126. Ibid., 257.

127. Ibid., 312.

128. Dowler, *Dostoevsky, Grigor'ev*, 104.

129. Leontyev, "The Average European," 276.

130. V. A. Tvardovskaia, "Tsarstvovanie Aleksandra III," in Grosul, *Russkii konservatizm*, 295; Thaden, *Conservative Nationalism*, 174.

131. Dowler, *Dostoevsky, Grigor'ev*, 98–100.

132. Katz, *Mikhail Katkov*, 156–57.

133. Ibid., 153–57.

134. Ibid., 110–16.

135. Chicherin, "On Serfdom," 73.

136. Chicherin, "Excerpts from Property and the State," 404.

137. Dowler, *Dostoevsky, Grigor'ev*, 111–14.

138. Danilevskii, *Rossiia i Evropa*, 195.

NOTES TO CHAPTER 6

1. Hans Heilbronner, "Alexander III and the Reform Plan of Loris-Melikov," *Journal of Modern History* 33, no. 4 (1961): 385.

2. Robert F. Byrnes, "Pobedonostsev's Conception of the Good Society: An Analysis of His Thought after 1880," *The Review of Politics* 13, no. 2 (1951): 172.

3. Robert F. Byrnes, *Pobedonostsev: His Life and Thought* (Bloomington: Indiana University Press, 1968), 55–63.

4. Ibid., 153.

5. Tvardovskaia, "Tsarstvovanie Aleksandra III," 277.

6. Ibid., 313.

7. Ibid., 317.

8. Ibid., 320–30.

9. Catherine Evtuhov and Richard Stites, *A History of Russia: Peoples, Legends, Events, Forces since 1800* (Boston: Houghton Mifflin, 2004), 147.

10. Evtuhov and Stites, *A History of Russia,* 149.

11. Edward H. Judge, *Plehve: Repression and Reform in Imperial Russia, 1902–1904* (Syracuse, NY: Syracuse University Press, 1983), 123–24; Ul'ianova, "Pochemu Rossii ne nuzhna modernizatsiia."

12. Richard Pipes divides conservatives of this era into church, noble, intelligentsia, and bureaucratic conservatives; Hans Rogger divides them into gentry, bureaucratic, and Pan-Slavic/Slavophile: Richard Pipes, "Russian Conservatism in the Second Half of the Nineteenth Century," *Slavic Review* 30, no. 1 (1971): 121; Hans Rogger, "Reflections on Russian Conservatism: 1861–1905," *Jahrbücher für Geschichte Osteuropas* 14 (1966): 207.

13. Thaden, *Conservative Nationalism,* 127; Pipes, *Russian Conservatism,* 117–18; Rogger, "Reflections," 207.

14. Byrnes, *Pobedonostsev,* 187–99.

15. Ibid., 205–7.

16. Ibid., 122–30.

17. Anders Henriksson, "The *St. Petersburg Zeitung*: Tribune of Baltic German Conservatism in Late Nineteenth-Century Russia," *Journal of Baltic Studies* 20, no. 4 (1989): 371–72.

18. Ibid., 372.

19. John Strickland, *The Making of Holy Russia: The Orthodox Church and Russian Nationalism before the Revolution* (Jordanville, NY: Holy Trinity Publications, 2013), 17.

20. Ibid., 9.

21. Ibid., 7.

22. Ibid., 73.

23. Nadieszda Kizenko, *A Prodigal Saint: Father John of Kronstadt and the Russian People* (University Park: The Pennsylvania State University Press, 2000), 2.

24. Ibid., 51–60.

25. Ibid., 84.

26. Grisbrooke, *Spiritual Counsels,* 214.

27. Ibid., 213.

28. Alfeyev, *Orthodox Christianity,* 205.

29. Kizenko, *A Prodigal Saint,* 236.

30. Bishop Alexander, *Father John of Kronstadt: A Life* (Crestwood, NY: St. Vladimir's Seminary Press, 1979), 133.

31. Strickland, *The Making of Holy Russia,* xviii.

32. Repnikov, *Konservativnye modeli,* 291–94.

33. Robert F. Byrnes, "Pobedonostsev on the Role of Change in History," *The Russian Review* 26, no. 3 (1967): 232.

34. Byrnes, "Pobedonostsev's Conception," 175.

35. John D. Basil, "Konstantin Petrovich Pobedonostsev: An Argument for a Russian State Church," *Church History,* 64, no. 1 (1995): 44.

36. Ibid., 44.
37. Byrnes, "Pobedonostsev on the Role of Change," 232.
38. Konstantin Pobedonostsev, "The Falsehood of Democracy," in *Readings in Russian Civilization, vol. 2, Imperial Russia, 1700–1917*, ed. Thomas Riha (Chicago: University of Chicago Press, 1964), 391.
39. Ibid., 395.
40. Byrnes, "Pobedonostsev on the Role of Change," 239.
41. Byrnes, "Pobedonostsev's Conception," 176.
42. Ibid., 177–82.
43. Basil, "Konstantin Petrovich Pobedonostsev," 56.
44. Arthur E. Adams, "Pobedonostsev and the Rule of Firmness," *The Slavonic and East European Review* 32, no. 78 (1953): 137–38.
45. A. Iu. Polunov, "Konstantin Petrovich Pobedonostsev—Man and Politician," *Russian Studies in History* 39, no. 4 (2001): 16.
46. Tvardovskaia, "Tsarstvovanie Aleksandra III," 290.
47. Dmitry Shlapentokh, "Forgotten Predecessors: The Russian Conservative Historians of the French Revolution," *International Journal of Politics, Culture, and Society* 9, no. 1 (1995): 65.
48. Judge, *Plehve*, 69.
49. Ibid., 51.
50. Ibid., 87–92.
51. Ibid., 176–78.
52. Repnikov, *Konservativnye modeli*, 203.
53. Mikhail Suslov, "'Slavophilism Is True Liberalism': The Political Utopia of S. F. Sharapov (1855–1911)," *Russian History* 38, no. 2 (2011): 293.
54. Don C. Rawson, *Russian Rightists and the Revolution of 1905* (Cambridge: Cambridge University Press, 1995), 41.
55. Suslov, "'Slavophilism Is True Liberalism,'" 297.
56. Repnikov, *Konservativnye modeli*, 203–8.
57. Suslov, "'Slavophilism Is True Liberalism,'" 299.
58. Gorokhov, "Konservatizm v Rossii," 139.
59. Lev Tikhomirov, *Pochemu ia perestal byt' revoliutsionerom* (Moscow: Tipografiia Vil'de, 1895), 10, 52–54, 104.
60. Ibid., 57.
61. Lev Tikhomirov, *Demokratiia liberal'naia i sotsial'naia* (Moscow: Universitetskaia tipografiia, 1896), 37.
62. Ibid., 40–42.
63. Ibid., 50.
64. Ibid., 50–51.
65. Ibid., 65–66.
66. Ibid., 80.
67. Ibid., 81.
68. Ibid., 82–84.
69. Ibid., 89.
70. Tikhomirov, *Pochemu ia perestal*, 65–66.
71. Rogger, "Reflections," 202.
72. Kotov, "Sovremennaia nefeodal'naia monarkhiia," 144.

73. Tikhomirov, *Pochemu ia perestal*, 122.
74. Lev Tikhomirov, *Monarkhicheskaia gosudarstvennost'* (Moscow: Izdatel'stvo "E," 2016), 493.
75. Repnikov, *Konservativnye modeli*, 184.
76. Tikhomirov, *Monarkhicheskaia gosudarstvennost'*, 511.
77. Ibid., 80.
78. Ibid., 430–34.
79. Ibid., 532.
80. Ibid.
81. Byrnes, "Pobedonostsev on the Role of Change," 245–50.
82. Repnikov, *Konservativnye modeli*, 143.
83. O. A. Milevskii, "Rossiiskie ekonomicheskie al'ternativy: Konservativnyi podkhod," *Tetradi po konservatizmu* 4 (2015): 110.
84. Mikhail Suslov, "The Lost Chance of Conservative Modernization: S. F. Sharapov in the Economic Debates of the Late Nineteenth Century to the Early Twentieth Century," *Acta Slavica Iaponica* 31 (2012): 37.
85. Tvardovskaia, "Tsarstvovanie Aleksandra III," 393–95.
86. Suslov, "The Lost Chance," 48–51.
87. Repnikov, *Konservativnye modeli*, 385.
88. Ibid., 355–56.
89. Byrnes, "Pobedonostsev on the Role of Change," 247–48.
90. Judge, *Plehve*, 78.
91. Ibid., 184.
92. Tvardovskaia, "Tsarstvovanie Aleksandra III," 340–50.
93. Milevskii, "Rossiiskie ekonomicheskie al'ternativy," 110.
94. Ibid., 113.
95. Ibid.
96. Ibid., 112.
97. Tikhomirov, *Demokratiia liberal'naia i sotsial'naia*, 180.
98. Ibid., 185–86.
99. Milevskii, "Rossiiskie ekonomicheskie al'ternativy," 109–10.
100. Judge, *Plehve*, 123–46.

NOTES TO CHAPTER 7

1. I. V. Omel'ianchuk, "Russkii konservatizm nachala XX veka v poiskakh partiinogo samoopredeleniia," *Tetradi po konservatizmu* 4 (2015): 148.
2. Jacob Langer, "Corruption and the Counterrevolution: The Rise and Fall of the Black Hundred" (PhD diss., Duke University, 2007), 63.
3. Omel'ianchuk, "Russkii konservatizm," 154.
4. Ibid., 154.
5. George Putnam, "P. B. Struve's View of the Russian Revolution of 1905," *The Slavonic and East European Review* 45, no. 105 (1967): 457–73; Boobbyer, "Russian Liberal Conservatism," 38–39.
6. Richard Pipes, *Struve: Liberal on the Right, 1905–1944* (Cambridge, MA: Harvard University Press, 1980), 81–84.
7. Ibid., 69–70.

8. M. Gershenzon, "Predislovie," in *Vekhi: Sbornik statei o russkoi intelligentsia*, by N. A. Berdiaev et al. (Moscow: Tipografiia V. M. Sablina, 1909), ii.

9. Nikolai Berdiaev, "Filosofskaia istina i intelligentskaia pravda," in Berdiaev, *Vekhi*, 2.

10. Ibid., 8.

11. Ibid., 22.

12. Sergei Bulgakov, "Geroizm i podvizhnichestvo (iz razmyshlenii o religioznoi prirode russkoi intelligentsii)," in Berdiaev, *Vekhi*, 24.

13. Ibid., 24–26.

14. Ibid., 47.

15. M. Gershenzon, "Tvorcheskoe samosoznanie," in Berdiaev et al., *Vekhi*, 70.

16. Ibid., 84.

17. Ibid., 82.

18. Ibid., 87.

19. B. Kistiakovskii, "V zashchitu prava (intelligentsiia i pravosoznanie)," in Berdiaev, *Vekhi*, 126.

20. Petr Struve, "Intelligentsiia i revolutsiia," in Berdiaev, *Vekhi*, 131.

21. Ibid., 142.

22. Semen Frank, "Etika nigilizma (k kharakteristike nravstvennogo mirovozzreniia russkoi intelligentsii)," in Berdiaev, *Vekhi*, 158, 162.

23. Ibid., 177–78.

24. Berdiaev, "Filosofskaia istina," 19, 21.

25. Bulgakov, "Geroizm i podvizhnichestvo," 51.

26. George Gilbert, *The Radical Right in Late Imperial Russia: Dreams of a True Fatherland?* (London: Routledge, 2016), 70.

27. Langer, "Corruption and the Counterrevolution," 36.

28. Abraham Ascher, *P. A. Stolypin: The Search for Stability in Late Imperial Russia* (Stanford, CA: Stanford University Press, 2001), 243.

29. Ibid., 309–20.

30. Repnikov, *Konservativnye modeli*, 307, 315.

31. Mikhail Luk'ianov, *Rossiskii konservatizm i reforma, 1907–1914* (Stuttgart: Ibidem-Verlag, 2006), 104.

32. Ibid., 103.

33. Repnikov, *Konservativnye modeli*, 309.

34. Ibid., 311.

35. Rawson, *Russian Rightists*, 92–95.

36. Strickland, *The Making of Holy Russia*, 129.

37. Ibid., 130–31.

38. Ibid., 132.

39. Pisiotis, "Orthodoxy versus Autocracy," 521.

40. Repnikov, *Konservativnye modeli*, 301.

41. Pisiotis, "Orthodoxy versus Autocracy," 40–41.

42. Strickland, *The Making of Holy Russia*, 123.

43. Ascher, *P. A. Stolypin*, 298–302.

44. The most strident comments to this effect were those of Mikhail Gershenzon. See: Gershenzon, "Tvorcheskoe samosoznanie," 88.

45. A. S. Tsipko, "Liberal'nyi konservatizm Nikolaia Berdiaeva i Petra Struve i zadachi dekommunizatsii sovremennoi Rossii," *Tetradi po konservatizmu* 2, no. 1 (2014): 33.

46. Pipes, *Struve*, 180.

47. Ibid., 375.

48. Pyotr Stolypin, "We Need a Great Russia," in Riha, *Readings in Russian Civilization*, 464.

49. Ascher, *P. A. Stolypin*, 11.

50. Ibid., 127.

51. Ibid., 218.

52. Ibid., 144.

53. Ibid., 150.

54. Ibid., 152.

55. Luk'ianov, *Rossiiskii konservatizm i reforma*, 27.

56. Ascher, *P. A. Stolypin*, 227–36.

57. Dominic Lieven, *Russia's Rulers under the Old Regime* (New Haven, CT: Yale University Press, 1989), 217.

58. For a discussion of Durnovo's opinions, see Dominic Lieven, "Bureaucratic Authoritarianism in Late Imperial Russia: The Personality, Career, and Opinions of P. N. Durnovo," *The Historical Journal* 26, no. 2 (1983): 391–402.

59. Luk'ianov, *Rossiiskii konservatizm i reforma*, 25.

60. Rawson, *Russian Rightists*, 31.

61. S. M. Sankova, "Partiia russkikh natsionalistov: Realnost' bez mifov," *Tetradi po konservatizmu* 4 (2015): 159–70.

62. Mikhail Loukianov, "Conservatives and 'Renewed Russia,' 1907–1914," *Slavic Review* 61, no. 4 (2002): 778.

63. Ibid., 765.

64. Luk'ianov, *Rossiiskii konservatizm i reforma*, 53–54.

65. Hans Rogger, "The Formation of the Russian Right: 1900–1906," *California Slavic Studies* 3 (1964): 91.

66. Luk'ianov, *Rossiiskii konservatizm i reforma*, 55–56.

67. Omel'ianchuk, "Russkii konservatizm," 152.

68. Luk'ianov, *Rossiiskii konservatizm i reforma*, 51.

69. Ibid., 51–52.

70. A. A. Kireev, *Dnevnik 1905–1910* (Moscow: Rosspen, 2010), 51.

71. Ibid., 29.

72. Ibid., 257.

73. Ibid., 135–36.

74. Loukianov, "Conservatives and 'Renewed Russia,'" 770.

75. Luk'ianov, *Rossiiskii konservatizm i reforma*, 33–35.

76. Ascher, *P. A. Stolypin*, 259.

77. Iu. I. Kir'ianov, *Pravye partii v Rossii, 1911–1917 gg.* (Moscow: Rosspen, 2001), 344.

78. For a discussion of conservatives' views of foreign policy, see Repnikov, *Konservativnye modeli*, 242–67.

79. David M. McDonald, "The Durnovo Memorandum in Context: Official Conservatism and the Crisis of Autocracy," *Jahrbücher für Geschichte Osteuropas* 44, no. 4 (1996): 481–502.

80. Peter Durnovo, "Memorandum to Nicholas II," in Riha, *Readings in Russian Civilization*, 476.

81. Ibid., 478.

82. Lieven, "Bureaucratic Authoritarianism," 400.

83. Kir'ianov, *Pravye partii*, 346.

84. Ascher, *P. A. Stolypin*, 156.

85. Milevskii, "Rossiiskie ekonomicheskie al'ternativy," 116; Sankova, "Partiia russkikh natsionalistov," 164–65.

86. Rawson, *Russian Rightists*, 44.

87. Luk'ianov, *Rossiiskii konservatizm i reforma*, 117.

88. Kireev, *Dnevnik*, 293.

89. Gilbert, *The Radical Right*, 71.

90. Ibid., 63.

91. I. V. Omel'ianchuk, "The Problems of Russia's Economic Development as Seen by Right-Wing Monarchists in the Early Twentieth Century," *Russian Studies in History* 48, no. 2 (2009): 87–88; Kir'ianov, *Pravye partii*, 330.

92. Luk'ianov, *Rossiiskii konservatizm i reforma*, 109.

93. Omel'ianchuk, "The Problems of Russia's Economic Development," 85–86.

94. Luk'ianov, *Rossiiskii konservatizm i reforma*, 109.

95. Omel'ianchuk, "The Problems of Russia's Economic Development," 80; Rawson, *Russian Rightists*, 41.

96. Omel'ianchuk, "The Problems of Russia's Economic Development," 81.

97. Ibid., 327.

98. Kir'ianov, *Pravye partii*, 326.

99. Ibid., 355.

100. Strickland, *The Making of Holy Russia*, 121.

101. Luk'ianov, *Rossiiskii konservatizm i reforma*, 132.

102. Milevskii, "Rossiiskie ekonomicheskie al'ternativy," 116.

103. Kir'ianov, *Pravye partii*, 331; Repnikov, *Konservativnye modeli*, 381.

104. Luk'ianov, *Rossiiskii konservatizm i reforma*, 112.

105. Ibid., 115.

106. Kireev, *Dnevnik*, 47.

Notes to Chapter 8

1. For an analysis of these events, see Paul Robinson, *The White Russian Army in Exile, 1920–1941* (Oxford: Clarendon Press, 2002).

2. For an examination of the causes and nature of the split in the church, see Dmitry Pospielovsky, *The Russian Church under the Soviet Regime, 1917–1982* (Crestwood, NY: St. Vladimir's Seminary Press, 1984), 1:113–42.

3. Nikolai Berdiaev, "Dukhi russkoi revolutsii," in *Iz glubiny: Sbornik statei o russkoi revolutsii*, ed. S. A. Askol'dov et al. (Paris: YMCA Press, 1967), 105.

4. Berdiaev, *Filosofiia neravenstva*, 15.

5. In 2014, Berdiaev's *Philosophy of Inequality* (*Filosofiia neravenstva*) was one of three books that the Kremlin sent to senior officials around Russia as suggested reading. The others were Vladimir Solovyov's *The Justification of the Good* (*Opravdanie dobra*) and Ivan Ilyin's *Our Tasks* (*Nashi zadachi*).

6. Berdiaev, *Filosofiia neravenstva*, 32.

7. Ibid., 81–82.

8. Ibid., 90.

9. Ibid., 100.

10. Ibid., 25.

11. Berdiaev, "Dukhi," 106.

12. Stuart Finkel, "Nikolai Berdiaev and the Philosophical Tasks of the Emigration," in *A History of Russian Philosophy 1830–1939: Faith, Reason, and the Defense of Human Dignity*, ed. G. M. Hamburg and Randall A. Poole (Cambridge: Cambridge University Press, 2010), 354.

13. Robinson, *The White Russian Army*, 174.

14. Petr Struve, "Istoricheskii smysl russkoi revolutsii i natsional'nye zadachi," in Askol'dov, *Iz glubiny*, 305.

15. For instance, Anton Barbashin and Hannah Thorburn, "Putin's Philosopher," *Foreign Affairs*, September 20, 2015, https://www.foreignaffairs.com/articles/russian-federation/2015-09-20/putins-philosopher.

16. Timothy Snyder, "Ivan Ilyin: Putin's Philosopher of Russian Fascism," *The New York Review of Books*, April 2018, https://www.nybooks.com/daily/2018/03/16/ivan-ilyin-putins-philosopher-of-russian-fascism/.

17. Timothy Snyder, *The Road to Unfreedom: Russia, Europe, America* (New York: Tim Duggan, 2018), 18, 22, 24, 47.

18. William E. Butler and V. A. Tomsinov, "Ivan A. Il'in: Russian Legal Philosopher," in *On the Essence of Legal Consciousness*, by Ivan Il'in, ed. and trans. W. E. Butler, P. T. Grier, and V. A. Tomsinov (London: Wildy, Simmonds & Hill, 2014), 87.

19. N. Poltoratskii, *Ivan Aleksandrovich Il'in* (Tenafly, NJ: Hermitage, 1989), 153; Iurii Lisitsa, "Il'in iskal sushchnost' svobody kak podobiia bozhiia v cheloveke: Interv'iu s Iuriem Lisitsei," *Samopoznanie* 2 (2015): 11.

20. Igor Evlampiev, "Nepriiatie idei Ivan Il'ina liberalami svidetel'stvuet tol'ko ob ikh neobrazovannosti: Interv'iu s Igorem Evlampievym," *Samopoznanie* 2 (2015): 12.

21. Egor Kholmogorov, "Pravyi gegel'ianets v okopakh Stalingrada," *Samopoznanie* 2 (2015): 24.

22. Liubov' Ul'ianova, "Skrytoe slavianofil'stvo v tvorchestve Il'ina," *Samopoznanie* 2 (2015): 38.

23. Ivan Il'in, *O soprotivlenii zlu siloiu*, with a commentary by P. N. Poltoratskii (London: Zaria, 1975).

24. For a discussion of Ilyin's book and the controversy that it created, see Paul Robinson, "On Resistance to Evil by Force: Ivan Il'in and the Necessity of War," *Journal of Military Ethics* 2, no. 2 (2003): 145–59.

25. Il'in, *O soprotivlenii*, 112–13.

26. Poltoratskii, *Ivan Aleksandrovich Il'in*, 162.

27. I. A. Il'in, *Osnovy bor'by za natsional'nuiu Rossiiu* (Narva: Izd. natsional'no-trudovo soiuza novogo pokoleniia, 1938), 27.

28. I. A. Il'in, *Nashi zadachi: Stat'i 1948–1954 gg.* (Paris: Izdanie Russkogo Obshche-Voinskogo Soiuza, 1956), 2:611–12.

29. Poltoratskii, *Ivan Aleksandrovich Il'in*, 190.

30. Il'in, *Nashi zadachi*, 2:613.

31. I. A. Il'in, *Rodina i my* (Belgrade: Izdatel'stvo Gl. Upravleniia O-va Gallipoliitsev, 1926), 4.

32. Ibid., 10.

33. Ibid., 15.

34. Il'in, *Nashi zadachi*, 1:51.

35. Ibid., 270.

36. Ibid., 272.

37. Ibid., 279.

38. I. A. Il'in, *O sushchnosti pravosoznaniia* (Moscow: Rarog, 1993), 101–2.

39. Il'in, *Nashi zadachi*, 1:50.

40. Ibid., 54.

41. Ibid., 317–18.

42. "Predislovie," in *Iskhod k vostoku*, ed. O. S. Shirokov (Moscow: Dobrosvet, 1997), 52.

43. David Schimmelpenninck van der Oye, "The East," in Leatherbarrow and Offord, *A History of Russian Thought*, 227–28.

44. Repnikov, *Konservativnye modeli*, 243–52.

45. N. V. Riasanovsky, "Prince N. S. Trubetskoy's 'Europe and Mankind,'" *Jahrbücher für Geschichte Osteuropas* 12, no. 2 (1964): 208.

46. Ibid., 214.

47. Ibid., 215.

48. N. S. Trubetskoi, "Verkhi i nizy russkoi kul'tury (etnicheskaia osnova russkoi kul'tury)," in Shirokov, *Iskhod k vostoku*, 220.

49. Petr Savitskii, "Povorot k vostoku," in Shirokov, *Iskhod k vostoku*, 54–55.

50. Gusev, *Russkii konservatizm*, 147.

51. N. S. Trubetskoi, "Ob istinnom i lozhnom natsionalizme," in Shirokov, *Iskhod k vostoku*, 183–85.

52. Georgii N. Florovskii, "O narodakh ne-istoricheskikh (strana otsov i strana detei)," in Shirokov, *Iskhod k vostoku*, 154, 159.

53. Petr Savitskii, "Migratsiia kul'tury," in Shirokov, *Iskhod k vostoku*, 119–38.

54. "Predislovie," in Shirokov, *Iskhod k vostoku*, 47.

55. Ibid., 50.

56. Savitskii, "Povorot k vostoku," 55.

57. P. Suvchinskii, "Sila slabykh," in Shirokov, *Iskhod k vostoku*, 64.

58. P. Suvchinskii, "Epokha very," in Shirokov, *Iskhod k vostoku*, 96–97.

59. Matthew Rendle, *Defenders of the Motherland: The Tsarist Elite in Revolutionary Russia* (Oxford: Oxford University Press, 2010).

60. Michael Kellogg, *The Russian Roots of Nazism: White Émigrés and the Making of National Socialism, 1917-1945* (Cambridge: Cambridge University Press, 2005), 145–47.

61. Robinson, *The White Russian Army*, 98–99.

62. Paul Robinson, *Grand Duke Nikolai Nikolaevich: Supreme Commander of the Russian Army* (DeKalb: Northern Illinois University Press, 2014), 322.

63. Ibid., 328.

64. Berdiaev, *Filosofiia neravenstva*, 104.

65. Ibid., 137–38.

66. Berdiaev's use of the word "cosmos" reflects the influence of the Russian Cosmist thinker Nikolai Fedorov. For an analysis of the thought of the Russian Cosmists, including both Fedorov and Berdiaev, see George M. Young, *The Russian Cosmists: The Esoteric Futurism of Nikolai Fedorov and His Followers* (Oxford: Oxford University Press, 2012).

67. Berdiaev, *Filosofiia neravenstva*, 40.

68. Ibid., 144.

69. John Stephan, *The Russian Fascists* (London: Harper & Row, 1978).

70. Robinson, *The White Russian Army*, 178–79.

71. For a fuller discussion of these matters, see Robinson, *The White Russian Army*, 165–83.

72. Pipes, *Struve*, 412–17, 432.

73. Il'in, *Rodina i my*, 7.

74. Butler and Tomsinov, "Ivan A. Il'in," 87.

75. Il'in, *Nashi zadachi*, 1:569, 571.

76. I. A. Il'in, *Osnovy gosudarstvennogo ustroistva: Proekt osnovnogo zakona Rossii* (Moscow: Rarog, 1996), 143.

77. *Rossiiskii Zarubezhyi S"ezd 1926: Dokumenty i materialy* (Moscow: Russkii put', 2006), 610–11.

78. Philip T. Grier, "The Complex Legacy of Ivan Il'in," in *Russian Thought after Communism: The Recovery of a Philosophical Heritage*, ed. James P. Scanlan (Armonk, NY: M. E. Sharpe, 1994), 167.

79. Philip T. Grier, "I. A. Il'in and the Rule of Law," in Il'in, *On the Essence*, 1.

80. Il'in, *O sushchnosti pravosoznaniia*, 41.

81. Philip T. Grier, "Adventures in Dialectic and Intuition: Shpet, Il'in, Losev," in Hamburg and Poole, *A History of Russian Philosophy*, 330.

82. Il'in, *O sushchnosti pravosoznaniia*, 50.

83. Ibid., 51–52.

84. Ibid., 82.

85. Ibid., 110.

86. Ibid., 112.

87. Ibid.

88. Il'in, *Nashi zadachi*, 1:122.

89. Ibid., 42.

90. Il'in, *O sushchnosti pravosoznaniia*, 130.

91. Il'in, *Nashi zadachi*, 1:133.

92. Ibid., 25.

93. Ibid., 44.

94. Ibid., 69.

95. Il'in, *O sushchnosti pravosoznaniia*, 137.

96. Il'in, *Osnovy gosudarstvennogo ustroistva*, 143.

97. Il'in, *Nashi zadachi*, 1:307.

98. Ibid., 307–8.

99. Il'in, *Nashi zadachi*, 2:415–17; Il'in, *Osnovy gosudarstvennogo ustroistva*, 71–73.

100. Ivan Solonevich, *Narodnaia monarkhiia* (Moscow: Algoritm, 2011), 23, 26.

101. Ibid., 27.

102. Ibid., 47.

103. Ibid., 62.

104. Ibid., 107, 119.

105. Mikhail Agursky, *The Third Rome: National Bolshevism in the USSR* (Boulder, CO: Westview, 1987), 256.

106. Hilde Hardeman, *Coming to Terms with the Soviet Regime: The "Changing Signposts" Movement among Russian Émigrés in the Early 1920s* (DeKalb: Northern Illinois University Press, 1994), 30.

107. N. V. Riasanovsky, "The Emergence of Eurasianism," *California Slavic Studies* 4 (1967): 51.

108. Françoise Lesourd, "Karsavin and the Eurasian Movement," in *Russia between East and West: Scholarly Debates on Eurasianism*, ed. Dmitry Shlapentokh (Leiden: Brill, 2007), 62.

109. Martin Beisswenger, "Eurasianism: Affirming the Person in an 'Era of Faith,'" in Hamburg and Poole, *A History of Russian Philosophy*, 371.

110. Ryszard Paradowski, "Absolutism and Authority in Eurasian Ideology: Karsavin and Alekseev," in Shlapentokh, *Russia between East and West*, 95.

111. Lesourd, "Karsavin," 79.

112. Marlene Laruelle, *Russian Eurasianism: An Ideology of Empire* (Washington, DC: Woodrow Wilson Center Press, 2008), 29.

113. Lesourd, "Karsavin," 89.

114. For instance, Laruelle, *Russian Eurasianism*, 49.

115. Il'in, *Osnovy gosudarstvennogo ustroistva*, 55; and *Nashi zadachi*, 1:207, 264–68.

116. Berdiaev, *Filosofiia neravenstva*, 44.

117. Ibid., 124–25.

118. Il'in, *Osnovy bor'by*, 55.

119. Solonevich, *Narodnaia monarkhiia*, 65.

120. Robinson, *Grand Duke Nikolai Nikolaevich*, 322.

121. *Rossiiskii Zarubezhnyi S"ezd*, 587.

122. Ibid., 591.

123. Ibid., 604.

124. Petr Savitskii, "Kontinent-okean (Rossiia i mirovoi rynok)," in Shirokov, *Iskhod k vostoku*, 226–62.

125. Ibid., 262.

126. Martin Beisswenger, "Metaphysics of the Economy: The Religious and Economic Foundations of P. N. Savitskii's Eurasianism," in *Between Europe and Asia: The Origins, Theories, and Legacies of Russian Eurasianism*, ed. Mark Bassin, Sergey Glebov, and Marlene Laruelle (Pittsburgh, PA: University of Pittsburgh Press, 2015), 105–6.

127. Ibid., 97.

128. Ibid., 109.

129. N. V. Rabotiazhev, "Mezhdu traditsiei i utopiei: Levyi konservatizm v Rossii," *Polis: Politicheskie issledovanie* 4 (2014): 118.

130. Raeff, *Russia Abroad*, 10.

NOTES TO CHAPTER 9

1. Anna Dickinson, "Quantifying Religious Repression: Russian Orthodox Church Closures and Repression of Priests 1917–41," *Religion, State and Society* 28, no. 4 (2000): 329–30.

2. David R. Shearer, "Crime and Social Disorder in Stalin's Russia," *Cahiers du monde russe* 39, nos. 1–2 (1998): 120.

3. Ibid., 129.

4. Nicholas S. Timasheff, *The Great Retreat: The Growth and Decline of Communism in Russia* (New York: E. P. Dutton, 1946).

5. Robert V. Daniels, *The Rise and Fall of Communism in Russia* (New Haven, CT: Yale University Press, 2007), 212.

6. Ibid., 216.

7. Vladimir Paperny, *Architecture in the Age of Stalin: Culture Two* (Cambridge: Cambridge University Press, 2002).

8. David L. Hoffmann, *Stalinist Values: The Cultural Norms of Soviet Modernity, 1917–1941* (Ithaca, NY: Cornell University Press, 2003), 3; Hoffmann, "Was There a 'Great Retreat' from Soviet Socialism? Stalinist Culture Reconsidered," *Kritika: Explorations in Russian and Eurasian History* 5, no. 4 (2004): 652.

9. Hoffmann, "Was There a 'Great Retreat'?" 654.

10. Ibid., 672.

11. Agursky, *The Third Rome*, 305.

12. Daniels, *The Rise and Fall*, 233.

13. Hoffmann, "Was There a 'Great Retreat'?" 670.

14. Timasheff, *The Great Retreat*, 180.

15. George Liber, "Korenizatsiia: Restructuring Soviet Nationality Policy in the 1920s," *Ethnic and Racial Studies* 14, no. 1 (1991): 15–23.

16. Peter A. Blitstein, "Nation Building or Russification? Obligatory Russian Instruction in the Soviet Non-Russian School, 1938–1953," in *A State of Nations: Empire and Nation-Making in the Age of Lenin and Stalin*, ed. Ronald Grigor Suny and Terry Martin (Oxford: Oxford University Press, 2001), 253–74.

17. Daniels, *The Rise and Fall*, 229.

18. Margaret A. Rose, *Marx's Lost Aesthetic: Karl Marx and the Visual Arts* (Cambridge: Cambridge University Press, 1984), 145.

19. Timasheff, *The Great Retreat*, 264–71; Hoffmann, "Was There a 'Great Retreat'?" 662–64.

20. Timasheff, *The Great Retreat*, 171.

21. Ibid., 230–31.

22. Ibid., 235–36.

23. Peter H. Solomon, *Soviet Criminal Justice under Stalin* (Cambridge: Cambridge University Press, 1996), 35.

24. Ibid., 64.

25. Ibid., 71.

26. Ibid., 153.

27. Daniels, *The Rise and Fall*, 234.

28. Timasheff, *The Great Retreat*, 255.

29. Solomon, *Soviet Criminal Justice*, 153.

30. Ibid., 187–88.

31. Ibid., 221, 227.

32. H. Kent Geiger, *The Family in Soviet Russia* (Cambridge, MA: Harvard University Press, 1968), 11–20.

33. Ibid., 40.

34. Ibid., 51.

35. Hoffmann, *Stalinist Values*, 89.

36. Ibid., 88.

37. Geiger, *The Family in Soviet Russia*, 47–48.

38. Cited in Igor Shafarevich, "Sotsializm," in *Iz-pod glyb*, ed. M. S. Agurskii et al. (Paris: YMCA-Press, 1974), 54.

39. Timasheff, *The Great Retreat*, 193–94.

40. Ibid., 196.

41. Hoffmann, *Stalinist Values*, 92.

42. Geiger, *The Family in Soviet Russia*, 61–62.

43. Hoffmann, *Stalinist Values*, 98.

44. Ibid., 100.

45. Timasheff, *The Great Retreat*, 196.

46. Ibid., 198.

47. Geiger, *The Family in Soviet Russia*, 94.

48. Timasheff, *The Great Retreat*, 201.

49. Ibid., 202.

50. Ibid.

51. Geiger, *The Family in Soviet Russia*, 89.

52. Ibid., 91.

53. Hoffmann, "Was There a 'Great Retreat'?" 659–60.

54. Daniels, *The Rise and Fall*, 216.

55. Timasheff, *The Great Retreat*, 201.

56. Geiger, *The Family in Soviet Russia*, 106.

57. Timasheff, *The Great Retreat*, 320.

58. Kees Boterbloem, "The Eternal Ensign: Andrei Zhdanov and the Survival of Tsarist Military Culture in the Soviet Union," *War and Society* 22, no. 1 (2004): 1–18.

59. Daniels, *The Rise and Fall*, 216, 239; Timasheff, *The Great Retreat*, 133–41.

60. Timasheff, *The Great Retreat*, 141.

61. Hoffmann, "Was There a 'Great Retreat'?," 658.

Notes to Chapter 10

1. McGuckin, *The Orthodox Church*, 53–54; John B. Dunlop, *The Faces of Contemporary Russian Nationalism* (Princeton, NJ: Princeton University Press, 1983), 32.

2. Stephen F. Cohen, "The Friends and Foes of Change: Reformism and Conservatism in the Soviet Union," *Slavic Review* 38, no. 2 (1979): 190.

3. Ibid., 195, 198.

4. Valentin Rasputin, "Your Son, Russia, and Our Brother: On Vasily Shukshin," in *Siberia on Fire: Stories and Essays*, by Valentin Rasputin (DeKalb: Northern Illinois University Press, 1989), 216–17.

5. David C. Gillespie, *Valentin Rasputin and Soviet Russian Village Prose* (London: The Modern Humanities Research Association, 1986), 7.

6. Valentin Rasputin, *Farewell to Matyora* (DeKalb: Northern Illinois University Press, 1995).

7. Gillespie, *Valentin Rasputin*, 8.

8. A. S. Tsipko describes village prose as "in essence anti-Soviet." See A. S. Tsipko, "Puti sovetskoi intelligentsia k rossiiskomu konservatizmu (O stikhiinom antikommunizme, podorvavshem ideologicheskie 'skrepy' SSSR)," *Tetradi po konservatizmu* 4 (2015): 194.

9. Dunlop, *Faces*, 38.

10. Duncan, *Russian Messianism*, 70.

11. Cited in Egor Kholmogorov, *Revansh russkoi istorii* (Moscow: Knizhnyi mir, 2016), 338.

12. Vladimir Soloukhin, "Pis'ma iz russkogo muzeia," *Molodaia gvardiia* 9 (1966): 243.

13. Ibid., 249.

14. Ibid., 260.

15. Ibid., 264.

16. Dunlop, *Faces*, 67.

17. Mark Bassin, "Narrating Kulikovo: Lev Gumilev, Russian Nationalists, and the Troubled Emergence of Neo-Eurasianism," in *Between Europe and Asia: The Origins, Theories, and Legacies of Russian Eurasianism*, ed. Mark Bassin, Sergey Glebov, and Marlene Laruelle (Pittsburgh, PA: University of Pittsburgh Press, 2015), 176.

18. Peter Duncan, "The Fate of Russian Nationalism: The *Samizdat* Journal *Veche* Revisited," *Religion in Communist Lands* 16, no. 1 (1988): 38; Dunlop, *Faces*, 43.

19. Dunlop, *Faces*, 60.

20. Charles Clover, *Black Wind, White Snow: The Rise of Russia's New Nationalism* (New Haven, CT: Yale University Press, 2016), 132.

21. Mark Bassin, "Lev Gumilev and the European New Right," *Nationalities Papers: The Journal of Nationalism and Ethnicity* 43, no. 6 (2015): 843–44.

22. L. N. Gumilev, *Etnogenez i biosfera zemli* (Leningrad: Izdatel'stvo Leningradskogo Universiteta, 1989), 27, 35.

23. Ibid., 143.

24. Ibid., 312.

25. Ibid., 344, 348.

26. Bassin, "Lev Gumilev," 856.

27. Ibid., 848.

28. Gumilev, *Etnogenez*, 109.

29. Ibid., 109–10.

30. Mark Bassin, *The Gumilev Mystique: Biopolitics, Eurasianism, and the Construction of Community in Modern Russia* (Ithaca, NY: Cornell University Press, 2016), 213–14.

31. Alexander Titov, "Lev Gumilev, Ethnogenesis and Eurasianism" (PhD diss., University College London, 2005), 151; Bassin, "Narrating Kulikovo," 171.

32. Ibid., 140.

33. Bassin, "Lev Gumilev," 855.

34. Bassin, *The Gumilev Mystique*, 195.

35. Duncan, "The Fate of Russian Nationalism," 37.

36. For a description of Dudko's life and its context, see Oliver Bullough, *The Last Man in Russia: The Struggle to Save a Dying Nation* (New York: Basic Books, 2013).

37. "To the Veche," *Veche* 1 (1971), in Dunlop, *Faces*, 296.

38. Duncan, "The Fate of Russian Nationalism," 41–42.

39. V. N. Osipov and V. S. Rodionov, "Back to the Land," *Veche* 1 (1971), in Dunlop, *Faces*, 297.

40. Dunlop, *Faces*, 166.

41. Duncan, "The Fate of Russian Nationalism," 43.

42. Ibid., 45.

43. Dunlop, *Faces*, 53–55.

44. Alix Holt, "The First Soviet Feminists," in *Soviet Sisterhood: British Feminists on Women in the USSR*, ed. Barbara Holland (London: Fourth Estate, 1985), 245.

45. Rochelle Ruthchild, "Sisterhood and Socialism: The Soviet Feminist Movement," *Frontiers: A Journal of Women Studies* 7, no. 2 (1983): 7.

46. Ibid., 10.

47. Holt, "The First Soviet Feminists," 246.

48. Ruthchild, "Sisterhood and Socialism," 11.

49. Duncan, *Russian Messianism*, 97; Walter Laqueur, *Black Hundred: The Rise of the Extreme Right in Russia* (New York: HarperCollins, 1993), 97.

50. Aleksandr Solzhenitsyn, "Pis'mo vozhdiam sovetskogo soiuza," in *Publitsistika v trekh tomakh* (Yaroslavl: Verkhne-Volzhskoe Knizhnoe Izdatel'stvo, 1995), 1:184.

51. Eric E. Ericson Jr., *Solzhenitsyn and the Modern World* (Washington, DC: Regnery Gateway, 1993), 208.

52. Aleksandr Solzhenitsyn, "Raskaianie i samoogranichenie kak kategorii natsional'noi zhizni," in Solzhenitsyn, *Publitsistika v trekh tomakh*, 1:64–65.

53. Ibid., 84.

54. Aleksandr Solzhenitsyn, "Kak nam obustroit' Rossiiu?" in Solzhenitsyn, *Publitsistika v trekh tomakh*, 1:542.

55. Aleksandr Solzhenitsyn, "Rech' v Garvarde," in Solzhenitsyn, *Publitsistika v trekh tomakh*, 1:312.

56. Ibid., 1:325

57. Ibid., 1:319–20.

58. Aleksandr Solzhenitsyn, "Templtonskaia lektsiia," in Solzhenitsyn, *Publitsistika v trekh tomakh*, 1:447, 449, 452.

59. Ericson, *Solzhenitsyn*, 126.

60. Duncan, *Russian Messianism*, 127.

61. Ibid., 128.

62. Tsipko, "Puti sovetskoi intelligentsii," 196.

63. Duncan, *Russian Messianism*, 101–2.

64. Ibid., 102–3.

65. Rabotiazhev, "Mezhdu traditsii i utopii," 120.

66. John B. Dunlop, *The Rise of Russia and the Fall of the Soviet Empire* (Princeton, NJ: Princeton University Press, 1993), 168.

67. Clover, *Black Wind, White Snow*, 171.

68. Dunlop, *The Rise of Russia*, 168.

69. Ibid., 173.

70. Ibid., 175.

71. Ibid.

72. Alexander Solzhenitsyn, *The Gulag Archipelago 1918–1956: An Experiment in Literary Investigation* (London: Collins Harvill, 1988), 457, 468.

73. Ibid., 452.

74. Aleksandr Solzhenitsyn, "Na vozvrate dykhaniia i soznaniia," in Solzhenitsyn, *Publitsistika v trekh tomakh*, 1:44–45.

75. Solzhenitsyn, *The Gulag Archipelago*, 306.

76. Solzhenitsyn, "Na vozvrate dykhaniia i soznaniia," 47.

77. Solzhenitsyn, "Pis'mo vozhdiam sovetskogo soiuza," 181.

78. Solzhenitsyn, "Kak nam obustroit' Rossiu?" 564.

79. Ibid., 583.

80. Ibid.

81. Ibid., 586–98.

82. David G. Rowley, "Alexander Solzhenitsyn and Russian Nationalism," *Journal of Contemporary History* 32, no. 3 (1997): 322.

83. Daniel J. Mahoney, *The Conservative Foundations of the Liberal Order: Defending Democracy against Its Modern Enemies and Immoderate Friends* (Wilmington, DE: ISI Books, 2010), 129.

84. Ericson, *Solzhenitsyn*, 5.

85. Dunlop, *The Rise of Russia*, 167.

86. Ibid., 172.

87. Valentin Rasputin, "Baikal," in Rasputin, *Siberia on Fire*, 193.

88. Valentin Rasputin, "Your Siberia and Mine," in Rasputin, *Siberia on Fire*, 178.

89. Gumilev, *Etnogenez*, 316.

90. M. Agurskii, "Sovremennye obshchestvenno-ekonomicheskie systemy i ikh perspektivy," in *Iz-pod glyb*, ed. M. S. Agurskii et al. (Paris: YMCA-Press, 1974), 79.

91. Ibid., 89.

92. Solzhenitsyn, "Raskaianie i samoogranichenie," 81.

93. Solzhenitsyn, "Pis'mo vozhdiam sovetskogo soiuza," 159.

Notes to Chapter 11

1. Izborskii Klub, "Ul'ianovskaia deklaratsiia izborksogo kluba," n.d., http://www.dynacon.ru/content/articles/901.

2. Ministerstvo Kul'tury Rossiiskoi Federatsii, *Osnovy gosudarstvennoi kul'turnoi politiki*, 2015, https://www.mkrf.ru/upload/medialibrary/3aa/3aa5ed08e6cfbb1c982fee861 8c4fa09.pdf, 6.

3. M. M. Mchedlova, "Tsennostnaia baza i sotsiokul'turnye proektsii sovremennogo rossiiskogo konservatizma," *Tetradi po konservatizmu* 3 (2014): 134.

4. Mikhail Remizov, *Russkie i gosudarstvo* (Moscow: Eksmo, 2016), 81–82.

5. Boris Mezhuev, "Konservativnaia demokratiia stanet glavnym opponentom liberal'nogo avtoritarizma," *Russkaia!dea*, January 9, 2016, http://politconservatism.ru/konservativnaya-demokratiya-stanet-glavnym-opponentom-liberalnogo-avtoritarizma.

6. Ibid.

7. *Russkaia doktrina*, 989.

8. Aleksandr Nagornyi, "Rossiia i zapadniki," Izborskii klub, December 1, 2015, https://izborsk-club.ru/7867.

9. Yulia Netesova, "What Does It Mean to Be Conservative in Russia?" *The National Interest*, August 10, 2016, http://nationalinterest.org/feature/what-does-it-mean-be-conservative-russia-17312.

10. Katharina Bluhm, "Modernization, Geopolitics, and the New Russian Conservatives," *Arbeitspapiere des Osteuropa-Instituts: Arbeitsbereich Soziologie* 1 (2016): 6.

11. *Russkaia doktrina*, 742

12. Tsipko, "Puti sovetskoi intelligentsii," 199.

13. Aleksandr Prokhanov, *Simfoniia "Piatoi Imperii"* (Moscow: Iauzma Eksmo, 2007), 27, 29–30, 33.

14. Gusev, *Russkii konservatizm*, 197.

15. Lavrov, "Russia's Foreign Policy."

16. Prokhanov, *Simfoniia "piatoi imperii*," 57.

17. Ibid., 24.

18. *Russkaia doktrina*, 102.

19. Vladimir Putin, "Interv'iu Vladimira Putina radio 'Evropa 1' i telekanalu TF1," June 4, 2014, http://kremlin.ru/events/president/news/45832.

20. Vladimir Putin, "Zasedanie mezhdunarodnogo diskussionnogo kluba 'Valdai,'" September 19, 2013, http://kremlin.ru/events/president/news/19243.

21. Remizov, *Russkie i gosudarstvo*, 72.

22. Ibid., 259.

23. Ibid., 247–49.

24. Ibid., 265–79.

25. Ibid., 285–88.

26. Ibid., 96.

27. Ibid., 26.

28. Ibid., 68.

29. Ibid., 85.

30. Ibid., 143.

31. Ibid., 145–46.

32. Ibid., 107–8.

33. Burgess, *Holy Rus'*, 9.

34. Ibid., 16. For a further analysis of this issue, see the tables and graphs in Thomas Bremer, "The Role of the Church in the New Russia," *Russian Analytical Digest* 47 (October 2008): 2–10.

35. Burgess, *Holy Rus'*, 53.

36. Ibid., 74.

37. *Russkaia doktrina*, 254.

38. For instance, Egor Kholmogorov, "Konservativnyi povorot v Rossii v zerkale global'noi istorii Fernana Brodelia," *Tetradi po konservatizmu* 3 (2015): 122; and Matveichev, "Klassifikatsiia vidov konservatizma," 80.

39. Putin, "Zasedanie."

40. Cai Wilkinson, "Putting Traditional Values into Practice: Russia's Anti-Gay Laws," *Russian Analytical Digest* 138 (November 2013): 6.

41. *Russkaia doktrina*, 829–30.

42. The Russian Orthodox Church, *Osnovy sotsial'noi kontseptsii Russkoi Pravoslavnoi Tserkvi*, 12.4, https://mospat.ru/ru/documents/social-concepts/.

43. John Anderson, *Conservative Christian Politics in Russia and the United States: Dreaming of Christian Nations* (London: Routledge, 2014), 75.

44. "Russian Church and State Sign Agreement to Prevent Abortion," *Russia Insider*, July 7, 2016, http://russia-insider.com/en/russia-church-and-state-sign-agreement-prevent-abortion/ri15445.

45. The Russian Orthodox Church, *Osnovy sotsial'noi kontseptsii*, 12.9.

46. Anderson, *Conservative Christian Politics*, 145.

47. Kholmogorov, *Revansh russkoi istorii*, 11.

48. Ibid., 239.

49. Burgess, *Holy Rus'*, 11.

50. Ibid., 14–15.

51. The Russian Orthodox Church, *Osnovy sotsial'noi kontseptsii*, 2.2.

52. Maria Engström, "Contemporary Russian Messianism and the New Russian Foreign Policy," *Contemporary Security Policy* 35, no. 3 (2014): 367.

53. Ibid., 368.

54. *Russkaia doktrina*, 70, 71, 78.

55. Mikhail Remizov, interview by Paul Robinson, Irrussianality, August 31, 2017, https://irrussianality.wordpress.com/2017/11/02/interview-with-mikhail-remizov.

56. "Obsuzhdenie doklada," *Tetradi po konservatizmu* 2, no. 1 (2014), 97.

57. Nataliia Narochnitskaia, *Russkii kod razvitiia* (Moscow: Knizhnyi mir, 2015), 230.

58. Ibid., 35.

59. Mikhail Remizov, interview; Narochnitskaia, *Russkii kod razvitiia*, 117.

60. Laruelle, *Russian Eurasianism*, 87.

61. M. A. Maslin, "Klassicheskoe evraziistvo i ego sovremennye transformatsii," *Tetradi po konservatizmu* 4 (2015): 204.

62. Marlene Laruelle, "The Two Faces of Contemporary Eurasianism: An Imperial Version of Russian Nationalism," *Nationalities Papers: The Journal of Nationalism and Ethnicity* 32, no. 1 (2004): 123–24.

63. Ibid.

64. Anastasia V. Mitrofanova, *The Politicization of Russian Orthodoxy: Actors and Ideas* (Stuttgart: Ibidem, 2005), 57.

65. Marina Peunova, "An Eastern Incarnation of the European New Right: Aleksandr Panarin and New Eurasianist Discourse in Contemporary Russia," *Journal of Contemporary European Studies* 16, no. 3 (2008): 407–19.

66. Clover, *Black Wind, White Snow*, 176.

67. For discussions of the New Right's influence on Dugin's thought, see: Mikhail Sokolov, "New Right-Wing Intellectuals in Russia: Strategies of Legitimation," *Russian Politics and Law* 47, no. 1 (2009): 47–75. See also: Bassin, "Lev Gumilev," 840–65.

68. Alexander Dugin, interview by Paul Robinson, Irrussianality, August 31, 2017, https://irrussianality.wordpress.com/2017/09/13/interview-with-alexander-dugin/.

69. Ibid.

70. Dmitry Shlapentokh, "Dugin, Eurasianism, and Central Asia," *Communist and Post-Communist Studies* 40, no. 2 (2007): 143–56.

71. Alexander Dugin, *The Fourth Political Theory* (London: Arktos Media, 2012), 165.

72. Alexander Dugin, interview.

73. Dugin, *The Fourth Political Theory*, 30.

74. Alexander Dugin, interview.

75. Aleksandr Dugin, *Osnovy geopolitiki: Geopoliticheskoe budushchee Rossii; Myslit' postranstvom* (Moscow: Arktogeia, 2000), 366.

76. Dugin, *The Fourth Political Theory*, 192–93.

77. Ibid., 193.

78. Dugin, *Osnovy geopolitiki*, 190.

79. Ibid., 219.

80. Viacheslav Nikonov, "Rossiia i mir: Konservatizm v rossiiskoi vneshnei politike," *Tetradi po konservatizmu* 1 (2014): 90; *Russkaia doktrina*, 919. For an academic analysis of this issue, see: Elena Chebankova, "Russian Fundamental Conservatism: In Search of Modernity," *Post-Soviet Affairs* 29, no. 4 (2013): 301–4.

81. Kholmogorov, *Revansh russkoi istorii*, 155.

82. Ibid., 297.

83. Ibid., 143.

84. Boris Mezhuev, "Putin priderzhivaetsia konservativnogo ponimaniia konservatizma," *Russkaia!dea*, April 16, 2016, http://politconservatism.ru/interview/putin-priderzhivaetsya-konservativnogo-ponimaniya-konservatizma.

85. Sergei Prozorov, "Russian Conservatism in the Putin Presidency: The Dispersion of a Hegemonic Discourse," *Journal of Political Ideologies* 10, no. 2 (2005): 125.

86. For instance, Vladimir Putin, "Poslanie prezidenta federal'nomu sobraniiu," December 12, 2012, http://kremlin.ru/events/president/transcripts/17118.

87. Vladimir Putin, "Vstrecha s uchastnikami mezhdunarodnogo diskussionogo kluba 'Valdai,'" September 14, 2007, http://kremlin.ru/events/president/transcripts/24537.

88. Vladimir Putin, "Poslanie federal'nomu sobraniiu Rossiiskoi Federatsii," April 25, 2005, http://kremlin.ru/events/president/transcripts/22931.

89. Putin, "Poslanie prezidenta federal'nomu sobraniiu," December 12, 2012.

90. Vladimir Putin, "Vystuplenia i diskussiia na Miunkhenskoi konferentsii po voprosam politiki bezopastnosti," February 10, 2007, http://kremlin.ru/events/president/transcripts/24034.

91. Putin, "Poslanie prezidenta federal'nomu sobraniiu," December 12, 2012.

92. Oleg Morozov, "Osnovnye polozheniia sotsial'no-konservativnoi ideologii," *Tetradi po konservatizmu* 1 (2014): 12.

93. Valentina Matvienko, "Pravovaia sistema strany dolzhna opirat'sia na natsional'nye traditsii i tsennosti," *Parlamentskaia gazeta*, August 12, 2016, https://www.pnp.ru/politics/2016/08/12/valentina-matvienko-pravovaya-sistema-strany-dolzhna-opiratsya-nanacionalnye-tradicii-i-cennosti.html.

94. Marlene Laruelle, *Inside and Around the Kremlin's Black Box: The Nationalist Think Tanks in Russia* (Stockholm: Institute for Security & Development Policy, 2009), 26–27.

95. Chestneishin, "Konservatizm i liberalizm," 170.

96. Tsipko, "Liberal'nyi konservatizm," 31–32.

97. Netesova, "What Does It Mean?"

98. Mikhail Remizov, interview.

99. For statements to this effect, see: A. Iu. Zudin, "Ocherki ideologii razvitiia," *Tetradi po konservatizmu* 2, no. 2 (2014): 9–10; B. V. Mezhuev, "Sovremennyi konservatizm: Parametry transformatsii," *Tetradi po konservatizmu* 2, no. 1 (2014): 81–82, 87; M. G. Deliagin, "Tsennostnyi krizis: Pochemu formal'naia demokratiia ne rabotaet," *Polis: Politicheskie issledovaniia* 1 (2008): 114.

100. Mezhuev, "Sovremennyi konservatizm," 81–82.

101. Ibid., 87.

102. Deliagin, "Tsennostnyi krizis," 114.

103. Boris Mezhuev, "Konservativnaia demokratiia stanet glavnym opponentom liberal'nogo avtoritarizma," *Russkaia!dea*, January 9, 2016, http://politconservatism.ru/konservativnaya-demokratiya-stanet-glavnym-opponentom-liberalnogo-avtoritarizma.

104. Oleg Barabanov, "Sotrudnichestvo velikoi konservativnoi Ameriki i velikoi konservativnoi Russii mozhet izmenit' mir," *Russkaia!dea*, November 10, 2016, http://politconservatism.ru/interview/sotrudnichestvo-velikoj-konservativnoj-ameriki-i-velikoj-konservativnoj-rossii-mozhet-izmenit-mir.

105. D. A. Iur'ev, "Konservatizm protiv nigilizma: Russkaia al'ternativa," *Tetradi po konservatizmu* 3 (2014): 210.

106. Poliakov, "Shans ob"edineniia," 44.

107. Vladimir Solov'ev, *Revolutsiia konservatorov: Voina mirov* (Moscow: Izdatel'stvo "E," 2017), 110, 113.

108. Boris Mezhuev, "Sud nad revolutsiei—sud nad peterburgskoi imperiei," *Russkaia!dea*, February 23, 2017, https://politconservatism.ru/articles/boris-mezhuev-sud-nad-revolyutsiej-sud-nad-peterburgskoj-imperiej.

109. Boris Mezhuev, "Island Russia and Russia's Identity Politics: Unlearned lessons from Vadim Tsymbursky," *Russia in Global Affairs* 2 (2017), http://eng.globalaffairs.ru/number/Island-Russia-and-Russias-Identity-Politics-18757. For more on Tsymbursky see A. P. Tsygankov, "Ostrovnaia geopolitika Vadima Tsymburskogo," *Tetradi po konservatizmu* 1 (2015):19; S. V. Khatuntsev, "Vspominaia Vadima Tsymburskogo," *Polis: Politicheskie issledovaniia* 3 (2013): 155–63.

110. V. L. Tsymburskii, "Osnovaniia rossiiskogo geopoliticheskogo konservatizma," *Tetradi po konservatizmu* 1 (2015): 41–44.

111. Boris Mezhuev, "In Russia, It's the Realists vs. the Ethno-Nationalists," *The American Conservative*, May 10, 2017, http://www.theamericanconservative.com/articles/in-russia-its-the-realists-vs-the-ethno-nationalists/.

112. Remizov, *Russkie i gosudarstvo*, 366.

113. Ibid., 122.

114. Kholmogorov, *Revansh russkoi istorii*, 7–8.

115. Ibid., 10. For a more detailed description of Kholmogorov's concept of "offensive isolationism," see: Egor Kholmogorov, interview by Paul Robinson, September 4, 2017, https://irrussianality.wordpress.com/2017/11/18/interview-with-egor-kholmogorov/.

116. Dugin, *The Fourth Political Theory*, 51–52.

117. Ibid., 65–66.

118. Ibid., 155.

119. Ibid., 196.

120. Dugin, *Osnovy geopolitiki*, 213.

121. Ibid., 343.

122. Ibid., 422.

123. Ibid., 436–37.

124. Alexander Dugin, interview.

125. Prokhanov, *Simfoniia "piatoi imperii,"* 41.

126. Ibid., 47.

127. Gusev, *Russkii konservatizm*, 179–80.

128. Vitalii Tret'iakov, "Konets partiinosti i soslovnaia demokratiia," in Shchipkov, *Po-drugomu*, 96–97.

129. Ibid., 99–101.

130. *Russkaia doktrina*, 314.

131. Ibid., 926.

132. Ibid., 314.

133. Ibid., 318.

134. Ibid., 322.

135. Ibid., 324–26.

136. Ibid., 314.

137. Ibid., 328.

138. Ibid., 917, 919.

139. Ibid., 159–60.

140. Ibid., 155.

141. Gusev, *Russkii konservatizm*, 175–76.

142. Ricky Twisdale, "A Conservative Russian Lion with Real Mass Influence— The Painter Ilya Glazunov," *Russia Insider*, September 11, 2016, http://russia-insider.com/en/culture/conservative-russian-lion-real-mass-influence-painter-ilya-glazunov/ri15339.

143. Aleksandr Prokhanov, "Ventsenosnyi Putin," Izborskii klub, July 5, 2017, https://izborsk-club.ru/13646.

144. TASS, "Mitropolit Ilarion: Monarkhiia imeet preimushchestva pered drugimi formami pravleniia," July 1, 2017, http:// tass.ru/obschestvo/4380573.

145. The Russian Orthodox Church, *Osnovy sotsial'noi kontseptsii*, 3.7.

146. Ibid., 3.2.

147. Ibid., 3.5.

148. Ibid., 3.3–4.

149. Mitrofanova, *The Politicization of Russian Orthodoxy*, 170.

150. Knox, "The Symphonic Ideal," 580.

151. Burgess, *Holy Rus'*, 41. For varying opinions on the church's attitude to the idea of symphony, see Irina Papkova, *The Orthodox Church and Russian Politics* (Washington, DC: Woodrow Wilson Center Press, 2011), 30; Knox, "The Symphonic Ideal," 582; and Zoe Knox and Anastasia Mitrofanova, "The Russian Orthodox Church," in *Eastern Christianity and Politics in the Twenty-First Century*, ed. Lucian N. Leustean (London: Routledge, 2014), 45.

152. Mitrofanova, *The Politicization of Russian Orthodoxy*, 18.

153. Papkova, *The Orthodox Church*, 124–32, 168.

154. Bremer, "The Role of the Church," 4.

155. For an analysis of the document, see Papanikolaou, *The Mystical as Political*, 94.

156. The Russian Orthodox Church, *Osnovy ucheniia Russkoi Pravoslavnoi Tserkvi o dostoinstve, svobode i pravakh cheloveka*, Section I, https://mospat.ru/ru/documents/dignity-freedom-rights/.

157. Ibid., 3.2.

158. Ibid., 3.3, 3.5.

159. Ibid., 4.1.

160. Ibid., 4.4–9.

161. Ibid., 5.2.

162. Burgess, *Holy Rus'*, 91.

163. Ibid., 119.

164. Chebankova, "Contemporary Russian Conservatism," 48.

165. Laruelle, "Inside and Around," 27–28.

166. Vladimir Putin, "Poslanie prezidenta federal'nomu sobraniiu," December 4, 2014, http://kremlin.ru/events/president/transcripts/47173.

167. Vladimir Putin, "Interv'iu telekanalu Russia Today," September 6, 2012, http://kremlin.ru/events/president/transcripts/16393.

168. Nigel Gould Davies, *Russia's Sovereign Globalization: Rise, Fall and Future* (London: Chatham House, 2016), 9, https://www.chathamhouse.org/sites/files/chathamhouse/publications/research/20160106RussiasSovereignGlobalizationGould DaviesFinal.pdf.

169. Morozov, "Osnovnye polozheniia," 14.

170. Remizov, *Russkie i gosudarstvo*, 96.

171. Ibid., 109.

172. Ibid., 98, 110.

173. Ibid., 373.

174. Dugin, *Osnovy geopolitiki*, 282.

175. The Russian Orthodox Church, *Osnovy sotsial'noi kontseptsii*, 7.2.

176. Ibid., 13.1.

177. Ibid., 13.3.

178. Dugin, *The Fourth Political Theory*, 65–66.

179. Prokhanov, *Simofoniia "piatoi imperii,"* 36.

180. *Russkaia doktrina*, 743.

181. For an analysis of left conservatism, see Rabotiazhev, "Mezhdu traditsii i utopiei," 114–30.

182. Ibid., 121–22.

183. For comments on Ziuganov's views, see: Prozorov, "Russian Conservatism," 134; Marlene Laruelle, *In the Name of the Nation: Nationalism and Politics in Contemporary Russia* (New York: Palgrave MacMillan, 2009), 91; Mitrofanova, *The Politicization of Russian Orthodoxy*, 60–64.

184. Duncan, *Russian Messianism*, 136.

185. Aleksandr Shchipkov, "Levyi konservatizm," in Shchipkov, *Po-drugomu*, 43–64.

186. Narochnitskaia, *Russkii kod razvitiia*, 212–13.

187. *Russkaia doktrina*, 409.

188. Ibid., 524, 527.

189. Ibid., 535.

190. Ibid., 631.

191. Ibid., 628.

192. Ibid., 698.

193. Ibid., 727.

194. Ibid.

195. Ibid., 718.

196. Ibid., 727.

197. See the banner on the Stolypin Club website: http://stolypinsky.club/.

198. Sergei Glaz'ev, "Konservatizm i novaia ekonomika," *Tetradi po konservatizmu* 1 (2014): 61, 62.

199. Ibid., 62.

200. Ibid., 66.

201. Ibid., 67.

202. Sergei Glaz'ev, "Doklad gruppy ekspertov pod rukovodstvom akademika Glaz'eva," Izborskii klub, June 24, 2014, https://izborsk-club.ru/3398.

203. Sergei Glaz'ev, "K strategii spravedlivosti i razvitii," Izborskii klub, August 3, 2015, https://izborsk-club.ru/6451.

204. Sergei Glaz'ev, "Predotvratit' voinu—pobedit' v voine (doklad Izborskomu klubu)," *Izborksii klub*, September 30, 2014, https://izborsk-club.ru/3963.

205. Glaz'ev, "K strategii."

206. Glaz'ev, "Predotvratit' voinu."

207. Glaz'ev, "Doklad gruppy ekspertov."

208. Ibid.

209. Glaz'ev, "Predotvratit' voinu."

210. Sergei Glaz'ev, "Vstat' v polnyi rost (doklad Izborskomu klubu)," *Izborskii klub*, November 23, 2014, https://izborsk-club.ru/4273.

211. Luke March, "Nationalism for Export? The Domestic and Foreign-Policy Implications of the New 'Russian Idea,'" *Europe-Asia Studies* 64, no. 3 (2012): 410.

212. Burgess, *Holy Rus'*, 207.

213. Papkova, *The Orthodox Church*, 93.

214. Ibid., 189.

215. For instance, March, "Nationalism for Export?" 410.

216. Vladimir Putin, "Vstrecha s uchastnikami XIX Vsemirnogo festivalia molodezhi i studentov," October 14, 2017, http://kremlin.ru/events/president/transcripts/55842.

217. See, for instance, Witold Rodkiewicz and Jadwiga Rogoza, "Potemkin Conservatism: An Ideological Tool of the Kremlin," *Point of View* 48 (2015): 1–25.

218. Vladimir Putin, "Interv'iu Pervomu kanalu i agentstvu Assoshieited Press," September 4, 2013, http://kremlin.ru/events/president/transcripts/19143.

219. Poliakov, "Shans ob"edineniia," 47.

220. Ibid., 47, 49.

BIBLIOGRAPHY

INTERVIEWS

Aleksandr Dugin, Moscow, August 31, 2017
Egor Kholmogorov, Moscow, September 4, 2017
Mikhail Remizov, Moscow, August 31, 2017

BOOKS, DISSERTATIONS, AND ARTICLES

Adams, Arthur E. "Pobedonostsev and the Rule of Firmness." *The Slavonic and East European Review* 32, no. 78 (1953): 132–39.
———. "Pobedonostsev's Religious Politics." *Church History* 22, no. 4 (1953): 314–26.
Agadjanian, Alexander. "Breakthrough to Modernity, Apologia for Traditionalism: The Russian Orthodox View of Society in Comparative Perspective." *Religion, State and Society* 31, no. 4 (2003): 327–46.
Agurskii, M. S., et al., eds. *Iz-pod glyb.* Paris: YMCA-Press, 1974.
Agursky, Michael. *The Third Rome: National Bolshevism in the USSR.* Boulder, CO: Westview, 1987.
Aksakov, K. "O sochineniiakh Zhukovskogo." In Brodskii, *Rannye slavianofily,* 117–18.
———. "Stat'i K. Aksakova iz 'Mol'vy.'" In Brodskii, *Rannye slavianofily,* 103–22.
———. "Svobodnoe slovo." In Brodskii, *Rannye slavianofily,* 171.
Alexander, Bishop. *Father John of Kronstadt: A Life.* Crestwood, NY: St. Vladimir's Seminary Press, 1979.
Alfeyev, Hilarion. *Orthodox Christianity: The History and Canonical Structure of the Orthodox Church.* Yonkers, NY: St. Vladimir's Seminary Press, 2011.
Anderson, John. *Conservative Christian Politics in Russia and the United States: Dreaming of Christian Nations.* London: Routledge, 2014.
Armstrong, Allan. "Foreword." In Brianchaninov, *On the Prayer of Jesus,* vii–xxxiv.
Ascher, Abraham. *P. A. Stolypin: The Search for Stability in Late Imperial Russia.* Stanford, CA: Stanford University Press, 2001.
Askol'dov, S. A. et al. *Iz glubiny: Sbornik statei o russkoi revolutsii.* Paris: YMCA-Press, 1967.
Avdeev, O. K. "Kakoi konservatizm nam nuzhen: Nasledie russkoi konservativnoi mysli i aktual'naia politika." *Tetradi po konservatizmu* 3 (2014): 80–84.
———. "Konservatizm kak faktor miagkoi sily Rossii." *Tetradi po konservatizmu* 2, no. 1 (2014): 66–77.
Avramenko, Richard, and Lee Trepanier, eds. *Dostoevsky's Political Thought.* Lanham, MD: Lexington Books, 2013.
Baburin, Sergei et al. "Imperativy natsional'nogo vozrozhdeniia." Pravaia.ru, March 21, 2006. http://www.pravaya.ru/look/7060.

Barabanov, Oleg. "Sotrudnichestvo velikoi konservativnoi Ameriki i velikoi konservativnoi Rossii mozhet izmenit' mir." Russkaia!dea, November 10, 2016. http://politconserva-tism.ru/interview/sotrudnichestvo-velikoj-konservativnoj-ameriki-i-velikoj-kon-servativnoj-rossii-mozhet-izmenit-mir.

Barbashin, Anton, and Hannah Thorburn. "Putin's Philosopher." *Foreign Affairs*, September 20, 2015. https://www.foreignaffairs.com/articles/russian-federation/2015-09-20/putins-philosopher.

Basil, John D. "Alexander Kireev: Turn-of-the-Century Slavophile and the Russian Orthodox Church, 1890–1910." *Cahiers du monde russe et sovietique* 32, no. 3 (1991): 337–47.

———. "Konstantin Petrovich Pobedonostsev: An Argument for a Russian State Church." *Church History* 64, no. 1 (1995): 44–61.

Bassin, Mark. *The Gumilev Mystique: Biopolitics, Eurasianism, and the Construction of Community in Modern Russia*. Ithaca, NY: Cornell University Press, 2016.

———. "Lev Gumilev and the European New Right." *Nationalities Papers: The Journal of Nationalism and Ethnicity* 43, no. 6 (2015): 840–65.

———. "Narrating Kulikovo: Lev Gumilev, Russian Nationalists, and the Troubled Emergence of Neo-Eurasianism." In Bassin, *Between Europe and Asia*, 165–86.

Bassin, Mark, Sergey Glebov, and Marlene Laruelle, eds. *Between Europe and Asia: The Origins, Theories, and Legacies of Russian Eurasianism*. Pittsburgh, PA: University of Pittsburgh Press, 2015.

Beisswenger, Martin. "Eurasianism: Affirming the Person in an 'Era of Faith.'" In Hamburg, *A History of Russian Philosophy*, 363–80.

———. "Metaphysics of the Economy: The Religious and Economic Foundations of P. N. Savitskii's Eurasianism." In Bassin, *Between Europe and Asia*, 97–112.

Berdiaev, Nikolai. "Dukhi russkoi revoliutsii." In *Iz glubiny: Sbornik statei o russkoi revoliutsii*, by S. A. Askol'dov et al. Paris: YMCA-Press, 1967.

———. *Filosofiia neravenstva: Pis'ma k nedrugam po sotsial'noi filosofii*. Berlin: Obelisk, 1923.

———. "Filosofskaia istina i intelligentskaia pravda." In Berdiaev, *Vekhi*, 1–22.

Berdiaev, N. A. et al. *Vekhi: Sbornik statei o russkoi intelligentsii*. Moscow: Tipografiia V. M. Sablina, 1909.

Blitstein, Peter A. "Nation-Building or Russification? Obligatory Russian Instruction in the Soviet Non-Russian School, 1938–1953." In *A State of Nations: Empire and Nation-Making in the Age of Lenin and Stalin*, edited by Ronald Grigor Suny and Terry Martin, 253–74. Oxford: Oxford University Press, 2001.

Bluhm, Katharina. "Modernization, Geopolitics, and the New Russian Conservatives." *Arbeitspapiere des Osteuropa-Instituts: Arbeitsbereich Soziologie* 1 (2016): 1–37.

Boobbyer, Philip. "Russian Liberal Conservatism." In *Russian Nationalism Past and Present*, edited by Geoffrey Hosking and Robert Service, 35–54. Basingstoke: Macmillan, 1998.

Boterbloem, Kees. "The Eternal Ensign: Andrei Zhdanov and the Survival of Tsarist Military Culture in the Soviet Union." *War and Society* 22, no. 1 (2004): 1–18.

———. *A History of Russia and Its Empire: From Mikhail Romanov to Vladimir Putin*. Lanham, MD: Rowman & Littlefield, 2014.

Bremer, Thomas. "The Role of the Church in the New Russia." *Russian Analytical Digest* 47 (October 2008): 2–10.

Brianchaninov, Ignatii. "Arkhipastyrskye vozzvaniia po voprosu osvobozhdeniia krest'ian ot krepostnoi zavisimosti." In *Polnoe sobranie tvorenii*, 2:430.

———. *Polnoe sobranie tvorenii*. Vol. 2. Moscow: Palomnik, 2001.

Brianchaninov, Ignatius. *The Field: Cultivating Salvation*. Jordanville, NY: Holy Trinity Publications, 2016.

———. *On the Prayer of Jesus*. Berwick, ME: Ibis, 2006.

Brodskii, N. L. "Slavianofily i ikh uchenie." In Brodskii, *Rannye slavianofily*, ix–lxv.

———, ed. *Rannye slavianofily: A. S. Khomiakov, I. V. Kireevskii, K. S. i I.S. Aksakovy*. Moscow: Tipografiia T-va I. D. Sytina, 1910.

Bulgakov, Sergei. "Geroizm i podvizhnichestvo (iz razmyshlenii o religioznoi prirode russkoi intelligentsii)." In Berdiaev, *Vekhi*, 23–69.

Bulgakov, Sergius. *The Orthodox Church*. Crestwood, NY: St. Vladimir's Seminary Press, 1988.

Bullough, Oliver. *The Last Man in Russia and the Struggle to Save a Dying Nation*. New York: Basic Books, 2013.

Burgess, John P. *Holy Rus': The Rebirth of Orthodoxy in the New Russia*. New Haven, CT: Yale University Press, 2017.

Butler, William E., and V. A. Tomsinov. "Ivan A. Il'in: Russian Legal Philosopher." In Il'in, *On the Essence*, 15–50.

Byrnes, Robert Francis. *Pobedonostsev: His Life and Thought*. Bloomington: Indiana University Press, 1968.

———. "Pobedonostsev on the Role of Change in History." *The Russian Review* 26, no. 3 (1967): 231–50.

———. "Pobedonostsev's Conception of the Good Society: An Analysis of His Thought after 1880." *The Review of Politics* 13, no. 2 (1951): 169–90.

———. "Russia and the West: The Views of Pobedonostsev." *The Journal of Modern History* 40, no. 2 (1968): 234–56.

Chaadaev, Petr. *Filosofskie pis'ma*. Kazan: Tipografiia D. M. Gran, 1906.

Chamberlain, Lesley. *Motherland: A Philosophical History of Russia*. New York: Rookery, 2007.

Chebankova, Elena. "Contemporary Russian Conservatism." *Post-Soviet Affairs* 32, no. 1 (2016): 28–54.

———. "Russian Fundamental Conservatism: In Search of Modernity." *Post-Soviet Affairs* 29, no. 4 (2013): 287–313.

Chernavskii, M. Iu. *Religiozno-filosofskie osnovy konservatizma v Rossii*. Moscow: Rossiiskii Zaochnyi Institut Tekstil'noi i Legkoi Promyshlennosti, 2004.

Cherniaev, A. V. "U istokov russkogo konservatizma: Ivan Pososhkov." *Tetradi po konservatizmu* 3 (2014): 32–35.

Chestneishin, N. V. "Konservatizm i liberalizm: Tozhdestvo i razvitie." *Polis: Politicheskie issledovaniia* 4 (2006): 168–73.

Chicherin, B. N. *Liberty, Equality, and the Market: Essays*. New Haven, CT: Yale University Press, 1998.

———. "Excerpts from On Popular Representation." In Chicherin, *Liberty, Equality, and the Market*, 149–206.

———. "Excerpts from Property and State." In Chicherin, *Liberty, Equality, and the Market*, 351–424.

———. "On Serfdom." In Chicherin, *Liberty, Equality, and the Market*, 69–109.

Christian, David. "The Political Ideals of Mikhail Speransky." *The Slavonic and East European Review* 54, no. 2 (1976): 192–213.

Christoff, Peter K. *An Introduction to Nineteenth-Century Russian Slavophilism: A. S. Xomjakov*. The Hague: Mouton, 1961.

———. *An Introduction to Nineteenth-Century Russian Slavophilism: Iu. F. Samarin*. Oxford: Westview Press, 1991.

———. *An Introduction to Nineteenth-Century Russian Slavophilism: I. V. Kireevskij*. The Hague: Mouton, 1972.

———. *K. S. Aksakov: A Study in Ideas*. Princeton, NJ: Princeton University Press, 1982.

Churkin, Aleksandr A. "St. Ignatius Brianchaninov and the Russian Religious Conservatism." Unpublished conference paper, Fifteenth Annual Aleksanteri Conference, University of Helsinki, 21–13 October 2015.

Clover, Charles. *Black Wind, White Snow: The Rise of Russia's New Nationalism*. New Haven, CT: Yale University Press, 2016.

Cohen, Stephen F. "The Friends and Foes of Change: Reformism and Conservatism in the Soviet Union." *Slavic Review* 38, no. 2 (1979): 187–202.

Coleman, Heather. "Introduction: Faith and Story in Imperial Russia." In Coleman, *Orthodox Christianity*, 1–21.

———., ed. *Orthodox Christianity in Imperial Russia: A Source Book on Lived Religion*. Bloomington: Indiana University Press, 2014.

Daniel, Wallace L. *The Orthodox Church and Civil Society in Russia*. College Station: Texas A&M University Press, 2006.

Daniels, Robert V. *The Rise and Fall of Communism in Russia*. New Haven, CT: Yale University Press, 2007.

Danilevskii, N. Ia. *Rossiia i Evropa: Vzgliad na kul'turnye i politicheskie otnosheniia slavianskogo mira k germano-romanskomu*. Moscow: Blagoslovenie, 2011.

Davies, Nigel Gould. *Russia's Sovereign Globalization: Rise, Fall and Future*. London: Chatham House, 2016.

Deliagin, M. G. "Tsennostnyi krizis: Pochemu formal'naia demokratiia ne rabotaet." *Polis: Politicheskie Issledovaniia* 1 (2008): 109–21.

Dickinson, Anna. "Quantifying Religious Repression: Russian Orthodox Church Closures and Repression of Priests 1917–41." *Religion, State and Society* 28, no. 4 (2000): 327–35.

Dostoevskii, F. M. "A. A. Romanovu (nasledniku)." In *Polnoe sobranie sochinenii*, 29:1:260–61.

———. "Adres Aleksandru II napisannyi Dostoevskim ot imeni Slavianskogo blagotvoritel'nogo obshchestva." In *Polnoe sobranie sochinenii*, 30:2:47–48.

———. *Dnevnik pisatelia*. In *Polnoe sobranie sochinenii*, vols. 21–27.

———. "Ob"iasnitel'noe slovo po povodu pechataemoi nizhe rechi o Pushkine." In *Polnoe sobranie sochinenii*, 26:129–36.

———. *Polnoe sobranie sochinenii v tridtsati tomakh*. 30 vols. Leningrad: Nauka, 1972–90.

———. "Pushkin." In *Polnoe sobranie sochinenii*, 26:136–49.

———. *Zimnie zametki o letnikh vpechatleniiakh*. In *Polnoe sobranie sochinenii*, vol. 5.

Dowler, Wayne. *Dostoevsky, Grigor'ev, and Native Soil Conservatism*. Toronto: University of Toronto Press, 1982.

———. "Herder in Russia: A. A. Grigor'ev and 'Progressivist-Traditionalism.'" *Canadian Slavonic Papers* 19, no. 2 (1977): 167–80.

———. "The 'Young Editors' of *Moskvityanin* and the Origins of Intelligentsia Conservatism in Russia." *Slavonic and East European Review* 55, no. 3 (1977): 310–27.

Drozdova, Oksana, and Paul Robinson. "In Others' Words: Quotations and Recontextualization in Putin's Speeches." *Russian Politics* 2, no. 2 (2017): 227–53.

Dugin, Aleksandr. *The Fourth Political Theory*. London: Artkos Media, 2012.

———. *Osnovy geopolitiki: Geopoliticheskoe budushchee Rossii; Myslit' prostranstvom*. Moscow: Arktogeia, 2000.

Duncan, Peter. "The Fate of Russian Nationalism: The *Samizdat* Journal *Veche* Revisited." *Religion in Communist Lands* 16, no. 1 (1988): 36–53.

———. *Russian Messianism: Third Rome, Revolution, Communism, and After*. London: Routledge, 2000.

Dunlop, John B. *The Faces of Contemporary Russian Nationalism*. Princeton, NJ: Princeton University Press, 1983.

———. *The New Russian Nationalism*. New York: Prager, 1985.

———. *The Rise of Russia and Fall of the Soviet Empire*. Princeton, NJ: Princeton University Press, 1993.

Dunn, Charles W., and J. David Woodard. *The Conservative Tradition in America*. Lanham, MD: Rowman & Littlefield, 1996.

Durman, Karel. *The Time of the Thunderer: Mikhail Katkov, Russian Nationalist Extremism and the Failure of the Bismarckian System, 1871–1887*. Boulder, CO: East European Monographs, 1988.

Eimontova, R. G. "V novom oblichii (1825–1855)." In Grosul, *Russkii konservatizm*, 105–91.

Emmons, Terence. *The Russian Landed Gentry and the Peasant Emancipation of 1861*. Cambridge: Cambridge University Press, 1968.

Engelstein, Laura. *Slavophile Empire: Imperial Russia's Illiberal Past*. Ithaca, NY: Cornell University Press, 2009.

Engström, Maria. "Contemporary Russian Messianism and the New Russian Foreign Policy." *Contemporary Security Policy* 35, no. 3 (2014): 356–79.

Ericson, Edward E. *Solzhenitsyn and the Modern World*. Washington, DC: Regnery Gateway, 1993.

Evans, Alfred. "Ideological Change under Vladimir Putin in the Perspective of Social Identity Theory." *Demokratizatsiya: The Journal of Post-Soviet Democratization* 23, no. 4 (2015): 401–26.

Evdokimov, Paul. *Orthodoxy: The Cosmos Transfigured*. Hyde Park, NY: New City Press, 2011.

Evlampiev, Igor. "Nepriiatie idei Ivan Il'ina liberalami svidetel'stvuet tol'ko ob ikh neobra-zovannosti: Interv'iu s Igorem Evlampievym." *Samopoznanie* 2 (2015): 12–17.

Evtuhov, Catherine, and Richard Stites. *A History of Russia: Peoples, Legends, Events, Forces since 1800*. Boston: Houghton Mifflin, 2004.

Fedotov, George P. *The Russian Religious Mind: Kievan Christianity, the Tenth to the Thirteenth Centuries*. New York: Harper Torchbooks, 1946.

Fedulov, Alexander et al. "The Phenomenon of 'Russian Soul' as a Reflection of Traditional Conservatism: New Theoretical and Methodological Approaches and Ordinary Perception of Conservatism." *Mediterranean Journal of Social Sciences* 6, no. 6 (2015): 113–21.

Florensky, Pavel. *The Pillar and Ground of the Truth*. Princeton, NJ: Princeton University Press, 2004.

Florovskii, Georgii. "O narodakh ne-istoricheskikh." In Shirokov, *Iskhod k vostoku*, 139–70.

Fonvizin, D. I. "Pis'ma iz vtorogo zagranichnogo puteshestviia (1777–1778)." In *Sobranie sochinenii*, 2:412–92. Moscow: Gosudarstvennoe Izdatel'stvo Khudozhestvennoi Literatury, 1959.

Frank. S. "Etika nigilizma (k kharakteristike nravstvennogo mirovozzreniia russkoi intelligentsii." In Berdiaev, *Vekhi*, 146–81.

Freeden, Michael. *Ideologies and Political Theory: A Conceptual Approach.* Oxford: Clarendon Press, 1996.

Freeze, Gregory L. "Handmaiden of the State? The Church in Imperial Russia Reconsidered." *Journal of Ecclesiastical History* 36, no. 1 (1985): 82–102.

——. "The Orthodox Church and Serfdom in Prereform Russia." *Slavic Review* 48, no. 3 (1989): 361–87.

Geiger, H. Kent. *The Family in Soviet Russia.* Cambridge, MA: Harvard University Press, 1968.

Gershenzon, M. "Predislovie." In Berdiaev, *Vekhi*, i–ii.

——. "Tvorcheskoe samosoznanie." In Berdiaev, *Vekhi*, 70–96.

Gilbert, George. *The Radical Right in Late Imperial Russia: Dreams of a True Fatherland?* London: Routledge, 2016.

Gillespie, David C. *Valentin Rasputin and Soviet Russian Village Prose.* London: The Modern Humanities Research Association, 1986.

Glaz'ev, Sergei. "Bol'shuiu Evraziiu stroit' bez dollara." Izborskii klub, April 11, 2017. https://izborsk-club.ru/13014.

——. "Doklad gruppy ekspertov pod rukovodstvom akademika Glaz'eva." Izborskii klub, June 24, 2014. https//izborsk-club.ru/3398.

——. "12 shagov dlia ekonomicheskogo razvitiia Rossii." Izborskii klub, March 27, 2017. https://izborsk-club.ru/12853.

——. "Konservatizm i novaia ekonomika." *Tetradi po konservatizmu* 1 (2014): 61–67.

——. "K strategii spravedlivosti i razvitiia." Izborskii klub, August 3, 2015. https://izborsk-club.ru/6451.

——. "Predotvratit' voinu—pobedit' v voine (doklad Izborskomu klubu)." Izborksii klub, September 30, 2014. https://izborsk-club.ru/3963.

——. "Vstat' v polnyi rost (doklad Izborskomu klubu)." Izborskii klub, November 23, 2014. https://izborsk-club.ru/4273.

Gogol', N. V. *Vybrannye mesta iz perepiski s druz'iami.* Moscow: Patriot, 1993.

Gorokhov, A. A. "Konservatizm v Rossii i osobennosti russkoi konservativnoi sotsial'no-politicheskoi mysli pervoi poloviny XIX veka." *Tetradi po konservatizmu* 2 (2016): 127–50.

Grenier, Paul. "Definitions and Dialogue: Reflections of a Reluctant Conservative on Russian and American Conservatism." Unpublished manuscript.

——. "The Varieties of Russian Conservatism." *The American Conservative*, June 19, 2015. http://www.theamericanconservative.com/articles/the-varieties-of-russian-conservatism/.

Grier, Philip T. "Adventures in Dialectic and Intuition: Shpet, Il'in, Losev." In Hamburg, *A History of Russian Philosophy*, 326–45.

——. "The Complex Legacy of Ivan Il'in." In *Russian Thought after Communism: The Recovery of a Philosophical Heritage*, edited by James P. Scanlan, 165–86. Armonk, NY: M. E. Sharpe, 1994.

————. "I. A. Il'in and the Rule of Law." In Il'in, *On the Essence*, 1–14.

Grisbrooke, W. Jardine, ed. *Spiritual Counsels of Father John of Kronstadt*. London: James Clarke, 1967.

Grosul, V. Ia., "V epokhu reform 1861 goda (1856–1866 gg.)." In Grosul, *Russkii konservatizm*, 192–230.

————. "Zarozhdenie rossiiskogo politicheskogo konservatizma." In Grosul, *Russkii konservatizm*, 18–104.

————. ed. *Russkii konservatizm XIX stoletiia: Ideologiia i praktika*. Moscow: Progress-Traditsiia, 2000.

Gumilev, L. N. *Etnogenez i biosfera zemli*. Leningrad: Izdatel'stvo Leningradskogo Universiteta, 1989.

Gusev, V. A. *Russkii konservatizm: Osnovnye napravleniia i etapy razvitiia*. Tver: Tverskoi gosudarstvennyi universitet, 2001.

Gvozdev, Nikolas. "Russia's Future." *Orbis* 53, no. 2 (2009): 347–59.

Hamburg, Gary M. "Peasant Emancipation and Russian Social Thought: The Case of Boris N. Chicherin." *Slavic Review* 50, no. 4 (1991): 890–904.

————. "The Revival of Russian Conservatism." *Kritika: Explorations in Russian and Eurasian History* 6, no. 1 (2005): 107–27.

————. *Russia's Path toward Enlightenment: Faith, Politics, and Reason, 1500–1801*. New Haven, CT: Yale University Press, 2016.

Hamburg, G. M., and Randall A. Poole, eds. *A History of Russian Philosophy 1830–1931: Faith, Reason, and the Defense of Human Dignity*. Cambridge: Cambridge University Press, 2013.

Hardeman, Hilde. *Coming to Terms with the Soviet Regime: The "Changing Signposts" Movement among Russian Emigres in the Early 1920s*. DeKalb: Northern Illinois University Press, 1994.

Hedlund, Stefan. *Russian Path Dependence: A People with a Troubled History*. London: Routledge, 2005.

Heilbronner, Hans. "Alexander III and the Reform Plan of Loris-Melikov." *Journal of Modern History* 33, no. 4 (1961): 384–97.

Henriksson, Anders. "The *St. Petersburger Zeitung*: Tribune of Baltic German Conservatism in Late Nineteenth-Century Russia." *Journal of Baltic Studies* 20, no. 4 (1989): 365–78.

Hierotheos of Nafpaktos, Metropolitan. "Personalism and Person." Discerning Thoughts, September 21, 2017. https://thoughtsintrusive.wordpress.com/2017/09/21/personalism-and-person/.

Hoffmann, David L. *Stalinist Values: The Cultural Norms of Soviet Modernity, 1917–1941*. Ithaca, NY: Cornell University Press, 2003.

————. "Was There a 'Great Retreat' from Soviet Socialism? Stalinist Culture Reconsidered." *Kritika: Explorations in Russian and Eurasian History* 5, no. 4 (2004): 651–74.

Holt, Alix. "The First Soviet Feminists." In *Soviet Sisterhood: British Feminists on Women in the USSR*, edited by Barbara Holland, 237–65. London: Fourth Estate, 1985.

Hosking, Geoffrey. *Russia and the Russians: A History*. Cambridge, MA: Belknap Press of Harvard University Press, 2001.

Hughes, Michael. "'Independent Gentlemen': The Social Position of the Moscow Slavophiles and Its Impact on Their Political Thought." *The Slavonic and East European Review* 71, no. 1 (1993): 66–88.

——. "State and Society in the Political Thought of the Moscow Slavophiles." *Studies in East European Thought* 52, no. 3 (2000): 159–83.

Huntington, Samuel. "Conservatism as an Ideology." *American Political Science Review* 51, no. 2 (1957): 454–73.

Il'in, I. A. *Nashi zadachi: Stat'i 1948–1954 gg.* Vols. 1 and 2. Paris: Izdanie Russkogo Obshche-Voinskogo Soiuza, 1956.

——. *On the Essence of Legal Consciousness,* edited and translated by W. E. Butler, P. T. Grier, and V. A. Tomsinov. London: Wildy, Simmonds & Hill, 2014.

——. *O soprotivlenii zlu siloiu,* with a commentary by P. N. Poltoratskii. London: Zaria, 1975.

——. *Osnovy bor'by za natsional'nuiu Rossiiu.* Narva: Izd. natsional'no-trudovo soiuza novogo pokoleniia, 1938.

——. *Osnovy gosudarstvennogo ustroistva: Proekt osnovnogo zakona Rossii.* Moscow: Rarog, 1996.

——. *O sushchnosti pravosoznaniia.* Moscow: Rarog, 1993.

——. *Problema sovremennogo pravosoznaniia.* Berlin: Izd. Ob-va "Presse," 1923.

——. *Rodina i my.* Belgrade: Izdanie Gl. Pravleniia O-va Gallipoliitsev, 1926.

Itenberg, B. S., "Ot aprelia 1866 do 1 marta 1881 goda." In Grosul, *Russkii konservatizm,* 230–75.

Iur'ev, D. A. "Konservatizm protiv nigilizma: Russkaia al'ternativa." *Tetradi po konservatizmu* 3 (2014): 203–10.

Ivanov, A. A. "Lozung 'Rossiia dlia russkikh' v konservativnoi mysli vtoroi poloviny XIX veka." *Tetradi po konservatizmu* 4 (2015): 34–42.

Izborskii klub. "Doklad Izborskogo kluba pod redaktsiei V. Aver'ianova." N.d. http://dynacon.ru/content/articles/4409/#a4.

——. "Kruglyi stol 'Gosudarstvo i Tserkov': K novoi paradigm." May 19, 2017. https://izborsk-club.ru/13335.

——. "Ul'ianovskaia deklaratsiia Izborskogo kluba." N.d. http://www.dynacon.ru/content/articles/901/.

Jakobson, Lev I., Boris Rudnik, and Stefan Toepler. "From Liberal to Conservative: Shifting Cultural Policy Regimes in Post-Soviet Russia." *International Journal of Cultural Policy* 24, no. 3 (2018): 297–314.

Judge, Edward H. *Plehve: Repression and Reform in Imperial Russia, 1902–1904.* Syracuse, NY: Syracuse University Press, 1983.

Karamzin, N. M. *Zapiska o drevnei i novoi Rossii v ee politicheskom i grazhdanskom otnosheniiakh.* Moscow: Nauka, 1991.

Katkov, M. "Chto nam delat' s Pol'shei?" *Russkii vestnik* 44 (March 1863): 469–506.

Katz, Martin. *Mikhail Katkov: A Political Biography, 1818–1887.* The Hague: Mouton, 1966.

Kaylan, Melik. "Kremlin Values: Putin's Strategic Conservatism." *World Affairs* 177, no. 1 (May–June 2014): 9–17.

Kekes, John. *A Case for Conservatism.* Ithaca, NY: Cornell University Press, 1998.

Kellogg, Michael. *The Russian Roots of Nazism: White Émigrés and the Making of National Socialism, 1917–1945.* Cambridge: Cambridge University Press, 2005.

Kelly, Aileen. "'What Is Real Is Rational': The Political Philosophy of B.N. Chicherin." *Cahiers du monde russe et soviétique* 18, no. 3 (1977): 195–222.

Kenez, Peter. *A History of the Soviet Union from the Beginning to the End.* Cambridge: Cambridge University Press, 2006.

Kenworthy, Scott M. *The Heart of Russia: Trinity-Sergius, Monasticism, and Society after 1825*. Washington DC: Woodrow Wilson Center Press, 2010.

Khatuntsev, S. V. "Vspominaia Vadima Tsymburskogo." *Polis: Politicheskie Issledovaniia* 3 (2013): 155–63.

Kholmogorov, Egor. "Konservativnyi povorot v Rossii v zerkale global'noi istorii Fernana Brodelia." *Tetradi po konservatizmu* 3 (2015): 121–23.

———. "Pravyi gegel'ianets v okopakh Stalingrada." *Samopoznanie* 2 (2015): 18–24.

———. *Revansh russkoi istorii*. Moscow: Knizhnyi mir, 2016.

Khomiakov, A. S. "Fifth Letter to William Palmer." In Khomiakov and Kireevsky, *On Spiritual Unity*, 154–59.

———. "Mechta." In Brodskii, *Rannye Slavianofily*, 146.

———. "Some More Remarks by an Orthodox Christian concerning the Western Communions, on the Occasion of Several Latin and Protestant Publications." In Khomiakov and Kireevsky, *On Spiritual Unity*, 117–34.

———. "Some Remarks by an Orthodox Christian concerning the Western Communions, on the Occasion of a Brochure by Mr. Laurentie." In Khomiakov and Kireevsky, *On Spiritual Unity*, 57–62.

———. "The Church is One." In Khomiakov and Kireevsky, *On Spiritual Unity*, 31–53.

———. "To the Serbians. A Message from Moscow." In Christoff, *A. S. Xomjakov*, 247–68.

Khomiakov, Aleksei, and Ivan Kireevsky. *On Spiritual Unity: A Slavophile Reader*, translated and edited by Boris Jakim and Robert Bird. Hudson, NY: Lindisfarne, 1998.

Khristoforov, I. A. *"Aristokraticheskaia" oppozitsiia Velikim reformam: Konets 1850–seredina 1870-kh gg*. Moscow: Russkoe slovo, 2002.

———. "Nineteenth-Century Russian Conservatism: Problems and Contradictions." *Russian Studies in History* 48, no. 2 (2009): 56–77.

Kireev, A. A. *Dnevnik 1905–1910*. Moscow: Rosspen, 2010.

Kireevsky, Ivan. "Fragments." In Khomiakov and Kireevsky, *On Spiritual Unity*, 276–91.

———. "On the Nature of European Culture and on Its Relationship to Russian Culture." In Khomiakov and Kireevsky, *On Spiritual Unity*, 189–232.

Kir'ianov, Iu. I. *Pravye partii v Rossii, 1911–1917 gg*. Moscow: Rosspen, 2001.

Kirk, Russell. *The Conservative Mind from Burke to Santayana*. Chicago: Henry Regnery Company, 1953.

Kistiakovskii, B. "V zashchitu prava (intelligentsiia i pravosoznanie)." In Berdiaev, *Vekhi*, 97–126.

Kizenko, Nadieszda. *A Prodigal Saint: Father John of Kronstadt and the Russian People*. University Park: The Pennsylvania State University Press, 2000.

Knox, Zoe. "The Symphonic Ideal: The Moscow Patriarchate's Post-Soviet Leadership." *Europe-Asia Studies* 55, no. 4 (2003): 575–96.

Knox, Zoe, and Anastasia Mitrofanova. "The Russian Orthodox Church." In *Eastern Christianity and Politics in the Twenty-First Century*, edited by Lucian N. Leustean, 38–66. London: Routledge, 2014.

Kochetkova, Natalya. *Nikolai Karamzin*. Boston: Twayne, 1975.

Kondakov, Iu. E. "Fotii (P. N. Spasskii): Filosofsko-religioznye vzgliady, obshchestvenno-politicheskaia i tserkovnaia deiatel'nost'." *Voprosy istorii konservatizma* 1 (2015): 67–131.

———. "Krizis gosudarstvenno-tserkovnykh otnoshenii i tserkovnyi konservatizm v pervoi polovine XIX veka." *Tetradi po konservatizmu* 4 (2015): 59–70.

Kotov, A. E. "'Sovremennaia nefeodal'naia monarkhiia': Russkaia konservativnaia pechat' kontsa XIX veka v poiskakh natsional'noi ideologii." *Tetradi po konservatizmu* 4 (2015): 130–46.

Langer, Jacob. "Corruption and the Counterrevolution: The Rise and Fall of the Black Hundred." PhD diss., Duke University, 2007.

Lanz, Henry. "The Philosophy of Ivan Kireevsky." *Slavonic Review* 4, no. 12 (1926): 594–604.

Laqueur, Walter. *Black Hundred: The Rise of the Extreme Right in Russia*. New York: HarperCollins, 1993.

Laruelle, Marlene. "Conservatism as the Kremlin's New Toolkit: An Ideology at the Lowest Cost." *Russian Analytical Digest* 138 (November 2013): 2–4.

——. *Inside and around the Kremlin's Black Box: The New Nationalist Think Tanks in Russia*. Stockholm: Institute for Security & Development Policy, 2009.

——. *In the Name of the Nation: Nationalism and Politics in Contemporary Russia*. New York: Palgrave MacMillan, 2009.

——. *Russian Eurasianism: An Ideology of Empire*. Washington, DC: Woodrow Wilson Center Press, 2008.

——. "The Two Faces of Contemporary Eurasianism: An Imperial Version of Russian Nationalism." *Nationalities Papers: The Journal of Nationalism and Ethnicity* 32, no. 1 (2004): 115–36.

Lavrov, Sergei. "Russia's Foreign Policy: Historical Background." *Russia in Global Affairs*, March 3, 2016. http://www.mid.ru/en/foreign_policy/news/-/asset_publisher/cKNonkJE02Bw/content/id/2124391.

Leatherbarrow, William. "Conservatism in the Age of Alexander I and Nicholas I." In *A History of Russian Thought*, edited by William Leatherbarrow and Derek Offord, 95–115. Cambridge: Cambridge University Press, 2010.

Leatherbarrow, William, and Derek Offord. *A History of Russian Thought*. Cambridge: Cambridge University Press, 2010.

Leont'ev, Konstantin. *Vizantizm i slavianstvo*. Moscow: Izdanie obshchestva istorii i drevnostei rossiiskikh pri Moskovskom Universitete, 1876.

Leontovitsch, Victor. *The History of Liberalism in Russia*. Pittsburgh, PA: University of Pittsburgh Press, 2012.

Leontyev, Constantine. "The Average European as an Ideal and Instrument of Universal Destruction." In *Russian Philosophy*, edited by James M. Edie, James P. Scanlan, and Mary-Barbara Zeldin, 2:271–80. Chicago: Quadrangle, 1965.

Lesourd, Françoise. "Karsavin and the Eurasian Movement." In *Russia Between East and West: Scholarly Debates on Eurasianism*, edited by Dmitry Shlapentokh, 61–94. Leiden: Brill, 2007.

Liber, George. "Korenizatsiia: Restructuring Soviet Nationality Policy in the 1920s." *Ethnic and Racial Studies* 14, no. 1 (1991): 15–23.

Lieven, Dominic. "Bureaucratic Authoritarianism in Late Imperial Russia: The Personality, Career and Opinions of P. N. Durnovo." *The Historical Journal* 26, no. 2 (1983): 391–402.

——. *Russia's Rulers under the Old Regime*. New Haven, CT: Yale University Press, 1989.

Lincoln, W. Bruce. *Nicholas I: Emperor and Autocrat of All the Russias*. Bloomington: Indiana University Press, 1978.

Lisitsa, Iurii. "Il'in iskal sushchnost' svobody kak podobiia bozhiia v cheloveke: Interv'iu s Iuriem Lisitsei." *Samopoznanie* 2 (2015): 7–11.

Loukianov, Mikhail. "Conservatives and 'Renewed Russia,' 1907–1914." *Slavic Review* 61, no. 4 (2002): 762–86.

———. "The Rise and Fall of the All-Russian National Union." *Kritika: Explorations in Russian and Eurasian History* 6, no. 1 (2005): 129–34.

Luk'ianov, Mikhail. *Rossiiskii konservatizm i reforma, 1907–1914*. Stuttgart: Ibidem-Verlag, 2006.

Lupareva, N. N. "'Zabytyi patriot 1812 goda': Obshchestvenno-politicheskaia deiatel'nost' Sergeia Nikolaevicha Glinki." *Voprosy istorii konservatizma* 1 (2015): 42–66.

Mahoney, Daniel J. *The Conservative Foundation of the Liberal Order: Defending Democracy against Its Modern Enemies and Immoderate Friends*. Wilmington, DE: ISI Books, 2010.

Makarychev, Andrey, and Alexandra Yatsyk. "A New Russian Conservatism: Domestic Roots and Repercussions for Europe." *Notes Internacionals CIDOB* 93 (June 2014): 1–6.

March, Luke. "Nationalism for Export? The Domestic and Foreign-Policy Implications of the New 'Russian Idea.'" *Europe-Asia Studies* 64, no. 3 (2012): 401–25.

Martin, Alexander M. *Romantics, Reformers, Reactionaries: Russian Conservative Thought and Politics in the Reign of Alexander I*. DeKalb: Northern Illinois University Press, 1997.

Maslin, M. A. "Klassicheskoe evraziistvo i ego sovremennye transformatsii." *Tetradi po konservatizmu* 4 (2015): 201–10.

Matthews, Owen. "Putin to Russia: We Will Bury Ourselves." *Newsweek*, June 12, 2014. http://www.newsweek.com/2014/06/20/putins-paranoia-card-254513.html.

Matveichev, O. A. "Klassifikatsiia vidov konservatizma: Novaia versiia." *Tetradi po konservatizmu* 2, no. 2 (2014): 74–80.

Matvienko, Valentina. "Pravovaia sistema strany dolzhna opirat'sia na natsional'nye traditsii i tsennosti." *Parlamentskaia gazeta*, August 12, 2016. https://www.pnp.ru/politics/2016/08/12/valentina-matvienko-pravovaya-sistema-strany-dolzhna-opirat-sya-nanacionalnye-tradicii-i-cennosti.html.

McDonald, David M. "The Durnovo Memorandum in Context: Official Conservatism and the Crisis of Autocracy." *Jahrbücher für Geschichte Osteuropas* 44, no. 4 (1996): 481–502.

McGuckin, John Anthony. *The Orthodox Church: An Introduction to Its History, Doctrine, and Spiritual Culture*. Oxford: Blackwell, 2008.

Mchedlova, M. M. "Tsennostnaia baza i sotsiokul'turnye proektsii sovremennogo rossiiskogo konservatizma." *Tetradi po konservatizmu* 3 (2014): 133–35.

Mendras, Marie. *Russian Politics: The Paradox of a Weak State*. New York: Columbia University Press, 2012.

Mezhuev, Boris. "In Russia, It's the Realists vs. the Ethno-Nationalists." *The American Conservative*, May 10, 2017. http://www.theamericanconservative.com/articles/in-russia-its-the-realists-vs-the-ethno-nationalists/.

———. "Island Russia and Russia's Identity Politics: Unlearned Lessons from Vadim Tsymbursky." *Russia in Global Affairs* 2 (2017). http://eng.globalaffairs.ru/number/Island-Russia-and-Russias-Identity-Politics-18757.

———. "Konservativnaia demokratiia stanet glavnym opponentom liberal'nogo avtoritarizma." Russkaia!dea, January 9, 2016. http://politconservatism.ru/interview/konservativnaya-demokratiya-stanet-glavnym-opponentom-liberalnogo-avtoritarizma.

———. "Putin priderzhivaetsia konservativnogo ponimaniia konservatizma." Russkaia!dea, April 16, 2016. http://politconservatism.ru/interview/putin-priderzhivaetsya-konservativnogo-ponimaniya-konservatizma.

———. "Sovremennyi konservatizm: Parametry transformatsii." *Tetradi po konservatizmu* 2, no. 1 (2014): 80–88.

———. "Sud nad revolutsiei—sud nad peterburgskoi imperii." Russkaia!dea, February 23, 2017. https://politconservatism.ru/articles/boris-mezhuev-sud-nad-revolyutsiej-sud-nad-peterburgskoj-imperiej.

Milevskii, O. A. "Rossiiskie ekonomicheskie al'ternativy: Konservativnyi podkhod." *Tetradi po konservatizmu* 4 (2015): 107–20.

Miliukov, Pavel. *Razlozhenie slavianofil'stva: Danilevskii, Leont'ev, Vl. Solov'ev.* Moscow: Tipo-lit. Vysochaishe utver. T-va I. N. Kushnerev, 1893.

Minakov, A. Iu. "Konservatizm—eto blistatel'noe intellektual'noe napravlenie." *Tetradi po konservatizmu* 1 (2014): 105–11.

———. "Konservativnaia 'russkaia partiia' nachala XIX veka." *Tetradi po konservatizmu* 4 (2015): 43–58.

———. "Rozhdenie russkogo konservatizma: Uroki proshlogo." *Tetradi po konservatizmu* 3 (2014): 12–26.

———. "Russian Conservatism in Contemporary Russian Historiography: New Approaches and Research Trends." *Russian Studies in History* 48, no. 2 (2009): 8–28.

———. "Russkie konservatory v poiskakh 'russkoi formuly.'" *Voprosy istorii konservatizma* 1 (2015): 33–41.

———. *Russkii konservatizm v pervoi chetverti XIX veka.* Voronezh: Izdatel'stvo Voronezhskogo gosudarstvennogo universiteta, 2011.

Ministerstvo Kul'tury Rossiiskoi Federatsii. *Osnovy gosurdarstvennoi kul'turnoi politiki.* 2015. https://www.mkrf.ru/upload/medialibrary/3aa/3aa5ed08e6cfbb1c-982fee8618c4fa09.pdf.

Mitrofanova, Anastasia V. *The Politicization of Russian Orthodoxy: Actors and Ideas.* Stuttgart: Ibidem, 2005.

Monas, Sidney. "Leontiev: A Meditation." *The Journal of Modern History* 43, no. 3 (1971): 483–94.

Morozov, Oleg. "Osnovnye polozheniia sotsial'no-konservativnoi ideologii." *Tetradi po konservatizmu* 1 (2014): 9–16.

Müller, Jan-Werner. "Comprehending Conservatism: A New Framework for Analysis." *Journal of Political Ideologies* 11, no. 3 (2006): 359–65.

Nagornyi, Aleksandr. "Rossiia i 'zapadniki.' Ot El'tsina do Naval'nogo: Chto dal'she?" *Izborskii klub,* December 1, 2015. https://izborsk-club.ru/7867.

Nagy, Levente. "The Meaning of a Concept: Conservatism." In *Reflections on Conservatism,* edited by Doğancan Özsel, 1–32. Newcastle upon Tyne: Cambridge Scholars Publishing, 2011.

Narochnitskaia, Nataliia. *Russkii kod razvitiia.* Moscow: Knizhnyi mir, 2015.

———. "Sredi zapadnykh konservatorov meniaetsia otnoshenie k Rossii." *Tetradi po konservatizmu* 1 (2014): 74–77.

Netesova, Yulia. "What Does It Mean to Be Conservative in Russia?" *The National Interest,* August 10, 2016. http://nationalinterest.org/feature/what-does-it-mean-be-conservative-russia-17312.

Nikonov, Viacheslav. "Rossiia i mir: Konservatizm v rossiiskoi vneshnei politike." *Tetradi po konservatizmu* 1 (2014): 88–93.

Oakeshott, Michael. "On Being Conservative." In *Rationalism in Politics and Other Essays*, 168–96. London: Methuen, 1962.

"Obsuzhdenie doklada." *Tetradi po konservatizmu* 2, no. 1 (2014): 95–97.

Odoevsky, Vladimir Fedorovich. *Russian Nights*. Evanston, IL: Northwestern University Press, 1997.

O'Hara, Kieron. *Conservatism*. London: Reaktion Books, 2011.

Omel'ianchuk, I. V. "The Problems of Russia's Economic Development as Seen by Right-Wing Monarchists in the Early Twentieth Century." *Russian Studies in History* 48, no. 2 (2009): 78–92.

——. "Russkii konservatizm nachala XX veka v poiskakh partiinogo samoopredeleniia." *Tetradi po konservatizmu* 4 (2015): 147–58.

O'Sullivan, Noel. *Conservatism*. London: J. M Dent & Sons, 1976.

Paert, Irina. "'The Unmercenary Bishop': St. Ignatii (Brianchaninov) (1807–1867) and the Making of Modern Russian Orthodoxy." *Slavonica* 9, no. 2 (2003): 99–112.

Papanikolaou, Aristotle. *The Mystical as Political: Democracy and Non-Radical Orthodoxy.* Notre Dame, IN: University of Notre Dame Press, 2012.

Paperny, Vladimir. *Architecture in the Age of Stalin: Culture Two*. Cambridge: Cambridge University Press, 2002.

Papkova, Irina. *The Orthodox Church and Russian Politics*. Washington, DC: Woodrow Wilson Center Press, 2011.

Papmehl, K. "Pososhkov as a Thinker." *Slavic and East European Studies* 6, no. 1 (1961): 80–87.

Paradowski, Ryszard. "Absolutism and Authority in European Ideology: Karsavin and Alekseev." In Shlapentokh, *Russia between East and West*, 95–108.

Perevezentsev, S. V. "Ideinye istoki russkogo konservatizma." *Voprosy istorii konservatizma* 1 (2015): 11–32.

Peunova, Marina. "An Eastern Incarnation of the European New Right: Aleksandr Panarin and New Eurasianist Discourse in Contemporary Russia." *Journal of Contemporary European Studies* 16, no. 3 (2008): 407–19.

Pipes, Richard. *Karamzin's Memoir on Ancient and Modern Russia: A Translation and Analysis*. New York: Atheneum, 1966.

——. *Russian Conservatism and Its Critics: A Study in Political Culture*. New Haven, CT: Yale University Press, 2005.

——. "Russian Conservatism in the Second Half of the Nineteenth Century." *Slavic Review* 30, no. 1 (1971): 121–28.

——. *Struve: Liberal on the Right, 1905–1944*. Cambridge, MA: Harvard University Press, 1980.

——. "The Background and Growth of Karamzin's Political Ideas to 1810." In Pipes, *Karamzin's Memoir*, 3–92.

Pisiotis, Argyrios K. "Between State and Estate: The Political Motivations of the Russian Orthodox Episcopate in the Crisis of Tsarist Monarchy, 1905–1917." *Canadian-American Slavic Studies* 46, no. 3 (2012): 335–63.

——. "Orthodoxy versus Autocracy: The Orthodox Church and Clerical Political Dissent in Late Imperial Russia, 1905–1914." PhD diss., Georgetown University, 2000.

Pliashchenko, T. E. "Konservativnyi liberalizm v poreformennoi Rossii: Istoriia odnoi neudachi." *Tetradi po konservatizmu* 4 (2015): 121–29.

Pobedonostsev, Konstantin. "The Falsehood of Democracy." In Riha, *Readings in Russian Civilization*, 390–401.

Pogodin, Mikhail. *Istoriko-politicheskie pis'ma i zapiski v prodolzhenii krymskoi voiny 1853–1856.* Moscow: Tipografiia V. M. Frish, 1874.

———. "Parallel' russkoi istorii s istoriei evropeiskikh gosudarstv otnositel'no nachala." In *Izbrannye trudy*, 250–64. Moscow: Rossiiskaia politicheskaia entsiklopediia, 2010.

Poliakov, L. V. "The Conservatism of Konstantin Leont'ev in Present-Day Russia." *Russian Studies in Philosophy* 35, no. 2 (1996): 51–60.

———. "Rossiiskii konservatizm na strazhe budushchego." *Tetradi po konservatizmu* 2, no. 1 (2014): 128–30.

———. "Shans ob"edineniia vlasti i naroda na odnoi tsennostnoi osnove." *Tetradi po konservatizmu* 1 (2014): 41–49.

———. "Vechnoe i prekhodiashchee v russkom konservatizme." *Tetradi po konservatizmu* 4 (2015): 219–29.

Poltoratskii, N. *Ivan Aleksandrovich Il'in*. Tenafly, NJ: Ermitazh, 1989.

Polunov, A. Iu. "Konstantin Petrovich Pobedonostsev—Man and Politician." *Russian Studies in History* 39, no. 4 (2001): 8–32.

Popov, A. A. "Istoriia russkogo konservatizma i slavianofily." *Tetradi po konservatizmu* 2, no. 1 (2014): 22–24.

———. "N. A. Berdiaev o konservatizme slavianofilov." *Tetradi po konservatizmu* 3 (2014): 54–59.

Popov, E. A. *Russkii konservatizm: Ideologiia i sotsial'no-politicheskaia praktika.* Rostov-on-Don: Izdatel'stvo Rostovskogo universiteta, 2005.

Pospielovsky, Dmitry. *The Russian Church under the Soviet Regime, 1917–1982.* Vol. 1. Crestwood, NY: St. Vladimir's Seminary Press, 1984.

Prokhanov, Aleksandr. *Simfoniia "Piatoi Imperii."* Moscow: Iauza Eksmo, 2007.

———. "Ventsenosnyi Putin." Izborskii klub, July 5, 2017. https://izborsk-club.ru/13646.

Prozorov, Sergei. "Russian Conservatism in the Putin Presidency: The Dispersion of a Hegemonic Discourse." *Journal of Political Ideologies* 10, no. 2 (2005): 121–43.

Putin, Vladimir. "Interv'iu Pervomu kanalu i agentstvu Assoshieited Press." Kremlin.ru, September 4, 2013. http://kremlin.ru/events/president/transcripts/19143.

———. "Interv'iu telekanalu Russia Today." Kremlin.ru, September 6, 2012. http://kremlin.ru/events/president/transcripts/16393.

———. "Interv'iu Vladimira Putina radio 'Evropa 1' i telekanalu TF1." Kremlin.ru, June 4, 2014. http://kremlin.ru/events/president/news/45832

———. "Poslanie federal'nomu sobraniiu Rossiiskoi Federatsii." Kremlin.ru, April 25, 2005. http://kremlin.ru/events/president/transcripts/22931.

———. "Poslanie prezidenta federal'nomu sobraniiu." Kremlin.ru, December 12, 2012. http://kremlin.ru/events/president/transcripts/17118.

———. "Poslanie prezidenta federal'nomu sobraniiu." Kremlin.ru, December 4, 2014. http://kremlin.ru/events/president/transcripts/47173.

———. "Vstrecha s uchastnikami XIX Vsemirnogo festivalia molodezhi i studentov." Kremlin.ru, October 14, 2017. http://kremlin.ru/events/president/transcripts/55842.

———. "Vstrecha s uchastnikami mezhdunarodnogo diskussionogo kluba 'Valdai.'" Kremlin.ru, September 14, 2007. http://kremlin.ru/events/president/transcripts/24537.

———. "Vystuplenia i diskussiia na Miunkhenskoi konferentsii po voprosam politiki bezopastnosti." Kremlin.ru, February 10, 2007. http://kremlin.ru/events/president/transcripts/24034.

———. "Zasedanie mezhdunarodnogo diskussionnogo kluba 'Valdai.'" Kremlin.ru, September 19, 2013. http://kremlin.ru/events/president/news/19243.

Putnam, George. "P. B. Struve's View of the Russian Revolution of 1905." *The Slavonic and East European Review* 45, no. 105 (1967): 457–73.

Pyziur, Eugene. "Mikhail N. Katkov: Advocate of English Liberalism in Russia, 1856–1863." *The Slavonic and East European Review* 45, no. 105 (1967): 439–56.

Rabotiazhev, N. V. "Mezhdu traditsiei i utopiei: Levyi konservatizm v Rossii." *Polis: Politicheskie Issledovaniia* 4 (2014): 114–30.

Rabow-Edling, Susanna. *Slavophile Thought and the Politics of Cultural Nationalism.* Albany: State University of New York Press, 2006.

Raeff, Marc. *Russia Abroad: A Cultural History of the Russian Emigration, 1919–1939.* Oxford: Oxford University Press, 1990.

———. "State and Nobility in the Ideology of M. M. Shcherbatov." *American Slavic and East European Review* 19, no. 3 (1960): 363–79.

Rancour-Laferriere, Daniel. *The Slave Soul of Russia: Moral Masochism and the Cult of Suffering.* New York: New York University Press, 1995.

Rasputin, Valentin. *Farewell to Matyora.* Evanston, IL: Northwestern University Press, 1995.

———. *Siberia on Fire: Stories and Essays.* DeKalb: Northern Illinois University Press, 1989.

Rawson, Don C. *Russian Rightists and the Revolution of 1905.* Cambridge: Cambridge University Press, 1995.

Remizov, Mikhail. *Russkie i gosudarstvo.* Moscow: Eksmo, 2016.

———. "Tri napravleniia razrusheniia sovremennoi tsivilizatsii i konservatizm." *Tetradi po konservatizmu* 2, no. 1 (2014): 100–103.

Rendle, Matthew. *Defenders of the Motherland: The Tsarist Elite in Revolutionary Russia.* Oxford: Oxford University Press, 2010.

Repnikov, A. V. "The Contemporary Historiography of Russian Conservatism." *Russian Studies in History* 48, no. 2 (2009): 29–55.

———. *Konservativnye modeli rossiiskoi gosudarstvennosti.* Moscow: Rosspen, 2014.

———. "Razmyshleniia o konservatizme." *Svobodnaia mysl'* 11–12 (2012): 103–16.

Rey, Marie-Pierre. *Alexander I: The Tsar Who Defeated Napoleon.* DeKalb: Northern Illinois University Press, 2012.

Riasanovsky, N. V. "The Emergence of Eurasianism." *California Slavic Studies* 4 (1967): 39–72.

———. *Nicholas I and Official Nationality in Russia, 1825–1855.* Berkeley: University of California Press, 1959.

———. "Prince N. S. Trubetskoy's 'Europe and Mankind.'" *Jahrbücher für Geschichte Osteuropas* 12, no. 2 (1964): 207–20.

———. *Russia and the West in the Teaching of the Slavophiles: A Study of Romantic Ideology.* Gloucester, MA: Peter Smith, 1965.

Riha, Thomas, ed. *Readings in Russian Civilization.* Vol. 2, *Imperial Russia, 1700–1917.* Chicago: University of Chicago Press, 1964.

Robinson, Paul. *Grand Duke Nikolai Nikolaevich: Supreme Commander of the Russian Army.* DeKalb: Northern Illinois University Press, 2014.

———. "On Resistance to Evil by Force: Ivan Il'in and the Necessity of War." *Journal of Military Ethics* 2, no. 2 (2003): 145–59.

———. *The White Russian Army in Exile, 1920–1941*. Oxford: Clarendon Press, 2002.

Rodkiewicz, Witold, and Jadwiga Rogoza. "Potemkin Conservatism: An Ideological Tool of the Kremlin." *Point of View* 48 (2015): 1–25.

Rogger, Hans. "The Formation of the Russian Right: 1900–1906." *California Slavic Studies* 3 (1964): 66–94.

———. "The 'Nationalism' of Ivan Nikitič Boltin." In *For Roman Jakobson: Essays on the Occasion of His Sixtieth Birthday, October 11, 1956*, edited by Halle Morris et al., 423–29. The Hague: Mouton, 1956.

———. "Reflections on Russian Conservatism: 1861–1905." *Jahrbücher für Geschichte Osteuropas* 14 (1966): 195–212.

Rose, Margaret A. *Marx's Lost Aesthetic: Karl Marx and the Visual Arts*. Cambridge: Cambridge University Press, 1984.

Rossiiskii Zarubezhnyi S"ezd 1926: Dokumenty i materialy. Moscow: Russkii put', 2006.

Rowley, David G. "Alexander Solzhenitsyn and Russian Nationalism." *Journal of Contemporary History* 32, no. 3 (1997): 321–37.

"Russian Church and State Sign Agreement to Prevent Abortion." Russia Insider, July 7, 2016. http://russia-insider.com/en/russia-church-and-state-sign-agreement-prevent-abortion/ri15445.

The Russian Orthodox Church. *Osnovy sotsial'noi kontseptsii Russkoi Pravoslavnoi Tserkvi*. 2000. https://mospat.ru/ru/documents/social-concepts/.

———. *Osnovy ucheniia Russkoi Pravoslavnoi Tserkvi o dostoinstve, svobode i pravakh cheloveka*. 2008. https://mospat.ru/ru/documents/dignity-freedom-rights/.

Russkaia doktrina: Gosudarstvennaia ideologiia epokhi Putina. Moscow: Institut russkoi tsivilizatsii, 2016.

Ruthchild, Rochelle. "Sisterhood and Socialism: The Soviet Feminist Movement." *Frontiers: A Journal of Women Studies* 7, no. 2 (1983): 4–12.

Sankova, S. M. "Partiia russkikh natsionalistov: Realnost' bez mifov." *Tetradi po konservatizmu* 4 (2015): 159–70.

Savitskii, Petr. "Kontinent-okean (Rossiia i mirovoi rynok)." In Shirokov, *Iskhod k vostoku*, 226–62.

———. "Migratsiia i kul'tury." In Shirokov, *Iskhod k vostoku*, 119–28.

———. "Povorot k vostoku." In Shirokov, *Iskhod k vostoku*, 52–56.

Schimmelpenninck van der Oye, David. "The East." In Leatherbarrow and Offord, *A History of Russian Thought*, 217–36.

Shcherbatov, M. M. *On the Corruption of Morals in Russia*, edited with a translation, introduction and notes by A. Lentin. London: Cambridge University Press, 1969.

Shchipkov, A. V. "Levyi konservatizm." In Shchipkov, *Po-drugomu*, 43–64.

———. "Tipologiia napravlenii konservativnoi mysli v sovremennoi Rossii." *Tetradi po konservatizmu* 2, no. 1 (2014): 114–17.

———, ed. *Po-drugomu: Sbornik statei o traditsii i smene ideologicheskogo diskursa*. Moscow: Abris, 2017.

Shearer, David R. "Crime and Social Disorder in Stalin's Russia: A Reassessment of the Great Retreat and the Origins of Mass Repression." *Cahiers du monde russe* 39, nos. 1–2 (1998): 119–48.

Shirokov, O. S., ed. *Iskhod k vostoku*. Moscow: Dobrosvet, 1997.

Shishkov A. S. *Rassuzhdenie o starom i novom sloge rossiiskogo iazyka.* St. Petersburg: Imperatorskaia tipografiia, 1803.

Shlapentokh, Dmitry. "Dugin, Eurasianism, and Central Asia." *Communist and Post-Communist Studies* 40, no. 2 (2007): 143–56.

———. "Forgotten Predecessors: The Russian Conservative Historians of the French Revolution." *International Journal of Politics, Culture, and Society* 9, no. 1 (1995): 57–85.

———. *Russia between East and West: Scholarly Debates on Eurasianism.* Leiden: Brill, 2007.

Snyder, Timothy. "Ivan Ilyin: Putin's Philosopher of Russian Fascism." *The New York Review of Books,* April 2018. https://www.nybooks.com/daily/2018/03/16/ivan-ilyin-putins-philosopher-of-russian-fascism/.

———. *The Road to Unfreedom: Russia, Europe, America.* New York: Tim Duggan, 2018.

Sokolov, Mikhail. "New Right-Wing Intellectuals in Russia: Strategies of Legitimization." *Russian Politics and Law* 47, no. 1 (2009): 47–75.

Solomon, Peter H. *Soviet Criminal Justice under Stalin.* Cambridge: Cambridge University Press, 1996.

Solonevich, Ivan. *Narodnaia monarkhiia.* Moscow: Algoritm, 2011.

Soloukhin, Vladimir. "Pis'ma iz russkogo muzeia." *Molodaia gvardiia* 9 (1966): 236–78.

Solov'ev, Vladimir. *Revolutsiia konservatorov: Voina mirov.* Moscow: Izdatel'stvo "E," 2017.

Solovyov, Vladimir. *The Justification of the Good: An Essay on Moral Philosophy.* Grand Rapids, MI: William B. Eerdmans, 2005.

Solzhenitsyn, Aleksandr. "Kak nam obustroit' Rossiiu?" In Solzhenitsyn, *Publitsistika v trekh tomakh,* 1:538–98.

———. "Na vozvrate dykhaniia i soznaniia." In Solzhenitsyn, *Publitsistika v trekh tomakh,* 1:26–48.

———. "Pis'mo vozhdiam sovetskogo soiuza." In Solzhenitsyn, *Publitsistika v trekh tomakh,* 1:148–86.

———. *Publitsistika v trekh tomakh.* Vol. 1. Yaroslavl: Verkhne-Volzhskoe Knizhnoe Izdatel'stvo, 1995.

———. "Raskaianie i samoogranichenie kak kategorii natsional'noi zhizni." In Solzhenitsyn, *Publitsistika v trekh tomakh,* 1:49–86.

Solzhenitsyn, Alexander. *The Gulag Archipelago 1918–1956: An Experiment in Literary Investigation.* London: Collins Harvill, 1988.

Starr, S. Frederick. *Decentralization and Self-Government in Russia, 1830–1870.* Princeton, NJ: Princeton University Press, 1972.

Stephan, John. *The Russian Fascists.* London: Harper & Row, 1978.

Strickland, John. *The Making of Holy Russia: The Orthodox Church and Russian Nationalism before the Revolution.* Jordanville, NY: Holy Trinity Publications, 2013.

Struve, Petr. "Intelligentsiia i revoliutsiia." In Berdiaev, *Vekhi,* 127–45.

———. "Istoricheskii smysl russkoi revolutsii i natsional'nye zadachi." In Askol'dov, *Iz glubiny,* 285–306.

Suslov, Mikhail. "The Lost Chance of Conservative Modernization: S. F. Sharapov in the Economic Debates of the Late Nineteenth to the Early Twentieth Century." *Acta Slavica Iaponica* 31 (2012): 31–54.

———. "'Slavophilism Is True Liberalism': The Political Utopia of S. F. Sharapov (1855–1911)." *Russian History* 38, no. 2 (2011): 281–314.

Suvchinskii, P. "Epokha very." In Shirokov, *Iskhod k vostoku,* 73–97.

———. "Sila slabykh." In Shirokov, *Iskhod k vostoku*, 57–64.

TASS. "Mitropolit Ilarion: Monarkhiia imeet preimushchestva pered drugimi formami pravleniia." July 1, 2017. https://tass.ru/obschestvo/4380573.

Teslia, A. A. "Slavianofil'skii 'konservatizm': Mezhdu natsionalizmom i liberalizmom?" *Tetradi po konservatizmu* 4 (2015): 23–32.

Thaden, Edward C. *Conservative Nationalism in Nineteenth-Century Russia*. Seattle: University of Washington Press, 1964.

Tikhomirov, Lev. *Demokratiia liberal'naia i sotsial'naia*. Moscow: Universitetskaia tipografiia, 1896.

———. *Monarkhicheskaia gosudarstvennost'*. Moscow: Izdatel'stvo "E," 2016.

———. *Pochemu ia perestal byt' revolutsionerom*. Moscow: Tipografiia Vil'de, 1895.

Timasheff, Nicholas S. *The Great Retreat: The Growth and Decline of Communism in Russia*. New York: E. P. Dutton, 1946.

Titov, Alexander Sergeevich. "Lev Gumilev, Ethnogenesis and Eurasianism." PhD diss., University College London, 2005.

Trubetskoi, N. S. "Ob istinnom i lozhnom natsionalizme." In Shirokov, *Iskhod k vostoku*, 171–95.

———. "Verkhi i nizy russkoi kul'tury. (Ethnicheskaia osnova russkoi kul'tury.)" In Shirokov, *Iskhod k vostoku*, 196–225.

Tsipko, A. S. "Liberal'nyi konservatizm Nikolaia Berdiaeva i Petra Struve i zadachi dekommunizatsii sovremennoi Rossii." *Tetradi po konservatizmu* 2, no. 1 (2014): 31–39.

———. "Puti sovetskoi intelligentsii k rossiiskomu konservatizmu (O stikhiinom antikommunizme, podorvavshem ideologicheskie 'skrepy' SSSR)." *Tetradi po konservatizmu* 4 (2015): 190–200.

Tsygankov, Andrei P. "In the Shadow of Nikolai Danilevskii: Universalism, Particularism, and Russian Geopolitical Theory." *Europe-Asia Studies* 69, no. 4 (2017): 571–93.

———. "'Ostrovnaia' geopolitika Vadima Tsymburskogo." *Tetradi po konservatizmu* 1 (2015): 12–20.

Tsymburskii, B. L. "Osnovaniia rossiiskogo geopoliticheskogo konservatizma." *Tetradi po konservatizmu* 1 (2015): 41–44.

Tvardovskaia, V. A. "Tsarstvovanie Aleksandra III." In Grosul, *Russkii konservatizm*, 276–360.

Twisdale, Ricky. "A Conservative Russian Lion with Real Mass Influence—The Painter Ilya Glazunov." Russia Insider, September 11, 2016. http://russia-insider.com/en/culture/conservative-russian-lion-real-mass-influence-painter-ilya-glazunov/ri15339

Tyneh, Carl S. *Orthodox Christianity: Overview and Bibliography*. New York: Nova Science, 2003.

Udalov, S. V. "Imperiia na iakore: Konservativnaia ideologiia v Rossii vtoroi chetverti XIX veka." *Tetradi po konservatizmu* 4 (2015): 80–94.

Ul'ianova, Liubov'. "Pochemu Rossii ne nuzhna modernizatsiia." Russkaia!dea, August 12, 2016. http://politconservatism.ru/articles/pochemu-rossii-ne-nuzhna-modernizatsiya.

———. "Skrytoe slavianofil'stvo v tvorchestve Il'ina." *Samopoznanie* 2 (2015): 38–42.

Valliere, Paul. "Vladimir Soloviev (1853–1900)." In *The Teachings of Modern Orthodox Christianity on Law, Politics, and Human Nature*, edited by John Witte and Frank S. Alexander, 33–75. New York: Columbia University Press, 2005.

Vasil'eva, Ol'ga. "Ob istokakh rossiiskogo konservatizma." *Tetradi po konservatizmu* 1 (2014): 28–37.

Walicki, Andrzej. *A History of Russian Thought from the Enlightenment to Marxism.* Stanford: Stanford University Press, 1979.

———. *The Slavophile Controversy: A History of a Conservative Utopia in Nineteenth-Century Russian Thought.* Oxford: Clarendon Press, 1975.

Walker, Franklin A. "Reaction and Radicalism in the Russia of Tsar Alexander I: The Case of the Brothers Glinka." *Canadian Slavonic Papers* 21, no. 4 (1979): 489–502.

Weeks, Richard. "The Attempted Reforms of Peter Andreevich Shuvalov." *The Historian* 51, no. 1 (1988): 64–77.

Whittaker, Cynthia. "The Ideology of Sergei Uvarov: An Interpretive Essay." *The Russian Review* 37, no. 2 (1972): 158–76.

———. *The Origins of Modern Russian Education: An Intellectual Biography of Count Sergei Uvarov, 1786-1855.* DeKalb: Northern Illinois University Press, 1984.

Wilkinson, Cai. "Putting Traditional Values into Practice: Russia's Anti-Gay Laws." *Russian Analytical Digest* 138 (November 2013): 5–7.

Woodburn, Stephen M. "The Origins of Russian Intellectual Conservatism, 1825–1881: Danilevsky, Dostoevsky, Katkov, and the Legacy of Nicholas I." PhD diss., University of Miami, 2001.

Wortman, Richard. "Koshelev, Samarin, and Cherkassky and the Fate of Liberal Slavophilism." *Slavic Review* 21, no. 2 (1962): 161–279.

Yanov, Alexander. *The Russian New Right: Right-Wing Ideologies in the Contemporary USSR.* Berkeley, CA: Institute of International Studies, 1978.

Young, George M. *The Russian Cosmists: The Esoteric Futurism of Nikolai Fedorov and His Followers.* Oxford: Oxford University Press, 2012.

Zacek, Judith Cohen. "The Russian Bible Society and the Russian Orthodox Church." *Church History* 35, no. 4 (1966): 411–37.

"Zapiska K. S. Aksakova 'o vnutrennem sostoianii Rossii,' predstavlennaia Gosudariu Imperatoru Aleksandru II v 1855 g." In Brodskii, *Rannye slavianofily*, 69–102.

Zudin, A. Iu. "Ocherki ideologii razvitiia." *Tetradi po konservatizmu* 2, no. 2 (2014): 7–18.

Zyrianov, P. N. *Russkoe monashestvo v xix i nachale xx veka.* (Moscow: Russkoe slovo, 1999).

INDEX

1905 Revolution, 113, 115–16, 124, 126, 128

abortion, 158, 163, 171, 189–90, 205
Agursky, Mikhail, 179
Akhmatova, Anna, 167
Aksakov, Ivan, 45, 59–60, 63, 83
Aksakov, Konstantin, 45, 59, 61, 64, 66, 68–71, 73, 80, 145
Aleksei, Metropolitan, 155
Aleksei, Patriarch, 173
Alexander I, Emperor, 23–25, 27, 29–36, 39, 41, 45
Alexander II, Emperor, 58, 70, 76–77, 83, 84, 86, 91–93, 97, 99, 101, 103, 186
Alexander III, Emperor, 3, 7, 81, 91, 99–101, 105, 107, 109, 129, 185
All-Russian National Union, 115, 123, 126
All-Russian Society for the Preservation of Historical and Cultural Monuments, 166
anarchism, 68
Anna, Empress, 23
anti-Semitism, 101, 118, 133
anti-Westernism, 2, 3, 16, 17, 59, 64, 135, 179, 183
Apraksin, Viktor, 87
Arakcheev, Count Aleksei, 38
aristocratic opposition, 19, 77, 86, 88–89, 94, 96, 213
asceticism, 47, 103
Ascher, Abraham, 120
atheism, 8, 29, 31, 46, 116–17, 130, 173
autocracy, 10, 17–19, 24, 26, 35–36, 45, 50–52, 55, 57–58, 69, 75, 87, 89, 91, 92, 97, 100, 105–9, 112–13, 116, 118, 122–24, 127, 139, 151; limited nature of, 15, 17, 19, 36, 39, 68, 74, 108, 128, 144, 176–77, 215

Barabanov, Oleg, 197
Belinsky, Vissarion, 3, 59

Benoist, Alain de, 193
Bentham, Jeremy, 63
Berdiaev, Nikolai, 7, 14, 116–17, 131–32, 134, 140–41, 147, 172, 196
Bismarck, Otto von, 195
Bolshevism, 1, 132–34, 145–46
Boltin, Ivan, 26–27
Bonaparte, Napoleon, 1, 23, 27, 29–30, 200, 214
Bondarev, Iury, 173
Brezhnev, Leonid, 163–65, 167, 174–75, 179–80
Brianchaninov, Ignaty, 44–48, 51–52, 56
Bulgakov, Sergei, 13, 15, 116–17
bureaucracy, 68, 87–88, 91, 195; dislike of, 101, 106, 108, 112, 123–24, 128, 184, 215
Burgess, John, 190, 205

caesaro-papism, 16, 109
capitalism, 153, 155; conservatives' attitude to, 9, 21, 39, 73, 96, 110, 148, 174, 177–79, 208–9
Catherine II, Empress, 15, 18, 24, 26–27
censorship, 32, 50–51, 53, 57, 69–71, 91
Chaadaev, Pyotr, 61
Chamberlain, Lesley, 1
change, conservatives' attitudes to, 6, 9, 44, 60, 74, 97, 104, 132, 149
Charles X, King, 44
Cherniaev, A. V., 26
Chernyshevsky, Nikolai, 3
Chicherin, Boris, 77, 89–91, 93, 96, 120, 214
Chizhov, Fyodor, 73
Churkin, Aleksandr, 46
civilizational realism, 199
civilizations, theories of, 77, 81–82, 85, 92, 137, 168, 170, 192–95, 199, 213
Cohen, Stephen, 164
Cold War, 1, 4, 169, 183
Coleman, Heather, 45